P9-DMM-822

A BAKER'S ODYSSEY

A Baker's Odyssey

GREG PATENT

CELEBRATING TIME-HONORED RECIPES FROM AMERICA'S
RICH IMMIGRANT HERITAGE

PHOTOGRAPHY by **Kelly Gorham**

VIDEOGRAPHY by **Dave McLean**

BICENTENNIAL
1807
WILEY
2007
BICENTENNIAL

JOHN WILEY & SONS, INC.

Copyright © 2007 by Greg Patent. All rights reserved

Published by John Wiley & Sons, Inc., Hoboken, New Jersey

Wiley bicentennial logo design by Richard J. Pacifico

No part of this publication may be reproduced, stored in a retrieval system, or transmitted in any form or by any means electronic, mechanical, photocopying, recording, scanning, or otherwise, except as permitted under Section 107 or 108, of the 1976 United States Copyright Act, without either the prior written permission of the Publisher, or authorization through payment of the appropriate per-copy fee to the Copyright Clearance Center, Inc., 222 Rosewood Drive, Dan MA 01923, (978) 750-8400, fax (978) 750-4470, or on the web at www.copyright.com. Requests to the Publisher forvers, permission should be addressed to the Permissions Department, John Wiley & Sons, Inc., 111 River Street, Hoboken, NJ 07030, (201) 748-6011, fax (201) 748-6008, or online at www.wiley.com/go/permissions.

Limit of Liability/Disclaimer of Warranty: While the publisher and author have used their best efforts in preparing this book, they make no representations or warranties with respect to the accuracy or completeness of the contents of this book and specifically disclaim any implied warranties of merchantability or fitness for a particular purpose. No warranty may be created or extended by sales representatives or written sales materials. The advice and strategies contained herein may not be suitable for your situation. You should consult with a professional where appropriate. Neither the publisher nor author shall be liable for any loss of profit or any other commercial damages, including but not limited to special, incidental, conse quential, or other damages.

Design by Vertigo Design, NYC

ISBN 978-0-7645-7281-4 (cloth)

Printed in the United States of America

Other Books by Greg Patent

Patently Easy Food Processor Cooking

Shanghai Passage

Food Processor Cooking Quick and Easy

New Cooking from the Old West

A Is for Apple

New Frontiers in Western Cooking

Baking in America

For my wife, Dorothy, who championed the idea for this book, and in honor of my late mother, Mabel, both of whom encouraged me to stay in the kitchen to bake and who always lavished praise on my efforts

With those old continents whence we have come to this new continent,

With the fading kingdoms and kings over there,

With the fading religions and priests,

With the small shores we look back to from our own large and present shores,

With countless years drawing themselves onward and arrived at these years,

You and me arrived—America arrived and making this year,

This year! sending itself ahead countless years to come.

—WALT WHITMAN, "With Antecedents," *Leaves of Grass*

Contents

8   Cakes, Tortes, Pies, and Other Desserts   274

Acknowledgments

This book could not have been written without the generosity of the more than sixty bakers who invited me into their homes to teach me their treasured recipes. Each person is listed along with her or his contributions in The Bakers and Their Contributions on page xvi. My life is immeasurably richer for having met and baked with them.

Finding the contributors was a major challenge, and I want to thank the following friends and family members for their roles in making this book possible:

Cookbook author and food journalist Ann Burckhardt, for introducing me to Carmela Hobbins, Daniela Ruggiero, Soile Anderson, and Elizabeth Germaine, and for housing and feeding me in Minneapolis.

Cookbook author and African culinary historian Jessica Harris, for introducing me to Nigerian cook and baker, Josephine Obianyo-Agu. Cammie Hinshaw, a contributor to this book, for putting me in touch with Yvonne Casalnuovo Braddick.

My agent and friend, Judith Weber, for enabling me to meet with the kransekake ladies of Brooklyn, Christine Fredricksen, Linda Qualben, and the late Alice Hansen. Judith championed this book through the five years it took to complete. Her wisdom and encouragement are rare, and I value them all the more.

Tony Cesare for suggesting I contact his sister Rosanna Aiuppa, who then arranged for a marathon baking session at her home in Albany, New York, with three other contributors to this book: Maria DeNitto, Santa Pasquini, and Rose Padula. Tony and Rosanna's parents, Rosina and Frank, for opening their home to me and insisting I stay with them during my time in Albany.

Writing coach and cookbook author, Antonia Allegra, for encouraging me to call Lebanese food writer Maureen Abood.

My daughter-in-law, Amy, for introducing me to her neighbor, Liz McDonald, whose housekeeper is the daughter of Krystyna Kawalec. Liz, for giving over her kitchen to Krystyna and me for two days of cooking and baking.

My son, Jason, for introducing me to Belen Flores, who then arranged for her mother, Maria Elena, to teach me three of her Mexican recipes.

Susana Arreda Arraial Ballantine, whom I met on the island of Terceira in the Azores, and who selflessly asked her housekeeper, Maria João, to teach me Portuguese recipes instead of cleaning house.

My brother, Phil, and his wife, Bobbi, for telling their Greek friend Kathy Salzetti about me and for hosting my stay in Phoenix.

David Harrington, for making the baking session with Evelyn Delly happen, and for arranging an Indian flatbreads lesson with Chitra Paresh through her daughter Nira Paresh.

Cooking store owner Sue Huffman, for suggesting Betty Groff as a source of Pennsylvania Dutch recipes.

College professor Julie Miller Jones, for putting out a mass e-mailing campaign resulting in an invitation to Leisha Ingdal's home for a lesson in Norwegian baking.

Micaela Musante, for befriending us when we were stranded at the Salt Lake City airport and introducing me to her friend and traveling companion, Marie Ocafrain, who then told me about her friend, Bernadette Iribarren, a Gâteau Basque specialist.

Jackie Vawter, whom I met in Washington, D.C., at an awards presentation for my wife, Dorothy, who told me that I simply must get in touch with Carol Lyons if I wanted a really terrific recipe for kolacky.

Restaurateur and cookbook author Jesse Z. Cool, for commanding me to meet German bakery owners Robert and Esther Nio, and their master baker Rudy Klopp, from whom I learned how to make Rudy's pretzels.

Food writer and cookbook author, Dianne Jacob, whose parents knew my parents in Shanghai, and who put me in touch with her cousin, Ellis Jacob. Ellis told me how to find his ex-wife, Jinni, who taught me a recipe for Iraqi chicken and potato pastries that she learned from Ellis's relatives.

Cookbook author Arthur Schwartz, for introducing me to strudel and matzoh maker Cindy Klotz, and for finding Vera Eisenberg when I told Arthur I needed a Hungarian baker for my book.

Pranee Halvorsen, in Seattle, and Arzu Yilmaz, in New Jersey, two cooks who responded to my plea at a meeting of International Association of Culinary Professionals to contribute to this book. Arzu also prepared a delicious Turkish lunch for my editor, Pam Chirls, and me, and Arzu's husband, Nevzat, related what their lives had been like in Turkey.

And deep gratitude to all of the following, who each played an essential role in this book:

Judith Sutton, whose uncanny eye for using just the right word and for spotting errors and inconsistencies is awesome.

John Keegan, Pam Adams, Marion Lavery, Pat and Mike Gray, and Linda Thompson, for providing the props and fabrics that my photographer, Kelly Gorham, and I used in styling the food.

Kelly Gorham, who came to my home and set up his studio to take all the beautiful pictures in this book. I feel extremely thankful that we found each other and that we had such a great working relationship.

David McLean, my videographer and friend for more than thirty years. Thank you for making me look so good on screen.

Cookbook author, Aglaia Kremezi, for clarifying historical details on layered pastries, especially phyllo.

Shirley Corriher, author of the now classic, Cookwise, for explaining why sunflower seeds turn green in Irish Soda Bread.

Chef, caterer, and hellenophile Harriet Eichenholz, for sharing her enthusiasm for melomakarona, Greek syrup-soaked cookies.

Cookbook author, Lisa Yockelson, for many stimulating conversations about baking.

Thanks also to everyone at John Wiley & Sons, for all their efforts in seeing this book through from concept to completion:

I want to give special thanks to my editor, Pam Chirls, who let me take this book where it led me, and who made many helpful suggestions for its content.

Publisher Natalie Chapman, who always expressed great enthusiasm for this book.

Senior production editor Ava Wilder, who made sure that the Polish words were rendered correctly and for her slavish attention to detail.

Assistant editor Christine DiComo, for gentle reminders when pages were due.

Christina Solazzo, editorial assistant to my editor, Pam, who responded instantly to any questions or problems.

Production assistant Doug Salvemini, for his extremely thorough attention to detail and cross-referencing.

And Alison Lew and Gary Philo at Vertigo Design for making this book so beautiful.

Special thanks to proofreaders Lilian Brady and Suzanne Fass for their amazing diligence.

The Bakers and Their Contributions

Maureen Abood *Lebanon*

Maureen is a talented cook and food writer who comes from a large Lebanese family where food and its preparation are central to life. Maureen learned from her family that so much happens at the table that it is much more than a place to eat. It is where food and conversation are shared, and it is a place to grow spiritually. "The table is a place where one learns to be civil, how to dialogue, how to love, a place where you can have disagreements and fierce discussions, but in the end you share love and nourishment through the food that you've made." For Maureen and her family, the table has always been a safe and welcoming place. "After arriving from a trip, it didn't matter how late, we'd always sit at the table and eat and drink and share stories. The food could be just a piece of fruit, but the important thing was that it was a time for us to be together." Maureen credits her grandmother with teaching her how to cook traditional Lebanese recipes.

Rosanna Aiuppa *Italy*

Rosanna was born in Sicily and emigrated to the United States as a child. She learned how to cook and bake from her mother, and preparing foods of her home country nourishes her both physically and spiritually. Rosanna recalls that her mother baked well into her eighties, sometimes changing a thing here and there to see if she could improve on a recipe.

Jody Anderson *Sweden*

An accomplished pianist and music teacher, Jody learned traditional Swedish recipes from her mother-in-law. Apples are one of her favorite fruits, and she has several trees in her backyard.

Soile Anderson *Finland*

A professional baker, Soile Anderson is owner/proprietor of a thriving catering company in Minneapolis. She bakes and cooks many Finnish dishes for parties and to sell in her store. Pulla, Finnish sweet coriander buns, are her biggest sellers.

Yvonne Casalnuovo Braddick *Italy*

Because Yvonne comes from a large Italian family, she bakes many traditional recipes learned from her mother and grandmother. Anise Yeast Sfinci, a hand-formed Sicilian doughnut, are an annual Christmastime treat.

Dee Butorac *Norway*

Dee, a professional fitness trainer, learned how to cook from her mother. Her specialty is lefse, a Scandinavian flatbread made from a potato-based dough, rolled very thin, and baked on a griddle. She makes it every year at Christmastime.

Germaine Doelle Conrad *Germany*

Germaine learned how to bake apple strudel from a Serbian neighbor in her apartment building many years ago. Her strudel is so good that people pay her to bake it for them. Every year she offers a few of her strudels as premiums to a fundraiser, and they're snapped up within minutes.

Dorothy Crocker *Norway*

Dorothy, a second-generation Norwegian American, remembers watching her uncle as he stirred the ingredients for limpa together and kneaded the sticky dough by hand until it held its shape when formed into a ball. She bakes it every week. He never parted with his recipe, so over the years Dorothy has developed her own version. She learned how to make the butter cookies from her mother, and now bakes them often.

Garnet Dahmer *Norway*

A second-generation Norwegian American, Garnet learned how to make lefse from her mother, who came to this country when a young bride. Over the years, she has tweaked the recipe, trying different types of potatoes to see which gave the best results. She has passed on this family tradition to her daughter, Dee Butorac (see page xvii).

Evelyn Delly *Iraq*

A woman of tremendous energy and vitality, Evelyn Delly cooks and bakes for her family of seven adult children and their spouses and offspring in Scottsdale, Arizona. Iraqi Meat Pies are among her most popular creations, which she has been making for more than forty years. She has a supply on hand at all times because she never knows when members of her family might drop in. Evelyn is comforted to know that her daughters and daughters-in-law will carry on her Iraqi baking traditions.

Maria DeNitto *Italy*

Owner of a bustling Italian deli in Albany, New York, Maria enjoys baking traditional Sicilian treats for the public and for her family. "I love to see the smiles on their faces," she says. Maria bakes with Rosanna Aiuppa (see page xvi), Rose Padula, and Santa Pasquini (see page xxvii) every holiday season.

Vera Eisenberg *Hungary*

A professional baker and food stylist, Vera Eisenberg prepares dishes from all over the world, but her passion is Hungarian food, which she learned from her mother in Hungary. Vera says, "My mother put ten eggs into everything she baked, so I follow her example."

Maria Elena Flores *Mexico*

Señora Flores, who emigrated from Mexico more than forty years ago, continues baking and cooking dishes she learned from her mother for her children and grandchildren. Buñuelos, wafer-thin fried pastries dusted with cinnamon sugar, and sweet, spiced, pumpkin-filled pastry turnovers are two of her most requested treats. She also makes flour tortillas every week.

Stella Fong *China*

Food writer Stella Fong's parents emigrated from China decades ago. Stella learned how to cook from her mother, and she regularly bakes the cakes and cookies she remembers eating as after-school treats. Stella says, "Mom was a really creative baker and learned how to get by with the simplest equipment, including whipping up eggs with chopsticks!"

Christine Fredricksen *Norway*

A second-generation Norwegian American, Chris bakes kransekake regularly. This tower of eighteen almond paste rings, held together with a confectioners' sugar icing, is often a centerpiece at weddings. Nowadays it's also made for just about any festive event.

Elizabeth Germaine *Australia*

Cooking teacher and cookbook author Elizabeth Germaine loves to bake, and she often prepares traditional Australian recipes for friends and family in Minnesota. Elizabeth's organization of her ingredients and equipment are exemplary. Three of the recipes she decided to share are classics, and the fourth, a Pavlova made with chocolate and cinnamon, is of her own invention.

Catherine Cavallaro Goodman *Italy*

Catherine, a second-generation Italian American, learned how to bake from her mother and several aunts. Because cookies are among her husband and sons' favorites, she bakes large batches of them and keeps them in the freezer. One of five children, Catherine was born and raised in upstate New York. Her grandfather came to the United States in the early 1900s and worked for several years, establishing himself financially before sending for his wife and child. Catherine's father was born in 1923 and as an adult worked in a shoe factory, like his father. Several of Catherine's uncles, and even her father, led lives that read like pages straight out of a Mario Puzo novel.

Betty Groff *Pennsylvania Dutch*

Cookbook author Betty Groff is a tenth-generation descendant of Pennsylvania Dutch immigrants. Cooking and baking are passions she inherited from her mother. She and her husband, Abe, own a golf course and bed-and-breakfast in Mt. Joy, Pennsylvania.

Mareth Gunstream *England*

Mareth is a descendant of Cornish immigrants who came to mine in the United States. She learned to make Cornish Splitters, a simple batter yeast bread, from her grandmother and bakes it frequently for her family.

Pranee Halvorsen *Thailand*

Pranee, a cooking teacher in Seattle, is passionate about sharing culinary traditions of her native country. Although Thailand does not have a baking tradition, fried savory fritters and desserts are extremely popular there. For effervescence in her rice flour batters, Pranee follows the traditional Thai custom of dissolving limestone in water.

Alice Hansen *Norway*

Alice, a second-generation Norwegian American, baked kransekake regularly with her friends Christine Fredricksen and Linda Qualben. I am sad to report she died early this year.

Jessica Harris *African American*

A university professor and prolific author of cookbooks on African cuisine, culture, and history, Ms. Harris has taught and mentored hundreds of students. Ms. Harris told me that Calas, the famous rice fritters of New Orleans, originally came from rice-growing regions in Africa, Liberia, and Sierra Leone. It was Ms. Harris who introduced me to Josephine Obianyo-Agu (see page xxvi), another contributor to this book.

Cammie Mitchell Hinshaw *Scotland*

A third-generation Scottish American, Cammie is a member of our family and is married to my wife's nephew, Michael Hinshaw. Her shortbread recipe originated with Cammie's great-grandmother, Mary McKirgan Mitchell, from Rothsay, Scotland. She passed the recipe on to Cammie's grandmother, Gertrude Kathleen Weatherby Mitchell, who taught it to Cammie.

Helena Hoas *Sweden*

Helena, a professor at the University of Montana, emigrated from Sweden decades ago. She loves to bake. "I don't know why," she says, "But I always seem to bake one of the recipes my mother taught me." It will be no surprise once you bake her recipes.

Carmela Tursi Hobbins *Italy*

A cooking teacher and cookbook author, Carmela delights in sharing her extensive knowledge of Italian cuisine with students, family, and friends. She regularly leads cooking tours to Italy.

Dan Hoffman *Slovenia*

Dan, a retired University professor, and I were students together at the University of California at Berkeley. He learned how to bake Potica, a walnut and honey-filled sweet yeast cake, from his mother more than forty years ago, and he bakes it at least twice a year for family and friends.

Leisha Ingdal *Norway*

Born in the United States of Norwegian parents, Leisha learned how to bake from a grandmother in Norway. As a teenager, she went to live in Norway to learn the language and culture of her heritage. She met her future husband there, and a few years later, they were married. She teaches cooking and baking to enthusiastic students in the Minneapolis area, and to her children, who carry on traditional Norwegian customs.

Bernadette Iribarren *France*

Bernadette came to San Francisco about fifty years ago as an au pair. There she met and married her Basque husband, had two sons, and continued cooking in the Basque tradition, which she learned from her mother. One of eight children, Bernadette was raised on a farm in the town of Macaye. Bernadette says, "We always had fresh eggs and butter, and I learned only to use the best ingredients."

Jinni Jacob *Iraq*

Not Iraqi by heritage, Jinni married an Iraqi man, Ellis Jacob (whom I knew in Shanghai as a child), and learned several traditional dishes from his mother and aunt. She often bakes sambouseks, filled savory pastry turnovers, for company. Jinni lives in Sedona, Arizona, where she teaches piano.

Maria João *Portugal*

Maria João is one of the most accomplished home cooks I've ever met. She lives on the island of Terceira in the Azores, where I met her and learned many traditional Portuguese dishes from her.

Krystyna Kawalec *Poland*

An exceptionally fine baker, Krystyna, a recent immigrant from Poland, taught me several of her favorite recipes that she continues to make for clients and for her family in Chicago.

Ryte Kilikeviciene *Lithuania*

A professional cook, baker, and caterer, Ryte is also an excellent teacher. She began cooking at the age of five and has been doing it ever since.

Noreen Kinney *Ireland*

An authority on Irish history and cuisine, Noreen generously shared her decades-old family recipe for Irish soda bread. Noreen is an indefatigable promoter of Irish cooking and leads culinary tours in Ireland every year.

Rudy Klopp *Germany*

A master baker from Germany, Rudy showed me the authentic way of making real German pretzels.

Cindy Klotz *Eastern Europe and Israel*

Cindy is the owner of a professional bakery that supplies many of New York City's premium stores with muffins, carrot cake, black-and-white cookies, and other delicious baked goods. Strudel is a particular passion of hers. She is a great cook and has a deft hand with everything she makes. Strudel, learned from her Russian grandmother, is a particular passion of hers.

Karin Knight *Norway*

Karin, an immigrant from Norway, maintains the baking traditions she learned from her mother in her native country. She bakes dozens of cookies and pastries every year at Christmas.

Fattigman   46

Krumkaker   246

Pamela Knutson *Sweden*

Of Swedish heritage, Pamela says she learned how to bake from her grandmother, who passed her love of baking to her and to her sister.

Cardamom Coffee Rolls   206

Gertrude Lackschewitz *Germany*

Gertrude, who emigrated to the United States after World War II, is a retired university professor of German. She learned how to cook from her mother and often bakes traditional German desserts for family and friends. Whenever she has a baking question, she calls her sister in Germany for clarification.

Nussplätzchen   260

Pfeffernüsse   262

Stollen   233

Sophie Lambros *Greece*

A first-generation descendant of Greek immigrants, Sophie carries on traditions learned from her mother, cooking and baking Greek foods almost every day. Her daughters do the same.

Melomakarona   248

Savaria Lisuzzo *Italy*

A native of Sicily, Savaria came to the United States decades ago. She makes Sfinci di Ricotta, sweet deep-fried fritters leavened with baking powder, almost every week.

Sfinci di Ricotta   70

Anna Lobonc *Czechoslovakia and Germany*

An immigrant from two European countries, Anna Lobonc makes recipes she learned from her mother and grandmother almost every day. Her repertoire includes some of the best examples in the German baking canon.

Carol Jalovec Lyons *Poland*

Carol's Polish mother taught her how to bake and cook, lessons Carol learned extremely well. Two of her specialties, the sweet yeast bread, babka, and the ethereal jam-filled pastries, kolacky, are outstanding.

Josephine Obianyo-Agu *Nigeria*

Josephine Obianyo-Agu came to the United States from Nigeria in 2004. Her husband and five children had preceded her arrival by a year or two. Trained in her native country in computer science, Josephine is studying for her master's degree in mathematics at Queens College, New York, and she is earning a teaching credential to teach high school math. Josephine says that in Nigeria people are always welcome into the home. When invitations to parties or weddings are sent out, RSVPs aren't necessary, because whoever shows up is an honored guest, and somehow enough food will be provided.

Geri Orsi *Germany*

Geri bakes lebkuchen, the spicy German honey cookies, every Christmas, something she learned from her husband's relatives. Geri says, "The cookies keep so well I make a huge batch, and they last for months and months."

Lebkuchen 272

Rose Padula *Italy*

A cousin of Rosanna Aiuppa (see page xvi), Rose is one of several Sicilian-American women friends who gather in the fall of each year to bake Sicilian holiday treats.

Cannoli 60

Casatelli 63

Chitra Paresh *India*

A recent immigrant from India, Chitra is a master maker of Indian flatbreads, which is something she does every morning. She shared many recipes with me, chapati being the most well known.

Chapati 92

Tottie Baines Parmeter *Wales*

Tottie, an excellent cook and baker, taught me several recipes she had learned in Wales from her mother. "I found it hard at first to make the recipes the way I remembered them tasting," Tottie said, "But when I tried different flours, I got the results I wanted."

Bara Brith 216

Welsh Christmas Cake 282

Welsh Griddle Cakes 160

Santa Pasquini *Italy*

A Sicilian American, and a friend of Rosanna Aiuppa, Maria DeNitto, and Rose Padula (see above), Santa is the designated pignoli expert, and she bakes them every year for the yuletide holidays.

Pignoli 264

Bipin Patel *India*

Bipin is the owner of Tipu's Tiger, an Indian restaurant in Missoula, Montana. He taught me the traditional Indian breads he learned from his mother and grandmother.

Mabel Patent *Iraq*

My mother, who died last year, spent years re-creating the Iraqi recipes she remembered her mother (my granny) making. She was most successful with the three included here.

Linda Qualben *Norway*

A kransekake expert and second-generation Norwegian American, Linda and her friends Christine Fredricksen and the late Alice Hansen (see page xxi) regularly baked this traditional Norwegian dessert to sell to eager patrons.

Ray and Susie Risho *Syria*

Retired chef Ray Risho and his artist wife, Susie, cook the dishes of Ray's heritage every day at home. Ray learned from his mother, as did Susie. Savory yeast breads are some of their favorites.

Daniela Ruggiero *Italy*

A cooking teacher and philosophy professor, Daniela regularly cooks the dishes of her native city, Naples, in her American home in Minneapolis.

Kathy Papastathis Salzetti *Greece*

A first-generation Greek American, Kathy learned how to cook from her mother and calls her often to clarify the details of a particular dish.

Eileen MacKerrow Sangster *Ireland*

Eileen learned the version of Irish soda bread included here from her grandmother. She bakes it often for her coworkers in California.

Bryony van derMerwe Schwan *South Africa*

A new American citizen from South Africa, Bryony now loves to cook the dishes she learned there in her home in Montana.

Kristine Soedal *Norway*

Kristine loves to bake all things Norwegian—and her husband and children show their appreciation by always asking for "more, please."

William Woys Weaver *Pennsylvania Dutch*

Noted scholar and historian Will Weaver has written many cookbooks on Pennsylvania Dutch food. He generously and unstintingly shared his knowledge with me for this book and for my previous book, *Baking in America*.

Carol Williams *England*

Montana Congresswoman Carol Williams's grandparents came to the United States from Cornwall because of the lucrative mining industry. Carol learned to bake from her grandmother, and the pasty, a turnover of meat and potatoes that miners took with them for lunch when they descended below ground to work, is something she still makes often.

Li Yanxiang *China*

Li, the housekeeper and cook working for my son Jason and his family in Beijing, makes all sorts of Chinese flatbreads and dumplings. Jian Bing, pork-filled flatbreads, is one of her specialties she taught me.

Arzu Yilmaz *Turkey*

Cooking teacher Arzu Yilmaz shares her vast knowledge of Turkish cuisine with students at the Institute of Culinary Education in New York City. She arrived in America some fifteen years ago and lives in New Jersey with her husband and children.

Luba Zeleniak *Russia*

My late auntie Luba helped me re-create two of my favorite childhood foods that Baba, her mother and my grandmother, made for Russian Easter—kulich, a tall sweet yeast cake, and paskha, a sweet molded cheese dessert.

Introduction

I remember being overcome by a feeling of sheer happiness when my parents told me we were moving to America. At the time, we were living in Shanghai, and my total knowledge of America came from movies, popular music, shortwave radio, and candy bars. I loved them all, and couldn't wait to leave. But why were we leaving? Shanghai had been my parents' home for twenty years. My mother had immigrated from Iraq and my father from Russia. They met and married in Shanghai, and all our relatives and friends lived there.

My father told me why we were leaving China. He said, addressing me by my nickname, "Gigi, America is the land of opportunity. It's where all things are possible." Before World War II, Shanghai had been the place of limitless possibilities, and thousands of expatriates from all over the world came to China's most progressive and fashionable city to make their fortunes. The foreigners with the highest status and power were the British. The French and Americans living there also had position, but some other nationalities, including the Iraqis and Russians, were not in the same league socially and economically. For these reasons, and also because my parents had expected that we'd spend our lives in Shanghai, they decided to have me born British, to give me all the advantages of a British citizen living in Shanghai. So shortly before I was due, my mom traveled by ship to the British Crown Colony of Hong Kong to give birth.

But the war changed everything. The Japanese, who occupied China, were at war with Great Britain, and I was a two-and-a-half-year-old enemy. My young age saved me from internment in a labor camp. Because Iraq and Russia were not at war with Japan, my parents were also spared internment.

Making a living while the war went on was extremely difficult. Mom had been employed as a secretary by an American firm, but they closed their offices when the war began. My parents could no longer afford their own place, so my mother's mother, Granny, took us in, and we all lived in her small one-room apartment in Shanghai's International Settlement. The money dad earned as an announcer and deejay on an English language radio station, XMHA, helped put food on the table.

Granny's food is what I remember most about the war years. What she created on a limited budget was astonishing. Besides soups, main dishes, and hand-made pastas, Granny baked all sorts of Jewish and Middle Eastern breads, cakes, cookies, and pastries. She always had a supply of *kahk* on hand, crunchy, savory bracelets of dough I'd munch on when I came home from school. When she made sponge cake, my eyes widened at the sight of billowy egg whites mounting to extraordinary heights as she whipped them with a fork on a large plate held on her lap. Granny made all these wonderful things using a small stove with a tiny oven in our twelve by fifteen foot apartment.

My dad's mother, Baba, who lived a few blocks away in the French Concession, was such an amazing baker that people paid her to make special desserts for them. Napoleons, rectangles of puff pastry filled with pastry cream, were a specialty of hers, and sometimes she brought a few to our home. Each time I bit into one, I'd look closely at all those crisp, paper-thin layers and wonder how they came about. Baba also made two traditional Russian Easter desserts, kulich, a sweet yeast cake, and paskha, a molded sweet cheese dessert, that are always eaten together. I'd spread a thick layer of the creamy paskha onto a slice of kulich and ask her, "Baba, how do you make the cheese so smooth?" I didn't know it then, but the seeds of a future baker had been planted.

As difficult as times were, life went on as normally as possible during the war. People threw parties, celebrated birthdays, and went on picnics. My mom and I took long walks all over the city, and once or twice we even had ice cream as a special treat. I played with my cousins at my uncle's house, visited dad at the radio station, and even got to sing "Somewhere over the Rainbow" on the air one day.

When the war ended, American businesses reopened their offices, mom began working for her old firm, and dad got a job as a bookkeeper at the YMCA. Dad met lots of American soldiers there, and he'd bring them home to meet the family. The soldiers gave my parents Spam and me candy bars. What wonderful food Americans eat, I thought. I began going to movies, American movies, and spent hours at the Uptown Theater just down the block. The cashier would take pity on me and let me sneak in after a movie started because I never had any money. Dad bought a shortwave radio and we were thrilled to listen to broadcasts coming directly from America.

Living in America had been a dream of my parents since the war began. Even though they'd be leaving family and friends behind, the chance of making a better life was something they couldn't resist. Soon after the war ended, my brother Bob was born. Having two children to support in a country that was becoming increasingly unstable politically made them determined to leave. And once the communists took over in 1949, it became imperative.

By the time we left China in 1950, many of our friends had already emigrated to various parts of the world, including Canada, Israel, Europe, Australia, and America. My parents chose San Francisco because, in the five years since the war ended, it had become a place where many of their Russian friends from Shanghai had settled. So many Russians were living in San Francisco, that within a few years, a cookbook, *Recipes from the Russians of San Francisco*, became a best seller.

One day while walking with my dad downtown on Market Street, we saw a crowd of people peering into a department store window. Curious, we went to have a look. What we saw was television. Here was this large wooden cabinet with a moving image on it, and it transfixed us just as it had everyone else watching. Dad was determined we'd have a set of our own as soon as possible, and within a couple of months, he bought one. It was like having our own personal movie theater.

Cooking shows were among the first regularly televised programs, and each of the three network stations featured one. But one show in particular, hosted by Edith Green, hooked me. She made cooking look like fun. She explained things clearly, made her share of mistakes—the show was televised live—and rolled with the punches. I wrote recipes she made onto sheets of paper so that I'd have them for future reference. I hadn't cooked anything myself yet, but Mom picked up on my keen interest and bought me a copy of the brand new *Betty Crocker Cookbook*. I read it like a novel, cover to cover, and imagined making all the delicious-looking cakes, pies, pastries, and cookies.

One day I got the courage to try my hand at baking and picked the easiest recipe I could find: baking powder biscuits. The results were a disaster. The biscuits hardly rose, and they were tough as rocks. I did the only thing a sensible child my age could do: I cried. But I decided not to give up because Edith Green always found a way to make things right. Sometimes she had to repeat a recipe to achieve this, so that's what I needed to do.

I ran upstairs to our landlady with my miserable biscuits to see if maybe she knew what I had done wrong. Being an excellent baker herself, she told me I had handled the dough too much. "Go easy, next time," she said. "Just toss the dough about for a few seconds until it holds together, then pat it gently before cutting out the biscuits." Her advice worked, and my next batch turned out looking just like the picture in the book. They also were tender and fluffy inside, just like the recipe said they should be. From then on, all I wanted to do was bake.

Baking is a form of alchemy. The ancients sought in vain to transform lead into gold. In baking, all you need to transform elemental ingredients—flour, sugar, eggs, liquid, flavorings—into an infinite number of baked goods, is heat. The result is completely different from the ingredients you start with. That, to me, is its magic, and it makes me want to do it over and over again. For me, it's not a question of wanting to bake. I *have* to bake.

Once we were settled in San Francisco, my parents were eager to participate in the culture of their new home, so we began celebrating Thanksgiving. But our holiday dinner consisted mostly of Russian appetizers, *zakuski*—platters of deli meats and cheeses and salads of beets and cucumbers in sour cream, with dark breads spread thickly with sweet butter and freezer-cold shots of vodka for the adults. The turkey came at the end, almost as an afterthought. No stuffing and no gravy—just canned cranberry sauce. Over time, the holiday bird gained in prominence at our feasts, but Russian foods and drinks always occupied center stage. What was familiar prevailed.

Food is like language. You grow up learning to speak your mother tongue, and at the same time you develop tastes for specific foods. If you move to a new country, you yearn for connection to the place you left, and food is the magical link. My parents were no different from other immigrants in wanting to connect with familiar foods in a foreign land.

That is why I wanted to write this cookbook. I knew why my mother and her Iraqi friends strove to re-create dishes their mothers had cooked for them, and why I wanted to bake my Russian baba's desserts, but did that same urge stir in other immigrants too? I decided the only way to find out was to travel around the country to meet these home bakers in their own kitchens, to bake with them, and to learn their stories of why they keep baking what they do. I did not want to work from written recipes, because often, something—a step deemed too simple to put down on paper—is left out. My plan was to sketch out each recipe as it was made; to make measurements of my own if the baker did it only by eye. I'd jot down notes on technique and take photos of the process step by step, to give myself the reminders I'd need to re-create the recipe in my kitchen.

In my latest cookbook, *Baking in America*, I told the history of America through two hundred years of baking. I delved into eighteenth- and nineteenth-century cookbooks in libraries all over the country to learn about the origins of America's baking, and to discover how recipes were modified and new ones were created over time. Simplicity, straightforwardness, and experimentation are the hallmarks of the American cook and baker. We are a people who love the new, and we celebrate it constantly.

The immigrant baker is completely different. She (it is almost always "she") wants to preserve tradition and bake things the way she learned from her mother or grandmother or aunt in her homeland. It is her way of honoring and connecting with her birthplace and the people she left behind. But she has often had to adapt her recipes to the ingredients she finds here. Maria Elena Flores uses Halloween pumpkins for her empanadas because the "water pumpkin" that grows in her native Mexico isn't available in the United States. Since Halloween pumpkins are around only for a short time in the fall, Maria Elena uses butternut squash at other times of the year, which she likes just as well. Tottie Parmeter uses cake flour in her Welsh Griddle Cakes because she has found it to be a fine substitute for the soft wheat flour she bought in Cardiff. It gives her the same taste and texture she remembers so clearly.

When I began this book, I didn't have a detailed roadmap. I knew I wanted a few specific recipes—Swedish Princess Torte, for example, an elaborate three-layer cake with raspberry jam and a custard and whipped cream filling, all enrobed in a thin sheet of pale green marzipan; apple strudel, the real thing, with paper-thin stretched strudel dough that crackles beneath a fork; kulich and paskha, the Russian Easter cake and the molded cheese that is spread on it with abandon that I knew from my own childhood; and Iraqi savory bracelets, the ones my Granny made—but beyond that, I'd let the book take me where it wanted to go.

Much would depend on the bakers I'd be able to find and their willingness to spend hours of their time working with me. Maria Elena Flores was the first. She lives near Sacramento, California, and how I found her was typical of the way I met most of the bakers in this book. My wife, Dorothy, and I were attending our son Jason's doctoral ceremony at the University of California, Berkeley. Jason was in the Linguistics department, and he introduced us to the director of the program, Belen Flores. Belen was born in California, but when I asked about her name, she told me that her mother had moved to the States from Mexico decades earlier. I sensed a possibility here, so I asked, "Does your mother bake?" "Oh, Mom's an excellent baker and cook. She's doing it all the time for us." That's all I needed. I learned from Belen that pumpkin empanadas was one of her mother's specialties, and that she made it often for her grandsons. She made buñuelos, paper-thin crisp fried wafers, for Christmas, but Belen said her mother would probably be happy to make them for me too. A few months later, on another trip to California, I arranged a baking date with Maria Elena, who turned out to be a total delight to work with. She speaks little English, so Belen acted as interpreter.

I found Krystyna Kawalec, a fabulous Polish cook and baker, through my daughter-in-law, Amy, who was living in the Chicago area at the time. Amy's neighbor, Liz McDonald, had a young Polish housekeeper. When Liz told her housekeeper I was looking for a great Polish baker, the housekeeper said, "My mom. He has to meet my mom." So I made a trip to Chicago, met briefly with Krystyna, and set a date and time to meet with her at Liz's home to bake. I went to a Polish grocery store and bought all the ingredients on Krystyna's list, and we set to work for two days of baking in Liz's large, well-equipped modern kitchen. Makowiec, a poppy seed roll, and Pączki, jam-filled doughnuts made just before Lent, are two of Krystyna's favorite recipes.

One thing that stands out about all the women I've worked with is the way they use their eyes and their hands in the kitchen. They reminded me of how Granny cooked. Most of them measure both dry ingredients and liquids by eye. It's how they learned, and they say it's quicker than taking the time to weigh or measure. For example, Krystyna dumped some flour from a sack onto the granite countertop, and announced it was 2 pounds. I weighed the 5-pound bag, and it now weighed 3 pounds. I was floored and awed by how well she knew her ingredients. Chitra Paresh measured her atta flour and water by eye for all of her Indian flatbreads. Maria Elena Flores did the same for the pumpkin empanadas dough and for her flour tortillas and buñuelos.

The women always adjusted the consistency of their doughs and pastries with liquid, depending on the humidity of the room and the dryness of the flour. They'd reach into the bowl with their hands, mixing, kneading, and squeezing the ingredients together, manipulating the mass until the consistency met their satisfaction. The whole process was one of give-and-take.

Many of the doughs I learned had to be shaped individually: some of the doughs for frying, all the flatbreads, many of the pastries and yeasted doughs, and lots of the cookies. There is much to be learned from shaping doughs and pastries by hand. Aside from literally putting you in touch with what you're making, it is a way to practice and develop a particular technique. It is an exercise of sorts, with food. Working with one's hands is also meditative—it takes you and what you're making into a spiritual place.

Many of the recipes I learned are traditionally made in quantity—8 to 10 dozen cookies, for example—which would be a real burden for just one baker. So a group of women from the same country would get together, often before a holiday, for a marathon session or two of baking. Several sets of hands speed the process along, and the women would chat and gossip and laugh and sip wine or coffee or tea and turn the baking into a special social occasion. I participated in one of these happy gatherings in Albany, New York, with a group of Sicilian-American women baking Christmas pastries and cookies. What impressed me during our weekend of baking was the warmth I saw between these women and how much they enjoyed just being together in the kitchen. This was something they did every year, yet each year seemed like a new beginning. The big payoff for them came on Sunday night, when all the family members gathered together for a gigantic dessert party and lavished praise upon them for their delicious efforts. Receiving their mothers' approval was what the women cherished the most.

While working on this book, I baked with about sixty women and five men. Dan Hoffman carries on his Slovenian mother's tradition of Potica, a super thin, sweet yeast dough filled with walnuts and honey; Bipin Patel, who owns an Indian restaurant, shared recipes for his family's stuffed flatbreads and samosas; and food historian William Woys Weaver, a tenth-generation Pennsylvania Dutch descendant, has been writing about the cooking and baking traditions of his family and culture for decades. From him I got the recipe for The Original Shoofly Pie.

In writing the recipes for this book, I have kept as true to the originals as possible. I have not added any new ingredients, but sometimes I've indicated a suggested variation at the end of recipes. In many cases, I had to scale the recipes down to make them manageable for one baker. Even so, you'll find some recipes that yield several dozen pastries, but these store well in the freezer and will be at the ready when you need them.

What a journey working on this book has been! Not only did I reconnect with my Iraqi and Russian heritage, I also became connected to about three dozen other cultures, and twice that many people, through all the marvelous bakers and their families who welcomed me into their homes to share their lives, stories, and recipes. A world of baking and discovery awaits you in these pages. Welcome, and have fun!

Ingredients

CHOCOLATE

Bittersweet Chocolate

Unsweetened chocolate with the addition of some sugar and vanilla flavoring, bittersweet chocolate is marvelous for baking because of its strong chocolate flavor.

Cocoa

Once all the cocoa butter (which is used to make chocolate) has been removed from roasted and ground cacao beans, the dried cake that's left, called cocoa liquor, is ground into a fine powder, cocoa. Cocoa powder is bitter because it contains no sugar, but it imparts a deep, rich chocolate flavor to baked goods and other desserts. Hershey's is probably the best-known natural, or nonalkalized, cocoa. Dutch-process cocoa is natural cocoa that's been treated with an alkali to neutralize its acidity. It is darker in color than natural cocoa and gives baked goods a smoother chocolate flavor.

Some baking recipes call specifically for one type of cocoa, and in that case, it's important you don't substitute one for the other. Since natural cocoa is acidic, it needs some alkali to work properly, and baking soda is usually used for that purpose. If you substituted a Dutch-process cocoa for natural in the recipe, you would need an acid, such as baking powder, not an alkali, to balance it.

Semisweet Chocolate

Semisweet chocolate has a lower percentage of cocoa solids and more sugar than bittersweet chocolate. Unless you like chocolate on the bitter side, semisweet makes the best eating chocolate.

Unsweetened Chocolate

The most concentrated of chocolate flavors in solid form, unsweetened chocolate is made from chocolate liquor with some cocoa butter added back, and nothing else. After the two are combined, the mixture undergoes a lengthy process, called conching, lasting from several hours to a week, which mixes, kneads, and beats air into the chocolate, giving it a smooth texture. The equipment originally used for the process, a long trough made of stone, was curved like a shell, hence the name. Unsweetened chocolate contains no sugar and is as bitter as cocoa; it has a fairly high fat content, about 14 grams per ounce. It must be melted before being used in cakes or cookies.

EGGS AND DAIRY PRODUCTS

Buttermilk

Buttermilk contributes tenderness and a delightful tang to baked goods. When butter used to be churned at home, the watery liquid left over after the cream solidified into butter was buttermilk. Today buttermilk is cultured. It has a thick, creamy texture but is low in fat. Buttermilk keeps well in the refrigerator for several weeks. Over time, it tends to separate into a heavier, thicker layer on the bottom with a thin, watery layer on top. Shake the milk carton a few times to mix the two before using.

Cream Cheese

Regular cream cheese comes in dense 3- and 8-ounce blocks. It's smooth and spreadable and contains at least 33 percent milk fat. Made with pasteurized milk, cheese cultures, and salt, with gum arabic as a stabilizer, regular cream cheese works better in recipes than "natural" cream cheeses made without stabilizers.

Eggs

All recipes in this book call for U.S. Grade A large eggs, which weigh about 2 ounces in the shell. Whenever possible, buy eggs laid by cage-free chickens fed organic feed. I buy eggs at a local health food store, where local purveyors make deliveries every few days.

The eggshells may be white, brown, green, or blue, depending on the breed of laying hen; the color of the shell has nothing to do with the quality of the egg.

Heavy Cream and Whipping Cream

Both these creams can be whipped, but heavy cream has a higher butterfat content (36 percent) than whipping cream (30 to 36 percent). The unfortunate practice of ultra-pasteurization, which extends shelf life, has a negative effect on the taste and texture of cream. Ultrapasteurized cream tastes less sweet than pasteurized cream, and it takes longer to whip. If you can find regular pasteurized cream, by all means buy it.

Milk

For baking, I always use whole milk. It makes pastry creams smooth and silky, gives custards body, and contributes a richer flavor to cakes, cookies, and other baked goods than low-fat milks.

Sour Cream

Real full-fat sour cream is cultured with lactic acid bacteria and has a butterfat content of about 14 percent. In baking, it adds tang, moistness, and richness. Low-fat sour cream is okay to use; avoid nonfat because of its additives.

Yogurt

A staple food for centuries in parts of Europe, the Middle East, and Asia, yogurt has made inroads into American baking as a lower-fat substitute for sour cream. In many cases, it works extremely well, especially if it is turned into "yogurt cheese" by putting the yogurt in cheesecloth and draining off the excess liquid. Yogurt is made by culturing lactobacillus or acidophilus bacteria in milk—whole, low-fat, or skim—causing it to thicken and turn sour. The milks of cows, goats, and sheep all make excellent yogurt, but in this country the most commonly available kind is made with cow's milk. Avoid yogurts that contain artificial gums. I use only plain unflavored yogurt in baking. Greek yogurt is particularly fine.

Butter

There is no substitute for butter. Its sweet flavor adds immeasurably to the taste of whatever you're baking. I prefer unsalted butter, because salt can mask the rich flavor. However, I do specify salted butter for some of the recipes in this book because that's what the bakers used. Over the years, I've tried many brands of butter, both regional and national, and the one with the most consistently good results has been Land O' Lakes. It has a marvelous sweet cream taste. If you do lots of baking, buy several pounds of butter when it's on sale and store it, well wrapped, in the freezer; thaw it in the refrigerator before you use it.

Many recipes in this book call for room-temperature butter, which means at a temperature from 65° to 70°F. Some professional bakers even take the temperature of the butter with an instant-read thermometer to make sure. What's important is that the butter be malleable, so that it creams and aerates when beaten with the sugar.

The microwave is handy for softening cold butter. Unwrap the butter, set it on a piece of waxed paper, and microwave at 30-percent power for 30 seconds. Test the butter to see if it feels cool and waxy and if your finger leaves an impression when you press it. If not, turn the stick(s) over and microwave again for a few seconds.

When butter is to be cut into flour to make pastry, it should be very cold, so that the pieces remain firm. During rolling, the butter flattens out, forming flakes arranged haphazardly throughout the dough. In the oven, the melting butter forms air pockets in the dough, making the pastry flaky.

Occasionally a recipe calls for clarified butter, as in Baklawa (page 140). To clarify butter, cut 3 sticks of butter into tablespoon-sized pieces and place them into a medium heavy saucepan. Melt the butter over low heat and bring it to a slow boil. Cook for 20 to 30 minutes. During this time the butter will be making noisy crackling, pinging, and sputtering sounds. While the butter cooks, skim off as much of the surface foam as you can with a teaspoon (you won't be able to get it all). You'll know the butter is clarified when it is silent. Watch and listen carefully near the end of the cooking time—it should be golden, not brown. Remove the pan from the heat. Carefully pour the clear golden butter through a very fine strainer into a 2-cup heatproof glass measure, leaving any buttery residue on the bottom of the saucepan. You should have slightly more than 1 cup of clarified butter. The butter can be clarified ahead. Let cool, cover, then refrigerate or freeze for up to 1 month. When ready to use, bring to room temperature and use in a solid form, or remelt the butter in a heavy small saucepan over low heat to use in cooking.

Lard

A little lard in combination with butter makes far flakier piecrusts than butter alone. Part of the reason is that lard is virtually water-free. Even small amounts of water produce gluten formation in wheat flour, and butter contains about 16 percent water. For delicious, flaky pastry, substitute lard for half the amount of butter.

For the best lard, you should render your own (see page 332), as our forbears did when they lived on farms and raised hogs. But you can order excellent home-rendered lard (see Sources, pages 342 and 343). Avoid blocks of supermarket lard, because they often contain undesirable trans fats and other additives. Store in the refrigerator or freezer.

Vegetable Oils

The oils most commonly used in cooking and baking are canola, corn, safflower, sunflower, and peanut. For frying, peanut oil is my first choice because it has a high smoking point, meaning it won't burn until the oil reaches very high temperatures. It also adds a mild nutty flavor to fried foods.

Vegetable Shortening

To make vegetable shortening, liquid vegetable oils are hydrogenated: through some chemical wizardry, extra hydrogen atoms are attached to the oils to turn them into a saturated fat. The addition of nitrogen gas to America's most popular brand, Crisco, helps extend its shelf life and contributes to its pure white color. Vegetable shortening is softer than butter, is easy to measure (Crisco comes in premeasured sticks), needs no refrigeration, and makes wonderfully flaky, tender pastries and fluffy cakes. The problem is that it has no taste, not even the new Crisco that contains no trans fat. For these reasons, when I use vegetable shortening, I use a higher proportion of butter to shortening in the recipe. And, when a recipe calls for vegetable shortening, I often substitute lard.

Almond and Anise Extracts and Oils

Be sure to use only pure almond or anise extract, readily available now in most supermarkets. Almond and anise oils, which come in small bottles and have a more concentrated flavor, are sold in ethnic food markets and can be ordered online (see Sources, page 343).

Lemon and Orange Extracts

Made by distilling concentrated solutions of essential oils from the fruit zests, these extracts add an authentic citrus flavor to all kinds of desserts. Always use pure extracts, readily available in supermarkets. Imitation extracts contain artificial substances and flavors.

Orange Flower Water

Orange flower water, also called orange blossom water, is distilled from the petals of orange blossoms. Like rose water, its use goes back centuries. I use it in custards, cakes, and cookies when I want a floral orange taste and aroma. In this book I use it in Baklawa (page 140), and sometimes I substitute it for rose water in Graibi (page 244), Lebanese butter crescents. Middle Eastern and Moroccan cooks use it in salads, syrups, and some savory foods. Middle Eastern stores and specialty markets, as well as some Italian delis, sell bottles of orange flower water. It can also be ordered by mail (see Sources, page 343). Store it in a cool, dark place after opening. It keeps indefinitely.

Rose Water

One of the oldest and most aromatic of all flavorings, rose water is distilled from the petals of roses. I love its sophisticated flavor and aroma and use it in pound cake, cookies, and other baked goods. In this book I use it in Graibi, Lebanese butter crescents (page 244) and in Date Babas (page 134). You can buy rose water in specialty food shops and in stores that sell Middle Eastern foods; it can also be ordered online (see Sources, page 343). It comes in small bottles and should be stored in a cool, dark place after opening. It keeps indefinitely.

Vanilla Beans and Extract

The fruit of an orchid native to Central America, vanilla must be hand-pollinated, making it quite costly. Once harvested, the pods (fruits) undergo a months-long process of fermentation and ripening before they are aged, for up to two years, and finally brought to market. Today we can buy vanilla from Mexico, Madagascar, Indonesia, Tahiti, and Hawaii.

Be sure to buy vanilla beans that are soft, plump, and pliable. They add an intense and concentrated flavor to sauces, cakes and other desserts, and sugar. For sauces, split the bean lengthwise, scrape out the small black seeds with a teaspoon, and add the seeds and pod to the milk or cream. Steeping over low heat for about 30 minutes releases vanilla's heady aromatic compounds. The pod can be rinsed, dried, and reused two or three times. For cakes, I sometimes make a quick vanilla sugar. I grind the bean with some of the sugar in the recipe in a coffee or spice grinder until both are pulverized and the sugar is saturated with vanilla's taste and aroma, then I cream the vanilla sugar with the butter. Vanilla sugar is delicious sprinkled over cookies hot from the oven or stirred into a steaming mug of tea, coffee, or cocoa. To store vanilla beans, wrap them tightly in plastic, seal them in a glass jar or in a resealable freezer bag, and place them in a cool cupboard. The beans will stay fresh for 4 to 6 months.

To make pure vanilla extract, the mature beans are chopped and steeped in a water-alcohol solution for a few months. Avoid imitation vanilla—it is made from artificial ingredients and contains no vanilla at all.

Wheat Flours

In the United States, which grows some of the world's best wheat, three main species are cultivated today, but they include more than 100 distinct varieties. Wheat is classified according to the season in which it's sown. Winter wheat is planted in the fall and reaped in the late summer or autumn of the following year. Spring wheat is sown in the spring and harvested in the fall of the same year.

A wheat kernel has three main parts: The endosperm, which makes up the bulk of the grain (80 to 85 percent), is mainly starch and protein. The tiny germ (2 to 3 percent of the kernel), or embryo of the plant, is packed with minerals, vitamins, including vitamin E, proteins, and fats. The bran (about 15 percent of the grain), or tough outer husk, is a rich source of fiber.

Winter and spring wheats can be "hard" or "soft," depending on their protein content. Generally speaking, the higher the amount of protein, the harder the wheat. The color of the wheat grain is another indicator of protein content. Hard red spring or hard red winter wheat is ideal for making bread, whereas soft red winter wheat is best used in cakes and pastries. Other soft wheats include winter and spring white wheats. The important point to keep in mind is to choose the proper flour for what you are going to bake. If it's a cake or pastry, you'll want a soft wheat flour, low in protein (8 to 9 percent). If you're baking a chewy, yeasty bread, then opt for a hard wheat flour (11 to 13 percent). As a rough guide, check the label on the flour package for protein content to determine if it's milled from soft or hard wheat. For each ¼ cup flour, soft wheat cake flour will have 2 grams protein, all-purpose bleached or unbleached flour 3 grams, and hard wheat bread flour 4 grams.

Wheat flour contains many kinds of proteins, but two of the main ones, glutenin and gliadin, are what give the wheat its "strength." When glutenin and gliadin come into contact with liquid, they knit together to form a network called gluten. The more there is of these proteins (the harder the wheat), the more gluten is formed, and the stretchier the dough becomes.

I use organic flours in baking whenever possible. They are better for the planet and more healthful for us. These flours are becoming increasingly available in supermarkets. The all-purpose brand I use routinely is Gold Medal Organic Unbleached Flour. For most breads, I use a hard wheat organic bread flour made by King Arthur. It can be ordered online or by mail if you can't find a local source (see Sources, page 341).

ALL-PURPOSE FLOUR

All-purpose flour is a blend of soft and hard wheat flours, with a medium percentage of protein. However, not all so-called all-purpose flours are equal. White Lily, for example, which is a wonderful flour milled in Knoxville, Tennessee, is labeled all-purpose, but it is really a soft wheat flour best suited for making cakes, biscuits, and pastries.

All-purpose flour may be bleached or unbleached. After the bran and germ have been removed from wheat, the resulting unbleached flour has a creamy cast. To make flour pure white, it is treated chemically with chlorine dioxide, benzoyl peroxide, and acetone peroxide. This bleaching, or whitening, process destroys vitamin E and members of the B-complex group, so bleached flour must then be "enriched" by adding these vitamins.

Bleached all-purpose flour contains slightly less protein than unbleached all-purpose flour. Many bakers prefer using bleached flour in cakes, cookies, and pastries because they say the results are more delicate.

Although all-purpose flour is supposed to be ideal for any use, that is not generally the case. I far prefer cake flour or unbleached soft wheat flour for cakes, and I often use a mixture of cake flour and all-purpose flour for pastries.

A Note to the Cook on Measuring Flour

For the recipes in this book, flour is measured either by the dip-and-sweep method or by the spoon-and-level method; in most cases, it is the dip-and-sweep method. To measure by the dip-and-sweep method, stir the flour in its container to aerate it slightly, then dip a dry measuring cup into the flour, filling it to overflowing, and sweep off the excess with a narrow metal spatula or a knife. To measure by the spoon-and-level method, after stirring to aerate the flour, spoon it into a dry measuring cup to overflowing and sweep off the excess with a narrow metal spatula or a knife. Unless the recipe specifies otherwise, use the dip-and-sweep method.

ATTA FLOUR

A very finely ground whole wheat flour passed through a fine sieve to remove the coarsest bran flakes. It is an even buff color and is used to make chapati and other Indian flatbreads. It is sold in Indian markets and South Asian grocery stores. You can also order it by mail (see Sources, page 343).

BREAD FLOUR

An unbleached hard wheat flour with a protein content of 11 to 13 percent, bread flour makes breads with a springy, chewy texture. I wouldn't use bread flour in cakes or pie doughs, but I do use it for strudel doughs.

CAKE FLOUR

Cake flour is a bleached soft wheat flour with a protein content of 8 to 9 percent. It makes light-textured, tender cakes and biscuits. It is too low in gluten to be used successfully in yeast breads. I use it in combination with bread flour to make puff pastry.

GRAHAM FLOUR

Graham flour is a coarsely ground whole wheat flour that gives breads a marvelous texture and a rich, nutty taste. Use it in yeast breads and quick breads.

WHOLE WHEAT FLOUR

If you can find stone-ground whole wheat flour, by all means buy it. Because less heat is generated during stone-grinding than with regular steel milling, more of the nutrients in the flour are preserved. And because it is ground between two stones, the flour has an uneven texture, which gives an interesting toothsome quality and richer, nuttier taste to breads.

Other Grains and Flours

OATMEAL

Oatmeal is highly nutritious because it contains the bran, germ, and endosperm of the grain; only the indigestible outer hull is removed in processing. I like to use old-fashioned or quick-cooking oats for the chewy texture and nutty taste they give to cookies and breads; I don't use instant oatmeal in baking.

RICE FLOUR

White rice flour is ground from husked rice kernels. It has an ultrafine texture and a pure white color. Since it doesn't contain gluten, there is no danger of overbeating batters made with rice flour. Rice flour is available in some supermarkets, usually in 2-pound bags, or it can be ordered by mail (see Sources, page 343). I use it in Thai Shrimp and Bean Sprout Fritters (page 128) and in Thai Fried Bananas (page 76). Rice flour is a good alternative for people who are sensitive to gluten.

RYE FLOUR

Rye flour can make dense, chewy, delicious breads, but because it is low in gluten, breads made with only rye flour turn out on the gummy side and hardly rise at all. In most cases, wheat flour (white or whole wheat) is added to the dough for texture and volume. Rye flour has a rich, nutty, slightly tart taste, and a little of it adds a marvelous tang to conventional doughs. Two basic types of rye flour are sold in the United States: dark, or pumpernickel rye, and light, or medium, rye. The whole grain is ground to make dark rye flour. It is coarse-textured and loaded with protein, vitamins, and minerals. I use it in Limpa (page 174). Because of its stronger taste and grittier texture, dark rye flour is great in bread doughs. Light rye has had the germ and sometimes the bran removed during milling, giving it a lighter color, finer texture, and less nutrition than dark rye. I use a little light rye flour in Schwabisch Pretzels (page 188).

Citron

Candied citron is made from the thick, knobby rind of a large lemon-like member of the citrus family. The fruit is cut in half and the flesh removed, then the rind is soaked in a brine, drained, and candied. It is often tinted a pale green color. Top-quality citron is tender and has a waxy texture (see Sources, page 342). Citron is sold chopped or as half-rinds. It's best to buy the larger pieces, which keep better, and cut them to suit your needs. Store citron tightly wrapped in plastic in a cool place for 4 to 6 months, or freeze it for up to 8 months.

Dried Fruits

The dried fruit available in supermarkets is most often sold in sealed packages. Dried fruit should be moist and supple when used in baking, so be sure to reclose the packages tightly after opening. Or, better yet, transfer the fruit to a resealable plastic bag, and store in the refrigerator, where it will keep better than at room temperature. If the fruit does dry out, you can soften it by steaming it in a wire strainer set over a pan of boiling water for a few minutes. Pat the fruit dry on paper towels, and it's ready to use. If you need diced or cut fruit, steam large pieces and cut them after steaming.

Fresh Apples

Even though some apple varieties can be kept in controlled-atmosphere holding chambers for a year, apples always taste best at harvest time. Use apples from New Zealand during our off-season. For baking, Braeburn is my favorite all-purpose apple. It is tart and sweet and firm-textured, and the slices hold their shape in baking. Honeygold is another excellent variety, usually available in October. I rarely use Granny Smith or Golden Delicious, since both of these varieties are picked underripe and never develop their full flavor potential. An apple strudel tastes better made with three or more varieties of fruit, each with a slightly different taste and texture. A combination of one-third each Braeburn, Gala, and Jonagold, for example, makes an excellent strudel. Try to use locally grown varieties whenever possible.

LEAVENERS: BAKING SODA, BAKING POWDER, AND YEAST

Leaveners are substances that make doughs or batters rise.

Baking Soda

Baking soda, or sodium bicarbonate, is one of the most potent chemical leaveners. It is used to neutralize acid ingredients in batters as well as to leaven them. Molasses, honey, chocolate, sour cream, and buttermilk, for example, are all acidic, and because it is alkaline (or basic), baking soda will counteract that acidity. In large amounts, baking soda can give an off taste to foods, so always use the amount specified in the recipe.

Double-Acting Baking Powder

Double-acting baking powder, the major kind sold today, contains baking soda, an alkali, and one or more acids. Some leavening action begins when the batter is mixed, but a second, stronger action, takes place in the oven under the influence of heat. One of the most commonly available brands is Calumet; its acidic ingredients include sodium aluminum sulfate, calcium sulfate, and monocalcium phosphate. Rumford baking powder contains only a single acid, calcium acid phosphate, and it is aluminum-free. Both these and other double-acting baking powders contain cornstarch, which acts to absorb moisture and to keep the acid and alkali ingredients separate from one another so they won't react in the can. I've used both aluminum and nonaluminum baking powders successfully, but I prefer Rumford, because aluminum baking powders can impart a slightly metallic flavor to baked goods. There are several brands of nonaluminum baking powder available nationally.

All baking powders have expiration dates printed on their containers. Once opened, they will lose their potency within a few months. I replace mine every 4 months or so. To test whether your baking powder still works or not, stir 1 teaspoon into ½ cup hot water. If it bubbles gently, it's fine. If you have a can that's been sitting in your cupboard for a year or more, toss it out.

Yeast

The three basic types of yeast available today are fresh, active dry, and rapid-rise. Fresh yeast is the purest form of yeast, and it has the highest amount of living cells—100 percent—of any type of yeast. Some supermarkets carry foil-wrapped cakes of refrigerated fresh yeast (0.6 ounce each), but it is not widely available. Fresh yeast is perishable; it must be stored in the refrigerator, and it should be used within 1 to 2 weeks of the expiration date on its wrapping, preferably sooner.

Active dry yeast contains fewer living yeast cells than fresh yeast. Most recipes call for dissolving it in warm water before using it, so that the dead yeast cells can fall away, exposing the living cells, but I have had good luck just mixing it into the flour and then adding the warm liquid. The major brands of active dry yeast available today are Fleischmann's and Red Star. Supermarkets everywhere carry them, and you can buy them in units of 3 conjoined packets containing ¼ ounce (2¼ teaspoons) each, in 4-ounce jars, or in 1-pound vacuum-packed bags. SAF also makes an active dry yeast, SAF Traditional Active Dry Perfect Rise Yeast. It can be dissolved in warm water before using or added directly to the dry ingredients.

Instant yeast is faster to use because you can add it directly to the flour. Once the liquid is incorporated, the yeast dissolves and becomes active. Because rapid-rise yeast has more living cells than active dry yeast, it causes doughs to rise faster. This isn't necessarily desirable, since doughs develop much more flavor when yeast acts slowly. However, doughs rich in butter, which are typically slow to rise, will profit from the addition of rapid-rise yeast.

Two major brands of instant yeast are SAF and Fermipan. I use SAF. It is sold under a couple of names: SAF Perfect Rise Gourmet Yeast and SAF Instant Yeast. The Perfect Rise yeast comes in double ¼-ounce (2¼-teaspoon) packets and in 3-ounce resealable packages. SAF Instant is available in 1-pound vacuum-packed bricks, handy if you bake a lot of bread. Many supermarkets carry SAF yeast. It can also be ordered by mail (see Sources, page 341).

Dry yeast, active or instant, should be stored in the refrigerator, where it will remain viable for up to 1 year. Check the expiration date before you buy.

The most important thing to remember about nuts is that they're perishable. They keep far better in the shell than out, and they'll stay fresh much longer if whole rather than chopped. Store shelled nuts in the freezer, and bring them to room temperature before using.

To chop nuts, I use a chef's knife, not a food processor, because the processor makes pieces that are very uneven in size, with lots of powder. It is also easy to overprocess the nuts and turn them into nut butter. A food processor is fine for grinding nuts, but process the nuts with a little of the recipe's sugar, just until you have a very fine, powdery mixture. Watch carefully so that you don't overprocess.

Almonds

Almonds are sold whole with skins on (unblanched or natural), whole without skins (blanched), slivered (without skin), or sliced (with or without skin). I usually buy slivered or sliced almonds. If you use a lot of almonds in cooking, buy whole unblanched nuts. They'll keep better than the blanched ones, and it's an easy job to remove the skins.

To blanch almonds, put them in a bowl and pour boiling water over them to cover. Let stand for a few minutes, then remove the almonds from the water with a slotted spoon a few at a time, and simply pinch off the skins. Drain the nuts on paper towels. To dry the almonds, spread them on a baking sheet and bake for about 20 minutes at 250°F, stirring or shaking them once or twice; do not allow them to brown. Cool completely and store in airtight plastic bags.

To toast almonds, bake them in a single layer on a baking sheet at 350°F until they turn a pale golden brown, 10 to 15 minutes, stirring them occasionally.

Black Walnuts

Black walnuts grow in the eastern United States. They have a very hard shell that's tough to crack, and unless you live near where they're grown, you're most likely to find them in your market shelled and chopped. Black walnuts have an intense, smoky flavor, and they lend distinction to many cookies and cakes. Try them in Lebkuchen (page 272).

Hazelnuts

Hazelnuts, also called filberts, are small acorn-shaped nuts with thin shells and brown inner skins. They should be toasted before using to bring out their deep, rich taste. To toast hazelnuts, spread them on a rimmed baking sheet and bake in a 350°F oven for about 10 minutes, until they begin to smell fragrant and their skins have partially split. Wrap the hot nuts in a clean kitchen towel and let them cool for a few minutes, then rub them vigorously through the towel to rub off most of the skins, which have a slightly bitter taste. A few patches of skin won't hurt. Hazelnuts are difficult to chop because of their shape. I use a meat pounder with a round, flat head and tap on the nuts gently, breaking them up into smaller pieces, then chop them finer if necessary.

Macadamia Nuts

Native to Australia, macadamias are now grown in Hawaii and in other tropical regions. They are tough to crack, which helps account for their high price. They are also the richest of all nuts, having the highest percentage of fat. Ounce for ounce, macadamia nuts have as much fat as butter, but the fat is mostly monounsaturated, good for our hearts.

Macadamia nuts are usually sold whole, either salted or unsalted; the salted ones are much more common. If you cannot locate unsalted ones, reduce the salt by at least half or eliminate it. Because of their round shape, macadamias, like hazelnuts, are hard to chop. I use a meat pounder with a flat, round head and tap the nuts gently until they break into smaller pieces. Because these nuts are so high in fat, they are especially perishable. Be sure to store them in the freezer, where they'll keep well for 6 months.

Pecans and Walnuts

The pecan is a native American nut, and the trees flourish in the central southern region of the United States, especially Texas and Georgia. Pecans are a type of hickory nut (as are walnuts), and their name comes from the Algonquin Indian *paccan*, which means hickory. The best time to buy pecans is when the nuts are gathered in late fall; November and December are peak months. Nuts in their shells keep well at room temperature for well over a year. Store shelled nuts in the freezer, where they keep for up to 1 year. Thaw before using.

Buy pecan and walnut halves rather than pieces, if possible, which will stay fresher longer. If a recipe calls for chopped or coarsely broken nuts, break them into smaller pieces with your fingers.

Both ordinary walnuts (not black walnuts) and pecans profit from a light toasting in the oven to bring out their rich flavor. Follow the instructions for almonds (page 23), and watch them closely. They should color only lightly. Your nose will be the best indicator of when they're ready.

SEEDS

Several of these recipes use seeds as flavorings. Many, such as anise, cumin, fennel, mustard, and sesame seeds, are available in supermarkets. Here are two others you will probably have to order by mail, unless you have access to Middle Eastern markets; see Sources, page 341.

Mahlab

Made from the pits of a sour cherry, mahlab (or mahleb) adds a wonderful aroma and faint sweetness to Middle Eastern cakes and breads. I use it in the dough for Assyrian Spinach Pies (page 166), Iraqi Meat Pies (page 184), Syrian Savory Bracelets (page 192), and Kleecha (page 180). You can buy mahlab whole or ground. Store in the freezer.

Nigella Seeds

Also known as black caraway, charnushka, or kalonji, nigella seeds are added to many Middle Eastern bread doughs and sometimes sprinkled on flatbreads. I use them in the dough for Iraqi Meat Pies (page 184), Syrian Savory Bracelets (page 192), and Kleecha (page 180).

Spices contain volatile aromatic oils, and over time they lose their flavor. Buy only small quantities of ground spices at a time and keep them in tightly closed small jars in a cool, dry place. Better yet, buy whole spices and grind what you need in a spice mill.

Asafetida

A combination of dried gum resins from the roots of certain plants, asafetida is used in Indian cooking for a strong onion flavor. When a little is added to hot oil, it fills the air with its pungent aroma. You can buy it in lump form or powdered; Indian cooks say the former is purer. I use it in the filling for the Indian flatbread Kachauri (page 96). It is available in Indian and South Asian markets and by mail order (see Sources, page 343).

Cinnamon

So-called true cinnamon is derived from the inner bark of an evergreen tree native to Ceylon (Sri Lanka) but is now grown in various parts of the world. The outer bark is stripped away and the inner bark is rubbed with a heavy brass rod to loosen it. Cuts are made around the bark, and it is carefully cut off the trunk in two sections. The bark is scraped clean, rolled into scrolls or quills, and dried. Then it's cut into cinnamon sticks of varying lengths or ground into a powder. Cassia cinnamon from China, Vietnam, and Sumatra is more intense and less fragrant than Ceylon cinnamon. The primary oil in all these cinnamons is cinnamic aldehyde, the main flavoring agent.

Garam Masala

Garam masala is a mixture of spices—typically cardamom, black pepper, cumin, coriander, cinnamon, and cloves—traditionally prepared fresh in Indian households but now available packaged and in jars. I use it in Samosas (page 118). See Sources, page 343.

Ginger

Ginger is a tropical or semitropical plant that grows as a rhizome, an underground stem; it is not a root. Stalks shoot up from the rhizome and produce beautiful big flowers. Fresh ginger can be grated and used in savory or sweet dishes. Dried and ground, it becomes the familiar spice in our kitchen cupboards. Turmeric, a spice used in Indian cooking, is related to ginger.

Nutmeg and Mace

Nutmeg grows on tall tropical trees. The seed of the tree's fruit, nutmeg is wrapped in a lacy red webbing of mace. (The fruit is sometimes made into a jam.)

Mace and nutmeg are not interchangeable. In large amounts, mace has a medicinal taste, but in small amounts, it adds a welcome sweetness and mild spicy flavor. In the American South, mace is a traditional flavoring in pound cakes.

Sumac

The red berry of a nonpoisonous sumac tree, this spice contributes a distinctive astringency with a lemony background to many foods of the Eastern Mediterranean. I use dried ground sumac in the filling for Iraqi Meat Pies (page 184). Store in the freezer, where it will keep for up to 1 year. Sumac is sold in Middle Eastern markets and can be ordered by mail (see Sources, page 343).

Zatar

A blend of thyme, sumac, and sesame, zatar (or zahtar) is used in Lebanese cooking as a topping for the flatbread Talami (page 183) and mixed with olive oil as a dip for pita. See Sources, page 343.

Brown Sugar

The most readily available brown sugars are light and dark brown sugar. Both are made from refined granulated white sugar with some of the extracted molasses replaced. Dark brown sugar has more molasses, giving it a deeper, richer taste than light brown sugar. In recipes where you want a delicate molasses flavor, use light brown sugar. The more assertive dark brown gives cakes and cookies a delicious toffee-like flavor. Brown sugar is moist and clumpy, and it is measured by packing it into dry measuring cups. Brown sugar has a tendency to dry out and become hard as a brick over time. You can soften it by adding a cut apple to the bag or box, closing it up, and waiting a day or two (in a warm climate, refrigerate the sugar after adding the apple). A quicker way is to smash the dried sugar into clumps, put them into a shallow pan, and spritz them lightly with water. Cover tightly with foil and heat in a warm oven (225°F) for about 15 minutes until the sugar has regained its softness. Cool before using. Brown sugar should always be stored in a tightly sealed container.

Confectioners' Sugar

Confectioners', or powdered, sugar is granulated white sugar that has been pulverized into a fine powder, with a small amount of cornstarch added to prevent clumping. It is used mostly to make icings and frostings and to dust baked cookies, cakes, or cupcakes. It may become lumpy, especially if you live in a humid environment. Be sure to store it airtight, and if it is very lumpy, sift it before measuring. Organic confectioners' sugar usually contains no cornstarch and should always be strained.

Corn Syrup

Corn syrup comes in light and dark varieties. It is made by combining cornstarch with an enzyme that converts the starch to sugar. Not as sweet as sugar, corn syrup adds moistness to baked goods and helps to prevent the crystallization of granulated sugar when it is cooked to make syrups and fondants. The primary sugar in corn syrup is dextrose, a form of glucose. Light corn syrup is a combination of dextrose and fructose. Dark corn syrup is a mixture of light corn syrup and a darker syrup produced during sugar refining. It is often used in pecan pie fillings, where a deeper, butterscotch-like taste is desirable.

Golden Table Syrup

This is a mild syrup with caramel overtones that is very popular with Pennsylvania Dutch bakers. I use it in Betty's Shoofly Pie (page 322) and in Amish Vanilla Pie (page 324). You can order it by mail (see Sources, page 342).

Granulated Sugar

Granulated white sugar is the most refined of sugars. There are two kinds of granulated sugar: cane, derived from tropical sugarcane, and beet, made from sugar beets. Beet sugar is cheaper than cane sugar. Chemically beet and cane sugar are the same sucrose molecule, made up of a glucose molecule joined to one of fructose, and they are interchangeable in baking. Containers of cane sugar will say "pure cane sugar." If a bag just says "sugar," it's most likely beet sugar.

Honey

Orange blossom, clover blossom, sage blossom, and buckwheat are among the most common honeys. Mild in flavor, they add moisture without dominating other flavorings. Honey sometimes crystallizes after prolonged storage. To liquefy it, put the jar of honey in a saucepan of water and heat it over low heat until the crystals dissolve.

Molasses

Molasses is a syrupy by-product of the refining of cane sugar. It is slightly more nutritious than white sugar. Molasses has a distinctive taste and aroma—assertive and inviting, with coffee and butterscotch nuances. I always use Grandma's Unsulphured Molasses because it has a pure flavor.

Equipment

BAKING PANS AND PAN LINERS

Baking Pan Liners

Cooking parchment, available in rolls or sheets, can be cut to fit any size baking sheet, and it makes an excellent natural nonstick surface for baking all kinds of cookies, pastries, and breads. I like reusable silicone sheets even better, especially for cookies. There's no buttering the pan or spraying it. Simply lay the sheet on your baking sheet, and when you're through, wash it in sudsy warm water, then rinse and dry it. Silpat is one popular brand.

Baking Sheets

Baking sheets may be rimmed or rimless. The rimmed ones can be used for jelly rolls, cinnamon rolls, and all sorts of cookies. The two most common sizes of rimmed baking sheets are 15½ × 10½ × 1 inch, which is the standard one for jelly rolls, and 18 × 12 × 1 inch (also called a half-sheet pan), for just about any kind of rolls or cookies. When making batches of cookies, it's convenient to have two of either size pan.

Rimless sheets are designed for cookies and for pastries that don't need sides to contain them. Rimless sheets, or sheets with one or two low rims, are often called cookie sheets; they come in many sizes. Heavy aluminum ones are my favorites. The most convenient are 17 × 14–inch pans, and it's nice to have two of them.

Insulated cookie sheets, with a layer of air between two layers of aluminum, prevent burning, but cookies tend to take longer to bake, and sometimes even when they finally do cook through, the texture is too soft. I don't recommend them.

Baking Stone

A preheated baking stone gives a sudden jolt of heat to yeast breads, making them rise higher than they would if baked on a baking sheet set on the oven rack. Baking stones come in round or rectangular shapes; I find the rectangular stone much more useful. A stone that is about 16 × 14 inches and ¾ inch thick fits perfectly on an oven rack with space to spare around the sides. These take a while to preheat, so plan on turning your oven on about 1 hour before your dough is ready. I like to bake sandwich loaves and free-form loaves this way. Baking stones are sold at specialty cookware shops and through mail-order (see Sources, page 341).

Loaf Pans

These come in several sizes and are used mostly for baking yeast breads and loaf cakes. The two most common sizes are the 6-cup (8½ × 4½ × 2¾ inches) and 8-cup (9 × 5 × 3 inches) pans. My preference for an 8-cup loaf cake is the LaForme pan made by Kaiser, a German company, which measures 10 × 4½ × 3 inches. It is a heavy dark gray non-stick pan, and because it is narrower than the standard 8-cup pan, the loaves bake taller and have a prettier shape (see Sources, page 341). It's a good idea to have two or three each of the standard 6- and 8-cup pans and one longer, narrower 8-cup pan.

Muffin Pans

Standard muffin pans have a single pan with either 6 or 12 cups. It's nice to have two of each kind of pan. I prefer nonstick muffin pans. The standard-size pans are also used for cupcakes, in which case I line the pans with paper cupcake liners.

Rectangular and Square Baking Pans

I like straight-sided pans made of sturdy, durable aluminum, with lips that make it easy to grasp them with a pot holder without touching the batter. The pans I have are made by Magic Line and by Doughmakers (see Sources, page 341). I've also used regular lightweight aluminum pans, with slightly sloping sides, and they work fine too. It's nice to have one or two each of the following pans: 8 × 8 × 2 inches, 9 × 9 × 2 inches, and 13 × 9 × 2 inches. You will also need three round 9-inch layer cake pans, 1½ to 2 inches deep, for the Hungarian Walnut Torte on page 279. Chicago Metallic makes heavy dark aluminum baking pans with a Silverstone coating in these sizes. Darker pans conduct heat better than light-colored pans, giving cakes a browner exterior.

Round Baking Pans

You will need a round 9 × 3-inch baking pan, sometimes called a cheesecake pan, for the Boschendal Pudding recipe on page 294. This is a seamless, one-piece pan.

Springform Pans

These round pans have removable sides that are fastened onto the flat base by means of a spring-loaded hinge. They are great for cheesecakes and other cakes that bake higher than 2 inches, or any cakes that would otherwise be difficult to unmold. They're made of shiny or dark aluminum or stainless steel. I use aluminum pans that are 2½ to 3 inches tall. Have one or two each with a diameter of 9 inches and 10 inches.

Tube Pans

The standard and most common tube pan, often called an angel food cake pan, is made of aluminum, with a removable central tube portion, and measures 10 × 4 inches. These pans are sold in supermarkets and in large chain stores. In addition to angel food, this pan is also used for sponge cakes, chiffon cakes, pound cakes, fruit cakes, and some sweet yeast cakes. Bundt pans are tube pans with scalloped sides. The most common size measures 10 inches across by almost 4 inches tall and has a 12-cup capacity.

Measuring Cups and Spoons

Dry and liquid ingredients must be measured in different kinds of cups. For liquids, use clear glass heatproof cups with a spout. These come in sizes ranging from 1 cup to 2 quarts. If you do a lot of baking, it's convenient to have at least two each of the 1-cup and 2-cup measures.

To measure sticky liquids like honey or molasses, either brush the inside of the cup lightly with flavorless vegetable oil or coat the cup very lightly with cooking spray: the liquid will then slide right out of the cup.

For dry ingredients, you'll need one or two sets of nested heavy stainless steel measuring cups with straight sides, ranging in size from ¼ cup to 1 cup. Some sets are sold now with odd measures, including ⅔ cup and ¾ cup. To measure dry ingredients, fill the cup, then sweep off any excess with a narrow metal spatula or any straight-edged knife. Measuring spoons come in sets of four and include ¼ teaspoon, ½ teaspoon, 1 teaspoon, and 1 tablespoon. Some sets include ⅛ teaspoon and ½ tablespoon measures. Heavy stainless steel spoons are best. To use measuring spoons, dip the spoon into the container, filling it to overflowing, and level it by sweeping off the excess. When measuring baking soda, cream of tartar, or ground ginger, which tend to clump, break up any lumps first with the spoon before measuring.

Scale

A kitchen scale, although an optional piece of equipment, is extremely useful for those times when you want to be absolutely accurate. And when making individual breads or rolls, it's a simple matter to weigh out portions of dough so that they will be the same size. Many kinds of scales are available from specialty gourmet stores and mail-order catalogs (see Sources, page 341).

Electric Mixers

A hand-held electric mixer is great for mixing cake and cookie batters and for whipping egg whites or cream. There are several powerful hand-held mixers on the market today, adjustable to several speeds.

If you don't already have one, you will bless the day you splurged on a heavy-duty mixer. I've had my KitchenAid for more than thirty-five years, and I would be lost without it. It has a 5-quart bowl, a whip attachment, a flat beater (also called a paddle attachment), and a dough hook. An extra bowl is a good idea, handy when a recipe calls for separately beaten egg whites and egg yolks. I use the whip attachment only for beating whole eggs, egg whites, egg yolks, or heavy cream. For pastries and streusel, I use the flat beater, and for yeast breads, the dough hook. KitchenAid mixers come in three sizes: 4½-quart, 5-quart, and a newer 6-quart model. Any one of these will cut the time for beating cake batters, whipping egg whites, and kneading heavy yeast doughs to mere minutes.

Food Processor

Pie crusts mixed in a food processor always bake up perfectly flaky and tender. When you need ground or finely chopped nuts, the machine will come through for you in a few seconds, provided you take a few precautions (see page 23). It can chop chocolate or puree fruits for sauces in moments. Two consistently highly rated and dependable brands are Cuisinart and KitchenAid.

Heatproof Rubber Spatulas

It's handy to have two medium and two large rubber or silicone spatulas for cooking, stirring, and folding batters. I buy only heatproof spatulas, instead of having some that are and some that are not, to save storage space and money. A large-bladed rubber spatula (4¼ inches long and 2¾ inches wide) is extremely useful for folding flour and egg whites into delicate cake batters.

ABOVE: *Zeppole* (page 52)

LEFT: *Welsh Griddle Cakes* (page 160)

ABOVE: *Calas (page 44)*

RIGHT: *Noreen Kinney's Irish Soda Bread*
(page 98)

ABOVE: *Koeksisters (page 72)*

RIGHT: *Kolacky (page 136)*

ABOVE: *Granny's Kahk (page 114) and Matzoh (page 80)*

RIGHT: *Traditional Cornish Pasty (page 125)*

ABOVE: *Kachauri (page 96)*

LEFT: *Thai Shrimp and Bean Sprout Fritters with Thai Chili Sauce (pages 128, 129)*

ABOVE: *Apple Strudel (page 142)*

LEFT: *Puff Pastry Squares with Lemon Buttercream (page 151)*

Stretching the strudel dough using the backs of the hands

Properly stretched dough—thin enough to read a newspaper through it

Arranging the apple filling on the strudel dough

Starting to roll up the strudle using the sheet and gravity as aids

The completely rolled-up strudel. The ends will be trimmed and sealed before shaping.

Shaping the strudel to fit the buttered baking sheet

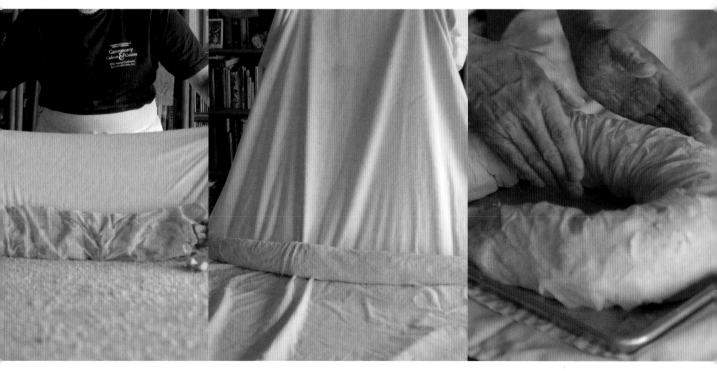

ABOVE: *Pumpkin Empanadas (page 146)*

RIGHT: *Assyrian Spinach Pie (page 166)*

Mixing Bowls

Stainless steel or glass bowls are best. You'll need a range of sizes. The following are especially useful: 2 cups, 1 quart, 1½ quarts, 2 quarts, 3 quarts, 4 quarts, 5 quarts, and 6 quarts. Plastic bowls tend to hang onto grease, no matter how thoroughly they're washed, inhibiting the beating of egg whites.

Whisks

Whisks are great for beating or for smoothing out lumpy mixtures, like cornstarch-thickened sauces or pastry cream. A small whisk is useful for mixing small amounts either in a small bowl or small saucepan. A medium one can be used for beating a few eggs or egg whites. A large whisk, or balloon whisk, is great for beating large amounts of batter, egg whites, or cream.

Wooden Spoons

You'll need two or three wooden spoons for stirring batters and sauces.

PASTRY TOOLS

Pastry Blender and Pastry Scraper

A pastry blender is a tool that consists of five or six curved blades attached to a wood, plastic, or metal handle. It does a quick job of cutting fats into flour when making a piecrust. Pastry blenders with flat stainless steel blades are sturdier than those with thin wire ones. An up-and-down chopping motion is the most efficient way to use it.

A pastry scraper, or bench scraper, is a flat piece of metal attached to a wooden or metal handle. If you roll doughs out on a countertop, these scrapers do a quick job of cleaning up any mess. Dough spatulas, super-large pastry scrapers, are very handy for moving large pieces of rolled-out dough or pastries.

Pastry Brushes

Pastry brushes are used to brush egg or sugar glazes onto yeast breads or cookies, to moisten doughs with water, and to dab strudel doughs with butter. Buy both a narrow (1 to 1½ inches) and a wide one (2 to 3 inches) made of natural bristles. Wash them in soapy water, rinse well, and shake out the excess water. Dry the bristles in a towel, and store the brushes in a cool, dry place. They should last for years. Silicone pastry brushes, which do a fine job, are also a good choice.

Pastry Cloth

A canvas pastry cloth is helpful for rolling out doughs without using too much flour, which can make the dough tough. It is particularly good for rolling out matzoh. A piece of canvas about 24 × 18 inches is big enough for just about any rolling job. You can purchase canvas at a fabric shop or online (see Sources, page 341). Rub flour thoroughly into the canvas before using it for the first time and shake off the excess. Before rolling out a pastry or cookie dough, dust the canvas lightly with flour, coat both top and bottom surfaces of the dough lightly with flour, and then roll away. After you have finished rolling, shake the canvas to remove any extra flour and particles of dough. Fold up the cloth and store it in a resealable plastic bag in a cool, dry place.

Rolling Pin

A large ball-bearing pin with two handles or a plain cylinder of boxwood is your best choice. Both types are excellent, and you should use what feels best for you. Avoid heavy marble rolling pins; they compress doughs too much.

PIE AND TART PANS

Pie Plates

Glass pie plates absorb heat readily instead of reflecting it, ensuring that crusts bake through and giving them a beautiful golden brown color.

Tartlet Pans

These are small round pans about 1 inch deep, usually with scalloped sides. It's handy to have two or even three dozen of these. You'll need them for Mazariner (page 156). Deeper tartlet pans with plain sloping sides are used for Pastéis de Nata (page 152).

THERMOMETERS

Candy Thermometer

Candy or deep-fry thermometers take the guesswork out of cooking sugar syrups and deep-fat frying. Two types are available: a rectangular stainless steel model and a digital probe electronic model, made by several manufacturers. The stainless steel thermometer has a sturdy clamp for attaching it to the side of your cooking vessel and it can measure up to 400°F. The digital model has a long straight stainless steel probe; it has a range of 14° to 392°F. The probe model is especially useful for small quantities of liquid: You can tilt the pan so that its contents pool into a corner, making it easier to dip the tip of the probe.

Instant-Read Thermometer

If you're not sure if the water's temperature is correct for your bread dough, an instant-read thermometer will give you the answer in a few seconds. The thermometer, a long metal probe topped by a dial, responds within seconds after being placed into a liquid. The thermometer should not be left in the liquid, or other food, once the reading has been made. Digital probe thermometers can also be used for this purpose.

Oven Thermometer

For accuracy's sake, you should take your oven's temperature before baking. You can use a digital probe or a stainless steel thermometer. I prefer the latter because I can leave it in the oven and monitor the temperature during baking.

Oven thermostats drift over the course of time. If you're unfamiliar with the way your oven heats, it's essential that you check it. Place a rack in the center position and place the thermometer in the center of the rack. Turn the oven on to 200°F and check the temperature on the thermometer after 15 to 20 minutes. Increase the thermostat in 25-degree increments every 15 to 20 minutes until you reach 450°F, and take the successive readings. If the thermometer and your oven dial are in agreement, you're in luck. If they're off by 25 to 50 degrees, you should have your oven recalibrated by a professional. Even if your oven seems to be behaving perfectly, it's a good idea to check it with an oven thermometer every once in a while.

OTHER USEFUL TOOLS

Cake Testers

Wooden toothpicks or skewers are best for testing the doneness of cakes. Stick the skewer into the center or the thickest part of the cake when you think it's done. The skewer should come out clean and dry. You can also use a clean broom straw as a tester.

Cookie Cutters

Cookie cutters come in all shapes and sizes. You can buy nested sets with a whole range of sizes from 1 to 4 or 5 inches, with smooth or scalloped sides. For most recipes, though, all you will really need are a 2-inch and a 3-inch round cutter. The cutting edges should be sharp and the cutter should be sturdy.

Double Boiler

A double boiler is a nested set of two pans. I use a double boiler to melt chocolate, to cook boiled icings, and to make certain custard sauces. It's easy to improvise a double boiler with two saucepans of different sizes or a heatproof bowl set over a saucepan.

Electric Griddles

For making Lefse (page 84), Bethany griddles and other tools are available in specialty gourmet stores or by mail order (see Sources, page 345). The griddles may also be used to cook pancakes, flatbreads, and Welsh Griddle Cakes (page 160).

Graters

Patterned after woodworking rasps, Microplane graters do the best job of removing zest (the colored rind) from citrus fruits without any of the bitter white pith. You run the fruit down the length of the rasp, and fine wisps of zest emerge on the underside. The graters come with holes of different sizes; if you buy only one, get the one designed for zesting. Microplane graters are sold at specialty cookware shops and may be ordered by mail (see Sources, page 341).

Nutmeg graters, inexpensive small metal graters with a curved suface of small grating holes, are sold at specialty cookware shops and even in some hardware stores. A Microplane grater is also fine for grating nutmeg.

Knives

A paring knife is useful for releasing baked cakes from the sides of pans, making slits in a pie's top crust, cutting dried fruits into smaller pieces, and cutting apples into quarters, coring, and peeling them. A chef's knife with an 8- or 10-inch blade is useful for chopping nuts and chocolate and for cutting cakes and pies into serving portions. A serrated knife with at least a 10-inch-long blade is wonderful for splitting cake layers horizontally and for slicing sponge-type cakes into portions. When dividing a cake layer, you want a blade that is longer than the diameter of the cake for the best control. A thin-bladed knife, such as a boning or filleting knife, is the best tool for loosening angel food cakes, sponge cakes, or chiffon cakes from a tube pan.

Nut Grinder

A nut grinder that can be clamped to the edge of a table or counter turns nuts into fluffy, dry powders that mix easily into batters. It is my first choice for grinding nuts because they will not turn pasty, as they can do in a food processor. But they are hard to find. I've found them at eBay.com. Also see Sources, page 343.

Pastry Bag and Tips

A 14-inch plastic-coated pastry bag is extremely useful for piping whipped cream, cream puff doughs, and ricotta into cannoli shells. The plain round or star pastry tips come in different sizes. A small, medium, and large one of each will allow you a wide range of uses. Wash the bag in hot soapy water, rinse it well, and stand it on a counter-top to drain and dry.

Scissors

Inexpensive kitchen shears do the best job of snipping dried dates into smaller pieces and cutting parchment or waxed paper for lining baking pans.

Sifters

Single-mesh sifters are straightforward: They have a single screen of wire mesh. You put the flour into the sifter and turn the handle, and a curved wire rotates, aerating the flour as it falls onto a sheet of waxed paper or other surface below. If some lumps of flour stay in the sifter, push them through with your fingers. Sifters do not need to be washed. Simply shake them out and store them in a dry place. If you live in a humid area, wrap airtight in a large plastic bag to keep the little critters away. Lacking a sifter, use a medium-fine strainer or sieve.

Strainers and Dredgers

A medium-mesh strainer is ideal for removing tiny lumps from sauces: they come in several diameters. To dust cocoa or confectioners' sugar over cakes or cookies, you can use a small fine strainer or a dredger.

Wire Cooling Racks

You'll want two or three round or rectangular wire racks for cooling cookies and cakes. Cake layers are often unmolded onto one rack, covered with another, and inverted again to cool right side up. The racks stand on short wire "feet" that allow air to circulate under them. A large rectangular wire rack is useful for oblong cakes and for large batches of cookies. Having two of them is a good idea.

1 | Fried Sweet Pastries and Doughs

*J*UST ABOUT EVERY CUISINE IN THE WORLD FRIES DOUGHS AND PASTRIES, because bubbling-hot fat is an excellent medium for quick-cooking and for making foods taste great. All you really need is a heat source and a heavy pot. This one simple technique has given rise to a dazzling variety of pastries that are favorites in so many societies. The sweet recipes here come from countries as different as Thailand, Mexico, Lebanon, and Italy, the last representing the lion's share of the recipes.

The fried pastries in this chapter display an incredible range of shapes, from blobs formed by pinching or stretching doughs by hand (Puff Puff, Anise Sfinci, Malasadas) to fancier rolled and braided treats (Koeksisters). The textures range from soft with crisp exteriors (Calas, Casatelli, Sfinci di Ricotta) to slightly chewy (Lebanese Fried Dough, Pączki) to crisp with a creamy cheese filling (Cannoli), very crisp (Fattigman, Buñuelos), and nice and crunchy (Chin Chin, Strufoli, Koeksisters).

A couple of these pastries, Pączki and Malasadas, were originally made just before Lent as a way of using up rich perishable ingredients such as eggs, cream, and butter. Today they're made year-round, but their popularity peaks around Fat Tuesday or Fat Thursday. Several others are Christmas specialties, while the remaining recipes are cooked throughout the year. Please feel free to make any of these sweets any time you want.

Calas

MAKES ABOUT 36 FRITTERS

CALAS (PRONOUNCED "ka-LA") *are not-too-sweet rice fritters with a heavenly light, slightly chewy texture. They were a traditional delicacy for decades in New Orleans, until the early 1900s, accompanying the morning cup of café au lait or coffee. African food authority Jessica Harris, in her marvelous cookbook* The Welcome Table, *says:*

> [Calas] *seem to have been the exclusive culinary preserve of African-American cooks who peddled them in the French Market and door to door, carrying their covered bowls of calas on their heads. Their cry, "Belles calas! Tout chaud! (Beautiful rice fritters! Nice and hot!)" is all that remains today of the cala.*

What is the African connection to a food so strongly identified with New Orleans? According to Jessica, the people of two rice-growing regions in West Africa, Liberia and Sierra Leone, make rice fritters—their word for rice is kala—*and Africans from those regions were recorded in the Southern slave census. I do not know how rice fritters from West Africa might compare with these calas, but I do know that these are sensational, and I am indebted to Jessica for allowing me to use her recipe. When you eat these, don't be surprised if you have a vision of a cala woman making her rounds, with her bandana tignon, guinea blue dress, and white apron, her cry piercing the morning air.*

BATTER

- ¾ cup long-grain rice
- 2¼ cups cold water
- 1½ packages (3½ teaspoons) active dry yeast
- ½ cup warm water (105° to 115°F)
- 4 large eggs, well beaten
- 6 tablespoons granulated sugar
- ¾ teaspoon freshly grated nutmeg
- ¾ teaspoon salt
- 2 cups all-purpose flour (spooned into the cup and leveled)

Vegetable oil for deep-frying

Confectioners' sugar for dusting

THE NIGHT BEFORE you plan to make the fritters, put the rice into a small heavy saucepan, add the water, and bring to a boil over medium-high heat. Stir once or twice with a fork, cover the pan, reduce the heat to very low, and cook for 25 to 30 minutes, without disturbing the rice, until it is very tender and the water is absorbed.

SCRAPE THE RICE into a large bowl and mash it with the back of a wooden spoon or wooden spatula to a mushy consistency. Let cool slightly.

MEANWHILE, in a small bowl, sprinkle the yeast over the warm water and give it a stir. Let stand until the yeast is dissolved, about 10 minutes.

WHEN THE RICE is lukewarm throughout, add the yeast and beat with a wooden spoon for 2 minutes. Place a damp towel over the bowl and leave the rice at room temperature overnight.

THE NEXT MORNING, stir the beaten eggs into the rice, followed by the sugar, nutmeg, and salt. Gradually stir in the flour. Cover the bowl with a damp towel and let the batter rise in a warm place for 30 minutes (or a bit longer). The batter will be very bubbly.

MEANWHILE, pour 3 inches of oil into a large heavy pot. Clamp a deep-fry thermometer to the side of the pot, or use a digital probe thermometer. Bring the oil to 375°F over medium to medium-high heat. Line a large baking sheet with several thicknesses of paper towels.

USE TWO SOUPSPOONS to shape the calas, one for dipping into the batter, the other for pushing the fritter off into the hot oil; take a well-rounded spoonful of batter for each cala. Fry the calas about 8 at a time for 6 minutes or so, until well browned. I get a tremendous kick out of watching the calas round up in the hot fat, sometimes forming spiky projections, and magically rolling themselves over from time to time. Remove them with a slotted spoon and set them on the paper towels to drain. Let the calas cool for a minute or so, and dust generously with confectioners' sugar. Make sure the oil returns to the proper temperature between batches. Serve the calas *tout chaud!* These are best when eaten within 3 or 4 hours.

Calas cooking in hot oil

Draining calas on paper towels

Dusting hot calas with confectioners' sugar.

Fattigman

MAKES ABOUT 60 PASTRIES

THESE QUINTESSENTIALLY NORWEGIAN CHRISTMAS PASTRIES, *thin, crisp, cardamom-scented diamond shapes, originated in the 1870s, when flour from Russia had become cheap and readily available and most city homes boasted a cast-iron range. The range made a safe place for a pot of boiling lard, far safer than hanging it from a metal rod in the fireplace, as in earlier times, and allowed the cook to regulate the temperature of the fat somewhat.*

"What I remember most as a child growing up in Norway was making Christmas cookies. This was right after World War II, and the years following, when the rationing and food shortages thankfully came to an end," Karin Knight, a petite, youthful grandmother with playful blue eyes, tells me as we roll, cut, and shape fattigman cookies. For seven days leading up to Christmas, her parents made a different cookie or pastry each day, and Karin and her sister helped. Some kinds of cookies were baked in an oven, others were cooked in an iron, and some, like fattigman, were deep-fried.

My first remembrance of making fattigman goes back to December 1945. I was seven years old. For the first time since I had been born, thanks to a Marshall-Aid package that contained, among many wonderful things, sugar, and to our friends on a nearby farm who brought us eggs and cream, my mother and father were making fattigman, the essential Norwegian Christmas pastry.

We made them in assembly-line fashion. My mother rolled the dough so thin I could see through it. I sat next to her, carefully cutting the dough into ribbons from a pattern. I passed the ribbons on to my sister, who cut them into diamond shapes and finished forming the cookies. In the meantime, my father heated a pot of lard on our electric stove. When the fat reached the correct temperature, he fried the fattigman three at a time. As soon as they were golden brown, which took only a few seconds, he removed them from the pot and set them aside to drain. We didn't have paper towels then, so he put them on unleavened bread, which soaked up the excess fat. The bread was delicious!

Just why these fried pastries are called fattigman, *which means "poor man's," is anybody's guess. "The name makes no sense," Karin says, "because the dough is rich with eggs and heavy cream. Of course, the name could be a kind of joke. There was a time when flour, cream, eggs, and spices were so costly that you'd be a 'poor man' if you made these!"*

And why the diamond shape? And why cut a slit in the dough and thread the tip of the dough through it? Some say the cookies were shaped to resemble a type of coin purse popular in Norway in the late 1800s, with the dough passing through the slit representing the purse's drawstring. The pastry itself might have symbolized something costly.

Whatever the story, the pastries are irresistible, and they melt in your mouth. Karin says, "Norwegian women often competed with one another to see whose fattigman were the best. Those that were the thinnest and crispest and had the best balance of flavors were always the winners."

The soft, sticky dough must be rolled on a well-floured surface until very thin and handled gently. It's best to work with one-quarter of it at a time; keep the rest covered in the refrigerator. Two or three people make quick work of fattigman, but I often make them by myself. Traditionally the pastries were fried in lard, but vegetable shortening or vegetable oil is a fine substitute. Be sure to keep the temperature of the fat between 360° and 370°F. Too low a heat will result in greasy pastries, and too high a heat will cause them to brown too much, losing the delicacy of their flavor. The pastries will keep well for several weeks in a tightly covered container at room temperature—but chances are they'll disappear way before then. Note that the dough must be made a day ahead and refrigerated overnight.

DOUGH

- 6 large egg yolks
- ¼ cup granulated sugar
- 1 tablespoon unsalted butter, melted
- 1 tablespoon Cognac or brandy
- 2 teaspoons pure vanilla extract
- 1 teaspoon cardamom, preferably freshly ground (see Note)
- ½ teaspoon salt
- ½ cup heavy cream
- 2 cups unbleached all-purpose flour, plus more for rolling

  Vegetable oil for deep-frying

  Granulated or confectioners' sugar for dusting (optional)

TO MAKE THE DOUGH, in a large bowl beat the egg yolks with an electric mixer on high speed for about 5 minutes, until thick and pale yellow. Add the sugar and beat for 5 minutes more, or until the mixture forms a slowly dissolving ribbon when the beaters are raised. On low speed, beat in the butter, Cognac, vanilla, cardamom, and salt.

IN A SMALL BOWL, beat the cream until it holds a soft shape. Fold the cream into the egg yolk mixture. With a wooden spoon, gradually stir in the flour to make a thick, sticky dough. Cover the bowl tightly with plastic wrap and refrigerate overnight.

TO MAKE THE FATTIGMAN, pour 3 inches of oil into a heavy 5- to 6-quart pot and clamp a deep-fry thermometer to the side of the pot, or use a digital probe thermometer. Bring the fat to 360° to 370°F over medium heat.

MEANWHILE, dust your work surface generously with flour. Scrape the dough onto the surface and divide it into quarters. Toss each piece to coat lightly with the flour, then return 3 of the pieces to the bowl, cover tightly, and refrigerate until needed. Roll the dough out until it is *very* thin, no thicker than ¹⁄₁₆ inch, preferably thinner. Handle it gently and flour the dough and work surface as necessary to prevent sticking; use a pastry brush to brush away excess flour—you only want to use enough flour to keep the dough from sticking. Don't be concerned about the shape of the dough or uneven edges.

USE A RULER to mark the dough into 2½-inch-wide strips. Cut the dough into strips with a large sharp knife or a bench scraper, making your cuts cleanly with a downward motion. Don't drag the blade through the dough, or the dough may stick to it. Cut the strips into diamond shapes with the same downward motion. Each diamond will be about 5 inches long. Use the tip of a small sharp knife to make a 1-inch-long slit in each one, starting in the center of the diamond and moving downward. Remove the scraps of dough from around the diamonds, wrap the scraps in plastic, and refrigerate.

LINE A LARGE BAKING SHEET with a silicone baking pan liner or cooking parchment. Carefully pick up one of the diamonds, fold the point nearest the slit over, push it through the slit, and bend it back down so that it forms a point at the tip of the pastry; set the fattigman on the prepared baking sheet. Repeat with the remaining diamonds, working quickly so that the dough doesn't soften. If the dough gets too soft to work with, refrigerate it for a few minutes.

WHEN THE FAT is at the correct temperature, carefully slip 3 fattigman, one at a time, into the pot. Wait about 5 seconds, and flip them over with chopsticks. Wait another 5 to 10 seconds, and flip them over again. Repeat the process, cooking the fattigman until they are blistery all over and golden brown with slightly darker edges. (The blisters indicate the pastries will be light and crisp.) Total cooking time is about 30 seconds. Immediately remove the fattigman from the fat with a large skimmer or slotted spoon and set them on paper towels to drain. Repeat with the remaining fattigman. Be sure to monitor the temperature of the fat so that it remains between 360° and 370°F; adjust the heat as necessary. Let the pastries cool for a few minutes before serving. If you wish (Karin says this is not traditional), give the warm fattigman a dusting of sugar just before serving. Roll, cut, shape, and fry the remaining dough one piece at a time, reserving the scraps. Gather all the scraps together and form them gently into a disk. Wrap in plastic and refrigerate for 30 minutes, then make more fattigman as described above. Do not use the scraps from this last rolling; the dough will be too tough.

Storing

Store the fattigman in layers in an airtight container, layered between sheets of waxed paper, at room temperature. They will stay fresh for 2 to 3 weeks.

Note

Cardamom, like all spices, loses its flavor over time. For the best flavor, buy cardamom pods (which keep well in an airtight jar). To use, husk them and pulverize the seeds in a mortar with a pestle or use a spice grinder. Pass through a fine strainer to remove coarser pieces, then measure. If you are able to buy decorticated cardamom seeds (just the seeds, without the pods), you can grind them.

Lebanese Fried Dough

MAKES ABOUT 12 PASTRIES

MAUREEN ABOOD, WHO TAUGHT ME THE LEBANESE RECIPES IN THIS BOOK, *says that home cooks often turned leftover scraps of yeast dough into fried sugared pastries as a reward for themselves, but especially for children. If you've made the full Basic Lebanese Yeast Dough recipe (page 182) for Fatayar (page 178) and Talami (page 183), you'll have about one-fourth of it remaining to turn into this simple treat. This is exactly what the recipe says it is: nothing fancy, just delicious. Fried dough is best when very fresh.*

¼ recipe Basic Lebanese Yeast Dough (page 182), allowed to rise once

Vegetable oil for deep-frying

Granulated sugar for sprinkling

PLACE THE DOUGH on a lightly floured surface and pat gently to remove air bubbles. Divide the dough into 12 pieces and shape each into a ball. Set the balls of dough slightly apart on the floured countertop and cover loosely with a kitchen towel. Let rest for 10 to 15 minutes.

ROLL A BALL OF DOUGH into a roughly oval shape slightly more than ⅛ inch thick; the dough should not be too thin. Use a fingertip to create a hole in the center of the oval and set the dough aside on the floured counter. Repeat with the remaining dough. Cover with a kitchen towel and let the dough rise for 30 to 45 minutes.

ABOUT 15 MINUTES before frying, pour 3 inches of oil into a large heavy pot and clamp a deep-fry thermometer to the side of the pot, or use a digital probe thermometer. Heat over medium heat until the temperature reaches 365° to 370°F. Line a baking sheet with a double thickness of paper towels.

BRUSH OFF the excess flour and carefully add 2 pastries to the hot oil. The dough will sizzle and bubble up. Fry until golden brown on both sides, turning the pastries once with kitchen tongs. Total cooking time is about 1 minute. Remove the pastries with the tongs, letting the excess oil drip back into the pot, and set the fried dough on the paper towels to drain. While they are still hot, sprinkle the pastries generously on both sides with sugar. Repeat with the remaining dough, making sure the temperature of the oil returns to 365° to 370°F between batches. Serve warm.

Chin Chin

MAKES ABOUT 4 CUPS OF SMALL NUGGETS

IT'S HARD TO STOP EATING THESE *spicy, crunchy-crispy nuggets, a classic fried dough treat that is made in just about all Nigerian households. Josephine Obianyo-Agu, a recent immigrant to this country, chose to share two recipes with me, this one and one for Puff Puff (page 54), yeasted Nigerian doughnut balls, because both are made in just about every home throughout the year. She says that chin chin is eaten as a snack at any time of the day, served as a nibble with drinks at parties or at weddings, and often given as a hostess gift.*

In Nigeria, it's common to make chin chin in large amounts—using more than 6 pounds of flour!—in assembly-line fashion. One person makes the dough and then everyone starts rolling and cutting as the oil heats up. Once the oil is ready, one person cooks the chin chin while the others continue with the shaping. "We make a party of it," said Josephine, "and with several of us, we can make lots of chin chin in practically no time." I've cut the quantities to make things manageable for one person.

Josephine always makes the dough by hand, and I recommend the same. It doesn't take long, and working with the dough will give you a better feel of the whole process. Shaping chin chin is a perfect activity for children. If you've got some kitchen helpers, you can double, triple, or quadruple the recipe.

DOUGH

- 2⅓ cups unbleached all-purpose flour, plus more for rolling
- ½ cup granulated sugar
- 1 teaspoon freshly grated nutmeg
- ½ teaspoon ground cinnamon
- ½ teaspoon baking powder
- 8 tablespoons (1 stick) cold salted butter, cut into tablespoon-sized pieces
- ½ cup water, plus more if needed

Vegetable oil for deep-frying

TO MAKE THE DOUGH, put the flour, sugar, nutmeg, cinnamon, and baking powder into a large wide bowl and mix well with your fingers. Add the butter pieces and work them into the flour with your fingers, pinching them at first to break them into smaller pieces, then rubbing the butter and flour between your palms until you have a fine sandy texture. Don't rush this step—it will take several minutes, and it is satisfyingly meditative. Gradually add the water, mixing it in with your fingers to make a soft, nonsticky dough. If necessary, add more water by the droplet.

TO SHAPE THE CHIN CHIN, divide the dough into 3 pieces. One at a time, roll each piece out on a lightly floured surface to a thickness of about ³⁄₁₆ inch; don't roll the dough too thin. Cut the dough into ¾-inch-wide strips, then cut the strips crosswise into ½-inch pieces. Since the dough is fairly soft, the pieces will round up slightly as you cut them, forming nuggets; that is as it should be. Set the chin chin aside on a lightly floured baking sheet, spreading the pieces out to keep them from sticking to each other. If some of them do stick, don't be concerned—when they're dropped into the hot fat and stirred, they will separate. Roll out and cut the remaining chin chin.

TO COOK THE CHIN CHIN, pour about 1½ inches of oil into a large heavy pot and clamp a deep-fry thermometer to the side, or use a digital probe thermometer. Heat the oil to 360° to 370°F over medium heat. Line a large baking sheet with several thicknesses of paper towels.

WHEN THE OIL reaches 360° to 370°F, using a slotted spoon, carefully add 2 or 3 handsful of chin chin to the hot oil without crowding. Cook, stirring almost constantly, until the chin chin are a uniform deep brown color with no light spots. This should take about 5 minutes, so regulate the heat as necesesary. Remove the chin chin from the fat with the slotted spoon, and set the chin chin on the paper towels to drain. Continue cooking the remaining chin chin; make sure to return the oil to the proper temperature between batches. Let cool completely.

Storing

Store the chin chin in resealable plastic bags at room temperature for 1 to 2 weeks.

Variation

Josephine sometimes cuts the dough into larger chin chin, about 1½ inches on a side. In that case, she makes a slit in each one to ensure that they cook through and become crisp throughout.

Zeppole

MAKES 24 FRITTERS

THESE ARE LUSCIOUS DEEP-FRIED FRITTERS, *made with cream puff dough, or pâte à choux, filled with a lemon cream, and topped with cherry jam or dusted with confectioners' sugar. A specialty of Naples, they are traditionally made for St. Joseph's Day, March 19, a very important Italian holiday. St. Joseph is the patron saint and protector of the family.*

Daniela Ruggiero, a teacher of philosophy and Italian literature, taught me how to make zeppole. Daniela came to the United States from Naples ten years ago, and she makes zeppole throughout the year to share with friends and to remind her of her home and family. In bakeries in Naples, the zeppole are shaped so that there's a depression in the top to contain the cherry jam. Daniela has never been able to make the zeppole that way, so she shapes the dough into balls before frying. They will not stay round during the cooking, but the shape avoids any rough edges that could brown too much and become too crisp.

If you've never fried cream puff dough, you have a treat in store. The zeppole seem to have minds of their own as they cook, and I find myself laughing out loud as they swim and roll themselves over in the oil. Limoncello is an Italian lemon liqueur. It adds a great lemon flavor to the zeppole cream filling. Fill the zeppole just before serving so that they remain crisp.

LEMON CREAM

- ⅓ cup granulated sugar
- 3 tablespoons unbleached all-purpose flour
- ⅛ teaspoon salt
- 2 teaspoons finely grated lemon zest
- 2 cups whole milk (1 to 2 tablespoons less if using limoncello)
- 2 large egg yolks
- 1 to 2 tablespoons limoncello (optional)

DOUGH

- 8 tablespoons (1 stick) salted butter, cut into tablespoon-sized pieces
- 1 cup water
- 1 cup unbleached all-purpose flour
- 4 large eggs

  Vegetable oil for deep-frying

  Confectioners' sugar for dusting or cherry jam for topping

TO MAKE THE LEMON CREAM, in a medium heavy saucepan whisk together the sugar, flour, salt, and lemon zest. Gradually whisk in ½ cup of the milk until smooth. Whisk in the egg yolks, then the remaining 1½ cups milk. Set the pan over medium heat and cook, stirring constantly with a heatproof rubber spatula, until the mixture comes to a boil and begins to thicken. Continue cooking, stirring, for 2 to 3 minutes more, until the filling is the consistency of a thick cream sauce. Remove the pan from the heat and set it into a larger pan or bowl of ice water. Stir occasionally until the lemon cream is cold; it will thicken even more. If desired, add the limoncello. Cover and refrigerate. (The filling can be made up to 1 day ahead.)

TO MAKE THE DOUGH, melt the butter in a medium heavy saucepan over medium heat. Add the water and bring to a rolling boil over medium-high heat. The entire surface of the liquid should be covered with bubbles, and the liquid level will begin to rise. Immediately remove the pan from the heat and dump in the flour. Stir vigorously with a wooden spoon or sturdy spatula until the dough gathers into a ball. Return the pan to the heat and stir the dough rapidly for a minute or two, just until it begins to film the bottom of the pan.

SCRAPE THE DOUGH into a medium bowl. Beat in the eggs one at a time with the spoon or spatula or with a hand-held electric mixer on medium speed, beating only until smooth after each addition. After the last egg is incorporated, beat about 1 minute with the spoon or 30 seconds with the mixer.

POUR 2 TO 3 INCHES of oil into a large heavy pot and clamp a deep-fry thermometer to the side of the pot, or use a digital probe thermometer. Bring the oil to a temperature of 370°F over medium heat. Line a baking sheet with cooking parchment and brush it lightly with oil or coat it lightly with cooking spray.

WHILE THE OIL IS HEATING, shape the zeppole. Use a regular teaspoon to scoop up a heaping spoonful of dough, about the size of a walnut, and, with another teaspoon, push the dough onto the prepared sheet. Repeat with the remaining dough, leaving an inch or two of space between the dough mounds. Coat the lumps of dough very lightly with cooking spray. Roll them between your palms into balls and replace them on the parchment.

WHEN THE OIL IS HOT, pick up a ball of dough, place it in a slotted spoon, and slip the dough into the oil. Working rapidly, add 5 more balls of dough to the oil. Do not crowd the pot; the zeppole need room to cook and expand. They will navigate through the oil on their own, rolling themselves over every now and then and making their way around the pot. Fry for about 10 minutes, until a deep golden brown color and completely cooked through. To make sure they cook evenly, turn the zeppole every so often using the slotted spoon. Do not stint on the cooking time, or the zeppole will collapse when you remove them from the oil. And be sure to monitor the oil's temperature and adjust the heat as necessary. Remove the zeppole with the slotted spoon and transfer them to paper towels to drain. Cook the remaining balls of dough in batches, making sure to return the oil to 370°F before each batch. The zeppole can stand at room temperature for several hours before being split and filled.

TO FILL THE ZEPPOLE, cut them horizontally in half with a sharp serrated knife. Spoon a generous amount of lemon cream onto each bottom, cover with the tops, and set the zeppole on a large platter. Dust with confectioners' sugar, or top with cherry jam, and serve as soon as possible.

Puff Puff

MAKES 40 TO 48 PUFFS

THESE ARE PUFFY, CHEWY, SPICY, SWEET *deep-fried balls of yeast dough. They rank with Chin Chin (page 50) as one of Nigeria's most beloved sweet treats. Puff puff are at their best when very fresh, but Josephine Obianyo-Agu, who taught me the recipe, refrigerates any leftovers for up to a day and then reheats them briefly in a microwave oven.*

DOUGH

3 cups unbleached all-purpose flour

1 package (2¼ teaspoons) instant or active dry yeast

⅓ cup granulated sugar

½ teaspoon salt

1 teaspoon freshly grated nutmeg

1 to 1½ cups hot water (120° to 130°F), or as needed

Vegetable oil for deep-frying

About 1 cup granulated sugar for coating

TO MAKE THE DOUGH, in a large bowl stir together the flour, yeast, sugar, salt, and nutmeg. Add 1 cup hot water and stir with a wooden spoon for about 5 minutes to make a smooth, thick batter with a pap-like consistency; gradually add more hot water as necessary. This is a very wet dough, not one that you can knead. Cover the bowl tightly with plastic wrap and let the dough rise at room temperature until it has almost tripled in bulk and is full of bubbles, about 1½ hours.

POUR about 3 inches of oil into a large heavy pot and attach a deep-fry thermometer to the side of the pot, or use a digital probe thermometer. Bring the oil to 360° to 370°F over medium-high heat. Line a large baking sheet with several thicknesses of paper towels. Put the sugar for coating in a small bowl.

TO COOK THE PUFF PUFFS, set a bowl of cool water near the bowl of risen dough. Dip your hand into the water, pinch off a walnut-sized piece of dough, and carefully add it to the oil. Working rapidly, form 7 more puff puffs this way. Cook for 5 to 8 minutes, or until the puff puffs are well browned and cooked through. Cut into one to make sure. Sometimes the puff puffs turn themselves over as they swim in the hot oil, but most likely they will not want to stay put if you turn them over with tongs or a fork. Josephine's solution is to use a long-tined meat fork to turn and spin the puff puffs in the oil once they've puffed and have begun to brown on the first side; she keeps the balls of dough rotating rapidly, going from one ball to the next, until the puff puffs are evenly browned and cooked. With a slotted spoon, transfer the cooked puff puffs to the paper towels to drain, then put them into the bowl of sugar and roll them about to coat with the sugar. Set them on a baking sheet to cool completely. Shape and cook the remaining dough, making sure to monitor the temperature of the oil so it doesn't get too hot or too cool. Serve as soon as possible.

Variation

Use about half the dough to make round puffs and the remaining half to make 16 square pastries. When the dough has risen, transfer half of it to a floured surface and coat liberally with flour. Pat the dough out to a thickness of about ¼ inch, and cut it into sixteen 2- to 3-inch squares with a sharp knife. Flour the knife as necessary to prevent sticking. Make a 1-inch slit in the middle of each square. Fry them 4 at a time in the hot oil for a total of 3 to 4 minutes per batch. Drain on paper towels, and roll in the sugar. Serve warm or cool.

Strufoli

MAKES 1 LARGE MOUND OR RING

DANIELA RUGGIERO TAUGHT ME this classic and beloved Neapolitan Christmas dessert. Deep-fried pasta dough nuggets are coated with a citrus-flavored honey sauce, then glacéed cherries, almonds, citron, and candied orange peel are added and the whole thing is shaped into a wreath or a mound. For a festive touch, the mound of strufoli is dusted with colored sprinkles.

DOUGH	HONEY SAUCE
3 large eggs	1¼ cups honey
½ teaspoon salt	Finely grated zest of 1 lemon
1 tablespoon limoncello (optional)	Finely grated zest of 1 orange
1 tablespoon extra-virgin olive oil	¼ cup glacéed cherries, finely diced
1 tablespoon granulated sugar	¼ cup slivered almonds, chopped
2½ cups unbleached all-purpose flour, plus more as needed	¼ cup finely diced candied citron
	¼ cup finely diced candied orange peel
Vegetable oil for deep-frying	Colored sprinkles

TO MAKE THE DOUGH, in a large bowl whisk together the eggs, salt, limoncello (if using), olive oil, and sugar just to combine well. Gradually add the flour, stirring to make a firm, slightly shaggy dough. Scrape the dough onto a floured work surface and knead until the dough gathers into a mass, then knead vigorously for 8 to 10 minutes. The dough should be smooth, dense, and no longer sticky. Wrap the dough in plastic wrap and let it rest at room temperature for about 1 hour.

TO SHAPE THE STRUFOLI, cut the dough into 8 pieces. Work with one piece at a time, keeping the rest covered. Roll one piece of dough beneath your palms into a rope about 18 inches long and ½ inch thick. If the dough continually shrinks back, set it aside for a few minutes, covered with a kitchen towel, then roll it out. Repeat with the remaining dough. With a sharp knife, cut each rope into ½-inch pieces,

and transfer the pieces to a baking sheet. Set them aside, uncovered, while you heat the oil.

TO COOK THE STRUFOLI, pour 2 inches of oil into a large heavy pot and attach a deep-fry thermometer to the side of the pot, or use a digital probe thermometer. Heat the oil over medium heat to 365° to 370°F. Line a large baking sheet (18 × 12 × 1 inch) with several thicknesses of paper towels.

PUT A HANDFUL of strufoli into a slotted spoon and lower the spoon into the hot oil. Add a second handful in the same way. Cook, stirring almost constantly to keep the pieces separate, until the strufoli have puffed to almost double their size and are golden brown and crisp, about 2 minutes. Some pieces will puff open and look like popped corn. Remove the strufoli with the slotted spoon, letting the excess oil drain back into the pot, and set them on the paper towels to drain. Cook the remaining strufoli in the same way in batches, making sure the temperature of the oil returns to 365° to 370°F.

TO MAKE THE HONEY SAUCE, put the honey and the lemon and orange zests in a large skillet, set the pan over medium heat, and bring to a boil, stirring occasionally with a wooden spoon or heatproof rubber spatula. The surface of the honey should be foamy all over. Add the strufoli, reduce the heat to medium-low, and cook for 8 to 10 minutes, stirring occasionally, so each piece of strufoli is completely coated. Stir in the glacéed cherries, almonds, candied citron, and candied orange peel, remove the pan from the heat, and let stand for about 5 minutes, stirring occasionally, until the honey has cooled and thickened slightly and has coated the strufoli even more.

SCRAPE THE HOT STRUFOLI onto a large platter and mold them into a pile or a wreath, using the two halves of a cut orange or a rubber spatula to help you shape them. Decorate the strufoli mound with a light dusting of colored sprinkles. Let cool.

WHEN THE STRUFOLI IS SET, people can pluck off pieces to munch on as they like. Eating strufoli is like eating popcorn. It's hard to stop.

Storing

Strufoli stay nice and crunchy at room temperature for several days uncovered, but it'll probably all be gone sooner than that.

Pączki

MAKES ABOUT 24 PASTRIES

IF IT'S POSSIBLE FOR ANYTHING TO BE TOO GOOD, *these luscious Polish doughnuts fill the bill in spades. Pączki (pronounced punch-key) are tender, so light you'd swear they could float, and not too sweet. Each one is filled with a small dollop of fruit preserves. Krystyna Kawalec, who immigrated from Poland several years ago, always makes these for Fat Thursday. In Poland, Fat Thursday takes place the Thursday before Ash Wednesday, which marks the beginning of Lent. In Chicago, where Krystyna lives, "Pączki Day" is the Tuesday before Ash Wednesday, known as Fat Tuesday, or Mardi Gras. The week or days before Lent are marked in many cultures by an almost orgiastic consumption of rich foods. It is because of Lent we can be grateful for the existence of pączki, as well as malasadas, kulich, paskha, and countless other treats.*

The heavenly dough for these pastries starts off with a sponge of flour, milk, yeast, and an egg. Then the dough is enriched with eight egg yolks, butter, sugar, sour cream, and a bit of brandy, which helps retard gluten development slightly, making the soft dough a dream to work with. The fruit filling must be thick enough to hold its shape. Krystyna's favorite preserve, Krakus Multifruit Powidła, is made with apples, plums, and aronia, red or black chokeberries, and flavored with rose hips. You can find it in Polish markets or order it online (see Sources, page 344). Lekvar, a paste of dried plums, is another good choice. It can be found in cans in supermarkets nationwide (Solo is the most popular brand).

Pączki, like most fried pastries, are best within a few hours of being made. They do not store well, so be sure to make them at a time when you've got plenty of eager eaters to gobble them down.

SPONGE

- 1 cup whole milk
- 1½ cups unbleached all-purpose flour
- 2 packages (1½ tablespoons) instant yeast
- 1 large egg, at room temperature

DOUGH

- 6 tablespoons (¾ stick) unsalted butter, at room temperature
- ½ cup granulated sugar
- 8 large egg yolks
- Finely grated zest of 1 large orange
- 3 tablespoons brandy or rum
- ½ cup sour cream
- 1 teaspoon salt
- 3¼ cups unbleached all-purpose flour, plus more as needed

- About ¼ to ½ cup thick fruit preserves, such as Krakus Multifruit Powidła, apricot or raspberry preserves, or lekvar
- Vegetable oil for deep-frying
- Confectioners' sugar for dusting

TO MAKE THE SPONGE, scald the milk in a small heavy saucepan over medium heat—you will see steam rising from the surface and small bubbles all around the edges. Remove the pan from the heat and let the milk cool until it registers between 120° and 130°F on an instant-read thermometer.

IN A MEDIUM BOWL, whisk together the flour, yeast, milk, and egg to make a thick batter. Bang the whisk against the side of the bowl to release any batter clinging to it, scrape the sides of the bowl with a rubber spatula, and cover the bowl tightly with plastic wrap. Let the sponge rise at room temperature until it is very bubbly and has more than doubled in volume and then collapsed back on itself, 1½ to 2 hours.

To make the dough by hand or with a hand mixer, beat the butter and sugar with a wooden spoon or hand-held electric mixer in a large bowl until fluffy. Add the egg yolks 2 at a time, beating until well incorporated, then beat in the orange zest. Beat in the sponge, the brandy or rum, sour cream, and salt. Gradually add 3 cups of the flour, first stirring it in with the spoon, then beating as the dough gets thicker. The dough will be quite sticky.

To make the dough using a stand mixer, put the butter and sugar into the mixer bowl, attach the flat beater, and beat on low speed until blended, then increase the speed to medium and beat for 3 to 4 minutes, until fluffy. Scrape the bowl and beater. Beat in the egg yolks 2 at a time, beating for about 1 minute after each addition. Stop to scrape the bowl and beater as necessary. Beat in the orange zest. Add the sponge, brandy or rum, sour cream, and salt and beat on low speed until smooth. Beat in 2 cups of the flour, then increase the speed to medium and beat for 3 minutes. Scrape the bowl and beater, and switch to the dough hook. Add 1 cup more flour and knead it in on low speed, then increase the speed to medium and knead 2 to 3 minutes more. The dough will be soft, wet, and sticky.

SPRINKLE THE remaining ¼ cup flour on your work surface and scrape the dough onto it. Knead the dough until all the flour has been incorporated. The dough should feel fairly soft and be a bit tacky. If it is too sticky, knead in up to ¼ cup more flour, but go easy here—the softer the dough, the more luscious the pączki.

WASH AND DRY the bowl you used and oil it lightly or coat it with cooking spray. Shape the dough into a ball and place it in the bowl, turning to coat all surfaces. Cover tightly with plastic wrap and let the dough rise at room temperature until doubled in size, about 1 hour.

TURN THE DOUGH OUT onto an unfloured work surface and pat it into a rectangle about 15 × 12 inches. Fold it in thirds, like a business letter, then pat it gently to extend it the long way to about 15 inches. Fold it again in thirds, to make a squareish packet. You'll notice the dough will have lost its stickiness and become firmer. Replace the dough in its bowl, seam side down, cover tightly with plastic wrap, and let rise at room temperature until doubled, about 1 hour.

TO SHAPE THE PĄCZKI, line two large baking sheets with cooking parchment or silicone baking pan liners. Place the dough on an unfloured work surface and pat it gently to deflate it. (This a wonderfully responsive dough; it will feel soft, puffy, and alive and will do what you ask of it.) Roll it to a thickness of between ½ and ¾ inch. If the dough sticks at any point, loosen it with a pastry scraper and dust the dough very lightly with flour. With a sharp 2¾- or 3-inch round cutter, stamp out circles of dough. If the dough sticks to the cutter, dip the cutter into flour before making the cuts. Gather the dough scraps from around the circles, shape them into a ball, and set them aside, covered with a kitchen towel.

MAKE A SHALLOW DEPRESSION in the center of a dough circle and place ½ to 1 teaspoon of the preserves in the depression. Pick up the circle of dough, pull the edges up around the filling, and pinch them together firmly to seal in the filling. (Because the dough is slightly tacky, it will stick to itself readily when pressed together.) Set the pączki seam side down on a lined baking sheet. Continue shaping the pączki, spacing them about 2 inches apart on the lined sheets. Reroll the scraps and make more pączki as described. Cover loosely with kitchen towels and let rise at room temperature about 45 minutes, until the pączki look light and are almost doubled in volume.

MEANWHILE, pour 3 inches of oil into a large heavy pot and attach a deep-fry thermometer to the side of the pot, or use a digital probe thermometer. Heat the oil over medium heat until it reaches 365° to 370°F. Line two large baking sheets with several thicknesses of paper towels.

TO FRY THE PĄCZKI, pick one up and set it on a heatproof spatula. Slip the spatula into the oil, and shake gently to float the pączki in the oil. Add 3 or 4 more pączki to the oil and cook for 1½ minutes on the first side. Turn them with tongs and cook on the second side for 1½ minutes, or until the pączki are a deep mahogany brown. Lift them out of the oil with a slotted spoon and set them on the paper towels to drain. While they are still hot, strain confectioners' sugar over the pączki. Cook and sugar the remaining pączki, returning the oil to 370°F between batches. Serve within an hour or two, when they will be at their very best.

Variation

Another way to shape the pączki is to roll the dough ¼ inch thick, and stamp out circles with a sharp 2-inch round cutter. Put a teaspoonful of jam on half the circles, moisten the exposed dough with a pastry brush dipped in water, and cover with the remaining circles. Press gently all around to seal in the filling.

Cannoli

MAKES ABOUT 24 PASTRIES

BAKERIES ALL OVER SICILY MAKE CANNOLI, *thin, crisp, tube-shaped pastry shells filled with sweetened sheep's-milk ricotta mixed with finely chopped candied citron or orange peel or with mini chocolate chips, or both, and dusted with confectioners' sugar. Cannoli have been made for centuries, and although they are decidedly Italian, various invading armies, particularly the Arabs, all had their influence on the cuisine of the area. Ricotta cheese may well owe its prominence in Italian cooking to the Arabs.*

These are the cannoli that are made every Christmas by Rosanna Aiuppa and her cousin Rose Padula. Because Rosanna and her Sicilian-American friends make many of the classic sweet Italian treats only once a year, she finds the recipes may change from year to year, as they are only sketched out and various additions or changes are not written down. This makes for some very lively and amusing discussions, but ultimately everything turns out "just like mamma made."

Rosanna likes to use pastry ricotta, made with cow's milk, which is drier than regular store-bought ricotta; she buys it at her local Italian deli in Albany, New York. Polly-O sells it as impastata ricotta; it is also called dry ricotta or ravioli ricotta. If you can't find it, drain supermarket ricotta in a cheesecloth-lined strainer overnight in the refrigerator, or make your own ricotta (see page 334); drain it first, then measure out what you need. Ricotta fresca, fresh ricotta in plastic drainage baskets, is also a good choice. I've found Cantare brand to be excellent.

You will need a pasta machine to roll out the dough, cannoli tubes, and a pastry bag and plain tip with a ½-inch opening.

In Sicily, many bakeries fill cannoli shells only when an order is

DOUGH	FILLING
1⅓ cups unbleached all-purpose flour	3 cups impastata ricotta (dry ricotta, also called pastry or ravioli ricotta) or 3 cups drained Homemade Ricotta (page 334) or whole-milk ricotta
¼ teaspoon salt	
1 tablespoon granulated sugar	
2 teaspoons unsweetened cocoa powder	1⅓ to 1½ cups confectioners' sugar
2 tablespoons vegetable shortening or lard	1½ teaspoons pure vanilla extract
6 to 7 tablespoons sweet Marsala or sweet vermouth	⅓ cup finely diced candied citron or candied orange peel, or a combination
Vegetable oil for deep-frying	⅓ cup miniature semisweet chocolate chips
1 to 2 large egg whites, lightly beaten (optional)	Finely chopped unsalted pistachios (optional)
	Confectioners' sugar for dusting

placed, because they lose their crispness on standing, and I recommend you do the same. You can make both the filling and the shells a day ahead, but once filled, cannoli should be eaten as soon as possible. See the companion DVD for a video demonstration of cannoli making.

To make the dough with a food processor, put the flour, salt, sugar, and cocoa into the work bowl of the food processor fitted with the metal blade, and process for 10 seconds. Add the shortening or lard and process for 10 seconds. With the machine running, gradually add 6 tablespoons of the Marsala or vermouth. Process for 1 full minute, or until most of the dough gathers into a ball, with a few small bits spinning around the sides of the work bowl; if necessary, gradually add some or all of the remaining 1 tablespoon of Marsala or vermouth. Transfer the dough to an unfloured work surface and knead for 2 to 3 minutes. The dough will firm up and may tear a bit as you work it, but that is all right. Shape the dough into a disk, wrap it in plastic wrap, and let rest at room temperature for 1 hour.

To make the dough with a stand mixer, put the flour, salt, sugar, and cocoa into the mixer bowl and stir to combine well. Add the vegetable shortening or lard, attach the flat beater, and mix on low speed for 2 to 3 minutes, until the mixture resembles fine crumbs. With the mixer on low speed, gradually add 6 tablespoons of the Marsala or vermouth, mixing to make a dough that is as stiff as pasta dough; if the dough doesn't gather into a mass, gradually add some or all of the remaining 1 tablespoon Marsala or vermouth. Transfer the dough to an unfloured work surface and knead for 2 to 3 minutes. Shape the dough into a disk, wrap in plastic wrap, and let rest at room temperature for about 1 hour.

TO ROLL AND CUT the dough, cut out a 4½-inch paper or cardboard oval, using the template at right. Divide the dough into quarters. Keep 3 pieces wrapped in plastic wrap while you work with the remaining piece. With a pasta machine set at its widest opening, pass the dough through the pasta rollers. If the dough is sticky, lightly flour it. Fold the dough in thirds and pass it through the widest setting again, starting with an open end.

Repeat the rolling and folding several times more to knead the dough, then gradually decrease the setting, passing the dough once through each thinner setting until you reach the next-to-last one. Lay the strip of dough on your work surface. If it is sticky, lightly flour the dough on both sides and brush off the excess flour with a pastry brush. Set the template on one end of the dough strip and use the tip of a sharp knife to cut out an oval. Set the oval aside on your work surface and repeat; do not overlap the ovals. Roll and cut the remaining dough, and cover the ovals with plastic wrap until needed.

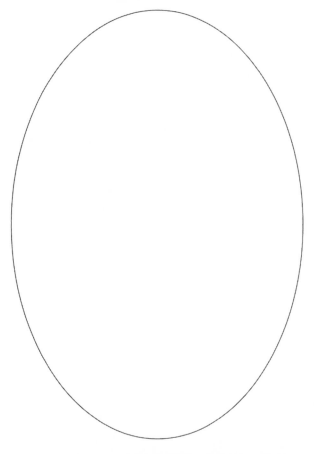

POUR 3 INCHES OF OIL into a large heavy pot and clamp a deep-fat thermometer to the side of the pot, or use a digital probe thermometer. Heat the oil over medium heat to between 350° and 360°F.

WHILE THE OIL HEATS, shape the cannoli shells. Wrap an oval of dough around an ungreased cannoli mold. Moisten one edge of the dough with water or lightly beaten egg white, overlap the other edge, and press gently to seal. Set on a baking sheet lined with plastic wrap. Repeat to shape as many cannoli as you have molds. Line another large baking sheet with several thicknesses of paper towels.

TO COOK THE CANNOLI SHELLS, slip 2 or 3 dough-wrapped tubes into the hot oil. When you place the tubes in the oil, they will sink. After a second or two, move them around with tongs, grasping the uncovered tube ends. You'll see that the dough has developed dozens of small blisters all over the surface, which is as it should be. After 1 minute or so in the oil, use the tongs to lift a tube out of the oil and gently shake the tube to release the cannoli shell back into the oil. If it is resistant, gently grasp the pastry with a pot holder or a wad of paper towels and twist to release it, then put it back into the hot oil. Set the metal tube aside on a heatproof surface to cool. (Be careful, the tube will be very hot.) Repeat with the other fried cannoli shells and continue cooking, moving them around with a fork, until the shells are golden brown, a total of 1½ to 2 minutes. Lift each one out of the oil with tongs or with the tines of a meat fork, letting the oil drain back into the pot, and stand on end on the paper-lined pan to drain. Cool completely before using. Wash cooled cannoli tubes thoroughly in hot soapy water,

and dry fully before reusing. Cook the remaining cannoli in batches, shaping more cannoli shells as soon as the metal tubes are cool. Be sure to return the oil to between 350° and 360°F between batches. (Once completely cool, the cannoli shells can be stored airtight at room temperature for 2 to 3 days.)

To make the filling with a food processor, combine the ricotta, 1⅓ cups of the confectioners' sugar, and the vanilla in the work bowl of the processor fitted with the metal blade, and process for 2 minutes, or until very smooth. Stop to scrape the sides of the work bowl 2 or 3 times. Taste and add more sugar if necessary. Transfer the filling to a medium bowl and stir in the citron or orange peel and chocolate chips. Cover and refrigerate (the filling can be made up to 1 day ahead).

To make the filling using a stand mixer, beat the ricotta with the flat beater on medium speed until smooth, 2 to 3 minutes. Add 1⅓ cups of the confectioners' sugar and the vanilla and beat until the filling is very smooth and fluffy. Taste and add more sugar if necessary. Stir in the citron or orange peel and chocolate chips. Cover and refrigerate (the filling can be made up to 1 day ahead).

TO FILL THE CANNOLI, fit a large pastry bag with a ½-inch plain tip. Spoon the filling into the bag. Carefully insert the tip of the bag into each cannoli shell and squeeze gently until the shell is half filled. Repeat on the other end of the shell. Smooth the exposed filling with the back of a spoon, and sprinkle it with pistachios, if using. Dust the cannoli shells with confectioners' sugar. Serve as soon as possible.

Casatelli

italian chickpea turnovers

MAKES ABOUT 40 PASTRIES

THESE FRIED PASTRIES WITH A SWEET AND SPICY GARBANZO FILLING *are a specialty of Rose Padula's Sicilian family. One November weekend, I joined Rose, her cousin Rosanna Aiuppa, and two other Sicilian-American friends for a marathon baking fest. Baking and freezing their family Christmas treats is a yearly ritual. Each was responsible for her own specialty, but we all pitched in when needed to speed up the work. I was given the task of removing the skins from six cans of garbanzo beans for the many dozens of casatelli we were making that day. The traditional way of pureeing the garbanzos is to put them through a food mill, and ridding them of their skins first makes the job easier. I have since found that simply shaking cooked garbanzos in a strainer and picking away the loose skins is sufficient. And a food processor works better than a food mill for pureeing them.*

Casatelli, also known as casateddi, are usually made to celebrate St. Joseph's Day, March 19, but this year the ladies had decided to make them for Christmas, too. The sweet, tender dough, which is excellent all by itself, fried and sprinkled with granulated sugar, makes a perfect case for the sweet, thick garbanzo puree. Ricotta cheese is also often used as a filling for casatelli, and I've included that version as a variation here.

Note that the dough must be made ahead and refrigerated overnight.

DOUGH

2½ cups unbleached all-purpose flour, plus more as needed

1½ teaspoons baking powder

½ teaspoon salt

6 tablespoons (¾ stick) unsalted butter, melted

3 tablespoons corn oil

½ cup granulated sugar

⅔ cup whole milk

1 large egg

1 teaspoon pure vanilla extract

1 teaspoon pure lemon extract

FILLING

1½ cups canned garbanzo beans (chickpeas)

3 tablespoons granulated sugar

⅛ teaspoon salt

2 tablespoons honey

¾ teaspoon ground cinnamon

⅛ teaspoon ground cloves

1 large egg white, lightly beaten

Vegetable oil for deep-frying

Granulated sugar, for sprinkling on the hot pastries

TO MAKE THE DOUGH, in a medium bowl stir together the flour, baking powder, and salt.

IN A LARGE BOWL, whisk together the melted butter, oil, sugar, milk, egg, and extracts until smooth. Add about half the dry ingredients and whisk until smooth. Add the remaining dry ingredients and stir with a wooden spoon or rubber spatula to make a thick, soft dough that holds its shape and is only slightly sticky. If your kitchen is warm, the dough may seem too soft, and you will be tempted to add more flour; don't. Cover the bowl tightly with plastic wrap and refrigerate the dough overnight. The dough will firm up and be easy to handle.

TO MAKE THE FILLING, drain the garbanzos in a sieve or colander and rinse under cold water. Shake or toss the garbanzos and remove and discard any loose skins. Put the beans into the work bowl of a food processor fitted with the metal blade and process until smooth and pasty, about 1 minute. Add the sugar, salt, honey, cinnamon, and cloves and process until smooth, about 1 minute more. Stop to scrape the work bowl as necessary. You will have about 1¼ cups.

LINE A LARGE BAKING SHEET with plastic wrap. Measure level tablespoons of the filling and place them in mounds on the plastic wrap. Cut each mound in half with a sharp knife. (Each ½ tablespoon will be used to fill 1 casatelli.)

TO SHAPE THE CASATELLI, lightly dust two large rimmed baking sheets (18 × 12 × 1 inch) with flour. Use half of the dough at a time, keeping the remainder covered and refrigerated. Shape the dough into a disk. Lightly flour your work surface and dust both sides of the dough with flour. Roll the dough to a roughly circular shape measuring between ¹⁄₁₆ and ⅛ inch thick (thin!). With a 3-inch plain or scalloped round cutter,

stamp out circles of dough, dipping the cutter into flour as necessary. With a pastry brush, lightly paint a dough circle with the beaten egg white. Shape one portion of filling into an oval about 2 inches long. Set the oval onto the center of the pastry round. Pick up the pastry, bring up the sides to meet in the center, enclosing the filling completely, and pinch the edges tightly to seal. Lay the casatelli on your work surface with the pinched edge facing you and pat the pastry gently to flatten it slightly. Put the pastry onto one of the prepared baking sheets and prick it with a fork 3 times down its length. Repeat filling and shaping the remaining circles of dough. Gather the scraps, wrap in plastic, and refrigerate. Roll, cut, and fill the second portion of dough.

COMBINE ALL THE DOUGH SCRAPS and reroll them. Cut enough circles to match the portions of filling you have left, and fill and shape as described above. Any leftover dough can be fried and dusted with granulated sugar for a snack. Cover the casatelli with kitchen towels.

TO COOK THE CASATELLI, line two large rimmed baking sheets with several thicknesses of paper towels. Heat 2 inches of oil in a large deep skillet over medium heat until the temperature registers between 365° and 370°F on a deep-fry or digital probe thermometer. Carefully slip 6 to 8 casatelli into the hot oil and cook for about 1 minute, until the undersides are a rich brown color. Turn the pastries over with a fork or chopsticks and cook for 1 minute on the second side, or until deeply browned. Remove the casatelli from the fat with a metal skimmer or slotted spoon and set the pastries onto one of the lined baking sheets. Dust the hot pastries with granulated sugar. Cook the remaining casatelli. Cool to room temperature before serving.

Storing

Casatelli are best when very fresh, but the pastries can be stored airtight for up to a day or so, then reheated in a preheated 325°F oven for 10 minutes to refresh them. Sprinkle again with sugar before serving.

They can also be frozen in heavy-duty resealable plastic bags for up to 3 weeks. To reheat, arrange the frozen pastries in a single layer on a baking sheet and put them into a preheated 350°F oven for about 15 minutes, until they are completely thawed and heated through. Sprinkle them with granulated sugar while hot, and let cool to room temperature before serving.

Variation

Rosanna also likes to use a ricotta filling for casatelli. If you can find ricotta fresca (Cantare is a good brand), an all-natural ricotta cheese in a 12-ounce container with the cheese in a plastic drainage basket, by all means use it. The cheese itself is 10 ounces, or 1¼ cups. Or use regular whole-milk ricotta or homemade ricotta (see page 344) drained overnight in a cheesecloth-lined strainer in the refrigerator. Measure or weigh the cheese after draining.

Put the cheese into the work bowl of a food processor fitted with the metal blade and process for 1 minute or so, until very smooth. Add ½ cup confectioners' sugar and ¾ teaspoon pure vanilla extract and incorporate into the cheese with 8 to 10 quick pulses. Transfer to a bowl and stir in 3 tablespoons very finely minced candied orange peel or citron and 1 teaspoon grated lemon or orange zest. Cover and refrigerate until ready to use.

Note

Traditionally the garbanzo filling for casatelli is made with dried beans. Put 1 cup dried garbanzos in a 3- to 4-quart saucepan and add enough cold water to cover the beans by 2 inches. Stir in ¼ teaspoon baking soda, cover the pan, and leave the garbanzos in a cool place overnight. The next day, drain off the soaking water and add fresh water to cover the garbanzos by 2 inches. Bring to a boil over medium heat, then reduce the heat to a simmer and cook until the garbanzos are tender, about 1½ hours. Drain and cool. Measure 1½ cups for the recipe. The garbanzos can be sealed in a plastic bag and refrigerated for up to 3 days before using.

Buñuelos

MAKES 24 LARGE WAFERS

THESE LARGE, SHATTERINGLY CRISP PAPER-THIN FRIED WAFERS *are fun to make and they're even more fun to eat. Be forewarned, they do take time—but your efforts will be well rewarded. The dough itself is a snap to put together, easily made by hand in just a few minutes. It is shaped into small balls that are allowed to rest for about 30 minutes, then each one is rolled out and stretched by hand until it almost reaches the size of a dinner plate. The stretching, akin to making strudel dough, is what takes time, but if you get a couple of family members or friends to help, the job will be done in about an hour.*

Maria Elena Flores, who taught me this recipe, learned how to make buñuelos from her mother and grandmother in Chihuahua, Mexico. The middle child in a family of seven children, she has been cooking and baking since she was a young girl. She and her husband immigrated to the United States in the early 1960s. Maria rarely measures anything when cooking. For her buñuelos, she needed 2½ pounds of flour, which she proceeded to dump into a bowl from a large sack. When I wanted to verify the amount with a measuring cup, she just smiled knowingly: exactly 8 cups, or 2½ pounds to the grain! To measure liquids she does use cup measures, but she adjusts these amounts to make sure the dough comes out just right. She measures spices, baking powder, and salt in the palm of a hand, and approximates the amount of shortening by eye. After cooking and baking this way for more than 60 years, all these things have become instinctive with her. Maria makes buñuelos at Christmastime and gets help with the shaping from her daughters and occasionally a grandchild or two.

A key to the recipe's success is having the correct working temperature. Like strudel dough, buñuelo dough is much easier to stretch in a warm room: 70° to 75°F is ideal. After each buñuelo is stretched, it is placed on a cloth to dry a bit before frying. A clean tablecloth or sheet draped over a dining table works fine, but if you're pressed for space, you can layer the buñuelos between pillow cases.

DOUGH

- 4 cups unbleached all-purpose flour
- 1 teaspoon baking powder
- ½ teaspoon salt
- 1 large egg
- 1 cup warm milk, plus more if needed
- 1 tablespoon vegetable shortening or soft butter, at room temperature

- 4 cups corn oil for deep-frying
- 1 cup granulated sugar
- 1 tablespoon ground cinnamon

TO MAKE THE DOUGH, mix the flour, baking powder, and salt together in a large bowl with your hands. Beat the egg in a small bowl with a fork just to combine the white with the yolk, then add the egg to the flour, along with the milk. Mix everything together with your hand to make a thick, wet dough. If the dough seems dry, add more warm milk a few droplets at a time, working them in until the dough holds together and feels wet and slightly sticky. In the bowl or on an unfloured work surface, knead the dough vigorously with both hands for about 5 minutes, until it is smooth, soft, elastic, and no longer sticky.

RUB YOUR HANDS with the shortening or butter and knead it into the dough until thoroughly blended. Divide the dough into 24 equal pieces, and shape them into balls. Place them back in the bowl in a single layer (it's fine if they touch each other) and cover the bowl tightly with plastic wrap. Let the dough rest for at least 30 minutes.

TO ROLL THE DOUGH, cover a large table with a tablecloth or sheet. Remove a ball of dough from the bowl, leaving the remaining balls tightly covered. Flatten the ball slightly between your hands and place it on a wooden board. Roll it into a 5-inch circle with a few swift strokes of a rolling pin and set it on the cloth. Cover with another cloth to keep the dough moist and supple. Repeat with the remaining balls of dough. As the circles rest, the gluten in the dough will relax, making the stretching quite easy.

TO STRETCH THE DOUGH, trim your fingernails if necessary, so they won't tear the dough. Starting with the dough circles you rolled first, remove a circle of dough from its cover and place it on a work surface. Carefully stretch it out from the center to the edge with the tips of your fingers. Grasp the dough by its edges, pull gently to stretch it some more, and hold it steady for a second or two, then rotate the dough slightly and repeat the stretching and holding. Continue the procedure, stretching slowly and gently and going all around the circle of dough. As the dough becomes thinner, begin stretching it from the thicker edges. Do your best not to tear the dough. Eventually the dough should be thin enough to see through;

it should have a final diameter of about 8 to 9 inches, with a paper-thin center and slightly thicker edges. Set the dough back on the cloth and leave it uncovered. Continue until all the dough circles have been stretched. By the time they all are shaped, the first ones will be almost dry enough to fry. They should feel slightly leathery when you run your fingers over them. Turn them over and let their undersides dry for a few minutes. If you are not ready to fry them, then cover them with a cloth. They can stand for a few hours before frying.

TO FRY THE BUÑUELOS, pour the oil into a large heavy skillet, preferably cast iron, and heat over medium heat until the oil registers 365° to 370°F. Combine the sugar and cinnamon in a small bowl. Line the bottom and sides of a large roasting pan with several thicknesses of paper towels.

SLIP A BUÑUELO INTO THE OIL and immediately press it down into the oil with a meat fork or wooden chopsticks. The buñuelo will puff and form blisters all over its surface, and it will begin to brown in a few seconds. Impale an edge of the buñuelo on the fork or grasp it with chopsticks and flip it over. Press it into the oil again and cook for a few seconds longer, until it is a deep golden brown all over. Total cooking time is 1 minute or less. Lift the buñuelo out of the oil by an edge and hold it above the oil for a few seconds to allow the excess to drip away, then stand the buñuelo upright in the lined pan to drain. Cook and drain 3 or 4 more buñuelos the same way. Sprinkle a little cinnamon sugar on both sides of the buñuelos and stack them on a dinner plate. Repeat with the remaining buñuelos, returning the heat to between 365° and 370°F between batches. The buñuelos are ready to eat as soon as they're cool. The edges will be slightly chewy, their centers very crisp and crackly.

Storing

Although buñuelos are best when freshly made, they keep well in an airtight container at room temperature for 2 to 3 weeks.

Anise Sfinci

MAKES ABOUT 48 PASTRIES

FOR AS LONG AS YVONNE CASALNUOVO BRADDICK, *who gave me this recipe, and her older siblings can remember, "Christmas Eve dinner at Nonna and Nunnu's in San Francisco always culminated with sfinci." Her seven siblings, along with her parents, cousins, aunt, and uncle, sat shoulder to shoulder at the extended tables in their cramped flat. At the end of the meal, platters of freshly fried anise-flavored sfinci were brought to the table. "Bowls of cinnamon sugar were always within arm's reach of even the youngest child," Yvonne says. "The sfinci disappeared quickly. No matter how full we were, we ate and ate until they were all gone."*

The name sfinci *is believed to come from* sfang, *an Arabic word meaning "fried pastry." Yvonne, who has done her own research, told me:*

> *Mary Taylor Simeti, in* Pomp and Sustenance, *mentions a type of sfinci made with mashed potatoes, sfinci di San Martino, made by the Benedictine Monks of Monreale.*

> *Pino Correnti, writing about Sicilian cuisine, also says that sfinci may be derived from the sweets the ancients made to greet the winter solstice, but he notes that some historians say they're Arab.*

The Casalnuovo family always hand-forms the dough into rustic doughnut shapes before dropping them into the hot oil, but you can simply make walnut-sized fritters if you prefer.

DOUGH

- 1 large russet potato (8 to 12 ounces)

- Water

- 1 package (2¼ teaspoons) active dry or instant yeast

- ¼ cup granulated sugar

- ½ cup whole milk

- 2 tablespoons unsalted butter, cut into pieces

- 1 large egg

- ¾ teaspoon salt

- 1 teaspoon anise seeds

- ½ teaspoon pure anise extract

- 3 cups unbleached all-purpose flour

- Vegetable oil for deep-frying

- 1 cup granulated sugar

- 1 to 2 teaspoons ground cinnamon

TO MAKE THE DOUGH, peel the potato and cut it into 1-inch chunks. Put them into a small heavy saucepan, add water to cover, and bring to a boil over medium-high heat. Reduce the heat to medium and cook, uncovered, until the potato is completely tender, about 15 minutes.

DRAIN THE POTATOES, reserving the water, and return the potatoes to the pan. Cook, stirring with a wooden spoon, over medium heat for about 1 minute to evaporate excess moisture. Pass the potatoes through a ricer. Measure ½ cup packed mashed potatoes, and set aside to cool.

WHEN THE POTATO WATER is just warm to your fingertip, measure ⅓ cup into a small bowl. Stir in the yeast and 1 teaspoon of the sugar. Let stand for about 10 minutes, until the yeast becomes very foamy and bubbly.

MEANWHILE, scald the milk in a small saucepan over medium heat—you will see steam rising from the surface and small bubbles forming around the edges. Remove the pan from the heat and stir in the remaining sugar and the butter. Let cool until the milk feels warm to your fingertip.

IN A LARGE BOWL, whisk together the mashed potatoes, egg, salt, anise seeds, and anise extract. Stir in the yeast and milk mixtures. Gradually add the flour, beating it in with a wooden spoon to make a soft, elastic dough. This may take 10 to 12 minutes. Scrape the sides of the bowl, cover tightly with plastic wrap, and let the dough rise at room temperature until doubled in volume, about 1 hour.

POUR 3 INCHES OF OIL into a large heavy pot and clamp a deep-fry thermometer to the side of the pot, or use a digital probe thermometer. Heat the oil over medium heat to 365°F.

Line two or three baking sheets with several thicknesses of paper towels.

To shape the sfinci into rings, using Yvonne's method, wet your hands and pinch off a golf-ball-sized piece of dough. Yvonne pinches the dough between her thumb and fingers, stretches some of it over the back of her fingertips, and joins the ends to create an odd-shaped ring, then drops it into the oil. Yvonne's sfinci have a bulbous ring shape, with some parts thicker and other parts somewhat knobby. She and her siblings and in-laws work rapidly, adding the hand-formed doughnuts to the oil as they form them. Cook no more than 8 sfinci at a time; do not crowd the pot. Turn them over with kitchen tongs or wooden chopsticks and cook until the sfinci are golden brown on both sides, a total of about 2 minutes. Remove them with a wire skimmer or slotted spoon and set on the lined pans. Cook the remaining dough, making sure to return the oil to 365°F before frying each batch.

To shape the sfinci into fritters, wet your hand and pinch off walnut-sized pieces of dough, dropping them into the oil as you go; don't crowd the pot. Cook about 2 minutes total, turning them once or twice, until the sfinci are nicely browned on both sides. Remove with a wire skimmer or slotted spoon and set on the lined pans.

COMBINE THE SUGAR AND CINNAMON, divide between two bowls, and set them on the table. Put the warm sfinci on one or two plates, and provide each diner with a dessert plate. Each person can dip and roll his or her own sfinci in as much cinnamon sugar as desired.

Sfinci di Ricotta

MAKES ABOUT 48 BEIGNETS

SFINCI (PRONOUNCED "SFEEN-gee") ARE ITALIAN BEIGNETS, *crisp on the outside and tender on the inside. This dough is made with ricotta and baking powder, but some cooks make sfinci with yeast and mashed potatoes (see page 68). So what's the difference between* sfinci *and* zeppole? *If made with cream puff paste, they're basically the same thing, differing only in choices of fillings and toppings. If made with a yeast dough, however,* sfinci *don't seem to have a* zeppole *counterpart.*

Savaria Lisuzzo, from Termini Imerese, Sicily, makes these often. She likes to use a packaged vanilla sugar, Vanillina, to flavor the sfinci. You can substitute 1 tablespoon homemade Vanilla Sugar (see page 337) or use 2 teaspoons pure vanilla extract. The thick pancake-like batter is simply spooned into the hot fat. These sfinci are quick to make, quick to cook, and very easy to eat. Serve them within an hour or two at most after frying.

Vegetable oil for deep-frying

BATTER

3 tablespoons granulated sugar

1 cup whole milk

2 cups unbleached all-purpose flour

2 teaspoons baking powder

½ teaspoon salt

2 large eggs

1 cup impastata ricotta (dry ricotta, also called pastry or ravioli ricotta) or drained Homemade Ricotta (page 334) or ricotta fresca

2 envelopes Vanillina (see headnote)

1 cup granulated sugar

2 teaspoons ground cinnamon

POUR 2 INCHES OF OIL into a large heavy pot and clamp a deep-fat thermometer to the side of the pot, or use a digital probe thermometer. Heat the oil over medium heat to 365°F.

TO MAKE THE BATTER, heat the sugar and milk in a medium heavy saucepan over medium heat, stirring occasionally, just until the sugar has dissolved and the milk is hot. Meanwhile, whisk together the flour, baking powder, and salt in a medium bowl.

REMOVE THE SAUCEPAN from the heat and whisk in the eggs, ricotta, and vanilla flavoring. Gradually whisk in the flour mixture to make a thick batter.

IN A MEDIUM BOWL, stir together the sugar and cinnamon. Line a large baking sheet with several thicknesses of paper towels.

TO COOK THE SFINCI, using regular teaspoons pick up a rounded teaspoonful of batter with one spoon and use the second spoon to push it off into the oil. Do not be concerned about the shapes: Sfinci should look rustic. Continue quickly adding sfinci to the pot until you have about 8 of them swimming in the oil. Cook for about 5 minutes, until the sfinci turn a deep brown color, stirring them to keep them moving and to brown them evenly. Remove them with a slotted spoon and set them on the lined pan to drain, then roll them in the cinnamon sugar and set them on a plate. Cook the remaining batter, making sure to return the oil to 365°F between batches. Serve as soon as possible.

Koeksisters

MAKES ABOUT 30 PASTRIES

THESE SOUTH AFRICAN DEEP FRIED PASTRIES *soaked in sugar syrup are a national favorite and enjoyed anytime of the day or year. I learned how to make them from Bryony van derMerwe Schwan. They are believed to have originated with Malayan slaves brought to South Africa's Cape Province by European settlers. The Malay cooks shaped the dough into balls and dipped them into a cold sugar syrup as soon as they came out of the hot fat. In this version, the dough is shaped into short braids, fried, and dunked into an ice-cold syrup flavored with cinnamon, ginger, and lemon. The pastries are crisp and sweet and fun to make and to eat.*

It's very important to keep the syrup as cold as possible so that the inside of the koeksisters remains crisp. Keep half of it in a bowl in the freezer while you dip the hot koeksisters into another bowl of syrup, nestled in crushed ice. When you notice the syrup has lost its chill, switch bowls. Leftover syrup can be stored in the refrigerator for a week or two to use on your next batch of koeksisters. The dough can also be made ahead and refrigerated for a day or two before shaping and cooking.

SYRUP	DOUGH
6 cups granulated sugar	4 cups unbleached all-purpose flour, plus more if necessary
3 cups water	1 tablespoon baking powder
½ teaspoon cream of tartar, mixed with 1 teaspoon water	1 teaspoon salt
1 cinnamon stick	1 tablespoon granulated sugar
Three ¼-inch-thick slices unpeeled fresh ginger	2 tablespoons cold unsalted butter
Zest of 1 lemon, removed in strips with a vegetable peeler	2 large eggs, lightly beaten
2 tablespoons fresh lemon juice	About 1 cup water
	Vegetable oil for deep-frying

TO MAKE THE SYRUP, with a wooden spoon stir all the ingredients together in a large heavy saucepan. Bring to a boil over medium-high heat, stirring occasionally to dissolve the sugar, then boil rapidly, without stirring, for exactly 10 minutes. Remove the pan from the heat and cool to room temperature. Cover and refrigerate for several hours, or overnight.

TO MAKE THE DOUGH, in a large bowl stir together the flour, baking powder, salt, and sugar. Add the butter and work it rapidly into the flour with your fingertips until the mixture resembles fine crumbs. Gradually add the eggs while tossing everything together with a fork. The mixture will still be crumbly. Gradually add the water, stirring with the fork, to make a firm yet soft dough that holds together; the dough may be slightly sticky.

TRANSFER THE DOUGH to an unfloured work surface and knead it briefly until it is smooth and no longer sticky, flouring the dough lightly if necessary. Wash and dry the bowl, and return the dough to it. Cover the bowl tightly with plastic wrap and let the dough rest in the refrigerator for at least an hour or two, or as long as overnight.

TO SHAPE THE KOEKSISTERS, divide the dough in half. Roll out half the dough on a lightly floured surface until it is about ⅛ inch thick—no thicker! Cut the dough into 2-inch-wide strips, then cut the strips into 4-inch lengths. Gather the scraps and cover them for later use. Cut each strip of dough lengthwise into 3 even strips, leaving them attached at one end. Braid the strips loosely, keeping them flat, then moisten the ends of the strips with a pastry brush dipped in water and seal the strips together. Set the koeksisters, uncovered, onto a wooden board. Repeat with the second half of the dough, and then with the scraps.

POUR 3 INCHES OF OIL into a large heavy pot and clamp a deep-fry thermometer to the side of the pot, or use a digital probe thermometer. Heat the oil over medium heat until the temperature is between 365° and 370°F. Meanwhile, set a large wire cooling rack over a large baking sheet (18 × 12 × 1 inch). Have two slotted spoons nearby. Remove the sugar syrup from the refrigerator and strain about half of it into another bowl. Put the bowl of unstrained syrup in the freezer, and put the bowl of strained syrup into a bowl of ice and water.

TO FRY THE KOEKSISTERS, slip 2 or 3 pastries into the hot oil and turn them about in the oil with one of the slotted spoons until they are puffed, crisp, and a deep golden brown; cooking time is about 1 minute. Remove the pastries from the oil with the same spoon, allowing the excess oil to drain back into the pot, and drop them one at a time into the bowl of cold sugar syrup. Use the second slotted spoon to submerge the pastries in the syrup for about 15 seconds, then remove them one at a time from the syrup and set onto the wire rack. Continue cooking and dipping the remaining koeksisters, making sure the oil returns to between 365° and 370°F between batches. When the first batch of syrup begins to lose its chill, place it in the freezer. Strain the remaining syrup into another bowl and set it into the ice water bath. Keep switching bowls of syrup as needed so the syrup is always cold.

Storing

Stored uncovered on a large tray, koeksisters will stay fresh at room temperature for 1 to 2 days, depending on the humidity. Never cover them or they'll turn soggy.

Malasadas

MAKES 16 LARGE DOUGHNUTS

IN PORTUGAL, THESE LIGHT-AS-AIR DOUGHNUTS *are made for carnival. The dough itself is very wet and full of bubbles. Susana Arreda Arraial Ballantine, a native of the Azores who now lives in the United States, learned how to make these from her housekeeper in the Azores, Maria João. I met Susana in the Azores, and she introduced me to Maria João, who gladly taught me several of her baking specialties. This was a thrilling experience, because it marked the first time I learned recipes not from the immigrant herself but from her original source in her home country.*

I watched Maria João and her sister, Maria do Natal (Mary Christmas!), make these scrumptious doughnuts on the island of Terceira. Maria João kneaded and beat the basic dough by hand in a large bowl, then she slowly worked in the eggs with her fingers and hands, beating the dough against the sides of the bowl until it was smooth, elastic, and very wet. After the dough had risen, she moistened her hands with oil and pinched off 2-inch balls of dough, which she stretched into odd shapes about 5 inches long with thin centers and thickish edges, and fried them until they were well browned. After draining them on paper towels, she dusted the hot malasadas lightly with cinnamon sugar.

Anywhere you find a community of Portuguese immigrants in the United States, you will find a bakery that makes malasadas. Some are glazed with a sugar icing, some offered plain, and some are split and stuffed with a cream filling. Oh, how a recipe can evolve!

Malasadas are at their supreme best while still hot or warm, so be sure to eat them that way. They do not keep well, but if you're making them for a crowd, you can double the recipe.

DOUGH

3½ cups unbleached all-purpose flour

4 tablespoons (½ stick) cold unsalted butter

¼ cup granulated sugar

1 package (2¼ teaspoons) instant yeast

⅔ cup whole milk

⅔ cup tepid water

½ teaspoon salt

1 large egg, lightly beaten

Vegetable oil for deep-frying

½ cup granulated sugar mixed with ½ teaspoon ground cinnamon, or plain sugar, or honey for drizzling

To make the dough by hand, put the flour into a large mixing bowl, add the butter, and cut it into the flour with a pastry blender or two knives until the mixture has the consistency of fine crumbs. Or, if you prefer, do as Maria João does, and work in the butter with your fingertips. Stir in the sugar and yeast.

To make the dough with a stand mixer, put the flour, butter, and sugar in the mixer bowl and attach the flat beater. Mix on low speed for about 3 minutes, until the mixture has the consistency of fine crumbs. Mix in the yeast.

SCALD THE MILK in a small heavy saucepan over medium heat—you will see steam rising from the surface and small bubbles forming around the edges. Remove the pan from the heat, add the tepid water and salt, and stir to dissolve the salt. The temperature of the liquid should be between 120° and 130°F. Add the liquid to the flour and stir with a wooden spoon to make a thick, wet dough.

If making the dough by hand, knead the dough right in the bowl, pressing the dough against the sides of the bowl, folding the dough over onto itself, and using your knuckles to knead vigorously, for 5 to 8 minutes. The dough should be soft and slightly sticky. Add the egg, lift the edges of the dough, and fold it over and over itself to incorporate and knead in the egg. Beat with your hand to make a thick, wet, elastic dough. Scrape the dough off your fingers.

If using a stand mixer, switch to the dough hook and knead on medium-high speed for a few seconds, until the dough masses on the hook. Reduce the speed to low and knead for 5 minutes. Raise the speed again to medium-high and knead briefly until the dough pulls away from the sides of the bowl. Add the egg and beat on low speed until incorporated. Increase the speed to medium or medium-high and knead for 3 to 4 minutes, until the dough is thick, wet, and elastic. Scrape the sides of the bowl and the dough hook.

COVER THE BOWL TIGHTLY with plastic wrap and let the dough rise at room temperature until almost tripled in volume, about 1½ hours. (The dough will come to the top of a 5-quart bowl.)

STIR THE DOUGH GENTLY to deflate it, cover the bowl again with plastic wrap, and let the dough rise a second time to almost tripled in volume, about 1 hour.

POUR 2 TO 3 INCHES of vegetable oil into a large heavy pot and clamp a deep-fry thermometer to the side of the pot, or use a digital probe thermometer. Heat the oil over medium heat to a temperature of 365°F. Set a small dish of oil nearby for shaping. Line the bottom and sides of a large roasting pan with paper towels.

TO SHAPE AND COOK the malasadas, rub a tablespoon or two of vegetable oil over the bottom of an 18 × 12 × 1–inch baking sheet. (To shape the dough as Maria João does, see the headnote.) Scrape the very soft dough onto the pan and flip it over to coat both sides with the oil. Pat the dough gently into a rough square measuring about 10 inches on all sides and ½ inch thick. Use a dough scraper to cut the dough into 4 equal strips, then cut the strips crosswise into 4 squareish shapes each. Stretch a piece of the dough with your fingers until it is about 5 inches long with a very thin center and thicker edges—the overall shape is not important—and slip the malasada into the hot oil. Working quickly, shape 3 more malasadas and add them to the pot. Cook, turning the malasadas once with tongs or wooden chopsticks after 1 minute, until nicely browned on the edges and cooked through, about 2 minutes total; the centers will still be pale. Use tongs to lift the malasadas one by one out of the oil, letting the excess oil drip back into the pot, and stand them on end in the lined pan. Continue frying the remaining malasadas, cooking no more than 4 at a time, and heating the oil to 365°F between batches.

DUST THE HOT OR WARM MALASADAS with cinnamon sugar or plain sugar, or place on plates and drizzle with honey. Enjoy the malasadas while they are warm.

Thai Fried Bananas

MAKES 6 TO 8 SERVINGS

THE THAI DO NOT HAVE A BAKING TRADITION, *but they do like sweets. Fruits, in particular the wide variety of bananas that exist in Thailand and in other tropical areas, are often dipped into a rice flour batter and deep-fried for a dessert. Pranee Halvorsen, who immigrated to the United States from the island of Phuket, likes to use the tiny bananas she can buy in Southeast Asian markets. Those are the ones that remind her most of her homeland. She simply peels them and uses them whole. Halved and quartered regular bananas work just as well. For the best flavor, be sure that the bananas you use are completely ripe. The yellow skins should be flecked with brown, but the flesh should still feel firm.*

This makes an excellent dessert for a party because the batter, which takes only a minute or two to whisk up, must be made ahead, and then the frying will take you less than 5 minutes. For a large gathering, simply double or triple everything. These bananas are delicious all by themselves or with vanilla ice cream.

Rice flour is sold in many supermarkets as well as in health food stores and in Asian markets. Thai cooks like to use naturally effervescent limestone water in fried batters because it makes them especially crisp. You can order solid limestone online and make limestone water yourself (see Note). Or, for equally good results, simply use sparkling mineral water.

BATTER

- 1 cup rice flour (spooned into the cup and leveled)
- 2 tablespoons all-purpose flour
- 2 tablespoons firmly packed light brown sugar
- ¼ teaspoon salt
- ¾ cup limestone water (see headnote) or sparkling mineral water, plus more if needed
- 3 tablespoons unsweetened shredded coconut

- 1 tablespoon sesame seeds

- Peanut or corn oil for deep-frying

- 18 to 24 small bananas, each about 3 inches long, peeled, or 4 to 5 large ripe regular bananas, peeled, halved lengthwise, and cut crosswise into quarters

- Confectioners' sugar for dusting

- Ice cream for serving (optional)

TO MAKE THE BATTER, whisk together the rice flour, all-purpose flour, brown sugar, and salt in a medium bowl. Add the limestone water or sparkling water and whisk to make a smooth batter the consistency of heavy cream. The batter shouldn't be too thick, or the coating on the bananas will be heavy. If necessary, gradually whisk in a little more water. Stir in the coconut and sesame seeds. Cover the bowl and let the batter rest at room temperature for about 1 hour.

ABOUT 20 TO 30 MINUTES before you're ready to cook the bananas, pour about 2 inches of oil into a large heavy pot and clamp a deep-fry thermometer to the side of the pot, or use a digital probe thermometer. Heat the oil over medium heat to 360°F. Line a large baking sheet with several thicknesses of paper towels.

GIVE THE BATTER A STIR. Add 8 small bananas or banana quarters to the batter and stir them about gently with a rubber spatula to coat them with a thin layer of batter. When the oil is ready, remove the bananas one at a time from the batter with your fingers, letting excess batter drip back into the bowl, and holding the fruit close to the oil, carefully let go of it so that it enters the oil without splashing. Working quickly, add the remaining batter-coated bananas. Cook, stirring occasionally with a slotted spoon, until the batter is a deep brown color and the bananas are cooked through, 2 to 3 minutes. Remove them with the slotted spoon, allowing excess oil to drain back into the pot, and set on the lined pan. Coat and cook the remaining bananas 8 pieces at a time, making sure to return the oil to 360°F between batches.

ARRANGE THE BANANAS on a platter and dust them with confectioners' sugar. If serving ice cream, put a generous scoop of vanilla ice cream into each serving bowl. Guests can help themselves to the fruit, placing a few pieces over the ice cream. Eat with a spoon.

Note

The limestone Pranee Halvorsen uses comes in small containers and is pink and pasty (see Sources, page 342). To make limestone water, put about 1 tablespoon of the limestone into a 1-quart screw-cap jar, add about 3 cups cold tap water, seal the jar, and shake well. The liquid will turn a murky pink. Let stand for 2 to 3 hours to allow the particles to settle. The water will be clear and effervescent. To use, slowly pour off what you need. Recap the bottle and refrigerate. The limestone water will be good to use as long as it's bubbly, about 3 or 4 days.

2 | Flatbreads and More

FLATBREADS ARE A BASIC FOOD IN MOST OF THE WORLD'S CULTURES. In some, they are made daily in the home and form the foundation of a meal, to be eaten with main dishes or side dishes. In India, for example, Chitra Paresh made flatbreads every morning to be eaten with a breakfast of cooked vegetables, yogurt, various chutneys, and hot pickles. Maria Elena Flores, from Mexico, prepares tortillas almost daily in her Sacramento kitchen. They are made most often into quesadillas, usually with cheese, and cooked on a griddle for lunch or a snack. The Lebanese serve pita breads with any meal, topping a round with meat or vegetables and yogurt and rolling it up to eat.

Some flatbreads are reserved for special times of the year. Lefse, a Scandinavian flatbread made with potatoes and flour, is baked in quantity, also on a griddle, during the Christmas season. One traditional way to eat it is wrapped around lutefisk. It is also served as a snack or a dessert, spread with butter, sprinkled with cinnamon sugar, and rolled up. Kids especially love it spicy.

Many Chinese cooks make flatbreads almost every day. These tend to be stuffed, either with vegetables or with meat, cooked on a griddle, and eaten out of hand. South African crumpets, really small sweet pancakes that welcome a guest to one's home, are also griddle-baked. They are served plain at any time of the day, on plates with forks.

One flatbread in this collection that is oven-baked is matzoh, the Jewish unleavened bread. Rolled out very thin and baked in an intensely hot oven, the matzoh dough cooks in about 2 minutes. Matzohs are crucial for the celebration of Passover, but they may also be eaten at any time of the year, at any time of day. Because they are large, matzohs are usually broken into smaller pieces. They can be spread with anything from butter and jam to chopped liver.

The two quick breads in this chapter, both from Ireland, are also baked in the oven. Irish soda bread is a staple in Irish homes and is eaten with meals. It is wonderful for sopping up gravies. A sweet soda bread, sometimes called spotted dog, is usually spread with butter and served with hot tea in the afternoon.

Some of these breads take a bit of time, but all of them will satisfy immensely.

Matzoh

MAKES 10 MATZOHS

THIS HISTORICALLY IMPORTANT JEWISH UNLEAVENED FLATBREAD, *as recounted in Exodus, sustained the Jews on their escape from Egypt. It is always served as part of a Passover seder. Cindy Klotz bakes matzoh once a year, with the aid of her young daughter and a few of her friends, as a way of honoring and preserving her Jewish heritage. To be considered truly kosher, matzoh must go into a very hot oven within 18 minutes of the time the water comes into contact with the flour. No fermentation of the dough is allowed to happen, and 18 minutes has been determined to be the limit.*

When Cindy showed me how she makes matzoh, she suspended the 18-minute rule. And when I make it, I don't set any time limit. Cindy places her rolled-out dough onto a wooden baker's peel and slides the matzoh right onto the oven rack, to simulate the ridged pattern in commercial matzoh. Because this can be a tricky process, I find it's best to bake the matzoh on a baking stone or on a heavy baking sheet, and I describe both of the procedures here. The matzohs turn out like super-crisp, ultrathin crackers with bubbly brown spots all over.

Matzoh is a wonderful multipurpose flatbread. You can eat it plain or put just about anything you like on it. Break it into pieces and top it with chopped liver, hummus, egg or tuna salad, soft cheese, deli meats, or whatever you like.

I've found the easiest way to roll the matzohs is on a canvas pastry cloth. The cloth absorbs the flour and gives traction to the dough so that it stays put as you roll it. And you will be able to get super-thin matzohs. See the companion DVD for a video demonstration of matzoh making.

> 1¾ cups unbleached all-purpose flour, plus more for rolling
>
> ¾ cup room-temperature water plus more if needed

IF USING A BAKING STONE, adjust an oven rack to the lower third position and set the stone on the rack. If using a baking sheet, set a large baking sheet (18 × 12 × 1 inch) on a rack in the center of the oven. Preheat the oven to 450°F at least 45 minutes before baking.

PUT THE FLOUR into a large bowl and gradually stir in the water to make a firm, slightly sticky dough. At first the dough will look shaggy, but as more water is incorporated into the flour,

the dough will gather into a mass. If the dough doesn't gather all together, work in droplets of additional water. Knead the dough for 2 to 3 minutes in the bowl, adding a little flour if necessary, to make a firm, slightly sticky dough.

DIVIDE THE DOUGH into 10 equal pieces. Set them on a floured surface to rest, covered with a kitchen towel, for a few minutes.

RUB FLOUR into your pastry cloth and have a bowl of flour nearby. Coat a piece of dough with flour and pat it out to a rough circle about 4 inches across. Dust again with flour, and roll from the center of the dough radiating outward with quick strokes of the pin, turning the dough over once or twice, until the dough is *very* thin, about $\frac{1}{32}$ inch thick, and about 10 inches across. Brush off excess flour with a pastry brush. Lift the dough onto a baker's peel or a cookie sheet, prick it all over with a fork, and slide the matzoh onto the baking stone or baking sheet. Bake for about 2 minutes, until the matzoh has brown-tinged bubbles all over its surface. The dough between the bubbles should remain white or a pale cream color, not brown. Remove the matzoh with tongs and set it on a wire rack to cool. While each matzoh bakes, roll and prick the next one, then slide it onto the baking stone or baking sheet as soon as you remove the baked matzoh. In this way, you will have 10 matzohs in about 25 minutes.

Storing

Store matzohs in a brown paper bag with the top rolled down at room temperature. In a dry environment, they will stay crisp and crackly for several days.

Variations

SALTED MATZOH Dissolve $\frac{3}{4}$ teaspoon salt in the water before mixing it into the flour.

HERB MATZOH Add 1 teaspoon finely crushed dried herbs, such as Italian seasoning or a mixture of thyme and oregano, to the flour.

OLIVE OIL MATZOH Add 1 tablespoon extra-virgin olive oil to the flour along with the water.

EGG MATZOH Beat 1 large egg in a 1-cup glass measure and add enough water to come to the $\frac{3}{4}$ cup line. Use this in place of the $\frac{3}{4}$ cup water, and adjust the consistency of the dough with a little more water, if necessary.

Lebanese Pita

lebanese pocket bread

MAKES 16 FLATBREADS

ALTHOUGH YOU CAN CUT THESE *kimaz or* khubz *(both words mean "bread") into half-circles and fill them with anything you like, that is not the Lebanese way, according to Maureen Abood, a wonderful and talented Lebanese cook and food writer. Instead, she uses the bread as wraps, putting a filling right onto a round, rolling it up, and eating it. You can also simply spread the breads with butter or yogurt, roll up, and eat. To the Lebanese, bread is an integral part of the meal because it is used as a case to enclose the food itself. Bread and food are thus entwined.*

Typically the dough for homemade pitas is rolled into rounds about 7 inches across and ¼ inch thick—which is a good thing if you do want to split and stuff the breads. With this method, you can bake 4 pitas at a time on a rectangular baking stone. Commercially made pitas are rolled much thinner, and you can try to do the same by rolling the balls of homemade dough into 10-inch rounds. Because they are thinner, these larger breads have a more refined texture, but you can only bake one at a time. I like both sizes, so I make them both ways.

You will need a baking stone for this recipe.

- 2½ cups warm water (105° to 115°F)
- 1 package (2¼ teaspoons) active dry yeast
- ¼ teaspoon granulated sugar
- 6 cups unbleached all-purpose flour, plus about ½ cup more
- 2 teaspoons salt
- 3 tablespoons olive oil

INTO A LARGE BOWL put ½ cup of the warm water and stir in the yeast and sugar. Let stand for about 10 minutes, until bubbly and frothy.

TO THE YEAST add 1 cup of the flour, the salt, and the remaining 2 cups water and beat well with a wooden spoon. Add 2 more cups flour and beat until the mixture is smooth and has the consistency of pancake batter. Beat in 2 tablespoons of the oil. Gradually stir in the remaining 3 cups flour to make a firm, slightly sticky dough.

SPRINKLE YOUR WORK SURFACE lightly with flour, and scrape the dough onto it. Knead for about 10 minutes, adding small amounts of flour as necessary, until the dough feels smooth, firm, elastic, and no longer sticky. You shouldn't need to add more than ½ cup additional flour.

WASH AND DRY the mixing bowl and rub it with the remaining 1 tablespoon oil. Shape the dough into a ball, place it in the bowl, and turn to coat all surfaces with oil. Cover the bowl tightly with plastic wrap and let the dough rise at room temperature until doubled in volume, about 2 hours. When you press a finger into the dough and remove it, the depression should remain.

ABOUT 1 HOUR BEFORE BAKING, adjust an oven rack to the lower third position and place a baking stone on the rack. Preheat the oven to 500° or 550°F.

MEANWHILE, line a large baking sheet (18 × 12 × 1 inch) with plastic wrap. Turn the dough onto your work surface and pat it gently to deflate. With a sharp knife or bench scraper, divide the dough into 16 equal pieces (a scant 3½ ounces each). Shape each into a ball and pinch the seam firmly to seal. Set the balls seam side down an inch or two apart on the lined baking sheet. Drape the balls loosely with a kitchen towel and let rest for about 20 minutes.

To make 7-inch breads, roll out balls of dough, one at a time, on a lightly floured surface into 7-inch rounds. Flip the dough over from time to time as you roll, which will help give the breads an even round shape. Set the rounds slightly apart on a kitchen towel, cover loosely with another kitchen towel, and let the breads rest for 10 to 20 minutes before baking.

To make 10-inch breads, roll out only one ball of dough at a time to a 10-inch round, flipping it over as necessary. Be patient—the dough is firm and elastic, and it will take a minute or two longer than it takes to roll a 7-inch round. Set the dough onto a kitchen towel, cover it with another towel, and let it rest for just 1 to 2 minutes before baking. Roll remaining 10-inch rounds as the previous one bakes.

BAKE THE BREADS

To bake the smaller breads, set 2 of them side by side on the end of a lightly floured baker's peel or end of a rimless cookie sheet, and quickly slide them off onto the far end of the baking stone. Immediately load 2 more 7-inch rounds and slide them off onto the near end of the baking stone. Work quickly to maintain the oven's intense heat. Bake for about 2½ minutes, until the breads are well puffed but the dough has not browned at all except for perhaps a few brownish spots on the undersides. The rounds of bread dough will puff up into taut pillows as the water in the dough converts to steamy pockets under the oven's intense heat. Slide the peel or cookie sheet under the breads and remove them from the oven (careful, the breads are hot), slide them onto a kitchen towel, and cover them with another towel. Using pot holders, gently press on the breads to deflate them, then stack the breads and wrap them in a kitchen towel to cool. Bake the remaining breads the same way.

To bake 10-inch breads, set the circle of dough near the edge of a lightly floured baker's peel or end of a rimless cookie sheet and slide the bread onto the center of the baking stone. Bake for about 1 minute, until the bread has puffed like a balloon but has not browned at all except for a few darker spots on its underside. Slide the peel or cookie sheet under the bread and remove it from the oven (careful, the bread is hot), slide it onto a kitchen towel, and cover with another towel. Using a pot holder, gently press on the bread to deflate it, and wrap it in a kitchen towel to cool. Bake and cool the remaining breads the same way.

Storing

The breads are best when very fresh, but they keep well in large resealable plastic bags in the refrigerator for up to 2 days. Let them stand at room temperature, still wrapped, for 30 minutes to 1 hour before serving. For longer storage, freeze the breads for up to 2 weeks. Thaw them in their wrapping, then unwrap, rewrap the breads in aluminum foil, and refresh in a preheated 325°F oven for 10 minutes.

Variation

You can use half whole wheat flour to make these breads, if you wish. Substitute 3 cups whole wheat flour for the white flour, and add this flour to the yeast mixture as directed. After beating in the olive oil, cover the bowl tightly with plastic wrap and let this sponge rise at room temperature until doubled in size, about 1 hour. Gradually stir in the 3 cups unbleached all-purpose flour and proceed as directed, using additional all-purpose flour for kneading.

PITA CHIPS Leftover pita can be split, cut into triangles, spread on a baking sheet, and toasted in a preheated 350°F oven until golden brown and crisp, about 10 minutes. Give them a spritz of olive oil spray and a sprinkling of kosher salt first, if you like. The chips are excellent to use as scoops for hummus. Toasted leftover pita can also be crumbled and used in fattoush, a Lebanese salad of bread and parsley.

Lefse

MAKES THIRTY TO THIRTY-SIX 12-INCH FLATBREADS OR FORTY TO FORTY-EIGHT 10-INCH FLATBREADS

GARNET DAHMER SAYS THESE THIN, CHEWY *potato Norwegian flatbreads are traditionally made at Christmas and served on Christmas Eve at a dinner featuring lutefisk. In the old days, the potatoes used for lefse had not been irrigated, so they weren't as "wet" as many kinds of potatoes available today. Red-skinned potatoes are less starchy and less moist than russets, so Garnet prefers them.*

5 pounds red-skinned potatoes (all about the same size), scrubbed
12 tablespoons (1½ sticks) salted butter, cut into tablespoon-sized pieces, at room temperature
⅔ cup evaporated milk
1 tablespoon granulated sugar
½ teaspoon salt
2 to 3 cups all-purpose flour, plus more for rolling

Garnet and her daughter, Dee Butorac, use special equipment from Bethany Housewares to make lefse: a cloth-lined lefse rolling board measuring 18 inches across, with small feet on the bottom for stability; a stockinet-covered ridged rolling pin; a thermostatically controlled griddle about 16 inches in diameter; and a lefse stick, which is about 2 feet long, flat, slightly concave on its top surface and convex on the bottom, and tapered slightly from handle to tip. If you begin making lefse regularly, you might want to invest in this equipment (see Sources, page 345). Otherwise, you can make great lefse with a pastry cloth, a 12-inch griddle (nonstick or not), two metal cookie spatulas, and a narrow wooden rolling pin cut from a dowel. If you have a stockinet cover for your rolling pin, by all means use it.

You can cut this recipe in half, if you wish. Note that you need to start making the dough a day ahead.

PUT THE POTATOES in a large pot, add water to cover by 1 inch, and bring to a boil. Cover and boil gently until very tender, about 30 minutes for 8-ounce potatoes. Drain the potatoes in a colander.

WHEN THE POTATOES are cool enough to handle, peel them and rice them into a large bowl. Add the butter pieces as you rice the hot potatoes so that they melt. Beat with a wooden spoon until smooth. Add the milk, sugar, and salt and beat well. Cool, uncovered, to room temperature, then cover tightly with plastic wrap and refrigerate overnight.

THE NEXT DAY, gradually mix 2 cups flour into the potatoes to make a stiff dough that may feel tacky but not sticky. If necessary, knead in additional flour so that the dough holds together.

IF USING AN ELECTRIC LEFSE GRIDDLE or other electric griddle, preheat it to 400°F. If using a nonelectric griddle, set it over medium heat.

WORK WITH ONE-QUARTER of the dough at a time, keeping the rest refrigerated. To prevent sticking, flour the lefse canvas and cloth-covered pin generously, or generously flour a pastry cloth and regular rolling pin. Be careful of overflouring, though—too much flour on the edges of the lefse can make them dry, and if there is too much flour sticking to the lefse, they may burn. If you have a large griddle, 15 to 16 inches in diameter, measure 1/3 cup of dough; if using a 12-inch griddle, use 1/4 cup. Toss the dough about on the floured cloth to coat it all over with flour. Shape it into a ball and flatten it into a 3- to 4-inch-wide disk. Roll it from the center outward in all directions, to make it as round as possible. Use a light, swift stroke, and don't roll over the edges or flip the dough or turn it while rolling. Roll the lefse very thin, about 1/16 inch or less, and about 12 inches across for 1/3 cup of dough or 10 inches across for 1/4 cup of dough.

INSERT THE LEFSE STICK between the lefse and the cloth, starting in the center of the lefse and moving it to the sides to loosen the lefse from canvas. (If the dough sticks to the pastry cloth and tears, simply gather up the dough, reshape it into a ball, and reroll.) Lift the lefse stick so that the lefse hangs down on both sides, move it to the griddle, and lay half the lefse on the griddle. Use the stick to quickly unroll the remaining half onto the griddle. Or, use two large spatulas, and slide them under the lefse from the left and right sides to meet in the middle. Transfer the lefse to the griddle and slowly slide the spatulas out from under the lefse.

COOK for 1 to 1½ minutes, until the underside of the lefse is dappled with brown spots and the top has many small bubbles. Use the lefse stick or a long narrow metal spatula to flip the lefse over and cook the second side for about 45 seconds, until dotted with larger brown spots. Brush off excess flour with a pastry brush. Do not overcook, or the lefse will be crisp instead of tender.

FOLD THE LEFSE into quarters on the griddle, using the lefse stick or spatula, and transfer to a kitchen towel. Cover with another towel and let it stand while you roll and bake the remaining lefse dough. Wait until each lefse is cooked before rolling the next one. As you add baked lefse to those already cooked, overlap them slightly between the towels. It takes about 2 hours to roll and cook a batch of lefse. It helps speed the process if one person rolls the dough and the other person cooks it.

Storing

Once cooled, lefse can be frozen. Place 5 or 6 folded lefse into a heavy-duty resealable plastic bag and freeze for up to 1 month. Thaw them in the bag. To refresh them, unwrap, rewrap in foil, and heat them in a preheated 300°F oven for about 10 minutes.

Note

It may take cooking a few lefse to get the hang of the process. On my first try, I succeeded making my first good lefse after 5 others didn't make the grade. Have patience. These flatbreads are well worth the effort.

Jian Bing

china

MAKES 4 STUFFED FLATBREADS; ENOUGH FOR 4 SERVINGS AS A MAIN DISH OR 8 SERVINGS AS PART OF A CHINESE MEAL

ONE OF THE MOST POPULAR STREET FOODS in northern China is a flatbread called jian bing. The vendor spreads a thin pancake batter in a perfect circle on a hot griddle. In a few seconds, after the batter has set, she cracks a raw egg onto it, breaks up the yolk, and spreads the egg all over the pancake. When it is set, she flips the whole thing over and quickly brushes various sauces onto the pancake, sprinkles it with some chopped scallions and cilantro, and centers a deep-fried, thin, crispy honeycombed rectangular cake made of flour, yeast, and water on top. With the edge of a spatula, she whacks the cake into a few pieces, then folds the edges of the pancake over, gives the whole thing another few whacks, and folds the jian bing into a small packet. After wrapping it in paper, she smiles and hands the bing to you. You pay her the equivalent of twenty-five cents and go off with your hot snack.

I learned how to make this homemade version of jian bing in Beijing from our son Jason's housekeeper, Li Ayi. She often makes a vegetarian version with garlic chives for his family, but she was happy to teach me her favorite pork-stuffed version. The flour Li uses is made from a soft wheat, specially milled for dumplings, which makes the flatbreads easy to roll out. I've substituted a mixture of all-purpose and cake flour for similar results. She chops the pork for the filling into tiny pieces with a large chef's knife; I usually use a food processor. After dividing the dough, she rolls a portion into a circle, fills it her own special way, and rolls it out to fit the bottom of a large skillet. Frying the bing takes only a few minutes, and as each one cooks, she shapes another.

DOUGH

1½ cups all-purpose flour, plus more for rolling

½ cup cake flour

¾ cup hot water

FILLING

1 pound lean pork (boneless sirloin chops or pork tenderloin)

3 scallions, trimmed and finely chopped

1-inch cube peeled fresh ginger, minced

3 garlic cloves, minced

2 tablespoons chicken broth or water

2 tablespoons soy sauce

1 tablespoon dry sherry

2 teaspoons roasted sesame oil

½ teaspoon Chinese five-spice powder

¾ teaspoon salt

½ teaspoon freshly ground black pepper

Vegetable oil, preferably peanut, for cooking

86   A BAKER'S ODYSSEY

The only really tricky part of the whole procedure is the final rolling. The filling will almost certainly break through the thin dough in one or more places. Do not panic—just flour the bing liberally, and everything will hold together nicely. Be sure to brush the excess flour off the bing before frying. After cooking, cut each bing into 4 or 6 wedges and serve. Some cooks like to slip a well-fried egg into each wedge. If you want, you can pass some hoisin sauce to be spread in a thin layer onto the bing, but this is not traditional.

TO MAKE THE DOUGH, put both flours into a large bowl and stir with a wooden spoon. Gradually add the hot water, stirring to make a firm but sticky dough. Lightly flour your work surface and scrape the dough onto it. Turn the dough to coat with flour and knead it, folding it over on itself and pushing it away with the heel of a hand as you rotate the dough. Once the dough develops some elasticity, pass it rapidly from hand to hand, squeezing and kneading it for a minute or two. The dough should feel firm and no longer be sticky. Wrap the dough in plastic wrap and let it rest at room temperature for about 1 hour.

To chop the meat with a very sharp Chinese cleaver or sharp chef's knife, cut the meat into coarse chunks on a cutting board. Put them in a pile and with a swift up-and-down motion, work your way from one end of the pile to the other. Flip the meat over with the knife or cleaver and repeat the chopping motion at right angles to the first chop. Chop the meat a few more times this way, making each chop at right angles to the previous chop, until the meat is in very small pieces. This whole process should take you 5 to 10 minutes.

To chop the meat in a food processor, cut the meat into 1-inch pieces, put them on a tray lined with plastic wrap, and freeze for 15 to 20 minutes to firm up the meat a bit; don't freeze the meat solid. Insert the metal blade into the work bowl of the processor, add the meat, and pulse rapidly, stopping to scrape the sides of the bowl as necessary, until the meat is cut into very small pieces.

TO MAKE THE FILLING, combine the pork with the remaining ingredients in a medium bowl and beat them together well with a wooden spoon. (The filling can be made 1 hour ahead and refrigerated, covered. Longer than that, and the ginger will start breaking down the meat, causing it to turn mushy. But if you hold back the ginger, you can make the filling a day ahead and refrigerate it; add the ginger before forming and cooking the bing.)

DIVIDE THE DOUGH into 4 equal pieces and shape each into a ball. Set them on a lightly floured surface and cover with an inverted bowl. Let the balls rest for 15 minutes or longer to relax the gluten and make them easy to roll.

ON A WELL-FLOURED SURFACE, roll a dough ball to a circle 9 to 9½ inches in diameter and about ⅛ inch thick. Treating the circle as the face of a clock, with the 6 o'clock position nearest you, spread one-quarter of the pork mixture in a thin layer to cover the circle from 9 o'clock all the way around to 6 o'clock, leaving the quadrant between 6 and 9 o'clock uncovered, as well as a ¾-inch border all around. Brush all exposed surfaces of dough with water. With a sharp knife, make a cut from the center of the circle and about ¼ inch to the left of the filling down through the 6 o'clock position. Lift the uncovered dough up and over the filling between 9 and 12 o'clock, covering it completely. Press firmly on the edges to seal. Fold this filled triangular section over the filling between 12 and 3 o'clock and pinch the seams firmly to seal. Fold the small strip of exposed dough between the center of the circle and the 6 o'clock position over the edge of the remaining section of exposed filling and brush with water, then fold the filled dough between 12 and 3 o'clock down to cover the filling completely. Pinch the edges firmly to seal, and tuck the seams underneath the triangle. With cupped hands, shape the triangle into a roughly circular shape.

GENTLY ROLL THE BING on a well-floured surface to an 8-inch circle about ¼ inch thick. The dough will become very thin and you'll be able to see the pork filling through it. The dough will probably tear at a few points, with the pork filling squeezing through—do not be alarmed. Simply flour everything liberally, flip the bing over from time to time, and roll to the specified size. Brush off excess flour with a pastry brush and set aside while the oil heats. (Shape each of the remaining bing as the previous one is being cooked.)

ADJUST AN OVEN RACK to the center position and preheat the oven to 250°F. Heat 2 tablespoons of oil in a large skillet over high heat.

WHEN THE OIL is very hot and almost smoking, slip the bing into the pan. It will sizzle. Cover the pan, reduce the heat to medium-high, and cook for 3 minutes. Uncover the pan, press down on the bing with a metal spatula (the bing will most likely have puffed during cooking), and turn it over. It will be nicely browned in patches. Add a bit more oil if necessary, cover the pan, and cook for 3 minutes longer. Uncover the pan and press down again on the bing with the metal spatula. Cook a few seconds, then transfer the bing to a baking sheet and put it into the oven to keep warm. Shape and cook the remaining bing, transferring them to the oven as they are done.

TO SERVE, cut the bing into quarters or sixths and eat them out of hand while they're hot.

Storing

The cooled flatbreads can be frozen in heavy-duty resealable plastic bags for up to 1 week. To serve, place the unwrapped frozen bing in a single layer on a baking sheet and reheat in a preheated 350°F oven for 10 to 15 minutes.

South African Crumpets *sweet pancakes*

MAKES 18 TO 20 CAKES

BRYONY VAN DERMERWE SCHWAN, *who was born in Zimbabwe, makes these sweet South African crumpets whenever unexpected company drops in. It is a way of welcoming guests into her home with something hot made specially for the occasion. She learned this recipe from her grandmother while growing up in Africa, and she carries on the tradition in the United States.*

These are not your typical chewy yeasted crumpets with large holes—they are light and tender pancakes. The batter is very quick and easy to make. The method is a bit untraditional in that you beat the sugar, a bit of oil, and egg together before mixing in the dry ingredients and milk, and it is this step that gives the crumpets their special texture. Because they're sweet, you don't need any syrup with them, but do serve the crumpets with softened or melted butter. Feel free to double or triple the recipe.

BATTER

1 cup unbleached all-purpose flour

1 teaspoon baking powder

¼ teaspoon salt

5 tablespoons granulated sugar

2 tablespoons vegetable oil

1 large egg

½ cup whole milk, plus more if needed

Butter for cooking and serving

TO MAKE THE BATTER, in a medium bowl combine the flour, baking powder, and salt with a whisk.

PUT THE SUGAR into another medium bowl, add the oil, and stir with a wooden spoon to make a damp, sandy-looking mixture. Stir in the egg and beat for about 30 seconds with the spoon, until creamy. In 4 additions, stir in the dry ingredients alternately with the milk, beginning and ending with the flour mixture. The batter should be the consistency of a thick pancake batter. It will thicken on standing; if necessary, adjust the thickness with droplets of milk as you cook the crumpets.

SET A LARGE HEAVY SKILLET or griddle over medium heat. When it is hot, add a dab of butter and rotate the pan to film the bottom lightly with butter. Place tablespoons of batter into the pan, without crowding, to make crumpets almost 3 inches in diameter, and cook for 1 to 2 minutes, until bubbly on top. Flip the crumpets over with a metal spatula—they should be golden brown on the bottom—and cook about 30 seconds more. Transfer the crumpets to a warmed platter and cover loosely to keep warm while you cook the rest of the batter.

SERVE HOT, with more butter on the side.

Flour Tortillas

MAKES 12 LARGE TORTILLAS

MARIA ELENA FLORES, *who immigrated to the United States from Mexico more than forty years ago, makes tortillas once or twice a week. She lives in Elk Grove, California, with one of her daughters, a son-in-law, and three growing grandsons, who have no trouble making quick work of any tortillas Maria Elena turns out. Watching her work is mesmerizing. It takes her a mere thirty seconds to roll a ball of dough into a tortilla—a perfect circle!—and less than a minute to cook it on a hot griddle. As one tortilla cooks, she rolls out another, and in about 20 minutes she has a stack of two dozen cooked tortillas. Just about every recipe involving dough that Maria Elena uses takes 2½ pounds of flour. I've cut her tortilla recipe in half, but feel free to double it if you want two dozen tortillas. They keep in the freezer for at least 2 weeks.*

A large cast-iron skillet or griddle is best for cooking tortillas because cast iron retains heat well and evenly, but a heavy stainless steel skillet will also do an excellent job.

DOUGH

- 4 cups unbleached all-purpose flour
- ½ teaspoon salt
- ½ teaspoon baking powder
- 2 tablespoons vegetable shortening or lard
- ¼ cup half-and-half
- ¾ cup warm water

Vegetable oil for cooking

TO MAKE THE DOUGH, in a large bowl stir the flour, salt, and baking powder with a whisk. Add the shortening or lard and work it into the flour with your fingertips. Combine the half-and-half and water and add it to the flour. Use your hand or a wooden spoon to form a stiff dough; your hand works best because you need to squeeze the mixture repeatedly to make it gather into a ball of dough.

TURN THE DOUGH OUT onto an unfloured surface and knead it until it becomes smooth, firm, and elastic, about 5 minutes. Shape the dough into a ball, wrap it in plastic wrap, and let it rest at room temperature for about 1 hour. (During this time the dough will become even smoother and more supple.)

UNWRAP THE DOUGH and divide it in half. Roll each half into a log about 9 inches long. Cut each log into six 1½-inch pieces. Roll each piece into a ball, and set the balls on your work surface. Cover loosely with plastic wrap and let the balls relax for 10 minutes.

LIGHTLY FLOUR your work surface. Set a ball of dough on it and flatten it with your fingertips into a circle measuring about 4 inches. Roll the dough out as evenly as you can, flouring it lightly as necessary, until it is 8 to 9 inches in diameter and less than ⅛ inch thick. Set the tortilla on a square of waxed paper, and cover with another square of waxed paper; if the weather is humid, dust the paper and tortilla lightly with flour. Roll the remaining balls of dough into tortillas, stacking them between squares of waxed paper.

SET A LARGE CAST-IRON SKILLET or griddle over medium heat. The griddle must get hot but not searing hot. Brush the hot pan very lightly with oil (Maria Elena uses a paper towel), and set a tortilla in the pan. In a few seconds, largeish bubbles will form on the surface. After 30 seconds or so, lift an edge of the tortilla with a fork to see if the bottom is flecked unevenly with golden brown spots. When it is, flip the tortilla over. Chances are the tortilla will puff up—use a kitchen towel to gently tap it flat. Cook for about 30 seconds more, until the second side is flecked with brown; regulate the heat if necessary. Remove the tortilla from the pan with kitchen tongs or a metal spatula and set it on a board or plate. Cover loosely with a kitchen towel. Cook the remaining tortillas, stacking them one on top of another as they're done and covering them with the towel.

Storing

If not serving the tortillas within an hour or so, put them in a resealable heavy-duty plastic bag and store in the refrigerator for up to 4 days. Or freeze them for up to 2 weeks. Thaw completely before removing the tortillas from their wrapping.

Variation

TORTILLA CHIPS Cut each tortilla into 8 wedges and arrange them on large baking sheets. Coat lightly on both sides with cooking spray and bake in a preheated 350°F oven until golden brown and crisp, about 10 minutes. Watch carefully to prevent them from burning. Cool before serving. These are excellent with guacamole.

Chapati

MAKES 16 FLATBREADS

CHAPATI ARE ONE OF THE BEST KNOWN *and easiest to make of the many Indian flatbreads. Made with only flour and water, the thin, wheaty breads are quickly cooked on a hot griddle and served with just about any meal. In India, chapati are prepared every day. They dry out within a few hours, so the dough is mixed, rolled, and cooked when wanted.*

Chitra Paresh makes Indian flatbreads at her home in Phoenix every day, and she uses atta flour for all of them. Made from durum wheat grown in Canada, atta flour is the nearest approximation to the wheat flour she used in India. If not available in your market, it can be ordered by mail (see Sources, page 343). Or simply substitute whole wheat flour—the breads will be browner in color and the texture a bit coarser, but they'll still have the characteristic chewiness.

Chitra mixes the dough by hand in a bowl. After letting it rest for 30 minutes to 1 hour, she divides the dough into 16 portions and shapes each into a ball. While the balls of dough rest, she heats up her cast-iron Indian griddle, called a tawa (pronounced "TA-va"), on her electric range to cook the chapati.

She sets up a wire cooling rack supported 3 to 4 inches above the heating element on another burner to give the cooked chapati their final puff. A wok ring or the sides of a springform pan will work nicely as a support for the wire rack. The idea is to have an intense radiating heat source.

Chitra uses an Indian rolling pin, a narrow rod with a fat middle and thinner tapered ends. As she rolls, the dough rotates magically underneath the pin, and in a few seconds, she has perfectly round chapati. A narrow dowel, about 1¼ inches in diameter works well, too, but any rolling pin will do.

---

2 cups atta flour or whole wheat flour, plus all-purpose flour for rolling

⅔ cup water, plus more if needed

PUT THE FLOUR into a medium mixing bowl. Add the water and work it into the flour with your fingers to form a firm dough. If necessary, add a little more water. Knead the dough in the bowl, folding it on itself and pushing it out, or knead it on an unfloured countertop, for about 5 minutes. The dough should feel smooth and resilient. Wrap the dough in plastic wrap and let it rest at room temperature for 30 minutes to 1 hour.

DIVIDE THE DOUGH into 16 equal portions. Shape each into a ball and cover with a towel or plastic wrap. Let the dough rest for another 10 to 20 minutes.

HEAT A GRIDDLE or cast-iron skillet over medium heat until very hot. Set a wire rack on a wok ring or the sides of a springform pan on another burner and turn the heat to medium (see Note). Set out a small bowl of all-purpose flour.

TO SHAPE THE CHAPATI, dip a ball of dough into the all-purpose flour, and roll the dough out to a 5½-inch round about ⅙ inch thick. Work rapidly so the dough doesn't dry out. Flip the dough over from time to time and flour it lightly as necessary to prevent sticking.

PUT THE CHAPATI on the griddle or skillet and cook for 10 seconds. Flip the chapati over with tongs—it will not have colored—and cook for 1 minute. During this time, you'll notice small bubbles beginning to form in the chapati, then becoming medium bubbles, and the edges may curl a bit. With tongs, lift the chapati out of the pan and flip it over onto the cake rack. You'll see that the cooked side facing you is studded with dark brown spots. Once it hits the wire rack, the chapati will puff almost immediately into a pillow. Amazing! Cook just a few seconds, then remove the chapati with tongs, and wrap it in a kitchen towel.

SHAPE AND COOK the remaining chapati one at a time. It's all right to leave the heat on under the griddle or cast-iron skillet and the wire rack as you work. Just regulate the heat if it's getting too hot. Serve as soon as possible.

Variation

Leftover chapati can be turned into chips, just like leftover tortillas—see page 91.

Note

If you don't want to bother with the wire rack setup, simply turn the chapati over after the 1-minute cooking time, and cook it on its second side for 1 minute more. To encourage the chapati to puff, use a wadded paper towel to press it down all around the outer edges. Sometimes the chapati puffs, sometimes it doesn't—no matter.

Puran Poori

MAKES 16 FLATBREADS

THESE STUFFED INDIAN FLATBREADS *are one of the many savory breads Bipin Patel remembers eating while growing up in East Africa. When Bipin, who owns an East Indian restaurant in Missoula, Montana, first told me about them, I was intrigued. The breads are stuffed with a sweet yellow split pea filling and fried in ghee, Indian clarified butter. "The dough is a basic dough for chapati, to serve with breakfast. These breads are more involved and you eat them with main dishes." For economic reasons, his family had emigrated to Africa from Gujarat, a province on the western coast of India near Pakistan. Bipin fondly recalls his mother and grandmother making these breads, and he learned how to make them himself at a young age. Although sweet, puran poori are meant to be eaten as part of a meal. The breads can be paired with all sorts of Indian dishes.*

The filling must be started the day before because the peas need an overnight soak in water. As with most Indian flatbreads, puran poori are best when very fresh.

FILLING

- ¾ cup yellow split peas
- ¼ cup ghee (see Sources, page 343) or clarified butter (see page 12)
- ½ teaspoon ground cardamom
- ½ teaspoon freshly grated nutmeg
- ⅛ teaspoon ground mace
- Pinch of ground cloves
- ¼ teaspoon saffron threads, soaked in 2 teaspoons warm water
- ½ cup firmly packed dark brown sugar

DOUGH

- 2 cups atta flour or 1 cup whole wheat flour plus 1 cup unbleached all-purpose flour, plus more for shaping
- ½ teaspoon salt
- 2 tablespoons vegetable oil
- ½ cup plus 2 tablespoons tepid water, plus more if needed

  About ½ cup ghee for frying

TO MAKE THE FILLING, pick over the split peas and remove any rocks or dirt fragments. Put the peas into a medium bowl, add 4 cups water, and let stand at room temperature overnight.

THE NEXT DAY, drain the split peas and put them into the work bowl of a food processor fitted with the metal blade. Process for 1 to 2 minutes, to a thick, smooth puree. Stop to scrape the sides of the work bowl as necessary.

MELT THE GHEE in a medium heavy skillet over medium heat. When hot, add the cardamom, nutmeg, mace, and cloves and stir once or twice with a wooden spoon, then add the ground split peas. Stir and cook for 1 to 2 minutes. Add the saffron, stir it in well, and add the brown sugar. Cook and stir for 1 to 2 minutes more. The puree will thin out a bit. Remove the pan from the heat and cool completely, then cover and refrigerate the filling for 1 to 2 hours to firm it up and make it easy to work with. (The filling can be made up to 1 day ahead and refrigerated. Bring to room temperature before using.)

TO MAKE THE DOUGH, put the flour and salt into a medium bowl and add the oil. Stir with a fork to disperse the oil, then work the mixture with your fingertips to coat the flour with the oil. Add ½ cup of the water and stir until the flour forms many largeish lumps. Add the remaining 2 tablespoons water and stir well. The dough may not gather into a cohesive mass. To test if it is moist enough, press the dough with your hands—it should stick together, feel firm, and not be sticky. Work in more water by the teaspoonful if needed, but don't add so much that the dough becomes wet or sticky.

TURN THE DOUGH OUT onto an unfloured work surface and knead for about 5 minutes. Wrap the dough in plastic wrap and let it rest at room temperature for 1 to 2 hours.

TO SHAPE the puran poori, divide the filling into 16 portions, and shape each into a ball. Set the balls of filling on a sheet of plastic wrap and cover loosely with another sheet of plastic wrap. Divide the dough into 2 equal pieces. Roll each into an 8-inch-long log. Cut the logs into 1-inch pieces and roll them into balls. Set them on your work surface and cover loosely with plastic wrap.

PUT A BALL OF DOUGH on your unfloured work surface and pat it into a 4-inch circle. If the dough feels tacky, dust it lightly with flour. Put a portion of filling in the center of the dough and bring up the edges of the dough to cover the filling completely; pleating the dough as you bring it up and over the filling makes this step go by quickly. Pinch the edges firmly to seal in the filling. Turn the puran poori seam side down onto a lightly floured surface and roll it out gently to a 4-inch circle about ¼ inch thick. Set the shaped bread onto a baking sheet lined with plastic wrap. Repeat with the remaining dough and filling.

LINE TWO BAKING SHEETS with several thicknesses of paper towels. Melt half the ghee in a large heavy skillet (cast iron is ideal, but any heavy large skillet will work) or a griddle with a rim over medium heat. When the ghee is hot, put 4 to 6 poori in the pan, leaving a little space between them. Cook for 3 to 4 minutes, until the dough is golden brown on the bottom, with a few darker spots. The breads may puff up during cooking. Turn the poori over with a large metal spatula and cook on the second side for 3 to 4 minutes. Transfer the cooked breads to a lined pan. If they puffed during cooking, they'll flatten out during cooling. Continue cooking the remaining breads the same way, adding more ghee to the pan as necessary. Serve warm or at room temperature.

Kachauri

MAKES 20 FLATBREADS

THIS INDIAN FLATBREAD, SIMILAR TO PURAN POORI, *is stuffed with a spicy filling of yellow split peas. It is delicious all by itself, but it can accompany any Indian vegetable or meat dish. Bipin Patel, who taught me this recipe, learned how to make it from his Gujarati mother and grandmother. Bipin likes to use atta flour for the dough, but you can use a mixture of whole wheat flour and unbleached all-purpose flour. Most of the spices in this recipe are available in well-stocked supermarkets, and they can also be ordered by mail (see Sources, page 341). Ghee, Indian clarified butter, is used in the filling and to fry the shaped kachauri.*

Begin this the night before, as the split peas need a good long soak in water to soften them.

FILLING

- ¾ cup yellow split peas
- ¼ cup ghee (see Sources, page 343) or clarified butter (see page 12)
- ½ teaspoon cumin seeds
- 1 small lump asafetida or ½ teaspoon asafetida powder
- ½ teaspoon fennel seed
- ½ teaspoon ground turmeric
- ¾ teaspoon salt
- 1 teaspoon finely grated peeled fresh ginger
- 1 teaspoon very finely minced jalapeño chile
- 1 tablespoon granulated sugar
- 6 tablespoons water, plus more if needed

DOUGH

- 2 cups atta flour or 1 cup whole wheat flour plus 1 cup unbleached all-purpose flour, plus more for shaping
- ½ teaspoon salt
- 2 tablespoons vegetable oil
- ½ cup plus 2 tablespoons tepid water, plus more if needed

About ½ cup ghee for frying

TO MAKE THE FILLING, pick over the split peas and remove any rock or dirt fragments. Put the peas in a medium bowl, add 4 cups water, and let stand at room temperature overnight.

THE NEXT DAY, drain the split peas and put them into the work bowl of a food processor fitted with the metal blade. Process for 1 to 2 minutes, to a thick, smooth puree. Stop to scrape the sides of the work bowl as necessary.

MELT THE GHEE in a medium heavy skillet over medium heat. When it is hot, add the cumin seeds and asafetida and stir

with a wooden spoon for a few seconds. Watch carefully so that the cumin doesn't burn. Add the fennel, turmeric, salt, grated ginger, and jalapeño and stir for about 30 seconds. Add the ground split peas and sugar and stir for about 1 minute. The peas may stick to the bottom of the pan in spots—that's okay. Remove the pan from the heat and stir in the water. The mixture will not form a cohesive mass, but when you place about a tablespoon of the seasoned split peas in your hand and press it firmly, it should hold together and not fall apart. Add water by the teaspoonful if the mixture is too dry. Let cool completely. (The filling can be made up to 1 day ahead. Cover tightly with plastic wrap and refrigerate; bring to room temperature before using.)

TO MAKE THE DOUGH, put the flour and salt into a medium bowl and add the oil. Stir with a fork to disperse the oil, then work the mixture with your fingertips to coat the flour with the oil. Add ½ cup of the water and stir until the flour forms many largeish lumps. Add the remaining 2 tablespoons water and stir well. The dough may not gather into a cohesive mass. To test if it is moist enough, press the dough with your hands. It should stick together, feel firm, and not be sticky. Work in more water by the teaspoonful if needed, but don't add so much that the dough becomes wet or sticky.

TURN THE DOUGH OUT onto an unfloured work surface and knead for about 5 minutes. Wrap the dough in plastic wrap and let it rest at room temperature for 1 to 2 hours.

TO SHAPE THE KACHAURI, divide the filling into 20 portions, and shape each into a ball; press firmly so that they hold their shape. Set the balls of filling on a sheet of plastic wrap and cover loosely with another sheet of plastic wrap. Divide the dough into 2 equal pieces. Roll each into a 10-inch-long log. Cut the logs into 1-inch pieces and roll them into balls. Set them on your work surface and cover loosely with plastic wrap.

PUT A BALL OF DOUGH on your unfloured work surface and pat it into a 4-inch circle. If the dough feels tacky, dust it lightly with flour. Put a portion of filling onto the center of the dough and bring up the edges of the dough to cover the filling completely; pleating the dough as you bring it up and over the filling makes this step go by quickly. Pinch the edges firmly to seal in the filling. Turn the kachauri seam side down onto a lightly floured surface and roll it out gently to a 4-inch circle a scant ¼ inch thick. Set the shaped bread onto a baking sheet lined with plastic wrap. Repeat with the remaining dough and filling.

LINE TWO BAKING SHEETS with several thicknesses of paper towels. Melt half the ghee in a large, heavy, straight-sided skillet (cast iron is ideal, but any heavy large skillet will work) or rimmed griddle over medium heat. When the ghee is hot, put 4 to 6 kachauri in the pan, leaving a little space between them. Cook for 3 to 4 minutes, until the dough is golden brown on the bottom, with a few darker spots. The breads may puff up during cooking. Turn the kachauri over with a large metal spatula and cook on the second side for 3 to 4 minutes. Transfer the cooked breads to a lined pan. If they puffed during cooking, they'll flatten out during cooling. Continue cooking the remaining kachauri the same way, adding more ghee to the pan as necessary. Serve warm or at room temperature. Kachauri are best fresh.

Noreen Kinney's Irish Soda Bread *ireland*

MAKES 1 ROUND LOAF

I AM INDEBTED TO IRISH FOOD EXPERT *and cookbook author Noreen Kinney, for sharing her family's Irish soda bread recipe. This bread is meant to be eaten plain with meals, or with cheese or with butter and jam, or used to sop up gravy. According to Noreen:*

Strictly speaking, there is no white Irish soda bread with raisins. Traditional Irish soda bread is brown, with a coarse texture and no fruit. It can also contain seeds and flax and bran, depending on the baker's desires. That is the reason I was shocked to see the white item passed off as Irish soda bread when I arrived in the States. However, in Ireland there is a famous old bread that was very popular with the poorer people in times past, and considered quite a treat for a special occasion or on Sundays. It is still popular today. Depending on which part of the country one is in, it is known as spotted dick or spotted dog. Basically it is derived from Irish soda bread, but it uses white flour in place of the traditional flours and other ingredients that go into the true Irish soda bread. To enrich the recipe, people added raisins when they became available, and they might add a full egg beaten into the milk, plus some white sugar. So it is the old Irish spotted dick that folks here call Irish Soda Bread [see recipe on page 100].

Everyone who makes Irish soda bread adds her or his own personal touches to the bread. To the mixture of whole wheat flour and white flour, Noreen, on any given day, might add wheat bran, oat bran, wheat germ, oats, sunflower seeds, flaxseeds, or poppy seeds. She varies proportions and grains depending on how she wants the bread to turn out. Think of the following proportions as guidelines, and feel free to vary the grain additions according to your tastes, adding from 4 to 5 ounces total by weight for each loaf.

The bread's crust is coarse and firm, while the inside is rather dense but moist. A cross indented (not cut) on top of the bread allows the bread to be easily separated into quarters. Oddly, the sunflower seeds change color during baking, flecking the bread with an emerald green. The unexpected appearance of flecks of green in the bread the first time I made it surprised me. I could tell the color came from the sunflower seeds, but why did this happen?

1 ¾ cups unbleached all-purpose flour

1 cup whole wheat flour or graham flour, plus more for shaping

3 tablespoons cold unsalted butter, cut into tablespoon-sized pieces

2 teaspoons baking soda

1 ¾ teaspoons salt

2 tablespoons granulated sugar

¼ cup wheat bran

¼ cup oat bran

¼ cup untoasted wheat germ

2 tablespoons flaxseed

⅓ cup raw sunflower seeds

1 large egg

About 1 ¾ cups buttermilk

Food chemist Shirley Corriher, author of the classic Cookwise, *had the answer. "Sunflower seeds are chock-full of good-for-you things," Shirley said, and by that she meant they're loaded with antioxidants. Among these are flavonoids, which turn yellow when they come into contact with an alkali (baking soda in the recipe). Other antioxidants, anthocyanins, react by turning blue. Put blue and yellow together, and you get green. Nifty.*

ADJUST AN OVEN RACK to the center position and preheat the oven to 425°F. Coat a heavy baking sheet with vegetable cooking spray or line it with a silicone baking pan liner or aluminum foil.

IN A LARGE BOWL, stir together the all-purpose flour and whole wheat flour. Add the butter and work it into the dry ingredients with your fingertips until the fat particles are very fine. Stir in the baking soda, salt, sugar, wheat bran, oat bran, wheat germ, flaxseed, and sunflower seeds.

BEAT THE EGG LIGHTLY with a fork in a 2-cup glass measure. Add enough buttermilk to come to the 2-cup line and stir with the fork to combine well. Add the liquid to the dry ingredients and stir with a wooden spoon or rubber spatula until the dough gathers into a thick, wet-looking mass.

SPRINKLE YOUR WORK SURFACE with whole wheat flour and scrape the dough onto it. Dust the dough with a bit more whole wheat flour. Pat the dough into a circular shape about 7 inches across and 2 inches high and transfer it to the prepared baking sheet. Don't be concerned about evenness—the loaf should look rustic. Make a cross-shaped indentation on top of

the loaf going right to the edges. I use a plastic bench scraper and press it into the dough very gently; don't actually cut the dough. During baking the indentation expands, giving the top of the loaf an attractive pattern.

BAKE THE BREAD for about 40 minutes, until it is well browned and sounds hollow when rapped on the bottom. An instant-read thermometer inserted into the center of the loaf should register 195° to 200°F. Cool the loaf on a wire cooling rack, and serve warm or at room temperature. Cut into quarters and slice each quarter with a sharp serrated knife. Delicious with butter.

Storing

The loaf keeps well at room temperature, wrapped in plastic wrap, for 2 to 3 days. The entire loaf or quarters of it can also be frozen when completely cool. Wrap in plastic wrap, place in heavy-duty resealable plastic bags, and freeze for up to 2 weeks. Thaw completely before unwrapping. If desired, refresh the bread in a preheated 300°F oven for 10 minutes.

Sweet Irish Soda Bread
(Spotted Dick or Spotted Dog)

ireland

MAKES 1 ROUND LOAF

4 cups all-purpose flour, plus more for shaping

½ cup granulated sugar

1 teaspoon salt

1½ teaspoons baking powder

4 tablespoons (½ stick) cold unsalted butter, cut into tablespoon-sized pieces

2 cups dark raisins

1 tablespoon caraway seeds

1 large egg

1⅓ cups buttermilk

1 teaspoon baking soda

RECIPES FOR IRISH SODA BREAD *are probably as varied as the people who bake it. The original, traditional bread, meant to be eaten with meals, contained nothing more than flour, salt, baking soda, and buttermilk. Some cooks also added seeds, flax, or bran as enrichments. The bread is believed to have originated in the mid-1800s. In rural areas of Ireland, bread was more likely to be made with baking soda than yeast. The reason is that the flour available was made from soft wheat, wheat low in gluten. Hard wheat flour, the kind usually used to make bread because of its high gluten content, was scarce there. Baking soda, in combination with an acid, worked better as a leavener in soft wheat breads than yeast. Or at least this is one theory as to how Irish soda bread originated.*

Over time, Irish soda bread has been transformed from a mainstay of the daily diet into a dessert bread. Butter, sugar, raisins, currants, orange zest, caraway seeds, various spices, and even whiskey can be found in recipes today. And these recipes call for all-purpose or whole wheat flour (in whole or in part), not cake flour (soft wheat flour).

Such flavor enrichments are certainly in no way bad, but purists maintain that to be called Irish soda bread, it should just be made from its original four ingredients. Be that as it may, this recipe, provided by Eileen MacKerrow Sangster, makes an excellent sweet bread that may be eaten for breakfast or with afternoon tea. Come to think of it, the bread is like a giant biscuit or scone, so treat it as such and eat it with whatever pleases you. The bread is delicious warm, spread with butter, jam, honey, or cream cheese. Eileen learned the recipe from her grandmother, who brought it with her from Ireland when she immigrated to the United States in the early 1900s. The bread is best when freshly baked, slightly warm even.

ADJUST AN OVEN RACK to the center position and preheat the oven to 375°F. Line a small baking sheet with silicone baking pan liner or cooking parchment.

IN A LARGE BOWL, whisk together the flour, sugar, salt, and baking powder well. Add the butter and cut it in with a pastry blender or two knives until the mixture is the consistency of fine meal. Fingertips also work well for this job; once the butter pieces have been slightly reduced in size, reach in with your hands and rapidly pinch and fluff the dry ingredients together until you have the texture you want. Add the raisins and caraway seeds and toss with your hands to distribute them evenly.

IN A MEDIUM BOWL, beat the egg with a fork. Stir in the buttermilk and baking soda. Make a well in the flour mixture and pour in all the liquid. Stir with the fork until the dough gathers into a thick, damp mass.

LIGHTLY FLOUR YOUR WORK SURFACE and scrape the dough onto it. Turn the dough to coat all surfaces with the flour, and knead it with a few gentle strokes into a ball. Flatten the ball into an 8-inch circle and place it on the center of your baking sheet. With a floured sharp knife, make a ½-inch-deep cross across the top of the dough, marking it into quarters.

BAKE FOR 45 MINUTES. Cover the bread loosely with foil and bake 8 to 10 minutes more, until a deep golden brown color. Cool the bread on a wire rack, and serve warm or at room temperature. Cut the bread into quarters, then cut each quarter into ½-inch-thick slices.

Storing

Store the bread in a plastic bag at room temperature for 2 to 3 days. It makes excellent toast. For longer storage, put the bread in a heavy-duty resealable plastic bag and freeze for up to 2 weeks. Thaw the bread in its wrapping, then unwrap the bread, set on a baking sheet, and refresh in a preheated 300°F oven for 10 minutes.

3 | Savory Pastries

STARTING WITH ONLY THE BASIC INGREDIENTS OF FLOUR AND WATER, with the occasional addition of milk or eggs, cooks from around the world have created a huge variety of doughs and pastries for savory treats, many of them stuffed with fillings of cheese, meat, seafood, vegetables, or some combination.

The doughs themselves are extremely versatile. For example, to make savory bracelets, an Iraqi dough is shaped into rings, but it can also be rolled thin and formed into cheese-filled turnovers, or sambouseks. Paper-thin strudel dough, most often enclosing a sweet filling of apples, is equally successful as a wrapping for savory fillings of all sorts of vegetables, including cabbage, potatoes, and mushrooms. The Indian dough for chapati is transformed into a croquette of sorts by wrapping it around a filling of spicy cooked vegetables and deep-frying it.

Many of these rolled and filled pastries have the same general formulas even in different cultures. What sets each apart is the kind of filling, the seasonings used, and manner of cooking. Cornish cooks make pasties, huge turnovers of pie pastry generously filled with meat, potatoes, and onions, seasoned simply with salt and pepper, and baked. The filling of the Iraqi chicken sambouseks is flavored with Indian spices, because the Iraqi cooks who made them lived in India for a time and incorporated seasonings of that country into their traditional foods. The Thai, like other Asians, do not have an oven-baking tradition, but they do wonderful things with fried rice flour batters, adding shrimp and bean sprouts or tofu to them before plunging them into hot fat and turning them into crusty fritters.

Cabbage Strudel

MAKES 1 LARGE STRUDEL; ABOUT 8 SERVINGS AS A MAIN COURSE, 16 AS A FIRST COURSE

LAYERS OF CRISP, BUTTERY PAPER-THIN STRUDEL DOUGH *conceal a sweet-sour filling made with caramelized onions, cabbage, raspberry vinegar, and sugar. Strudel means "whirlpool" in German, and when Cindy Klotz makes strudel, she personifies the name. Her Russian grandmother was a master strudel maker, and Cindy learned the technique from her. Watching Cindy stretch the dough on her long cloth-covered dining room table reminded me of a roiling ocean. Her hands move over each other and stretch the dough apart rapidly and repeatedly as Cindy moves all around the table and down its length. In less than 10 minutes, the sheet of dough is paper-thin and about 6 feet long by 3 feet wide. After cutting away the thick edges of the dough and placing the filling in a 2-foot-long column along the short side of dough nearest her, Cindy lifts the cloth, causing a single thin layer of dough to flop over the filling and cover it completely. Then she lifts the sheet higher, and by force of gravity, the strudel rolls over and over itself in a blur until the filling is enclosed in all the dough—layers and layers of it. See the photos accompanying Apple Strudel on page 145 and in the color plates to envision the strudel-making process. Also, see the companion DVD for a video demonstration of strudel-dough making.*

Strudel is really a type of phyllo dough, which originated in Turkey a thousand or so years ago. Early in strudel's history, the dough wasn't paper-thin, as it is today. That refinement took place centuries later, in the Ottoman sultans' kitchens in Istanbul. After Suleyman the Great defeated the Hungarians in 1526 at the battle of Mohacs, the Turks annexed a large part of Hungary. During 200 years of Turkish rule, the Hungarians adopted and adapted many of the Turkish culinary traditions. Strudel dough, which the Turks used to make baklava, was one of them.

In Hungary, a new ingredient was introduced to strudel: the apple. Plentiful in that part of the world, apples were almost completely absent in Turkey then. When Austria conquered Hungary in 1699, strudel's journey extended into northern Europe. And there it has developed into a high form of culinary art. The Austrians don't limit themselves to sweet strudels. Savory strudels with meat, mushrooms, or cheese are often made in the home as a main dish.

If you haven't made it before, strudel dough can be one of the most intimidating of pastries.

There are a few things to keep in mind. You have to use the right kind of flour, a flour with the right proportion of elastic protein. I've found that Gold Medal organic unbleached all-purpose flour and King Arthur bread flour or unbleached all-purpose flour work extremely well. Gold Medal is slightly lower in protein content than King Arthur, but strudel dough made from it stretches like a dream. Do not use bleached flour—it does not work well for strudel dough.

Another important thing to keep in mind is the temperature of the room. Strudel dough likes it when your kitchen is warm, about 75°F, since the elastic proteins are then easier to stretch. A slightly humid room also helps to prevent the stretched dough from drying out.

This strudel can be served as a first course or as a main dish. As the former, it can stand all by itself. For a main dish, serve it with a tossed green salad and rice or potatoes. You can bake the strudel 2 or 3 hours before serving, and the pastry will remain wonderfully crisp.

FILLING

- 8 tablespoons (1 stick) unsalted butter
- ½ cup extra-virgin olive oil
- 4 or 5 large yellow onions (about 2½ pounds total), cut into ¼-inch-thick slices
- ¼ to ½ cup granulated sugar
- 1 large head cabbage (about 2½ pounds), core removed and cut into ¼-inch-wide slices
- 1 tablespoon salt, or to taste
- ½ cup wine vinegar (white wine, raspberry, or champagne vinegar), or to taste

DOUGH

- 2¾ cups bread flour or unbleached all-purpose flour, plus more if needed
- ½ teaspoon salt
- 4 tablespoons (½ stick) unsalted butter, at room temperature
- 1 large egg
- About ¾ cup water
- ½ teaspoon distilled white vinegar or fresh lemon juice
- 12 tablespoons (1½ sticks) unsalted butter, melted
- About ⅔ cup fine dry bread crumbs

TO MAKE THE FILLING, melt the butter with the oil in a large wide heavy pan, such as a 5- to 6-quart sauté pan or a Dutch oven, over medium heat. Add the onions, stir well, cover, and cook, stirring frequently, until the onions are light golden and have cooked down, about 15 to 20 minutes.

ADD ¼ cup sugar and cook and stir for a few minutes, until the onions begin to caramelize. Add the cabbage, stir well, and cover the pan. After 5 minutes, uncover the pan and give the vegetables a big stir. Cover the pan and continue cooking, stirring occasionally, until the cabbage cooks down and is

slightly caramelized. Uncover the pan and cook, stirring frequently, until the cabbage and onions are well caramelized and a rich brown color. This may take about 1 hour.

ADD the salt and vinegar and taste the filling. If it seems too sour, add up to ¼ cup more sugar. Cook, stirring, until the liquid is absorbed. There will be about 5 cups of filling. Taste again carefully. The onions and cabbage should taste sweet and sour. Adjust the seasoning as necessary with more salt, sugar, or vinegar. Let cool completely. (The filling can be made up to a day ahead; cover and refrigerate.)

TO MAKE THE DOUGH, put the flour and salt into the work bowl of a food processor fitted with the metal blade and process for 5 seconds. Add the butter and process for 8 to 10 seconds, until the mixture is the consistency of very fine meal. Beat the egg in a 2-cup glass measure and add enough water to reach the 1-cup level. Add the vinegar or lemon juice. Combine well with a fork. With the machine running, slowly add the liquid in a steady stream, taking about 10 seconds to do so. The dough will gather into a ball that cleans the sides of the work bowl. Process for 30 seconds. Stop the machine to push the dough about with a plastic scraper—it may be sticky at this point—and then process for another 30 seconds. Remove the dough from the work bowl and work it between your hands for a few seconds. It should be smooth, elastic, and no longer sticky. If it is sticky, replace it in the work bowl, add 1 tablespoon flour, and process for 10 seconds. Check the consistency again and repeat if the dough is still too wet.

TO DEVELOP THE GLUTEN, slap the dough on your countertop 50 to 100 times: throw the dough down, pick it up, throw it down again; repeat. Coat a medium bowl lightly with cooking spray or vegetable oil, add the dough, and turn to coat all surfaces. Cover tightly with plastic wrap and let the dough rest at room temperature for 2 to 3 hours to relax the gluten. Developing and then relaxing the gluten may seem contradictory, but it is not. For strudel dough, the gluten proteins must be tightly bonded to allow the dough to be stretched until it is paper thin. Letting the dough rest prior to stretching relaxes the gluten bonds, facilitating the stretching.

ADJUST AN OVEN RACK to the center position and preheat the oven to 450°F. Brush some of the melted butter onto the bottom of a large baking sheet (18 × 12 × 1 inch).

TO STRETCH THE DOUGH You will need a table 5 to 6 feet long and 2½ to 3 feet wide and a tablecloth or sheet large enough to allow several inches of overhang on all sides when doubled. Drape the cloth over the table and rub a thin layer of all-purpose flour into the cloth (except for the overhanging portion). Unwrap the dough and feel it. If it is tacky, dust it all over with flour. Pick up the dough and stretch it a bit. This dough is very responsive and will do what you ask of it. Put the dough on the center of the cloth, pat it gently to flatten slightly, and brush the top with a little melted butter. Roll the dough into an oval shape about 18 inches long and 12 inches wide. Gently tug on the edges of the dough, one edge at a time, until the dough is about 24 by 18 inches. Don't turn the dough over; just check on it periodically to make sure it is not sticking to the cloth, and sprinkle additional flour under it if necessary.

REACH UNDER THE DOUGH, with the backs of your hands against the dough, and gently pull your hands apart slightly and toward you, stretching the dough as you do so. Work your way around the table, repeating the process. Stretch the dough further by grasping the outer part of a thick edge and gently tugging on it. When the dough has been stretched a few inches more on all sides, repeat the hand movements described above. In a few minutes more of stretching, the paper-thin dough will reach the edges of the table. Continue tugging on the thicker edges to make about 6 inches of overhanging dough on all sides. Cut off the thick edges with kitchen shears. If the dough tears at any point, just leave it alone. Any tears will be covered up when the strudel is rolled up.

BECAUSE THE DOUGH is so thin, there's a danger of tearing it if you brush on the butter with a pastry brush. Instead, dip the brush into the butter and dab the butter all over the dough. Another way is to drizzle the butter onto the dough with a teaspoon: Dip the spoon into the butter and, holding it a few inches above the dough, wave the spoon from side to side to sprinkle drops of butter all over the dough. In either case, dab or drizzle the dough with about three-quarters of the remaining melted butter. Sprinkle about ½ cup bread crumbs evenly over the butter, just to make a very light dusting. Arrange the cabbage filling in an 18- to 20-inch-long horizontal column about 8 inches from the short side of the dough nearest you. Lift the end of the pastry-lined cloth nearest you and carefully flip it over to cover the cabbage completely with a layer of dough. Keep lifting the edge of cloth nearest you, and gravity will cause the strudel to roll over and over until it has formed a long log at the opposite end of the table. The strudel will be about 22 inches long, too long to fit onto your baking sheet, but there will be quite a bit of excess pastry at either end of the strudel. Pinch the ends of the pastry together near the filling, and cut them away with kitchen shears. Pinch the cut ends again to seal in the filling.

CAREFULLY LIFT THE STRUDEL (don't be afraid, it won't break) and place it on the baking sheet, curving it into a gentle C shape so that it will fit. Brush the strudel all over with the remaining butter and sprinkle lightly with more bread crumbs.

BAKE FOR 15 MINUTES. Reduce the temperature to 400°F and bake for about 20 minutes more, until the strudel is well browned and the pastry is crisp. Cool the strudel on its baking sheet, and serve warm or at room temperature. Cut into portions with a sharp serrated knife.

Storing

Strudel is at its best when very fresh. You can wrap leftovers in foil and refrigerate them for a day or two. To reheat, pull back the top of the foil but leave it against the cut ends. Pop into a preheated 400°F oven for about 15 minutes.

Potato Porcini Strudel

MAKES 1 LARGE STRUDEL; ABOUT 8 SERVINGS AS A MAIN COURSE, 16 AS A FIRST COURSE

THIS IS ONE OF CINDY KLOTZ'S FAVORITE STRUDELS, *made with a filling of boiled and "smashed" Yukon Gold potatoes seasoned with cooked onions, shallots, garlic, fresh mushrooms, and dried porcini mushrooms. Baked to a crisp golden brown, the strudel makes a fine first course or main dish. For the latter, serve with a salad, some steamed asparagus, and sliced tomatoes, if in season.*

The strudel can be baked 2 to 3 hours before serving—in fact, it will be at its best then. The pastry will remain crisp and crackly and the filling will still be a tad warm. See the photos accompanying Apple Strudel on page 145 and in the color plates to envision the strudel-making process. Also, see the companion DVD for a video demonstration of strudel-dough making.

FILLING

- 1 ounce best-quality dried porcini mushrooms
- 1 cup very hot water
- 5 pounds Yukon Gold potatoes (all about the same size), scrubbed
- Salt and freshly ground black pepper
- 6 tablespoons (¾ stick) unsalted butter
- ⅓ cup extra-virgin olive oil
- 3 large yellow onions, thinly sliced
- 3 shallots, finely chopped
- 6 ounces cremini or white mushrooms, washed and thinly sliced
- 3 garlic cloves, finely chopped

DOUGH

- 2¾ cups bread flour or unbleached all-purpose flour, plus more if needed
- ½ teaspoon salt
- 4 tablespoons (½ stick) butter, at room temperature
- 1 large egg
- About ¾ cup water
- ½ teaspoon distilled white vinegar or fresh lemon juice
- 12 tablespoons (1½ sticks) unsalted butter, melted
- About ⅔ cup fine dry bread crumbs

TO MAKE THE FILLING, put the porcini mushrooms in a small bowl with the hot water, and set aside to soak.

MEANWHILE, put the potatoes in a large pot and add cold water to cover by about 2 inches and 2 teaspoons salt. Bring the water to a boil over high heat, then reduce the heat slightly, partially cover the pot, and cook until the potatoes are completely tender, 25 to 30 minutes. Drain the potatoes in a colander and let them stand until easy to handle, about 20 minutes; set the pot aside.

SCRAPE THE SKINS off the potatoes and return the potatoes to their pot. Smash the potatoes with a pastry blender: use an up-and-down chopping motion to partially mash the potatoes and to cut most of them into medium pieces. Season to taste with salt and pepper.

IN A LARGE SKILLET, melt the butter with the oil over medium heat. Add the onions, shallots, and a sprinkling of salt, stir well, and cover the pan. Cook for 5 minutes. Uncover the pan and cook, stirring frequently, until the onions look translucent and are light golden, 10 to 15 minutes. Add the sliced mushrooms and garlic and cook, stirring occasionally, until the onions are a deep golden brown and the mushrooms are lightly browned, about 15 minutes.

LIFT THE PORCINI MUSHROOMS out of their liquid and squeeze gently to remove excess liquid; reserve the liquid. Chop the porcini, add them to the onions and mushrooms, and cook for 3 to 5 minutes, until the porcini are tender. Taste, and adjust the seasoning with salt and pepper.

ADD THE ONIONS AND MUSHROOMS to the smashed potatoes and combine well. The mixture will be thick and dense. Carefully add about half the porcini liquid to the potatoes, pouring slowly to avoid any dirt that may have settled in the bottom of the bowl. Add enough liquid to loosen the potato mixture a little—you may need to add almost all the liquid. Taste again and adjust the seasoning with more salt and pepper. Let cool, then cover and refrigerate until ready to use. (The filling can be made up to a day ahead).

TO MAKE THE DOUGH, put the flour and salt into the work bowl of a food processor fitted with the metal blade. Add the butter and process for 8 to 10 seconds, until the mixture is the consistency of very fine meal. Beat the egg in a 2-cup glass measure and add water to reach the 1-cup level. Add the vinegar or lemon juice. Combine well with a fork. With the machine running, slowly add the liquid in a steady stream, taking about 10 seconds to do so. The dough will gather into a ball that cleans the sides of the work bowl. Process for 30 seconds. Stop the machine to push the dough about with a plastic scraper—the dough may be sticky at this point—and then process for another 30 seconds. Remove the dough from the work bowl and work it between your hands for a few seconds. It should be smooth, elastic, and no longer sticky. If it is sticky, replace it in the work bowl, add 1 tablespoon flour, and process for 10 seconds. Check the consistency again and repeat if the dough is still too wet.

TO DEVELOP THE GLUTEN, slap the dough on your countertop 50 to 100 times to fully develop the gluten: throw the dough down, pick it up, throw it down again; repeat. Coat a medium bowl lightly with cooking spray or vegetable oil, add the dough, and turn to coat all surfaces. Cover tightly with plastic wrap and let the dough rest at room temperature for 2 to 3 hours to relax the gluten. Developing and then relaxing the gluten may seem contradictory, but it is not. For strudel dough, the gluten proteins must be tightly bonded to allow the dough to be stretched until it is paper thin. Letting the dough rest prior to stretching relaxes the gluten bonds, facilitating the stretching.

ADJUST AN OVEN RACK to the center position and preheat the oven to 450°F. Brush some of the melted butter onto the bottom of a large baking sheet (18 × 12 × 1 inch).

TO STRETCH THE DOUGH, you will need a table 5 to 6 feet long and 2½ to 3 feet wide and a tablecloth or sheet large enough to allow several inches of overhang on all sides when doubled. Drape the cloth over the table and rub a thin layer of all-purpose flour into the cloth (except for the overhanging portion). Unwrap the dough and feel it. If it is tacky, dust it all over with flour. Pick up the dough and stretch it a bit. This dough is very responsive and will do what you ask of it. Put the dough on the center of the cloth, pat it gently to flatten slightly, and brush the top with a little melted butter. Roll the dough into an oval shape about 18 inches long and 12 inches wide. Gently tug on the edges of the dough, one edge at a time, until the dough is about 24 by 18 inches. Don't turn the dough over; just check on it periodically to make sure it is not sticking to the cloth, and sprinkle additional flour under it if necessary.

REACH UNDER THE DOUGH, with the backs of your hands against the dough, and gently pull your hands apart slightly and toward you, stretching the dough as you do so. Work your way around the table, repeating the process. Stretch the dough further by grasping the outer part of a thick edge and gently tugging on it. When the dough has been stretched a few inches more on all sides, repeat the hand movements described above. In a few minutes more of stretching, the paper-thin dough will reach the edges of the table. Continue tugging on the thicker edges to make about 6 inches of overhanging dough on all sides. Cut off the thick edges with kitchen shears. If the dough tears at any point, just leave it alone. Any tears will be covered up when the strudel is rolled up.

BECAUSE THE DOUGH IS SO THIN, there's a danger of tearing it if you brush on the butter with a pastry brush. Instead, dip the brush into the butter and dab the butter all over the dough. Another way is to drizzle the butter onto the dough with a teaspoon: Dip the spoon into the butter and, holding it a few inches above the dough, wave the spoon from side to side to sprinkle drops of butter all over the dough. In either case, dab or drizzle the dough with about three-quarters of the remaining melted butter. Sprinkle about ½ cup bread crumbs evenly over the butter, just to make a very light dusting. Arrange the potato filling in an 18- to 20-inch-long horizontal column about 8 inches from the short side of the dough nearest you. Lift the end of the pastry-lined cloth nearest you and carefully flip it over to cover the potato completely with a layer of dough. Keep lifting the edge of cloth nearest you, and gravity will cause the strudel to roll over and over until it has formed a long log at the opposite end of the table. The strudel will be about 22 inches long, too long to fit onto your baking sheet, but there will be quite a bit of excess pastry at either end of the strudel. Pinch the ends of the pastry together near the filling, and cut them away with kitchen shears. Pinch the cut ends again to seal in the filling.

CAREFULLY LIFT THE STRUDEL (don't be afraid, it won't break) and place it on the baking sheet, curving it into a gentle C shape so that it will fit. Brush the strudel all over with the remaining butter and sprinkle lightly with more bread crumbs.

BAKE FOR 15 MINUTES. Reduce the temperature to 400°F and bake for about 20 minutes more, until the strudel is well browned and the pastry is crisp. Cool the strudel on its baking sheet, and serve warm or at room temperature. Cut into portions with a sharp serrated knife.

Storing

Strudel is at its best when very fresh. You can wrap leftovers in foil and refrigerate them for a day or two. To reheat, pull back the top of the foil but leave it against the cut ends. Pop into a preheated 400°F oven for about 15 minutes.

Cheese Sambouseks

MAKES 24 PASTRIES

MY IRAQI GRANDMOTHER OFTEN MADE SAMBOUSEKS, *half-moon-shaped pastries, which can be sweet or savory. The Iraqi version of empanaditas, they were often served with tea in the afternoon. Granny used a mixture of feta and ricotta cheeses, while my mother used sharp Cheddar. You can use just about any cheese you like, but be sure to include one strong-tasting cheese in the combination. Muenster and extra-sharp Cheddar are very good together. I've even made them with a mixture of Gouda and Petit Basque.*

Sambouseks are best when very fresh, but they also freeze well.

Dough for Granny's Kahk (page 114)

FILLING

12 ounces cheese, shredded (see headnote for suggestions)

Pinch of salt

Pinch of cayenne pepper

1 large egg

1 large egg white

1 large egg yolk, beaten with 1 teaspoon water for egg wash

DIVIDE THE KAHK DOUGH into 24 pieces and shape into balls. Let the dough rest, covered with a kitchen towel, for about 30 minutes.

MEANWHILE, make the filling. Place the cheese, salt, cayenne, egg, and egg white in the work bowl of a food processor fitted with the metal blade and pulse very rapidly 20 to 30 times, until the mixture just begins to gather into a mass. Turn out onto a sheet of waxed paper or plastic wrap and pat into a 6 × 4–inch rectangle. Cut the cheese mixture into 1-inch squares.

ADJUST TWO OVEN RACKS to divide the oven into thirds and preheat the oven to 350°F. Line two 14 × 17–inch baking sheets with silicone baking pan liners or cooking parchment.

TO SHAPE THE SAMBOUSEKS, pat a ball of dough into a 4-inch circle on your unfloured work surface. Place a square of the cheese mixture slightly below the center of the circle and pat it into a semicircular shape, leaving a bottom border of dough a scant ½ inch wide. Fold the top half of the dough over the cheese and press the edges firmly to seal. Use a fingertip to crimp the edge of the dough back on itself, forming a fluted border. Place the sambousek on the prepared sheet. Repeat with the remaining dough and cheese, placing 12 sambouseks about 2 inches apart on each sheet.

PAINT THE SAMBOUSEKS with the egg wash. Bake 30 minutes, or until golden brown. Rotate the pans top to bottom and front to back once during baking to ensure even browning. Use a wide metal spatula to transfer the sambouseks to wire cooling racks, and serve warm or at room temperature.

Storing

To freeze sambouseks, once they are cool, arrange them on a baking sheet and freeze until solid, then transfer them to heavy-duty resealable plastic bags and freeze for up to 1 month. Thaw the sambouseks in their bags, then arrange them on a baking sheet and refresh in a preheated 300°F oven for 10 minutes.

Chicken and Potato Sambouseks

MAKES ABOUT 30 PASTRIES

THESE ARE FLAKY CHICKEN-AND-POTATO-FILLED IRAQI PASTRIES *with decidedly Indian overtones. Many Sephardic Jewish Iraqis traveled to India when they left their native country. Some made their homes there permanently, while others used it as a way station to other parts of the world. It was only natural that they started to incorporate the local flavors into their Iraqi dishes, and these sambouseks are clear evidence of that.*

There's a story behind this recipe. Someone I had known in Shanghai, Ellis Jacob, sent me an e-mail after reading my childhood memoir, Shanghai Passage. *It had been more than fifty years since we'd seen each other, and he wanted to catch up. When I told him I was working on this book, he said, "You must include those chicken and potato sambouseks. My ex-wife, Jinni, can show you how to make them." Ellis doesn't cook, but Jinni had learned how to make several Iraqi recipes from his mother and aunt. I learned that Jinni now lived in Sedona, Arizona, and as it happened, my wife and I were planning a driving trip there as a break from winter's grip on Montana. I called Jinni, and she welcomed my wife and me to her home most warmly.*

Jinni likes to have these sambouseks on hand for special occasions, especially parties. These make excellent appetizers to serve with drinks, and they can also be served as a main course with a salad. You can make both the dough and filling ahead of time and then assemble and bake the pastries on the day you want to serve them.

DOUGH

2½ cups unbleached all-purpose flour

1 teaspoon salt

1 tablespoon baking powder (yes, 1 tablespoon)

1 large egg

1 large egg yolk

½ cup olive oil

½ teaspoon ground turmeric

4 to 5 tablespoons ice water

FILLING

2 tablespoons olive oil

1 medium onion, chopped medium-fine

¾ teaspoon salt, or to taste

¼ teaspoon freshly ground black pepper, or to taste

½ teaspoon dried sage

½ teaspoon dried oregano leaves

½ teaspoon ground cumin

¼ teaspoon dried thyme

¼ teaspoon ground turmeric

¼ teaspoon ground coriander

1 cup diced (¼-inch) peeled russet potato (one 10-ounce potato)

½ pound ground chicken breast meat

½ cup frozen peas

1 large egg, lightly beaten

¼ cup chopped flat-leaf parsley

TO MAKE THE DOUGH, in a large bowl stir together the flour, salt, and baking powder.

IN A SMALL BOWL, beat the egg and egg yolk with a fork to combine well. Add the olive oil and turmeric and beat for about 30 seconds, until the mixture is creamy. Add the liquid to the dry ingredients and stir with the fork until the oil and eggs are absorbed. The mixture will not hold together. Reach in with your hands and rub everything together between your palms until the dough is crumbly and the particles are the size of small peas. Add the water 1 tablespoon at a time, stirring in each addition well with the fork. As the dough gets wetter, it will form large clumps, but will not form into a ball. After the fourth tablespoon of water is thoroughly mixed in, press the clumps of dough together. If they form a cohesive mass, you've added enough water. If the dough wants to fall apart, stir in droplets of additional water until the dough holds together when pressed and is no longer sticky. Wrap the dough in plastic wrap and let it rest an hour or so in the refrigerator while you make the filling. (The dough can be made up to 2 days ahead and refrigerated. Bring to room temperature before using.)

TO MAKE THE FILLING, heat the olive oil in a large skillet over medium heat. When hot, add the onion and cook, stirring occasionally, for about 10 minutes, until lightly browned and tender. While the onion cooks, combine the salt, pepper, sage, oregano, cumin, thyme, turmeric, and coriander in a small cup.

ADD THE SPICE MIXTURE to the onions and stir and cook for 1 minute. Add the potatoes, stir well, and cook for 1 to 2 minutes. Add the chicken and cook, stirring frequently, until the chicken is cooked through and potatoes are tender, 8 to 10 minutes. Stir in the peas and remove the pan from the heat. Taste and adjust the seasoning with more salt or pepper if necessary. Let the filling cool for 10 minutes.

ADD THE BEATEN EGG and parsley to the filling and stir well. Cool completely before using. (The filling can be made a day ahead, covered when cool, and refrigerated. Bring to room temperature before using.)

ADJUST TWO OVEN RACKS to divide the oven into thirds and preheat the oven to 375°F. Line two large baking sheets (18 × 12 × 1 inch) with silicone baking pan liners or cooking parchment.

TO SHAPE THE SAMBOUSEKS, divide the dough into 4 portions. Roll one piece between two sheets of waxed paper until very thin, between 1/16 and 1/8 inch thick. Flip the sheets over from time to time, then peel off the top sheet of waxed paper, replace the paper, and continue rolling to the proper thickness. Remove the top sheet of waxed paper. Cut the dough into 3½-inch rounds with a sharp cookie cutter. Transfer the rounds of dough to a cutting board. Wrap the dough scraps in plastic wrap and reserve.

PLACE 1 level tablespoon of filling slightly below the center of each dough round. One at a time, brush the exposed dough lightly with cool water, fold the dough over the filling, and pinch the edges firmly to seal. Press the tines of a table fork gently on the seal for insurance. Place the sambouseks 1 inch apart on one of the prepared baking pans. Make more sambouseks with the remaining 3 portions of dough and filling. Each sheet should have 15 sambouseks. If you have leftover filling, gather all dough scraps together, reroll, and fill as before. (Do not prick the sambouseks with a fork.)

BAKE FOR 15 TO 20 MINUTES, until the sambouseks are golden brown. Rotate the sheets top to bottom and front to back halfway during baking to ensure even browning. Cool the sambouseks on their baking sheets.

Storing

Sambouseks are best when very fresh, but they freeze well. When they are completely cool, freeze on a baking sheet, then place the pastries in heavy-duty resealable plastic bags, and freeze for up to 1 month. Thaw the pastries in their bags, then arrange on a baking sheet and refresh in a preheated 300°F oven for 10 minutes.

Granny's Kahk (Savory Bracelets)

MAKES 24 RINGS

MY MOTHER AND HER MOTHER EMIGRATED TO SHANGHAI *from Iraq in 1930. My grandmother had been widowed many years earlier. Over the intervening years, her three older children had all found their way to Shanghai, and her only son, Jason, eventually sent for Granny and my mom once he was able to support them. At the time, thousands of Iraqi Jews resided in Shanghai, one of the most cosmopolitan cities in the world. The Iraqis did what they could to maintain their customs. Granny, the widow of a rabbi, went to synagogue twice a day.*

We all lived together in her one-room apartment during World War II. Granny was a fabulous cook and baker. Her kitchen only had room enough for one person, so my mother wasn't able to learn from her. What my mom and I remember best are the smells, tastes, and textures of Granny's food. The two pastries that stand out as the sine qua non *of her repertoire are kahk and cheese sambouseks (see page 111). When my family immigrated to San Francisco in 1950, we had to leave Granny behind in Shanghai. She eventually traveled with my uncle Jason and his family to Israel and then to Canada, but she died without us ever seeing her again.*

It then became my mom's job to try to re-create some of our most treasured memories of Granny's cooking. She experimented with doughs for kahks and fillings for sambouseks and finally succeeded in making what we both think taste very close to what Granny made. When we make kahk and sambouseks, we feel as if Granny's with us again.

These savory bracelets of dough remind me of breadsticks: dry, crunchy and addictive. Kahk are eaten any time of the day as a delicious nibble. In Shanghai, it's the first thing I'd reach for every day when I came rushing home from school. The dough may be plain or flavored with fennel, cumin, or caraway seeds. Granny often made some of each type, and she brushed the tops of the kahk with an egg wash and sprinkled them with sesame seeds. Making this dough is a breeze with the food processor, and it is very easy to work with.

DOUGH

2½ cups unbleached all-purpose flour (spooned into the cups and leveled)

¾ teaspoon salt

1½ teaspoons baking powder

1 teaspoon granulated sugar

9 tablespoons cold unsalted butter, cut into tablespoon-sized pieces

½ cup cool water

2 teaspoons fennel, cumin, or caraway seeds (optional)

1 large egg, beaten with a pinch of salt for egg wash

Sesame seeds for sprinkling

TO MAKE THE DOUGH, combine the flour, salt, baking powder, and sugar in a food processor fitted with the metal blade and process for 5 seconds. Add the butter and pulse 10 times, or until the mixture is the consistency of fine meal. With the machine running, add the water in a steady stream, taking about 10 seconds to do so. Process for 1 minute. The dough will gather into a ball and form a mass that whirls around the blade. Feel the dough. It should be smooth, soft, elastic, and no longer sticky. If necessary, adjust the texture with droplets of water or small amounts of flour, processing a few seconds after each addition. If you want to add seeds to the dough, knead them in by hand on your work surface.

DIVIDE THE DOUGH into 24 pieces and shape into balls (¾ ounce each). Cover the balls of dough loosely with a kitchen towel and let stand for 20 minutes.

ADJUST TWO OVEN RACKS to divide the oven into thirds and preheat the oven to 350°F. Line two 17 × 14-inch cookie sheets with silicone baking pan liners or cooking parchment.

ROLL EACH PIECE OF DOUGH beneath your palms into a log about 7 inches long and ½ inch wide, with tapered ends. Bring the ends together, overlapping them by about 1 inch, and pinch tightly to seal; each ring will be about 2 inches in diameter. Set the rings on the prepared sheets, spacing them about 2 inches apart. Paint each bracelet with the egg wash and sprinkle with sesame seeds.

BAKE FOR ABOUT 30 MINUTES, until the kahk are golden brown. Rotate the sheets top to bottom and front to back once during baking to ensure even browning. Cool the kahk completely on the baking sheets.

Storing

Kahk keep well stored in an airtight container at room temperature for 2 to 3 weeks. To freeze, pack them into heavy-duty resealable plastic bags and freeze for up to 1 month. Thaw them in their bags, then arrange on a baking sheet and refresh in a preheated 300°F oven for 10 minutes. Cool before eating.

Empadas

MAKES 24 TARTLETS

THESE SAVORY PORTUGUESE TARTLETS, *crunchy, buttery pastry shells enclosing a filling of tuna, onion, olives, and a bit of cayenne for some heat, are a specialty of Maria João, a fabulous Portuguese cook and baker I met on the island of Terceira in the Azores. Maria says the filling can be anything savory, but she loves to use canned tuna packed in olive oil, both for its taste and because it is a traditional recipe she's been making ever since she can remember.*

Empadas make excellent appetizers. To make bite-sized empadas, cut them into quarters. Or serve a few empadas for lunch or a light supper with a tossed green salad. The filling can be made a day or two ahead and refrigerated. The dough should be refrigerated for an hour or two or up to a day before using.

You will need 3-inch-diameter tartlet pans with sloping sides, measuring about 1¼ inches deep and 1½ inches across the bottom. Lacking them, use standard muffin cups.

FILLING

- 3 tablespoons extra-virgin olive oil
- 1 medium onion, chopped medium-fine
- ⅓ cup finely chopped flat-leaf parsley
- ¼ cup chopped pimento-stuffed olives
- One 7-ounce can tuna packed in olive oil, drained
- Pinch of cayenne pepper
- ½ cup canned tomato puree
- 1 Knorr chicken bouillon cube
- 2 tablespoons all-purpose flour
- 3 tablespoons whole milk
- Salt and freshly ground black pepper

DOUGH

- 3½ cups unbleached all-purpose flour, plus more for kneading
- ¼ cup granulated sugar
- 1 tablespoon baking powder
- ½ teaspoon baking soda
- 1 teaspoon salt
- 8 tablespoons (1 stick) cold unsalted butter, cut into tablespoon-sized pieces
- ½ cup cold vegetable shortening or home-rendered lard (page 332; or see Sources, pages 342 and 343), cut into 4 to 6 pieces
- 3 large eggs, beaten with 1 tablespoon water
- Olive oil, to coat molds
- About 2 tablespoons whole milk
- 24 Kalamata olives, pitted

TO MAKE THE FILLING, heat the olive oil in a medium saucepan over medium heat until hot. Add the onion, stir well, and cook, stirring occasionally, for 8 to 10 minutes, until it is tender and lightly browned. Add the parsley, olives, and tuna and cook, stirring occasionally, for 3 minutes. Stir in the cayenne and tomato puree, then crumble in the bouillon cube. Continue cooking, stirring occasionally, for a minute or two.

MEANWHILE, in a small bowl, whisk together the flour and milk to make a paste. Scrape the mixture onto the tuna and stir and cook until thickened, 1 to 2 minutes. The filling should hold a soft shape in the bowl of a spoon. Taste, and adjust the seasoning with salt and pepper if necessary. Remove the pan from the heat and cool completely. (The filling can be cooled, covered tightly, and refrigerated for 1 to 2 days; bring to room temperature before using.)

TO MAKE THE DOUGH, in a large bowl stir the flour, sugar, baking powder, baking soda, and salt together with a whisk. Add the butter and shortening or lard and cut them in with a pastry blender until the size of small peas. Gradually add the eggs and water, tossing with a fork. The dough will look clumpy. Reach into the bowl with your hands and squeeze and knead the dough gently until it gathers into a cohesive mass. If the dough seems too dry, work in droplets of additional water.

FLOUR YOUR WORK SURFACE and scrape the dough onto it. Turn the dough to coat with flour, then shape it into a log and start to smear portions of the dough away from you with the heel of your hand. (This ensures an even blending of fat and flour.) When all the dough has been smeared, gather it together and form it into a disk about 1 inch thick. Wrap tightly in plastic wrap and refrigerate for 1 to 2 hours, or overnight.

ADJUST AN OVEN RACK to the center position and preheat the oven to 350°F. Brush 24 tartlet molds or muffin cups lightly with olive oil.

TO SHAPE THE TARTLETS, divide the dough into 24 equal pieces about the size of golf balls. If using individual tartlet molds, place a ball of dough in each mold and press the dough with your thumbs to line the mold evenly and to extend ¼

inch above the rim. If using muffin cups, flatten the balls of dough on a lightly floured surface into 4-inch circles (don't be concerned with rough edges) and line the muffin cups with them. The dough should just reach the rims of the cups or extend slightly above. Try to make the pastry shells as even as possible and especially not too thick on their bottoms or in the corners.

PUT A LEVEL TABLESPOON of filling into each tartlet shell and, with your fingertips, carefully pull the edges of dough toward the center, covering the filling completely. Press gently to seal. The molds or muffin cups will be about half-full. Brush the tops of the empadas with milk and press an olive into the center of each one, leaving about half the olive showing. Arrange the tartlet pans, if using, on a large (18 × 12 ×1 inch) rimmed baking sheet.

BAKE FOR 30 TO 40 MINUTES, until the empadas are golden brown. Leave the empadas in their molds for about 5 minutes, then loosen them from their pans with the tip of a small sharp knife and remove them. Set the empadas on wire cooling racks to cool to room temperature.

Storing

The empadas can be assembled and frozen before baking. In that case, do not brush their tops with milk and do not insert the olives. Put the empadas on a baking sheet and freeze until solid, then wrap them airtight in several layers of plastic wrap and a layer of heavy-duty aluminum foil, and freeze for up to 2 weeks. To bake, preheat the oven, unwrap the frozen empadas, and brush them with the milk. Bake for 20 minutes. Quickly remove them from the oven, insert the olives into their centers as described above, and continue baking until they're golden brown, another 25 to 40 minutes. Cool as directed.

Samosas

MAKES 32 PASTRIES

THESE CRISP, FLAKY, CONE-SHAPED PASTRIES *are a ubiquitous snack in India. They are so good you can even make a meal of them. A dough made from atta flour (see Sources, page 343) or a combination of whole wheat and white flour is rolled thin and wrapped around a spicy filling of potatoes and other vegetables before being deep-fried. Bipin Patel, who was born in Uganda to parents from the Indian province of Gujarat, modified this classic Indian pastry by including African ingredients in its filling. Bipin says, "Indians would never put corn or cabbage into a samosa, but I do because I like the combination." Bipin opened Tipu's Tiger, an Indian vegetarian restaurant in Missoula, Montana, more than ten years ago, and the dishes he serves there reflect his African roots and Indian upbringing. See Sources (page 343) for Indian spices.*

Serve the samosas with the Cucumber Raita or your favorite chutney, or both.

FILLING

- 1 pound red-skinned potatoes (about 3 medium), peeled and cut into ½-inch dice
- ⅓ cup vegetable oil
- 2 teaspoons black mustard seeds
- 2 teaspoons cumin seeds
- 1 cup finely chopped white or yellow onion
- 2 tablespoons minced, peeled fresh ginger
- ½ to 1 tablespoon very finely chopped jalapeño chiles
- 2 teaspoons garam masala
- ½ teaspoon ground turmeric
- 1½ teaspoons salt, or to taste
- 1 cup chopped (medium-fine) green cabbage
- 1 cup frozen peas
- 1 cup frozen corn kernels
- 2 tablespoons fresh lemon juice, plus more if needed
- ½ cup chopped cilantro
- ½ cup finely chopped red onion

DOUGH

- 1½ cups atta flour or ¾ cup unbleached all-purpose flour plus ¾ cup whole wheat flour, plus more for rolling
- ¾ teaspoon salt
- 3 tablespoons vegetable oil
- ½ cup tepid water

Vegetable oil for deep-frying

Cucumber Raita (recipe follows; optional)

TO MAKE THE FILLING, drop the potatoes into a pot of lightly salted boiling water and cook, uncovered, until just tender, about 8 minutes. Drain and set aside.

HEAT THE OIL in a large (12-inch) skillet over medium heat. Add the mustard seeds and cook for a few seconds, until the seeds give off a popping sound. Add the cumin and cook for a few seconds, stirring, just until the seeds turn golden brown and crackle. Watch carefully to prevent burning. Immediately add the onion, stir well, and cook, stirring occasionally, until the onion is tender but not browned, 3 to 4 minutes. Add the ginger, jalapeño, garam masala, turmeric, and salt and stir well. Stir in the cabbage, cover the pan, and cook over medium-low heat, stirring occasionally, for 5 minutes. Add the potatoes, peas, corn, and lemon juice, stir well, and cook for 2 to 3 minutes, until the corn and peas are thawed and heated through. Remove the pan from the heat and add the cilantro and red onion. With the back of a spoon or a potato masher, break up the potatoes into smaller pieces, but do not mash them. Taste the filling and add more lemon juice and salt if needed. Set the filling aside, uncovered, until ready to use. (The filling can be made a day ahead. When cool, transfer to a container, cover, and refrigerate.)

TO MAKE THE DOUGH, combine the flour and salt in a large bowl. Add the oil and work it into the flour with your fingertips. Gradually add the water, stirring it into the flour with a fork. The dough should form moist-looking clumps. Press the clumps of dough together to form one cohesive mass. If the dough seems too dry, gradually work in small amounts of water until you have a firm dough that is pliable and not sticky. Wrap the dough tightly in plastic wrap and let it rest at room temperature for at least 1 hour. (The dough can be made a day ahead and refrigerated. Bring to room temperature before using.)

TO SHAPE THE SAMOSAS, divide the dough in half. Roll each half into an 8-inch-long log. If the dough is sticky, lightly flour it with all-purpose flour. Cut each log into 1-inch pieces, and shape each piece into a ball. Set the balls of dough on your work surface and cover them loosely with plastic wrap. Let the dough rest for about 10 minutes.

SET A SMALL CUP OF WATER and another of all-purpose or atta flour near your rolling surface. Lightly flour a ball of dough and pat it with your fingertips into a 2- to 3-inch circle. Roll it into a 6-inch circle, flouring the dough as necessary if it is sticky. Cut the circle in half. Shape each semicircle into a cone. Dampen half of the semicircle's straight edge with a finger dipped in water, and bring the other half of the straight edge over it to overlap, by about ¼ inch. Press firmly to seal. Hold the dough cone with one hand (it will be soft and floppy), and spoon a generous tablespoon of filling into it, packing it in gently. Do not overfill the cone—there should be about ⅓ inch of exposed dough above the filling. Moisten the edges of the dough and pinch the top of the cone firmly to seal, making a samosa that is triangular in shape, resembling a clamshell. It is important that the seams be completely sealed, or the samosas may break open during frying. Dust your work surface lightly with flour and set the samosa down on it. Shape the remaining samosas the same way. (If you have leftover filling, it makes a delicious snack with plain yogurt.) Let the samosas dry on your countertop for about 1 hour, turning them over once or twice. Check the seams when you turn the samosas to make sure they are well sealed.

TO COOK THE SAMOSAS, pour about 3 inches of vegetable oil into a 4- to 5-quart, deep, heavy pot. Clamp a deep-fat thermometer to the side of the pot, or use a digital probe thermometer. Heat the oil over medium heat to 350°F. Line a large baking sheet with several thicknesses of paper towels.

WHEN THE OIL IS HOT, carefully slip in 5 or 6 samosas. The samosas will sink to the bottom of the pot but will rise to the surface in a few seconds. Turn the samosas about with a slotted spoon occasionally, and cook them for about 5 minutes, until they develop bubbles all over their surface and are a deep golden brown color. Remove from the oil, draining the samosas in the slotted spoon, and set them on the paper towels to drain further. Let them cool for 5 to 10 minutes before serving. Repeat with the remaining samosas, making sure to return the oil to 350°F between batches. Serve warm, with the raita, if desired.

Storing

Cooled leftover samosas can be wrapped in plastic wrap and refrigerated for 1 or 2 days. To reheat, arrange them on a baking sheet and pop them into a preheated 350°F oven for 8 to 10 minutes. Samosas can also be frozen before or after cooking. Freeze in a single layer on a baking sheet lined with plastic wrap until solid, then transfer to heavy-duty resealable plastic bags and freeze for up to 1 month. Thaw cooked frozen samosas in their bags, then arrange them on a baking sheet and reheat them in a preheated 350°F oven for 8 to 10 minutes. Remove frozen uncooked samosas from their bags while still frozen and set them in a single layer on a lightly floured baking sheet. When completely thawed, cook them according to the instructions above.

Cucumber Raita

MAKES ABOUT 1½ CUPS

1 large seedless cucumber

Salt

1 cup full-fat or low-fat plain yogurt

½ teaspoon ground cumin

2 tablespoons chopped mint or cilantro

Freshly ground black pepper

Peel and shred the cucumber. Toss it with 1 teaspoon salt in a medium bowl, and let stand for 30 minutes to 1 hour. Transfer the cucumber to a strainer and squeeze firmly to extract excess liquid. Return the cucumber to the bowl (wiped dry) and stir in the yogurt, cumin, and mint or cilantro. Taste and adjust the seasoning with salt and pepper. Serve, or cover tightly with plastic wrap and refrigerate for 1 to 2 hours.

Shrimp Rissois

MAKES ABOUT 48 TURNOVERS

SHRIMP RISSOIS (*pronounced "ree-SOY-ish"*) *are savory deep-fried turnovers shaped into half-moons. The dough is essentially an eggless cream puff dough made with water, milk, butter, flour, and salt, cooked in a saucepan on top of the stove. The contrast of the soft dough with the shrimp filling and crispy bread crumb coating has justifiably made this one of Portugal's favorite appetizers. Maria João, who made these for me on the island of Terceira in the Azores, says the filling can be just about anything. One of her favorites is her tuna filling for Empadas (page 116), another is this shrimp version.*

Serve the rissois hot, warm, or at room temperature, with drinks.

FILLING

- 12 ounces medium shrimp in the shell
- 4 cups boiling water
- 2 tablespoons olive oil
- ½ cup finely chopped onion
- 2 tablespoons unbleached all-purpose flour
- 1 cup whole milk, heated until very hot
- Pinch of cayenne pepper
- ½ teaspoon salt, or to taste
- ½ teaspoon freshly ground black pepper, or to taste
- Droplets of fresh lemon juice
- 2 tablespoons finely chopped flat-leaf parsley

DOUGH

- 4 tablespoons (½ stick) unsalted butter
- 1½ cups water
- ½ cup whole milk
- ½ teaspoon salt
- 2 cups unbleached all-purpose flour, plus more for rolling

COATING

- 2 large eggs
- 1 large egg white
- 2 cups fine dry bread crumbs

- Vegetable oil for deep-frying

FOR THE FILLING, put the shrimp in a medium bowl and add the boiling water, cover, and leave the shrimp for 10 minutes. Take a shrimp out of the water, peel it, and cut into it to make sure it is cooked through—it should look opaque throughout. If it is not quite cooked, leave the shrimp in the hot water for another minute or two. Drain the shrimp, cool them slightly, and peel them. Coarsely chop the shrimp.

HEAT THE OLIVE OIL in a medium heavy saucepan over medium heat. When it is hot, add the onion and cook,

stirring occasionally with a wooden spoon, until tender and golden brown, 6 to 8 minutes. Add the flour and cook, stirring, for 2 minutes. The onion will gather into several masses. Scrape the onion off the spoon, take the pan off the heat momentarily, and pour in all the hot milk at once. Stir vigorously with a wire whisk, then return the pan to the heat and cook, whisking, until the sauce comes to a boil and thickens to the consistency of heavy cream. Cook for 1 to 2 minutes more, whisking constantly. Remove the pan from the heat and whisk in the cayenne, salt, and pepper. Taste, and adjust the seasoning if necessary. Stir in a little lemon juice, and taste again. Stir in the shrimp and parsley. Cool, then cover tightly and refrigerate until chilled. (The filling can be made up to 1 day ahead.)

TO MAKE THE DOUGH, melt the butter in a medium heavy saucepan over medium heat. Add the water, milk, and salt and bring to a full rolling boil over medium-high heat. Remove the pan from the heat and immediately dump in the flour. Stir well with a wooden spatula or spoon to form a dough. Set the pan over medium heat and beat and stir the dough vigorously for about 2 minutes to evaporate excess moisture. The dough should film the bottom of the pan. Scrape the dough out onto your work surface, cover it loosely with a kitchen towel, and let it cool for about 20 minutes.

TO MAKE THE RISSOIS, knead the dough gently for 1 to 2 minutes to make sure it is perfectly smooth. Divide the dough in half and work with half the dough at a time; keep the rest covered with the towel. Lightly flour your work surface, coat the dough lightly on both sides with flour, and roll it to a thickness of ⅛ inch. Turn the dough over occasionally to make sure it isn't sticking. Stamp out circles of dough with a 3-inch round cutter. Place about 1 teaspoon of filling in the center of a circle. Pick up the dough, lift the edges of the dough to cover the filling, and pinch the edges firmly to seal; since the dough is moist, it should seal easily. Set the rissois on a baking sheet lined with plastic wrap. Fill the remaining circles of dough. Gather the dough scraps and place them under the kitchen towel. Roll, cut, and fill the second portion of dough, then reroll, cut, and fill the scraps.

TO COAT THE RISSOIS, beat the eggs and egg white in a shallow dish or pie plate with a fork until thoroughly combined. Put the bread crumbs into another shallow dish or pie plate. Place 4 rissois at a time in the eggs and turn them over carefully with two forks to coat them. One by one, lift the rissois out of the eggs and set them onto the crumbs. Turn to coat the rissois with a thin layer of crumbs, and set them onto one or two large baking sheets.

TO COOK THE RISSOIS, pour about 2 inches of oil into a large heavy wide pan about 3 inches deep, such as a 5- to 6-quart sauté pan or a large pot. Bring the oil to 350° to 360°F over medium heat; monitor the temperature with a deep-fry or digital probe thermometer. Line two large baking sheets with several thicknesses of paper towels.

ADD 10 TO 12 RISSOIS to the hot oil and cook them, turning them over halfway during cooking, for a total of about 3 minutes, until they turn a deep golden brown. Remove the rissois from the fat with a slotted spoon or skimmer and drain them on the paper towels. Cook the remaining rissois the same way, making sure to return the oil to 350° to 360°F between batches. Let the rissois cool for at least 10 minutes before serving. The filling will be very hot.

Storing

Cooked rissois can be frozen for up to 2 weeks. When cool, arrange in a single layer on a large baking sheet or cookie sheet and freeze until solid. Transfer to heavy-duty resealable plastic bags and freeze. To serve, arrange the frozen pastries on a baking sheet and pop into a preheated 350°F oven for 15 to 20 minutes, until hot and crisp.

Cheese and Potato Pierogi

MAKES 60 TO 72 DUMPLINGS; 5 TO 6 SERVINGS

PIEROGI ARE PERHAPS THE BEST KNOWN *Polish dish in America. They are half-moon-shaped dumplings of tender pasta dough enclosing a variety of fillings. After boiling, the pierogi can be served in any number of ways. Krystyna Kawalec, a recent Polish immigrant, has been making pierogi for almost forty years. She's experimented with many dough and filling formulas, and these cheese and potato pierogi are one of her favorites. Krystyna makes almost everything by hand, and she always makes enormous quantities. With pierogi, you need to make a lot because people seem to have an infinite capacity for them. For a pleasant task, enlist the aid of one or two helpers. If you want, double the quantities and freeze the leftovers for another day.*

To serve, give the cooked pierogi a quick sauté in melted butter until lightly browned and crisp. Or ladle hot chicken broth over them or top them with crumbled crisp bacon and a drizzle of bacon fat.

FILLING

- 2 tablespoons olive oil
- 2 medium yellow onions, chopped medium-fine
- 2 pounds russet potatoes
- 12 ounces farmer's cheese or dry-curd cottage cheese (if using cottage cheese, force it through a sieve)
- 2 teaspoons salt
- 1 teaspoon freshly ground black pepper

DOUGH

- 4 cups unbleached all-purpose flour, plus more for rolling
- 1⅓ cups warm water
- 1 large egg yolk
- 3 tablespoons olive oil

TO MAKE THE FILLING, heat the olive oil in a large skillet over medium heat. Add the onions and cook, stirring occasionally, until they are golden brown, tender, and beginning to caramelize, 10 to 15 minutes. Remove from the heat.

MEANWHILE, peel the potatoes and cut them into 2-inch chunks. Add them to a large pot of salted boiling water and cook, uncovered, until very tender, about 20 minutes.

DRAIN THE POTATOES WELL and put them through a ricer into a large bowl. The potatoes must be very smooth. Add the cheese, salt, pepper, and cooked onions and mix well. (The filling can be made a day ahead; cover tightly with plastic wrap and refrigerate.)

TO MAKE THE DOUGH, put the flour in a large bowl and make a well in the center. In a medium bowl, stir the warm water, egg yolk, and olive oil with a fork just to combine. Add the liquid to the flour well and stir with the fork, gradually incorporating the flour from the sides, to make a soft but firm dough. If necessary, adjust the consistency of the dough by gradually adding small amounts of warm water.

TURN THE DOUGH onto your work surface and knead a few minutes, until it is smooth and elastic. It should feel firm, but not as firm as pasta, and not be at all sticky. Cover the dough loosely with a kitchen towel or an inverted bowl and let it rest for about 30 minutes.

TO SHAPE THE PIEROGI, cut the dough in half and keep the unused portion covered with the towel. Roll the dough on a lightly floured surface until it is about ⅛ inch thick. Stamp out circles with a 2½- to 3-inch round cutter. Put a heaping teaspoonful of filling onto the center of a circle, and bring up the edges of the dough to cover the filling completely. Pinch firmly to seal, making a half-moon shape, then crimp the edge of the dough in 4 or 5 places to give the pierogi a pleated look. Set the pierogi on a lightly floured baking sheet. Repeat with the remaining dough and filling.

TO COOK THE PIEROGI, bring a large pot of salted water to a boil. Add 8 to 10 pierogi. They'll settle to the bottom—carefully dislodge them with a heatproof rubber spatula.

When the pierogi float to the surface, cook them for 3 minutes. Remove them with a skimmer or slotted spoon and set them on a lightly oiled baking sheet. Cook the remaining pierogi. (The pierogi can be cooked an hour before serving. When cooled, cover loosely with plastic wrap. Serve as described in the headnote.)

Storing

Once cool, pierogi can be stored in resealable plastic bags in the refrigerator for 2 to 3 days. Reheat them in boiling water and follow one of the serving suggestions above. To freeze, arrange the cooled pierogi in a single layer on plastic-lined baking sheets and freeze until solid, then transfer to heavy-duty resealable plastic bags and freeze for up to 1 month. To serve, add the frozen pierogi to boiling water and cook for a few minutes to thaw and reheat them; drain.

Traditional Cornish Pasties

england

MAKES 4 LARGE TURNOVERS

THESE LARGE BEEF AND POTATO TURNOVERS, *pronounced "PASS-tees," were a traditional food of miners in many of our northern states. But Montana claims the pasty as its own, because it was a mainstay for the thousands of Cornish miners who lived and worked in Butte during the last decades of the nineteenth century and the first part of the twentieth century. Cornish housewives brought the tradition of making this quintessential miners' dish— a letter from 'ome, as it was affectionately called—with them from Cornwall, England. The women who made pasties were known as Cousin Jennies, and the hard-working miners were called Cousin Jacks.*

A rich lard pastry was wrapped around a generous amount of potatoes and a few slices of meat, with some seasoning, and baked. Pasties were made large enough to fit in the bottom of the miner's lunch pail. Although the traditional Cornish way is to use sliced meat in the pasty, in Butte, Montana, where the pasty became as popular as pizza, diced meat was sometimes substituted. But Carol Williams, who grew up in Montana and learned how to make pasties from her Cornish grandmother, says, "The meat is always sliced, never diced, and everything that goes into a pasty must be raw. Baking takes care of all the cooking." Carol makes pasties often, and she showed me how to make two traditional versions, one with beef, onion, and potatoes, another with ham and egg, as well as a vegetarian pasty made with Stilton cheese that she tried on a recent visit to Cornwall.

DOUGH

3 cups unbleached all-purpose flour

1½ teaspoons salt

1 cup cold home-rendered lard (page 332 or see Sources, pages 342 and 343)

About ⅔ cup ice water

FILLING

One 1¼-pound top round or sirloin steak

Meat tenderizer

1 large yellow onion (about 12 ounces)

3 large russet potatoes (about 2 pounds total)

Salt and freshly ground black pepper

8 tablespoons (1 stick) cold unsalted butter

2 large egg yolks, beaten with 1 teaspoon cold water for egg wash

GRAVY (OPTIONAL)

3 cups beef stock or canned unsalted beef broth

3 tablespoons unsalted butter

3 tablespoons unbleached all-purpose flour

Salt and freshly ground black pepper

Finely chopped flat-leaf parsley (optional)

Pasties may be eaten warm or at room temperature. Make them fresh and eat them that way. The pastry and filling lose some of their integrity when refrigerated or frozen.

Miners couldn't eat their pasties with gravy, but when you order a pasty in a restaurant, it almost always comes with gravy ladled over it. I've included a gravy recipe in case you want to try your pasties that way. I highly recommend it.

TO MAKE THE DOUGH, stir together the flour and salt in a large bowl. Cut the chilled lard into small chunks and add to the flour. Using a pastry blender or two knives, cut the lard into the flour until the fat is in pea-sized pieces. Gradually add the ice water while tossing the dry ingredients with a fork. Add only enough water so the dough gathers into a cohesive, slightly moist mass. Press the dough together with the palms of your hands. It should stay in one piece. If it is too dry, sprinkle on droplets of ice water and work them in with the fork just until the dough holds together.

DIVIDE THE DOUGH into 4 equal pieces and shape each into a 1-inch-thick disk. Enclose each disk securely in plastic wrap and refrigerate for 1 hour, or longer.

WHILE THE DOUGH CHILLS, trim any sinews and visible fat off the meat and cut the steak lengthwise into 12 strips about ¼ inch thick. Sprinkle the meat lightly with meat tenderizer. Put it onto a plate and refrigerate for about 1 hour, uncovered.

CUT THE ONION into ½-inch dice. You should have about 2 cups. Put the onion into a small bowl and cover tightly with plastic wrap. Peel the potatoes, quarter them lengthwise, and slice them crosswise into thin (about ⅛-inch-thick) slices. Put the potatoes into a bowl and leave them uncovered. Don't be concerned if they turn brown.

ADJUST AN OVEN RACK to the lower third position and preheat the oven to 400°F. Line an 18 × 12 × 1–inch baking sheet with a silicone baking pan liner or cooking parchment, or coat with cooking spray.

ON A LIGHTLY FLOURED SURFACE, roll one of the chilled dough pieces into a rough oval about 12 inches long and 10 inches wide. The pastry will be about ⅛ inch thick. Don't be concerned about shaggy edges. Starting about ½ inch to one side of the center of the oval, arrange a thick layer of potatoes (½ inch or so) lengthwise over half the oval, leaving about 1½ inches of pastry exposed on the curved edge. The potato layer should be in a half-moon shape with the flat side of the "moon" near the center of the pastry. Sprinkle generously with salt and pepper. Scatter about ¼ cup of the onion over the potatoes and sprinkle with more salt and pepper. Repeat with another layer of potatoes and onion, sprinkling each with salt and pepper. Arrange 3 strips of meat lengthwise on top and salt and pepper the meat. Put 2 tablespoons of the butter, cut into 3 or 4 chunks, over the meat. The pile of meat, onion, and potatoes will be about 3 inches high. Moisten the edge of dough around the filling with a pastry brush dipped in water. Carefully lift the uncovered half of the pastry over the filling and gently pat the edges together, then press firmly to seal. Trim away any rough edges of dough with a sharp knife, leaving about a ½-inch border of pastry. Beginning at one end of the pasty, fold the pastry border back on itself, crimping it at intervals to make a scalloped pattern. Carefully lift the pasty with your hands or a pastry scraper and place at one end of the prepared baking sheet. Shape the remaining pasties in the same way and set them on the baking sheet, leaving 1 to 2 inches between them. Brush the pasties with the egg wash, and make 3 small slits in the top of each with the tip of a sharp paring knife.

BAKE THE PASTIES for 10 minutes. Reduce the temperature to 325°F and bake for 1 hour longer, or until well browned. Let the pasties cool on the baking sheet for 10 to 15 minutes, then transfer them to wire cooling racks with a large metal spatula. Serve hot, warm, or at room temperature, plain or with the gravy.

TO MAKE THE OPTIONAL GRAVY, put the beef stock or broth into a small heavy saucepan and bring to a simmer over medium heat. Meanwhile, in a heavy medium saucepan, melt the butter over medium heat. When bubbly, add the flour and cook, stirring, for 2 minutes. Remove the pan from the heat and pour in the hot liquid all at once. Stir well with a wire whisk until smooth. Return the pan to medium heat and continue cooking and stirring until the gravy is smooth and slightly thickened. Season with salt and pepper. Pour into a gravy boat and pass at the table. Sprinkle the pasties with parsley, if desired.

Variations

HAM AND EGG PASTIES Omit the steak and butter in the filling; you'll also need 2 cups diced (½-inch) thick-sliced ham and 4 eggs. In a large bowl, combine the ham, potatoes, onion, and salt and pepper to taste. For each pasty, use one-quarter of the ham mixture. Pile the filling onto each pastry oval as directed, and make a depression in the center of the mixture large enough to contain an egg. One at a time, crack an egg into a small cup and slide the egg into each depression. Don't be concerned if the egg yolks break—just continue on with the recipe and bake as directed.

STILTON, CORN, AND RED PEPPER PASTIES Omit the steak in the filling and reduce the butter to 6 tablespoons. You'll also need 1 cup fresh corn kernels, 1 cup diced (¼-inch) red bell pepper, and 6 to 8 ounces Stilton cheese. In a large bowl, combine the potatoes, onion, corn, red bell pepper, butter, and salt and pepper to taste. For each pasty, use one-quarter of this mixture. Pile the filling onto each pastry oval as directed. Cut the Stilton into thin slices and arrange on top of the vegetable mixture. Proceed as described above.

Thai Shrimp and Bean Sprout Fritters *thailand*

MAKES 12 LARGE FRITTERS

THESE DELECTABLE FRITTERS COME FROM PRANEE HALVORSEN, *a charming, energetic teacher of Thai cooking. Packed with shrimp and bean sprouts, they have an especially crisp exterior. Pranee says one of the secrets to crispy coatings on fish and vegetables is rice flour. The other is using limestone water for the liquid. Pranee buys small jars of a pasty pink limestone in Southeast Asian markets (see Sources, page 342, and Note, page 77). The day before cooking the fritters, she soaks a tablespoon or so of the limestone in a screw-cap 1-quart jar with about 3 cups of water. She shakes the jar vigorously, turning the liquid pink. After settling, the water is clear and has tiny bubbles. The carbonation, Pranee says, contributes to the crispiness. I've used both limestone water and sparkling mineral water (Pellegrino) and find the results to be indistinguishable. But using the limestone is fun and authentic, and if you're willing to seek it out, you'll get a kick out of working with it.*

These fritters make great appetizers. You can make the batter 30 minutes before adding the remaining ingredients, and the fritters cook in just a few minutes. For best results, serve them right away, with the Thai Chili Sauce. You can also cook the fritters ahead and freeze them, then reheat in a hot oven. Having a dozen or so fritters in the freezer is a definite asset, so you may want to double or triple the recipe.

See the companion DVD for a video demonstration of fritter making.

BATTER

- 1 cup rice flour (spooned into the cup and leveled)
- 6 tablespoons cake flour (dip and sweep)
- ½ teaspoon salt
- ¾ cup limestone water (see headnote) or sparkling mineral water, plus more if needed

FILLING

- 4 ounces bean sprouts
- 8 ounces shrimp, peeled, deveined, and cut into ½-inch pieces
- 3 scallions, trimmed and thinly sliced, or ½ cup thinly sliced garlic chives
- 2 garlic cloves, minced

  Peanut or corn oil for shallow-frying

  Thai Chili Sauce (recipe follows)

TO MAKE THE BATTER, put the rice flour, cake flour, and salt into a medium bowl. Stir with a whisk to combine well. Add the limestone water or sparkling water and whisk to make a smooth batter the consistency of heavy cream. The batter shouldn't be too thick. If necessary, gradually whisk in a little more water. Let stand for 30 minutes, uncovered.

TO MAKE THE FRITTERS, add the bean sprouts, shrimp, scallions or chives, and garlic to the batter and stir to coat thoroughly with the batter. Line a baking sheet with several thicknesses of paper towels.

POUR about ½ inch of oil into a 12-inch skillet and heat over medium-high heat. When the oil is very hot and on the verge of smoking, quickly spoon 6 heaping tablespoonfuls of the fritter batter into the oil, using half the fritter mixture and leaving a bit of space between the fritters. Cook for about 1 minute, until the bottoms of the fritters are golden brown and crisp. Turn the fritters over with a metal spatula and cook the second side the same way. Transfer the fritters to the paper towels to drain, and cook the remaining fritters. Serve as soon as possible, with the chili sauce.

Storing

You can cook the fritters ahead and freeze them. Put the cooled fritters on a tray lined with waxed paper or plastic wrap and freeze until solid. Transfer to heavy-duty resealable plastic bags and freeze for up to 2 weeks. To serve, arrange the frozen fritters on a baking sheet and reheat them in a preheated 450°F oven until sizzling hot, 5 to 8 minutes. Serve as soon as possible.

Thai Chili Sauce

MAKES 1 GENEROUS CUP

PRANEE IMMIGRATED TO THE UNITED STATES *in 1991 from Phuket Island. One thing that her mother always had on hand was some sort of chili sauce. At home, Pranee says, they put chili sauce on practically everything. So one of the first challenges to her here was duplicating as best she could the chili sauce she loved the most. After much testing, this is the recipe she makes, and she always keeps a supply of it. It's easy, it can be made as hot as you like, and it keeps for months in the refrigerator.*

5 dried New Mexico or guajillo chiles

6 large garlic cloves

¼ teaspoon salt

¼ to ⅓ cup tamarind concentrate (see Sources, page 347)

¼ cup seasoned rice vinegar (Pranee uses Marukan Seasoned Gourmet), plus more if needed

3 tablespoons firmly packed light or dark brown sugar, plus more if needed

Remove and discard the stems from the chiles. Cut the pods into 1-inch pieces with scissors and place them, seeds and all, into a medium heatproof bowl. Add boiling water to cover and let the chiles steep until they are very soft, about 1 hour.

Put the garlic, salt, tamarind, rice vinegar, and brown sugar into the work bowl of a food processor fitted with the metal blade. Remove the softened chiles from the water with a slotted spoon, allowing the excess water to drain back into the bowl, and add the chiles to the food processor. Some seeds will come along with the chiles; if you like your sauce really hot, strain the water and add some or all of the remaining seeds to the food processor. Process until smooth. The sauce can be served as is, but cooking it briefly will make it even hotter. Scrape it into a medium saucepan and cook, stirring frequently, over medium heat, for about 5 minutes.

Taste the sauce and adjust the seasoning with more brown sugar or rice vinegar if necessary. If the sauce seems too thick, thin it with a little water. Let the sauce cool, then transfer it to an airtight container. Store in the refrigerator for up to 2 months.

Flaky Turkish Feta Turnovers (Puaça) turkey

THESE ARE SAVORY TURNOVERS WITH A TANGY FETA CHEESE FILLING *enclosed in a tender, flaky dough that gets its special texture and taste from a combination of butter, yogurt, and olive oil. Arzu Yilmaz, who taught me the recipe, learned how to make puaça from her grandmother in Turkey. These pastries make great party food. Because the turnovers are on the salty side, they are good with drinks. The shaping takes a bit of time, so a second pair of hands will be welcome.*

DOUGH

3½ cups unbleached all-purpose flour, plus more for kneading

1 teaspoon salt

1 teaspoon baking powder

½ cup olive oil

8 tablespoons (1 stick) unsalted butter, melted

½ cup plain yogurt

1 large egg

FILLING

10 ounces feta cheese

½ cup finely chopped dill

2 large eggs

2 large egg yolks, beaten with 1 teaspoon water for egg wash

TO MAKE THE DOUGH, in a large bowl whisk together the flour, salt, and baking powder.

IN A MEDIUM BOWL, whisk together the olive oil, melted butter, yogurt, and egg. Add the liquid to the dry ingredients and stir well with a wooden spoon until the dough gathers into a mass. Scrape the spoon clean and add any bits of dough to the dough in the bowl.

SCRAPE THE DOUGH onto an unfloured work surface and knead briefly until it forms a cohesive mass. The dough may not look completely smooth and it may want to break apart; do not be concerned. Slip the dough into a large resealable plastic bag, seal the bag, and let the dough rest at room temperature for 1 to 2 hours. During this time the dough will become supple and feel soft, and it will be easy to work with. (The dough can be made a day ahead and refrigerated overnight. Bring it to room temperature before using.)

TO MAKE THE FILLING, crumble the feta into a medium bowl. Add the dill and eggs and stir to combine well.

ADJUST TWO OVEN RACKS to divide the oven into thirds and preheat the oven to 350°F. Line two large baking sheets (18 × 12 × 1 inch) with silicone baking pan liners, cooking parchment, or aluminum foil.

TO SHAPE THE TURNOVERS, divide the dough into 30 equal pieces (each piece of dough will weigh about 1 ounce). Roll each piece between your palms into a ball and set the balls on an unfloured work surface. Cover loosely with plastic wrap. Flatten one ball of dough with your fingertips to make a circle about 3½ inches in diameter. Don't be concerned with any rough edges. If the dough sticks, use a bench scraper to release the dough from the work surface, and pat the dough back into the proper size if necessary. Place a generous teaspoonful of filling just below the center of the dough

ABOVE: *Limpa (page 174)*

LEFT: *Schwabisch Pretzels (page 188)*

ABOVE LEFT: *The Original Shoofly Pie (page 320)*

ABOVE: *Princess Torte (page 289)*

LEFT: *Kransekaker (page 298)*

ABOVE: *Turkish Semolina Sponge Cake*
(page 318)

RIGHT: *Gâteau Basque (page 284)*

ABOVE: *Lamingtons (page 306)*

RIGHT: *Hungarian Walnut Torte (page 279)*

circle. Fold the top half of the dough over the filling to form a half-moon shape, and press the edges of the dough together firmly to seal. The sealed edges will be thinner than the rest of the dough; fold the outer edge of the dough over on itself to even out the thickness. Place the turnover onto one of the prepared pans. Repeat with the remaining dough and filling, placing 15 turnovers on each sheet, 1 to 2 inches apart. Paint the turnovers with the egg wash.

BAKE FOR ABOUT 30 MINUTES, until the turnovers are a deep golden brown color. Rotate the sheets top to bottom and front to back halfway during baking to ensure even browning. With a wide metal spatula, transfer the pastries to wire cooling racks. Serve warm or at room temperature.

Storing

These are best when very fresh, but they can be frozen when completely cool. Place in heavy-duty resealable plastic bags and freeze for up to 2 weeks. To serve, thaw the pastries in their bags until completely thawed, then arrange on one or more baking sheets and reheat in a preheated 300°F oven for 10 minutes.

4 Sweet Pastries

*a*LL THE PASTRIES IN THIS CHAPTER, which come from ten different countries, call for much the same basic dough ingredients, yet the results range from flaky to crunchy, tender to chewy. It's the proportions of flour, butter, and some binding liquid (egg, water, or milk) and the techniques that vary, creating completely different results. For example, the apple strudel dough is kneaded vigorously and allowed to rest for an hour or two to enable it to be stretched so thin you can read a newspaper through it, but most of the other doughs are worked just enough to hold together, so they remain tender. Puff pastry starts off as a plain dough made from flour, water, and salt, but it achieves its flakiness and crispness through rolling and folding the butter between multiple dough layers rather than incorporating it into the dough.

The preferred fat in most of these doughs is butter, but the addition of other fats such as cream cheese (in rugelach) or sour cream (in szarlotka) can give another dimension of tenderness to a dough. Baking powder serves to lighten some of the doughs. The Welsh griddle cakes, for example, wouldn't have their melt-in-your-mouth texture without it.

Almost half the recipes contain fruit, from apples (szarlotka), dates (date babas), and plums (german plum cake) to fruit jams (kolacky), illustrating what a great partnership fruit and dough can be. About half the recipes are for individual pastries. Many of the bakers I worked with like to make individual things because it keeps them connected to the food in a repetitive way, and they have a chance to experiment and try some modifications. Baking this collection of recipes is like taking a pastry course at a culinary school. After making all of them, you'll be equipped to handle just about any pastry recipe that comes your way.

Date Babas

MAKES 30 PASTRIES

THESE ARE THE CLASSIC IRAQI DATE-FILLED LITTLE CAKES *that my Granny made all the time. A crunchy and tender butter pastry subtly flavored with rose water encloses a generous filling of pureed dates. These babas were so much a part of my childhood I can't remember a time when we didn't have them. Granny cooked the dates with butter to soften them and mash them. I use the food processor to make the pastry in about 1 minute, and to puree the dates in about 2 minutes, with no cooking necessary.*

The dough and filling can both be prepared a day ahead and refrigerated. Making the babas takes a bit of time because each is shaped individually, but put on some music and the time will pass quickly.

DOUGH

- 2¼ cups unbleached all-purpose flour, plus more for shaping
- 1 tablespoon granulated sugar
- ½ teaspoon salt
- 1 teaspoon baking powder
- 12 tablespoons (1½ sticks) cold unsalted butter, cut into tablespoon-sized pieces
- ½ cup cold water
- 1 tablespoon rose water

FILLING

- 1 pound pitted dates (check carefully—these sometimes contain a pit or two)
- 2 tablespoons unsalted butter, at room temperature
- 1 large egg, lightly beaten with 1 teaspoon water for egg wash
- Sesame seeds for sprinkling

TO MAKE THE DOUGH, put the flour, sugar, salt, and baking powder into the work bowl of a food processor fitted with the metal blade and process for 5 seconds. Add the butter and pulse 5 or 6 times to begin cutting the butter into the flour. Combine the water and rose water. As you pulse the machine rapidly, add the liquid to the dry ingredients in a steady stream, then pulse about 30 times until you have several large clumps of dough. Remove the dough and knead the pieces together briefly. Wrap the dough in plastic wrap and refrigerate for 1 hour or up to overnight.

TO MAKE THE FILLING, wipe out the work bowl of the food processor and clean the blade. Insert the blade, add the dates, and pulse several times, until the dates are finely chopped. Add the butter and process to a paste. Stop as necessary to scrape the work bowl and redistribute the dates. There may be some small date pieces remaining—this is fine. Scrape the paste onto a sheet of plastic wrap. Divide the paste into 30 portions and roll each between your palms into a ball.

ADJUST AN OVEN RACK to the center position and preheat the oven to 400°F. Line two large baking sheets (18 × 12 × 1 inch) with silicone baking pan liners or cooking parchment.

TO SHAPE THE BABAS, divide the dough into 30 equal portions and shape each into a ball. This dough is pliable and very easy to work with; if it is at all tacky, dust it with flour as needed. Shape a dough ball into a cup, rotating the dough between your fingertips as your thumbs open the dough to create a cup almost 1 inch deep. Put a ball of filling into the cup and use your fingertips to bring the dough around the filling, covering it completely. Pinch to seal. Set the baba seam side down on your work surface and press gently to flatten slightly. The shaped baba should be about 2 inches across and ½ inch thick. Place the baba onto one of the lined sheets. Shape the remaining babas, arranging 15 on each baking sheet spaced 1 to 2 inches apart. Cover one sheet of babas loosely with plastic wrap. Brush the remaining sheet of babas—top and sides—lightly with the egg wash and sprinkle with sesame seeds.

BAKE FOR 20 TO 25 MINUTES, until the babas are golden brown. Cool the babas on the baking sheet. Meanwhile, uncover the remaining sheet of babas, brush the top and sides of each with egg wash, sprinkle with sesame seeds, and bake.

Storing

Babas keep well stored airtight at room temperature for about 1 week. To freeze, arrange the babas on a baking sheet lined with waxed paper and freeze until solid. Transfer to heavy-duty resealable plastic bags and freeze for up to 1 month. Thaw completely in the bags before serving.

Kolacky

MAKES 60 TO 70 PASTRIES

FILLING

½ cup golden raisins

One 8-ounce package regular cream cheese, at room temperature

1 large egg yolk

3 tablespoons confectioners' sugar

DOUGH

4½ cups unbleached all-purpose flour (spooned into the cups and leveled), plus more as needed

¼ teaspoon salt

1 package (2¼ teaspoons) rapid-rise yeast

2 tablespoons granulated sugar

1 pound (4 sticks) salted butter, at room temperature

½ cup whole milk, warmed

3 large egg yolks

Canned fillings: apricot, prune, raspberry, or almond paste (see Note)

Confectioners' sugar, to dust baked kolacky

DO NOT CONFUSE THESE EXQUISITELY TENDER *and delectable Polish pastries with kolaches, Czech yeast pastries topped with fruit or jam. Kolacky ("ko-LAHTCH-key") are melt-in-your-mouth pastries, like a small turnover in appearance, with a jam, cream cheese and raisin, poppy seed, prune, or almond filling. The dough is rolled out and cut into circles, a spoonful of filling is placed in the center of each circle, and the edges folded up and over the filling and pinched together. After baking, the pastries are dusted generously with confectioners' sugar. Carol Jalovec Lyons, who taught me how to make these, proclaims that they are the best kolacky in the world. And after having sampled several different recipes, I completely agree with her.*

As a child, Carol watched her mother make these kolacky many times, but never actually made them with her. It was only after her mother died that Carol learned to re-create the pastries, using her mother's recipe and her aunt's guidance. Unlike her mom, who made the dough by hand, Carol uses a KitchenAid mixer.

Carol usually makes these pastries with several different fillings. She buys Solo brand canned fillings and also makes her mother's cream cheese and raisin filling. She often substitutes farmer's or ricotta cheese for the cream cheese in this recipe. Because she doesn't have four large baking sheets, she bakes her kolacky on disposable aluminum foil jelly-roll pans, which she washes and reuses.

TO MAKE THE FILLING, put the raisins into a small bowl and cover them with hot water. Leave them for 5 to 10 minutes to plump up, then drain and pat them dry on paper towels.

IN A MEDIUM BOWL, beat the cream cheese with a wooden spoon until smooth. Beat in the egg yolk and confectioners' sugar. Stir in the raisins. Cover the bowl tightly with plastic wrap, and refrigerate for at least 1 hour to firm the filling. (The filling can be made up to a day ahead.)

To make the dough using a stand mixer, put 4 cups of the flour into the mixer bowl and stir in the salt, then the yeast and sugar. Attach the flat beater and beat on low speed for 30 seconds. Still mixing on low, add the butter about 4 tablespoons (½ stick) at a time, beating for a few seconds after each addition. Continue mixing until the dough masses onto the beater and looks smooth. In a small bowl, stir the warm milk and egg yolks together to mix well. With the mixer on low speed, slowly add the liquid to the dough and beat until incorporated. Gradually add the remaining ½ cup flour and mix briefly to make a firm, not sticky dough. Transfer the dough to a large bowl, packing it in firmly. Cover tightly with plastic wrap and let the dough rest at room temperature about 40 minutes, or until you're ready for it.

To make the dough by hand, use a wooden spoon to stir together 4 cups of the flour with the salt in a large bowl. Stir in the yeast and sugar. Cut in the butter with a pastry blender to make a crumbly dough. In a small bowl, stir the warm milk and egg yolks together to mix well. Add to the flour and mix with the wooden spoon to make a smooth dough. Gradually stir in the remaining ½ cup flour to make a firm, not sticky dough. Cover tightly with plastic wrap and let the dough rest at room temperature about 40 minutes, or until you're ready for it.

TO SHAPE AND BAKE THE KOLACKY, adjust an oven rack to the center position and preheat the oven to 400°F. Have ready four large baking sheets (18 × 12 × 1 inch) or 4 disposable aluminum foil baking sheets of about the same dimensions.

LIGHTLY FLOUR your work surface. Remove about one-quarter of the dough from the bowl and roll it to a scant ¼-inch thickness. Dust the dough with flour as necessary to prevent sticking. (If your kitchen is very warm, chill the dough before rolling, keeping the unused portions of the dough refrigerated.) Stamp out cookies with a 2½- or 3-inch round cutter. Gather the dough scraps and set them aside to reroll later. (This dough does not toughen on rerolling.) Put a rounded teaspoonful of the filling of your choice onto the center of a round of dough, bring two opposite sides up to the middle, and pinch firmly to seal. The filling will be exposed at the ends of the kolacky. Place on a baking sheet and continue making kolacky, using the remaining dough and then the scraps; arrange the cookies about 1 inch apart on the baking sheets, putting 16 to 18 pastries on a sheet.

BAKE THE KOLACKY one sheet at a time for about 15 minutes, until the cookies are an even, light golden color. Rotate the sheet back to front after 10 minutes to ensure even browning. Leave the kolacky on the sheet to cool—they are very fragile. When completely cool, sprinkle them liberally with confectioners' sugar.

Storing

Kolacky keep well in an airtight container at room temperature for 3 to 4 days. Carol freezes some of her kolacky, layering them in deep disposable aluminum foil containers between sheets of waxed paper. She wraps the containers in aluminum foil and puts them in large resealable plastic bags. They keep well in the freezer for up to 2 months. Thaw the kolacky in their wrapping, then dust them again with confectioners' sugar before serving.

Note

You'll use only a portion of each can of filling. Cover and refrigerate leftovers for another use.

Szarlotka

MAKES 16 TO 18 SERVINGS

THIS OLD POLISH APPLE PIE RECIPE *has been handed down in Krystyna Kawalec's family for generations. A generous layer of cinnamon-scented apples is sandwiched within a cookie-like dough rich with butter, sugar, egg yolks, and sour cream. Krystyna learned how to make szarlotka (pronounced "shar-LOT-ka") from her grandmother decades ago and has been making it ever since. She likes Granny Smith apples, but feel free to use whatever firm cooking apples you prefer. A combination, one third each of Macoun or McIntosh, Rome Beauty, and Granny Smith, is excellent. Braeburns (my favorite) and Cameos are also good together.*

Krystyna makes the dough by hand, piling all of the ingredients on her counter top and working them together until they gather into a smooth, cohesive mass. I've modified her procedure a little by rubbing the butter into the dry ingredients first, then mixing in the yolks and sour cream. I've also given directions for making the dough with a heavy-duty mixer.

Make the szarlotka a day before you want to serve it. It's far better after an overnight rest at room temperature, because then the pastry and apples meld together into a unified whole.

DOUGH

- 5 cups unbleached all-purpose flour
- 1 teaspoon baking powder
- 1 teaspoon salt
- 1 cup granulated sugar
- ½ pound (2 sticks) cold unsalted butter, cut into tablespoon-sized pieces
- 6 large egg yolks
- ½ cup sour cream

FILLING

- 3½ pounds (about 7 large) cooking apples (see headnote)
- ½ cup granulated sugar
- 1 teaspoon ground cinnamon
- ¼ teaspoon salt

Confectioners' sugar for dusting

To make the dough by hand, stir together the flour, baking powder, salt, and sugar in a large bowl. Add the butter and work it into the flour with your fingertips to make a coarse, flaky mixture, then rub the mixture rapidly between your palms to make fine crumbs. In a small bowl, whisk the egg yolks and sour cream together until smooth. Add to the dry ingredients and work everything together with your hands to make a firm, smooth, not sticky dough.

To make the dough using a stand mixer, put the flour, baking powder, salt, and sugar into the mixer bowl. Add the butter and mix on low speed with the flat beater until the mixture is the consistency of fine crumbs, about 3 minutes. In a small bowl, whisk the egg yolks and sour cream together until smooth. Add to the dry ingredients and mix on low speed for 2 to 3 minutes, or until a firm, not sticky dough masses on the blade. Be patient; it may seem to you that a cohesive dough will never form, but it will. If your kitchen is very warm, the dough will gather together more quickly.

DIVIDE THE DOUGH into 2 pieces, making one piece slightly larger. Pat each portion into a 1-inch-thick rectangle. You can work with the dough right away or wrap it tightly in plastic wrap and refrigerate it. (The dough can be made up to a day ahead and refrigerated; bring to room temperature before rolling.)

TO MAKE THE FILLING, quarter, core, and peel the apples. You can either cut the apples crosswise into very thin slices and then cut the slices into short matchstick shapes, which is what Krystyna does, or shred the apples with a box grater or the shredding disk of a food processor. Put the apples into a large bowl. Stir together the sugar, cinnamon, and salt; set aside to add to the apples later. (If the apples discolor a bit as they wait, don't be concerned.)

ADJUST AN OVEN RACK to the center position and preheat the oven to 375°F. Butter a 13 × 9 × 2–inch baking pan, preferably nonstick. (Do not use cooking spray—you want the dough to adhere to the butter, and it will not stick to cooking spray.)

PINCH OFF SMALL PIECES of dough from the larger dough portion, using about one-third of it, and press them onto the sides of the pan, going up halfway. The thickness of the dough should be slightly more than ⅛ inch thick. Don't be concerned about uneven edges, but try to not make the corners too thick. Roll the remaining portion of this piece of dough on a lightly floured surface to fit the bottom of the pan. If the dough tears, just pinch it together. Carefully lift the dough into the pan—use a giant pastry spatula or a cookie sheet to help you—and press the dough with your fingertips to join with the sides. The bottom crust will be slightly thicker than the sides.

LIGHTLY DUST YOUR WORK SURFACE with flour and coat both sides of the smaller piece of dough with flour. If the dough feels very firm, tap it gently with a rolling pin to soften it a

bit. Roll the dough to a rectangle the size of the top of the baking pan. Use a ruler to make sure. The dough will be about ¼ inch thick. Check frequently during rolling to make sure the dough isn't sticking to the work surface; if it is, loosen it with a pastry scraper. During rolling, the dough is likely to crack in several places, particularly along its sides; simply pinch the dough together, squaring off any rough edges. Add the sugar mixture to the apples and toss to combine well. Transfer the apples to the dough-lined pan, distribute them evenly, and pat them gently into place. The apples will just reach the upper edge of the dough. Slide a giant pastry spatula or a cookie sheet under the top crust and carefully slip it onto the apples. Pinch the edges of the top and bottom crust with your fingertips to seal the two together (this dough is very amenable to being pinched and sealed). Prick the top crust at 1-inch intervals with a fork.

BAKE FOR 45 TO 55 MINUTES, until the pastry is a rich golden brown color, the apples smell fragrant, and a paring knife inserted into the apples passes through them with no resistance. Set the pan on a wire rack to cool for 20 to 30 minutes.

RUN THE TIP OF A SMALL SHARP KNIFE all around the pastry to release it. Cover it with a wire rack, grasp the pan and rack together, and invert the two. Slowly lift off the pan. Cover the bottom of the szarlotka with another wire rack and invert again so that it is right side up. Cool completely, then slide the szarlotka onto a platter or wooden cutting board, cover loosely with plastic wrap, and let stand overnight at room temperature.

TO SERVE, dust the top of the szarlotka with confectioners' sugar and cut into portions with a sharp serrated knife.

Storing

Store leftovers in the refrigerator, but bring to room temperature before serving. Dust again with confectioners' sugar if necessary.

Baklawa

MAKES ABOUT 30 DIAMONDS

THIS IS A LEBANESE VERSION OF BAKLAVA, *the classic Greek dessert, which I learned from food writer Maureen Abood. Lebanon is historically a Christian nation, and baklawa (pronounced "bahk-LAY-wa") was always made at Christmas. Today it is also prepared for special occasions such as weddings, anniversaries, and birthdays. Layers of phyllo dough are brushed with clarified butter and topped with walnuts flavored with sugar and orange blossom water, and then with more buttery layers of dough. After baking, the dessert is saturated with a cold lemon-scented sugar syrup. Maureen says that for maximum absorption, a cold syrup must be poured onto a hot baklawa or a room-temperature baklawa should be doused with a hot syrup.*

Many cooks prepare the various parts of the baklawa over several days. The butter can be clarified days ahead and refrigerated. The walnut filling can be made ahead and refrigerated or frozen for a week or more before assembling and baking. And the sugar syrup should be made at least 1 day ahead, because it needs to be cold.

When working with phyllo dough, always keep it covered to prevent it from drying out and crumbling; it must remain flexible. Orange flower water is sold in Middle Eastern markets and can also be ordered by mail (see Sources, page 341).

SYRUP

- 3 cups granulated sugar
- 2 cups water
- 2 tablespoons orange flower water
- 1 tablespoon fresh lemon juice

FILLING

- 1 pound walnuts
- ½ cup granulated sugar
- 1 to 2 tablespoons orange flower water (to taste)
- ¾ pound (3 sticks) unsalted butter, clarified (see page 12), tepid
- 1 pound phyllo dough, thawed if frozen

TO MAKE THE SYRUP, combine the sugar and water in a medium heavy saucepan and bring to a boil over medium heat, stirring occasionally. Cover the pan and cook for 3 minutes. Uncover the pan, reduce the heat to medium-low, and cook for several minutes, until the syrup registers 200°F on an instant-read thermometer. Remove the syrup from the heat and stir in the orange flower water and lemon juice. Let cool completely, then cover and refrigerate until thoroughly chilled. (The syrup can be refrigerated for up to 3 days.)

TO MAKE THE FILLING, chop the walnuts with a large chef's knife into medium pieces—you want a range of textures. You can also chop the walnuts in batches in a food processor, pulsing 4 to 5 times to achieve the proper texture. Transfer the chopped walnuts to a large bowl and stir in the sugar and orange flower water. Cover tightly and refrigerate. (The filling can be refrigerated for up to 2 days or frozen for up to 1 month.)

TO ASSEMBLE AND BAKE THE BAKLAWA, adjust an oven rack to the center position and preheat the oven to 350°F. Unwrap and unroll the phyllo sheets and cover them with a dry towel, then a damp towel.

LIGHTLY BRUSH THE BOTTOM AND SIDES of a 13 × 9 × 2–inch baking pan with clarified butter. Place 1 phyllo sheet in the pan and brush lightly with butter. Fold the overhanging edges of phyllo into the pan. Repeat, using half the phyllo sheets. Distribute the walnut filling evenly over the phyllo, spreading it with your fingers. Cover with a sheet of phyllo, and brush it lightly with the butter. Repeat until all the phyllo has been used. With a small sharp knife, score the pastry into diamond shapes, dividing it first into 5 lengthwise strips, then on the bias into sixths. After scoring, use a sharp heavy knife to cut into portions going all the way to the bottom of the pan. The baklawa is very dense and firm, and you'll have to use a fair amount of pressure to cut through it. Brush the top of the baklawa generously with clarified butter, and pour any remaining butter into the cuts.

BAKE FOR 30 MINUTES. Reduce the temperature to 300°F and continue baking until the baklawa is golden brown and crisp throughout, another 45 to 60 minutes. If in doubt, err on the side of a longer stint in the oven—do not underbake.

WHILE THE BAKLAWA BAKES, check the consistency of the cold syrup. It must be liquid and pourable, like maple syrup, not as thick as honey or corn syrup. If it is too thick, thin it to the correct consistency with gradual additions of very small amounts of cold water. Refrigerate until needed.

REMOVE THE PAN from the oven and immediately pour the cold syrup slowly and evenly all over the top of the baklawa. It will sizzle and crackle. Let the baklawa stand until completely cool, 2 to 3 hours, before serving.

Storing

Stored at room temperature, loosely covered with a sheet of waxed paper and a layer of foil, baklawa keeps well for up to 1 week.

Apple Strudel

MAKES 1 LARGE STRUDEL; 12 TO 16 SERVINGS

THIS IS THE CLASSIC APPLE STRUDEL, *layer upon layer of paper-thin buttery pastry rolled around a generous amount of apples and cinnamon, with raisins and walnuts rounding out the taste and texture. Germaine Doelle Conrad, whose parents were German, learned to make strudel in Detroit from a Serbian lady, Mrs. Lambic, who had immigrated there. And what a fabulous strudel she makes! At one time, Serbia was part of the Austro-Hungarian empire, and strudel was a national dish, something every woman was expected to be able to make, and make well. Apple strudel, with its enticing aromas of butter and cinnamon, was something Mrs. Lambic made often. "I lived next door to Mrs. Lambic," Germaine said. "And the smells that came from her kitchen made me so hungry I had to find out what she was cooking. I never saw how she made the dough, only how she turned it into strudel, but she described the process, and I took it from there. When I finally figured out how to make the dough myself, it was incredible to me. Smelling the strudel as it bakes always drives me wild."*

Because this strudel is a celebration of apples, I urge you to use two or three different varieties to balance tartness and sweetness. For contrast with a softer apple, you might add one or two first-of-the-season McIntosh or Macoun. But use whatever is best and available in your area.

Germaine uses Crisco in her strudel dough instead of the traditional butter because she's found it makes the dough easier to stretch and less apt to tear, and the dough is a dream to work with. You make it in a food processor, and after a rest of one or two hours (longer is better), it becomes

DOUGH

2¾ cups bread flour or unbleached all-purpose flour, plus more as needed

½ teaspoon salt

¼ cup vegetable shortening

1 large egg

About ¾ cup cool water

½ teaspoon distilled white vinegar or fresh lemon juice

FILLING

8 medium-to-large apples (4 pounds total; see headnote)

1 lemon, cut in half

¾ cup granulated sugar, mixed with 1 tablespoon ground cinnamon

½ cup dark raisins

½ cup golden raisins

12 tablespoons (1½ sticks) salted butter, melted and kept warm

¾ cup fine dry bread crumbs or finely ground walnuts (about 3 ounces)

Confectioners' sugar for dusting (optional)

very supple and stretchable. If you have never made strudel before, you're in for an adventure. Your hands do all of the stretching, and it is fascinating to watch them move beneath the transparency of the strudel dough. Since the dough is stretched paper thin, be sure to remove any rings and trim your nails to lessen the possibility of tears.

Strudel dough stretches best in a warm room; a temperature of about 75°F is ideal. You will need a table 5 to 6 feet long and 2½ to 3 feet wide, an old clean sheet or other large cloth, and kitchen shears. See the companion DVD for a video demonstration of strudel-dough making.

Apple strudel is delicious plain, but it is even better with a dollop of sweetened whipped cream or a scoop of vanilla ice cream.

TO MAKE THE DOUGH, put the flour and salt into the work bowl of a food processor fitted with the metal blade and process for 5 seconds. Add the shortening and process for 8 to 10 seconds, until the mixture is the consistency of very fine meal. Crack the egg into a 2-cup glass measure and beat it lightly with a fork just to combine the white with the yolk. Add water to reach the 1-cup level, then add the vinegar or lemon juice and stir with the fork. With the machine running, slowly add the liquid in a steady stream, taking about 10 seconds to do so. The dough will gather into a ball that cleans the sides of the work bowl. Process for 30 seconds. Stop the machine to push the dough about with a plastic scraper—it may be sticky at this point—then process for another 30 seconds. Remove the dough from the work bowl and work it between your hands for a few seconds. It should be smooth, elastic, and no longer sticky. If it is sticky, replace it in the work bowl, add 1 tablespoon flour, and process for 10 seconds. Check the consistency again and repeat if the dough is still too wet.

TO DEVELOP THE GLUTEN, slap the dough on your countertop 50 to 100 times: throw the dough down, pick it up, throw it down again; repeat.

COAT A MEDIUM BOWL lightly with cooking spray or vegetable oil. Add the dough and turn to coat all surfaces. Cover tightly with plastic wrap and let rest for 2 to 3 hours to relax the gluten.

MEANWHILE, PREPARE THE FILLING Quarter, core, and peel the apples. Cut each quarter lengthwise in half, then cut crosswise into thirds or fourths, making ½-inch chunks. Drop the apples into a large bowl as you go, add a squeeze of lemon, and toss the apples with the juice. Continue with the remaining apples. (Have the remaining filling ingredients ready.)

ADJUST AN OVEN RACK to the center position and preheat the oven to 450°F. Brush some of the melted butter over the bottom of a large baking sheet (18 × 12 × 1 inch).

DRAPE A DOUBLE THICKNESS of cloth (an old sheet or a tablecloth) over a 5- to 6-foot-long table 2½ to 3 feet wide, making sure there is about 1 foot of overhanging cloth on all sides. Dust about 1 cup flour over the cloth (not the overhang) and rub it in gently. Unwrap the dough and feel it. If it is tacky, dust it all over with flour. Pick up the dough and stretch it a bit. This dough is very responsive and will do what you ask of it. Put the dough on the center of the cloth, pat it gently to flatten slightly, and brush the top with a little melted butter. Roll the dough into an oval shape about 18 inches long and 12 inches wide. Gently tug on the edges of the dough, one edge at a time, until the oval is about 24 inches long and 18 inches wide. Don't turn the dough over; just check on it periodically to make sure it is not sticking to the cloth, and sprinkle additional flour under it if necessary.

REACH UNDER THE DOUGH, with the backs of your hands against the dough, and gently pull your hands apart slightly and toward you, stretching the dough as you do so (see photos on page 145 and in the color plates). Work your way around the table, repeating this process. Stretch the dough further by grasping the outer part of a thick edge and gently tugging on it. When the dough has been stretched a few inches more on all sides, repeat the hand movements described above. In a few minutes more of stretching, the paper-thin dough will have reached the edges of the table. Continue tugging on the thicker edges of the dough so you have a few inches of overhanging dough on all sides. Cut off the thick edges with kitchen shears. If the dough tears at any point, just leave it alone. Any tears will be covered up when the strudel is rolled.

BECAUSE THE DOUGH IS SO THIN, there's a danger of tearing it if you brush on the butter with a pastry brush. Instead, dip the brush into the butter and dab the butter all over the dough with a gentle touch. Another way is to drizzle the butter onto the dough with a teaspoon: Dip the spoon into the butter and, holding it a few inches above the dough, wave the spoon from side to side to sprinkle drops of butter all over the dough. In either case, dab or drizzle the dough with about three-quarters of the butter. Sprinkle the bread crumbs or nuts evenly over the butter, just to make a very light dusting.

TO ASSEMBLE THE STRUDEL, add the cinnamon sugar and raisins to the apples and mix well. Arrange the filling in an 18- to 20-inch-long horizontal column about 8 inches from the short side of the dough nearest you (see photos on page 145 and in the color plates). Lift the end of the pastry-lined cloth nearest you and carefully flip it over to cover the apple filling completely with a layer of dough. Keep lifting the edge of cloth nearest you, and gravity will cause the strudel to roll over and over until it has formed a long log at the opposite end of the table. The strudel will be too long to fit onto your baking sheet, and there will be quite a bit of excess pastry at either end of the strudel. Pinch the ends of the pastry together near the apple filling, and cut them away with kitchen shears. Pinch the cut ends again to seal and tuck them under the strudel log.

CAREFULLY LIFT UP THE STRUDEL (don't be afraid, it won't break) and place it on the baking sheet, curving it to fit: You can make a C, J, or U shape. Brush any remaining butter all over the strudel.

BAKE FOR 15 MINUTES. Reduce the temperature to 350°F and bake another 30 to 35 minutes, until the strudel is golden brown and the apples are tender. Test by piercing the strudel with the tip of a sharp knife. Remove the pan from the oven. If you see the strudel has released juices, carefully tip the pan, keeping the strudel in place with a pot holder, and drain them off into a small bowl—they're delicious. Cool the strudel on the baking sheet, and serve warm or at room temperature. Dust with confectioners' sugar before serving, if desired, and cut into portions with a sharp serrated knife.

Storing

Strudel is at its best when very fresh, but you can wrap leftovers in foil and refrigerate them for a day or two. To reheat, pull back the top of the foil, but leave it against the cut ends. Pop into a preheated 400°F oven for about 15 minutes.

ABOVE: *stretching the dough using your fingers and palms;* ABOVE RIGHT: *placing the apple filling onto the nut-sprinkled strudel dough;* RIGHT: *completing the shaping of the rolled-up strudel by hand*

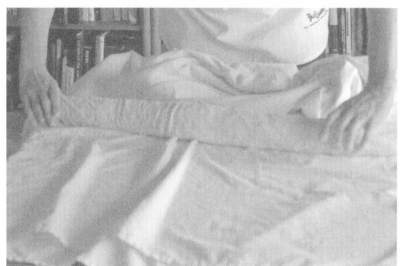

Pumpkin Empanadas

MAKES 20 PASTRIES

THESE GREAT PASTRIES ARE A SPECIALTY OF MARIA ELENA FLORES, *who started making them as a young girl in Chihuahua, Mexico. A delicious tender dough encloses a smooth, spicy filling made with pumpkin or butternut squash. It makes a great out-of-hand munch. Maria Elena bakes these empanadas from October to Christmas because she likes to use Halloween pumpkins, which come closest in texture to the "water pumpkins" that grow in her native Mexico.*

Maria Elena has a fear of knives, so one of her three grandsons drops the pumpkin onto the concrete to crack it. Then she breaks it apart with her hands into large chunks. She scoops out the seeds and fibers with a spoon and cooks the pumpkin in a large pot. Maria Elena makes the dough by hand in a large bowl set into the sink for leverage. She leans her tiny body over the edge of the sink and beats the shortening to cream it, beats in the sugar, spices, and egg, and then works in the flour and milk by hand. She doesn't measure anything but uses her eyes and her fingers to guide her through the process. I've cut Maria Elena's quantities in half, but because the empanadas freeze well, feel free to double the recipe.

FILLING

- 2½ pounds Halloween pumpkin or butternut squash
- 1 cinnamon stick
- 1 cup firmly packed dark brown sugar
- 1 teaspoon ground cinnamon
- ⅛ teaspoon ground cloves

DOUGH

- 3 cups unbleached all-purpose flour, plus more as needed
- ½ teaspoon baking powder
- ½ teaspoon salt
- ¾ cup home-rendered lard (page 332; or see Sources, pages 342 and 343) or vegetable shortening
- ¼ cup granulated sugar
- ½ teaspoon ground cinnamon
- ¼ teaspoon ground cloves
- 1 large egg
- ½ cup warm milk

Evaporated milk or heavy cream for brushing

TO COOK THE PUMPKIN, cut the (unpeeled) pumpkin or squash into large chunks. Scrape out the seeds and fibers and discard. Put the chunks into a large pot, add 2 to 3 cups water, cover the pot, and bring to a boil over high heat. Reduce the heat to medium and cook for about 45 minutes, or until the pumpkin is soft but not completely tender. Test with the tip of a sharp knife—you should feel a bit of resistance the deeper the knife goes in. Drain in a colander and let cool for 20 to 30 minutes; set the pot aside.

TO MAKE THE FILLING, with a spoon, scrape off any remaining fibers from the pumpkin. Cut off the skin and cut the flesh into 1½-inch chunks. You should have about 4 packed cups. Return the pumpkin to the pot, add the cinnamon stick, and sprinkle on the brown sugar. Cover the pot and set it over medium heat. The sugar will melt slowly and the pumpkin will release some of its juices. When the liquid comes to a boil, reduce the heat to medium-low and cook, stirring occasionally, for 10 minutes. Uncover the pot and boil, stirring occasionally, for another 20 to 30 minutes, until the pumpkin is completely tender and the liquid is syrupy and almost completely absorbed.

REMOVE FROM THE HEAT and discard the cinnamon stick. Mash the pumpkin with a potato masher to make it very smooth. Stir in the ground cinnamon and cloves. You'll have a scant 3 cups of filling. Let cool completely. (The filling can be prepared 2 to 3 days ahead; when cool, cover tightly and refrigerate.)

TO MAKE THE DOUGH, in a medium bowl stir the flour, baking powder, and salt together with a whisk.

IN A LARGE BOWL, beat the lard or shortening with an electric mixer on medium speed just until smooth and creamy, less than 1 minute. Add the sugar, cinnamon, and cloves and beat well. Add the egg and beat for 1 minute. With a wooden spoon, add the flour in 3 additions alternating with the milk in 2 additions, beginning and ending with the flour and stirring only until each addition is incorporated. The dough should be firm, pliable, and not sticky. If it is too wet, knead

in up to ¼ cup additional flour on your work surface. Wrap the dough in plastic wrap and let it rest for 30 minutes to 1 hour.

ADJUST TWO OVEN RACKS to divide the oven into thirds and preheat the oven to 375°F. Line two large baking sheets (18 × 12 × 1 inch) with silicone baking pan liners or cooking parchment.

TO SHAPE THE EMPANADAS, divide the dough into 20 pieces (about 1½ ounces each) and shape each into a ball. Flatten a ball of dough slightly and roll it out on a wooden board (flour the surface lightly only if the dough sticks) to a 5-inch circle. This dough is very easy to work with; it rolls smoothly, and you can even the edges with your fingertips. Put 2 level tablespoons of filling slightly below the midpoint of the circle, and fold the dough over the filling. Pinch the seam to seal, and press firmly with a fork or fold the edge decoratively. Prick the top of the empanada 3 times with the fork and set the pastry on one of the prepared sheets. Repeat with the remaining dough and filling, spacing the empanadas 1 to 2 inches apart on the sheets. Brush the tops of the pastries with evaporated milk or cream.

BAKE FOR 40 TO 45 MINUTES, until the empanadas are a deep golden brown color. Rotate the sheets top to bottom and front to back once during baking to ensure even browning. Cool for 1 minute on the baking sheets, then, with a wide metal spatula, transfer the pastries to wire cooling racks to cool completely.

Storing

The empanadas keep well at room temperature, stored airtight, for 2 to 3 days. To freeze, when completely cool, place the empanadas on baking sheets and freeze until solid. Transfer to heavy-duty resealable plastic bags and freeze for up to 1 month. Thaw the empanadas completely in their wrapping, then arrange on a baking sheet and refresh in a preheated 300°F oven for 10 minutes. Cool before serving.

Folhados

MAKES A SCANT 3 POUNDS; ENOUGH FOR 8 PUFF PASTRY SQUARES AND 24 TARTLETS

FOLHADOS (PRONOUNCED "fool-YA-doosh") *is Portuguese puff pastry, and I learned it from Maria João, a marvelous baker on the island of Terceira in the Azores. If you've never made puff pastry, or if you've only made what is called fast puff pastry, you're in for a baking adventure. Puff pastry is nothing more than butter rolled into a dough that is folded and rolled repeatedly until it contains hundreds of thin layers. When baked, the dough puffs to magical heights. It is crisp and flaky and utterly irresistible. The technique is not complicated, but it does take time, most of which involves rests in the refrigerator for the dough.*

In Portugal, puff pastry is made with a special margarine. Maria João makes a basic dough with "tipo 65" flour, water, and salt. After kneading it well and allowing it to rest, she slams it down 100 times on her counter to strengthen the gluten, then lets the dough rest again. She rolls the dough into a large square and spreads one-quarter of the fat on the dough. She actually smears the margarine, which has a clay-like consistency and tan color, onto the dough with her fingertips. She folds up the dough into a 9-layered square packet and rerolls it immediately, then repeats the process of spreading on the fat, folding the dough, and rolling it out three more times with no rests in between. By the final rolling, the dough is difficult to roll out, but Maria João says she always makes folhados this way, with no rests between rollings, because this is how she learned it from her mother. The firm yet pliable consistency of Portuguese folhados margarine does not change at room temperature. And because the Azores lie in the North Atlantic about 650 miles west of Lisbon, it never gets very hot there—so I am guessing that maybe this is why Maria João can make folhados her way year round.

I found Maria João's technique fascinating because it is completely contrary to how the French make classic puff pastry. In that method, all the fat (usually butter) is enclosed within a basic dough and the successive rollings and foldings are carried out with prolonged refrigerated rests in between to allow the gluten in the dough to relax and to make sure the dough and butter are the same degree of firmness. The chilling and relaxing of the dough also make it easy to roll.

DOUGH

- 3 cups unbleached all-purpose flour, plus more as needed
- 1 cup cake flour
- 1 cup warm water, plus more if needed
- 1 teaspoon salt
- 1 pound unsalted butter, slightly softened but still cold

I cannot buy the specially formulated margarine Maria João uses, so I chose butter, both for its taste, and because it is firmer than our margarine. Kneading a little flour into the butter makes it easier to roll with the dough and less likely to soften too much and turn oily. I've approximated the Portuguese "tipo 65" flour that Maria João uses by using a combination of unbleached all-purpose flour and cake flour. Refrigerating the dough between rollings and foldings also makes the dough easy to handle and prevents the butter from becoming too soft.

For maximum puff during baking, it's very important not to tear the dough during the repeated rollings. If the dough gets too soft, tears are more likely to occur—so refrigerate the dough frequently if your kitchen is very warm. But even if it tears, don't worry. You will still have a crisp, delicious, and flaky pastry that could not have been made any other way.

Folhados lends itself to both sweet and savory uses. Maria João showed me two sweet recipes: Puff Pastry Squares with Lemon Buttercream (page 151) and Pastéis de Nata (page 152), fabulous custard tartlets.

TO MIX THE DOUGH, in a large bowl whisk both flours together. Remove and reserve ½ cup of the flour mixture to work into the butter.

IN A 1-CUP GLASS MEASURE or a medium bowl, stir the water and salt together until the salt is dissolved. Make a well in the center of the flour, add all the water, and stir with a wooden spoon until the dough forms large, shaggy-looking masses. Reach into the bowl with your hands and squeeze the dough together. If it seems too dry, add warm water a teaspoonful at a time, working it until the dough forms a firm mass that is not sticky. (This is a firm dough, firmer than a bread dough.) Knead the dough on your work surface, without adding any more flour, for about 5 minutes, until it feels smooth and firm; the dough may still look a bit rough. Shape the dough into a ball, wrap it in plastic wrap, and let it rest at room temperature for about 1 hour.

THE NEXT STEP helps to strengthen the gluten in the flour. Maria João slams the dough down on her countertop 100 times—she doesn't fold the dough after each slam, she simply slams it down. I've made the dough her way, but I've also simply given the dough a vigorous kneading for 5 to 8 minutes. Either way works, so take

your pick. Rewrap the dough in plastic wrap and let the dough rest for 30 minutes to 2 hours at room temperature.

MEANWHILE, PREPARE THE BUTTER. The butter should be cold but firm; your aim is to have the dough and butter the same consistency. While the dough is resting for the second time, put the butter on your countertop (granite, marble, or laminate is fine, but wood is not) and tap it gently with a rolling pin to flatten it a bit and soften it slightly. Smear it out quickly with the heel (not palm) of your hand, then scrape up the butter with a bench scraper held in your other hand and smear it out again rapidly. Sprinkle on the reserved flour and knead it into the butter with the heel of your hand. Work rapidly so that the butter doesn't soften too much and get oily. Scrape up the butter again, form it into a 6-inch square, and wrap it in plastic wrap. Refrigerate for about 30 minutes.

TO ROLL THE DOUGH, dust the dough lightly with flour and roll it to a 16-inch square. Divide the butter into 4 equal portions. With an offset spatula or a table knife, spread one portion in a thin layer evenly over the dough to within ¼ inch of the edges. Fold the dough in thirds like a business letter;

with each fold, use a pastry brush to brush off any excess flour. Fold the dough again into thirds, making a square 9-layer packet. Wrap in plastic wrap and refrigerate for 1 hour. If your kitchen is cool, the remaining butter can rest at room temperature; if it is warm, wrap and refrigerate the butter.

WITH AN OPEN END of the dough away from you, tap the dough lightly with a rolling pin to flatten it slightly, and roll the dough again to a 16-inch square. Don't flip the dough over during rolling; simply dust with flour as necessary by lifting it up periodically. Spread the dough with one-third of the remaining butter, and fold it again into a 9-layer packet. Wrap and refrigerate for 1 hour.

REPEAT THE ROLLING and folding procedure twice more, wrapping and refrigerating the dough for 1 to 2 hours between the last two rollings. If you will be using the dough for the Puff Pastry Squares (page 151) or Pastéis de Nata (page 152), cut the dough crosswise in half. Cover and refirgerate or freeze until ready to use.

Storing

The dough can be refrigerated overnight or frozen, well wrapped, for up to 2 weeks.

Puff Pastry Squares with Lemon Buttercream

portugal

MAKES 8 PASTRIES

THESE CRISP, FLAKY PASTRIES ARE MADE *by filling baked puff pastry squares with a thin layer of a lemon-flavored buttercream, and giving them a dusting of confectioners' sugar. Maria João taught me how to make them on the island of Terceira in the Azores. Bakeshops there and throughout Portugal, she says, always sell them because they are a national favorite. They are one of the best ways to enjoy puff pastry in its purest form. These are best the day they are made but may be assembled one or two hours before serving. Although you can serve them with a knife and fork, it's more traditional to eat the pastries out of hand.*

½ recipe Folhados (page 148)

BUTTERCREAM

8 tablespoons (1 stick) unsalted butter, at room temperature

½ cup confectioners' sugar

Pinch of salt

1 teaspoon pure lemon extract

Confectioners' sugar for dusting

TO MAKE THE PASTRIES, line a large baking sheet (18 × 12 × 1 inch) with silicone baking pan liner or cooking parchment. The dough will be very firm. To make it easier to roll, press the rolling pin gently on the dough to flatten it slightly, then roll the dough on a lightly floured surface into a 13 × 7–inch rectangle about ⅓ inch thick. Square the edges periodically to keep the shape as even as you can. Brush off the excess flour.

WITH A LARGE SHARP KNIFE, trim the edges of the pastry to make a 12 × 6–inch rectangle. Cut the dough lengthwise into two 3-inch-wide strips, then cut each strip crosswise into four 3-inch squares, making a total of 8 squares. Place the squares about ½ inch apart on the prepared sheet, and prick each 3 times with a fork. (The folhados won't spread sideways—it rises straight up.) Refrigerate, loosely covered with plastic wrap, for 1 hour.

ADJUST AN OVEN RACK to the center position and preheat the oven to 450°F while the pastries chill.

UNCOVER THE PASTRIES and place the pan (straight from the refrigerator) into the oven. Bake for about 25 minutes, until the pastries are puffed—they'll be about 2 inches tall—and very brown. With a wide metal spatula, transfer the pastries to a cooling rack. Cool completely.

TO MAKE THE FILLING, beat the butter in a small bowl with a hand-held electric mixer until smooth. Beat in the confectioners' sugar, salt, and lemon extract.

TO ASSEMBLE THE PASTRIES, split the cooled squares horizontally in half with a sharp serrated knife. Spread the bottom halves with a thin layer of the lemon buttercream and replace the tops. Dust generously with confectioners' sugar before serving.

Pastéis de Nata

MAKES 24 TARTLETS

½ recipe Folhados (page 148)

FILLING

2 large eggs

6 large egg yolks

1 cup granulated sugar

3 tablespoons unbleached all-purpose flour

¾ cup whole milk

2 cups heavy cream

2 teaspoons pure vanilla extract

Confectioners' sugar for dusting

Ground cinnamon for sprinkling

THESE MAY WELL BE THE BEST OF ALL PORTUGUESE SWEET PASTRIES. *Thin puff pastry tart shells are filled with rich custard, baked in a very hot oven for just a few minutes, and sprinkled with confectioners' sugar and cinnamon. The contrast of the crisp, flaky pastry with the creamy custard is extraordinary. A famous pastry shop, the Antiga Confeitaria de Belém, on the outskirts of Lisbon, is credited with originating the recipe in the mid-1800s. The bakery has become a tourist destination, and thousands of the tartlets are made there every day. Practically every pastry shop in Lisbon sells pastéis de nata, but the quality is highly variable. This recipe comes closest to those served in Belém.*

Maria João (see Folhados, page 148), who taught me this recipe, uses aluminum tartlet molds with sloping sides that measure 3 inches in diameter and 1¼ inches deep. Nonstick standard-sized muffin pans work equally well. These pastries are best when slightly warm, before they lose their crispness. However, they also freeze beautifully.

THE DOUGH WILL BE VERY FIRM. To make it easier to roll, press the rolling pin gently on the dough to flatten it slightly, then roll the dough on a lightly floured surface into an 18 × 9–inch rectangle. Square the edges periodically to keep the shape as even as you can. Brush off the excess flour. Starting from an 18-inch side, roll the dough into a tight log. Moisten the far edge of the dough with water, and pinch the edges firmly to seal. Wrap tightly in plastic wrap, set the log of dough on the bias on an 18 × 12 × 1–inch baking sheet and refrigerate for 1 to 2 hours.

HAVE READY twenty-four ungreased individual tartlet molds (see headnote) or two nonstick standard-sized muffin pans, each with 12 cups. Remove the dough from the refrigerator and unwrap it. If the roll is now less than 18 inches long, roll it back and forth gently on your countertop to extend it to that length. With a sharp knife, cut the dough into twenty-four ¾-inch-thick slices.

To line the molds using the classic method, place a circle of dough into each ungreased mold and let stand for about 5 minutes to soften slightly. Have a small cup of cool water nearby. Dip your thumbs into the water and press them straight down into the spiral of dough to flatten the dough against the bottom of the mold to a thickness of about ⅛ inch. Then press to extend the dough up against the sides of the pan, reaching all the way to the rim.

To roll out the dough to line the molds (I find this method easier), dust a circle of dough lightly with flour and roll it into a 4-inch circle, less than ⅛ inch thick. Set the circle of dough in a mold and press it onto the bottom and up the sides with your thumbs and fingertips; press firmly so that the dough adheres to the sides of the mold. The pastry should reach the rim of the mold or just slightly above it. Repeat with the remaining pastry circles.

IF USING TARTLET PANS, set the molds slightly apart on two heavy baking sheets. Drape a sheet of plastic wrap loosely over the tartlet shells and refrigerate for about 1 hour.

MEANWHILE, about 45 minutes before baking, adjust an oven rack to the center position. If you have a baking stone, set it on the rack. Preheat the oven to 550°F.

WHILE THE PASTRY SHELLS ARE CHILLING, make the filling. Whisk the eggs and yolks together in a medium bowl for about 30 seconds. Gradually whisk in the sugar, beating well. In another medium bowl, whisk together the flour and milk until smooth.

SCALD THE CREAM in a medium heavy saucepan over medium heat—you will see steam rising from the surface and small bubbles all around the edges. Remove the pan from the heat and gradually whisk the hot cream into the flour and milk; set the saucepan aside. Then gradually whisk the cream mixture into the eggs and sugar. Pour the custard back into the saucepan, set it over medium-low heat, and cook, stirring constantly with a heatproof rubber spatula or wooden spoon, for 8 to 10 minutes, until the custard thickens to the consistency of heavy cream and the temperature is 175° to 180°F. Shortly before this point is reached, you'll notice that lumps of custard have formed on the end of the spatula or spoon—remove the pan from the heat and scrape the spatula or spoon clean with the whisk, then return the pan to the heat and continue cooking, whisking rapidly, until the custard reaches the desired temperature; do not allow the custard to boil. Pass the custard through a strainer into a medium bowl and stir in the vanilla. Stir occasionally as the custard cools slightly, to keep it smooth. The custard should be warm when poured into the pastry shells. (The custard can be made ahead and, once cool, refrigerated, covered, for up to 2 days. To rewarm it, use a double boiler or put the custard into a medium saucepan and set it into a larger pan of hot water over medium heat. Whisk occasionally until the custard feels warm to a fingertip.)

WHEN READY TO BAKE the tartlets, remove one pan of pastry shells or one muffin pan from the refrigerator and let stand at room temperature for about 5 minutes. Uncover the pastry shells and fill each one two-thirds to three-quarters full (about 3 tablespoons custard per cup); the easiest way to do this is to transfer the custard to a 4-cup glass measure with a spout.

PLACE THE PASTRIES in the oven and bake for about 10 minutes on the stone or 10 to 15 minutes without the stone, until the edges of the dough are well browned and the custard is puffed and set. The custard may appear jiggly when done. Ideally, the top of the tartlets should be flecked with brown—if you've baked the pastéis on a stone, they will almost certainly develop spots; if not, the tartlets might have just a few brown spots. Cool the pastéis for 5 minutes in their pans. Fill and bake the remaining pastries.

CAREFULLY TAKE THE TARTLETS out of their pans, using the tip of a small paring knife to help you, and set them on a baking sheet to cool for 20 to 30 minutes, until warm, then dust generously with confectioners' sugar and sprinkle lightly with cinnamon. Serve as soon as possible, or within 2 to 3 hours.

Storing

These tartlets freeze very well. When they are completely cool (leave them plain), place them on a baking sheet lined with waxed paper or cooking parchment and freeze until solid. Transfer them to heavy-duty resealable plastic bags and freeze for up to 1 month. To serve, remove as many pastries as you want from the bags and thaw completely, then put them on a baking sheet and reheat in a preheated 300°F oven for 10 minutes. Serve warm, dusted with confectioners' sugar and cinnamon.

Polish Poppy Seed Pastry

MAKES 16 TO 20 SERVINGS

I LEARNED HOW TO MAKE THIS INTRIGUING POPPY SEED DESSERT *from Krystyna Kawalec, an exceptionally fine baker who immigrated to the United States from Poland a few years ago. When I asked its name, she said that in Polish it was called* makowiec na francuskim ciescu, *"poppy seed pastry in the French manner." The* mak *in* makowiec *means "poppy seed." The contrast of the tender, buttery pastry and the sponge cake–like interior, loaded with poppy seeds, is nothing short of sublime. It is also one of the most unusual desserts I've ever eaten.*

All this needs is a dusting of confectioners' sugar, but a dollop of lightly sweetened whipped cream flavored with vanilla makes a nice accompaniment. This is best served the day it is made.

PASTRY

- 2¼ cups unbleached all-purpose flour
- ¼ teaspoon salt
- ½ pound (2 sticks) cold unsalted butter, cut into tablespoon-sized pieces
- ¼ cup ice water
- 3 large egg yolks

FILLING

- ½ cup poppy seeds
- 6 large eggs, separated
- 6 tablespoons granulated sugar
- 1½ cups canned poppy seed filling
- 3 tablespoons unbleached all-purpose flour
- 4 tablespoons (½ stick) unsalted butter, at room temperature
- 1 teaspoon almond oil or pure almond extract
- 1 teaspoon baking powder
- 2 large egg whites
- ⅛ teaspoon salt

Confectioners' sugar for dusting

To make the pastry using a food processor, insert the metal blade into the work bowl and add the flour, salt, and butter. Pulse 4 or 5 times to cut the butter into small pieces. Pour the ice water into a 1-cup glass measure, add the egg yolks, and mix with a fork to combine well. While pulsing, slowly pour the liquid through the feed tube, then pulse very rapidly (a fraction of a second per pulse) about 30 times, until the pastry forms large clumps but not a coherent mass. Turn the pastry out onto an unfloured work surface and press the lumps of dough together. The dough will be firm.

To make the pastry by hand, combine the flour and salt in a large bowl. Add the butter and cut it in with a pastry blender or two knives until the butter is in pea-sized pieces. Pour the ice water into a 1-cup glass measure, add the egg yolks, and mix with a fork to combine well. Gradually add the liquid to the dry ingredients while tossing with a fork. Stir with the fork until the pastry just gathers into a firm mass. Turn the pastry out onto an unfloured work surface.

To make the dough using a stand mixer, add the flour, salt, and butter to the mixer bowl. Attach the flat beater and mix on low speed for 3 to 4 minutes, until the butter is in pea-sized pieces. Pour the ice water into a 1-cup glass measure, add the egg yolks, and mix with a fork to combine well. Gradually add the liquid to the dry ingredients while mixing on low speed. Continue mixing for a few seconds, until the pastry masses onto the blade. Turn the pastry out onto an unfloured work surface and press together.

FLATTEN THE DOUGH and shape it into a rough rectangle. Dust the dough and work surface lightly with flour and roll the dough to a rectangle measuring about 15 × 10 inches. Fold the dough in thirds like a business letter. Wrap securely in plastic wrap and refrigerate for at least 2 hours. (The dough can be made up to 1 day ahead.)

TO SHAPE THE DOUGH, cut it crosswise in two, making one piece slightly larger than the other. Let the dough stand at room temperature for about 5 minutes to soften slightly. Roll the larger piece to a 15 × 12–inch rectangle, using as little flour as possible. (This is a lovely dough to work with; it rolls like a dream.) Butter a 13 × 9–inch baking pan and carefully fit the dough into the pan, trying to avoid stretching it, especially in the corners. Once the dough is in the pan, lift and nudge the sides to fit, pressing the dough so it adheres to the sides, without stretching. If necessary, use your fingertips to even the dough's thickness. Don't be concerned if the corners of the dough are a bit thicker than the sides. With a small sharp knife, trim the dough on the sides to a height of about 1½ inches.

MEASURE THE TOP OPENING of the pan. Roll the smaller piece of dough to a 14 × 10–inch rectangle, then trim it to a size about ¼ inch larger on all sides than the pan opening. Set the dough on a baking sheet and refrigerate.

ADJUST AN OVEN RACK to the lower third position and preheat the oven to 400°F.

MEANWHILE, MAKE THE FILLING. Grind the poppy seeds in a coffee or spice grinder for 15 to 20 seconds, until they are finely ground and starting to become pasty. Beat the 6 yolks in a medium bowl with an electric mixer on medium-high speed until thick and lemon colored, about 5 minutes. While beating, gradually add the sugar and continue beating until the yolks are very thick and pale, about 5 minutes more. Beat in the canned poppy seed filling, the ground poppy seeds, and the flour. Add the butter, almond oil or extract, and baking powder and beat them in well.

IN A LARGE CLEAN BOWL, with clean beaters, beat the 8 egg whites with the salt until they form stiff shiny peaks that curl slightly at their tips when the beaters are raised. Fold the whites into the poppy seed batter in 3 installments, just until no whites show. Spread the batter in the pastry-lined pan. Carefully place the chilled rectangle of dough over the filling. With a fingertip, gently press the edges of the dough onto the bottom crust to make a snug fit; work carefully and slowly to avoid tearing the crust. Do not prick the crust.

BAKE FOR 30 TO 35 MINUTES, until the crust is golden brown. During baking, the pastry will rise and puff slightly and the top crust may separate from the bottom—this is all right. Cool the pastry in its pan on a wire rack for 15 minutes. During this time, the top crust will level itself.

RUN THE TIP of a sharp knife around the sides to release the pastry from the pan. Cover the pan with a wire rack and invert the two. Carefully lift off the pan, and leave the pastry top side down to cool completely. To serve, dust with confectioners' sugar and cut the pastry into portions with a sharp serrated knife.

Storing

This pastry will stay fresh for 2 to 3 days in the refrigerator, wrapped airtight. Bring to room temperature before serving.

Mazariner

MAKES 24 TARTLETS

THESE IRRESISTIBLY DELICIOUS ALMOND TARTLETS, made of a meltingly tender butter and sugar pastry filled with a cream and almond filling, were taught to me by Helena Hoas, who came to this country many years ago from Sweden. She makes them for festive occasions. Helena uses a food processor to quickly prepare both the pastry and the filling, which is also what I do, but lining the tartlet molds with the dough takes time, so don't make these when you are in a rush. Better still, enlist a second pair of hands to speed the process. You will need two dozen scalloped or fluted tartlet tins measuring 2½ inches × ¾ inch. I use Swedish ones made of stainless steel (see Sources, page 341).

PASTRY

½ cup granulated sugar

14 tablespoons (1¾ sticks) cold salted butter, cut into tablespoon-sized pieces

1 large egg

2¼ cups unbleached all-purpose flour

FILLING

4 ounces (about ¾ cup) blanched slivered or whole almonds

¾ cup granulated sugar

2 large eggs

¾ cup heavy cream

½ teaspoon pure almond extract

GLAZE

1 cup confectioners' sugar

1½ tablespoons water

½ teaspoon fresh lemon juice

TO MAKE THE PASTRY, put the sugar, butter, and egg into the work bowl of a food processor fitted with the metal blade. Process for 1 to 2 minutes, until smooth and creamy, stopping to scrape the work bowl as necessary. Add the flour and pulse rapidly 5 times. Scrape the sides of the work bowl and continue pulsing rapidly until the dough almost gathers into a ball. Scrape the dough onto a sheet of plastic wrap and press it together to form a 6 × 4–inch rectangle. Wrap tightly in the plastic wrap and refrigerate for at least 1 hour. (The pastry can be made a day ahead.)

HAVE READY twenty-four ungreased 2½ × ¾–inch scalloped tartlet pans. Cut the rectangle of dough into twenty-four 1-inch squares. Roll each between your palms into balls. If the dough is too firm to roll, let it stand at room temperature a few minutes to soften a bit. Press the dough into the ungreased molds, lining them evenly and extending the dough a scant ⅛ inch above the rims. Arrange the lined molds on an 18 × 12 × 1–inch baking sheet, spacing them about ½ inch apart. Set aside.

ADJUST AN OVEN RACK to the center position and preheat the oven to 400°F.

MEANWHILE, MAKE THE FILLING. Put the almonds into the work bowl of a food processor fitted with the metal blade. Add the sugar and process until the nuts are finely ground, about 1 minute. Add the eggs, heavy cream, and almond extract and process for 10 seconds. Scrape the work bowl and process for 5 seconds more.

SCRAPE THE FILLING into a 2-cup measure with a spout. Slowly pour the filling into each mold, to come within ⅛ inch from the top of the pastry.

BAKE THE TARTLETS for about 15 minutes, until the filling has risen and is nicely browned. It may crack here and there, which is fine. The pastry should be a pale golden color. Remove the pan from the oven and set it on a wire cooling rack. Allow the tartlets to cool for 10 minutes, until you can hold a mold comfortably, then carefully remove the tartlets from the molds and set them onto the baking sheet to cool completely. The filling will level itself as it cools.

TO PREPARE THE GLAZE, whisk all the ingredients together in a small bowl to make a thick, creamy glaze. Divide it evenly among the tops of the tartlets and spread it carefully with the back of a demitasse spoon to reach the edges of the pastry. You'll be able to see the dark tartlet tops through the glaze. Let stand until set, about 30 minutes, before serving.

Storing

The tartlets keep well at room temperature in tightly covered containers for 2 to 3 days. The unglazed baked tartlets can be frozen. Place them on a baking sheet and freeze until solid, then seal in heavy-duty resealable plastic bags and freeze for up to 2 weeks. Thaw them completely in their wrapping, then unwrap and glaze.

German Plum Cake *german pflaumenkuchen*

MAKES 12 SERVINGS

THIS TENDER CAKE TOPPED WITH PRUNE PLUMS *(pflaumenkuchen) is easy to make and can be served just about anytime. Italian prune plums ripen in late summer, and their season is rather brief, so you might make several of these cakes while the fruit is at its peak and freeze them (see Note). Wrapped airtight, they freeze well for up to 3 months. Anna Lobonc, who grew up in the former Czechoslovakia, taught me this recipe. She also uses a yeast dough as the base for this kuchen; see German Yeast Fruit Kuchen (page 200).*

DOUGH

1½ cups unbleached all-purpose flour

1 teaspoon baking powder

6 tablespoons (¾ stick) unsalted butter, at room temperature, plus a little extra

⅓ cup granulated sugar

Finely grated zest of 1 lemon

1 large egg

⅓ cup whole milk

TOPPING

2 pounds Italian prune plums (about 21), halved and pitted

2 tablespoons unsalted butter, melted

⅓ cup granulated sugar

½ teaspoon ground cinnamon

WHIPPED CREAM (OPTIONAL)

2 cups heavy cream

2 tablespoons confectioners' sugar

½ teaspoon pure vanilla extract

ADJUST AN OVEN rack to the center position and preheat the oven to 400°F. Butter a 13 × 9 × 2–inch baking pan (do not use cooking spray; the dough must adhere to the pan).

TO MAKE THE DOUGH, in a medium bowl whisk the flour and baking powder together to combine well.

IN ANOTHER MEDIUM BOWL, beat the butter briefly with a hand-held electric mixer until smooth. Add the sugar and beat for 2 to 3 minutes on medium speed, until fluffy. Add the lemon zest and egg and beat in well. On low speed, alternately add the flour mixture in 3 additions and the milk in 2 additions, beginning and ending with the flour and beating only until smooth after each. The dough will be stiff.

PLACE TABLESPOON-SIZED GOBS of the dough all over the bottom of the prepared pan. Lightly butter your fingers, and pat the dough into an even layer, covering the pan bottom completely; it will be a thin layer.

ARRANGE THE PLUMS skin side up in tightly packed rows on top of the dough. Brush with the melted butter. Stir together the sugar and cinnamon in a small cup and sprinkle evenly over the plums.

BAKE FOR 35 TO 40 MINUTES, until the plum juices bubble very slowly and a toothpick inserted into the cake comes out clean. Cool the kuchen in the pan on a wire rack, and serve warm or at room temperature.

TO MAKE THE OPTIONAL WHIPPED CREAM, in a large bowl beat the cream, confectioners' sugar, and vanilla until the cream holds a soft shape. Place a spoonful of cream alongside each portion of kuchen.

Note

If you want to freeze the kuchen, butter the baking pan, line it with aluminum foil, and butter the foil. After the kuchen has cooled in its pan, grasp the edges of foil, carefully lift the cake out of the pan, and set it on a cookie sheet. Place in the freezer. When it is solidly frozen, peel off the foil, then wrap the cake tightly in plastic wrap and heavy-duty foil. Store in the freezer for up to 3 months. To reheat, unwrap the frozen cake and set it on a baking sheet. Tent the still-frozen cake loosely with the foil and place into a preheated 300°F oven for 20 to 30 minutes, until it is completely thawed and slightly warm.

Welsh Griddle Cakes

MAKES 20 TO 24 TEA CAKES

THESE LEMON-FLAVORED TEA CAKES, *made with golden raisins or currants, have a deliciously crumbly texture and melt in your mouth. Tottie Parmeter, who grew up in Cardiff, learned how to make them from her mother, who often would serve the cakes warm with afternoon tea. "I always looked forward to these cakes, because my mother had such a deft hand with them," she says. "And the smell of lemon, wafting up from the griddle, just made my mouth water." Tottie's mother used a combination of lard and butter. The lard contributes its own special flavor and makes the cakes especially tender. Use homemade lard (page 332) or order a top-quality lard by mail (see Sources, pages 342 and 343). Or, if you wish, substitute butter for the lard.*

This recipe dates back to the eighteenth century or earlier. In Wales, the cakes were traditionally cooked on a bakestone, a heavy cast-iron sheet that was set on coals in the fireplace. Today most bakers use an electric griddle. The dough has barely enough liquid to hold it together, which accounts for the cakes' sublime texture.

These griddle cakes are quick and easy to make. They cook in just a few minutes and are delicious with steaming-hot tea.

4 cups cake flour	½ teaspoon freshly grated nutmeg
2 teaspoons baking powder	¼ teaspoon ground allspice
¼ teaspoon salt	1 cup golden raisins or currants, or a mixture
8 tablespoons (1 stick) cold unsalted butter plus ½ cup cold home-rendered lard (page 332; or see Sources, pages 342 and 343), cut into tablespoon-sized pieces, or ½ pound (2 sticks) cold unsalted butter, cut into tablespoon-sized pieces (see headnote)	Finely grated zest of 1 large lemon
	1 large egg
	3 tablespoons fresh lemon juice
	1 tablespoon whole milk, plus more if needed
¾ cup granulated sugar, plus extra for sprinkling	All-purpose flour for rolling

To make the dough by hand, put the flour, baking powder, and salt in a large bowl. Add the butter and lard, if using, and cut into the flour with a pastry blender or two knives until the fat particles are about the size of small peas. Reach into the bowl with both hands and rub the dry ingredients rapidly between your fingers until the consistency is like coarse sand.

For the best texture, the fat must be in very small pieces. Stir in the sugar, spices, raisins or currants, and lemon zest.

To make the dough using a food processor, in a large bowl stir together the flour, baking powder, and salt. Insert the metal blade into the food processor, add about two-thirds of the dry ingredients to the work bowl, and scatter the fat on top. Pulse 5 or 6 times, then process continuously for about 10 seconds. Rub a little of the dry ingredients rapidly between your fingertips; the mixture should feel like fine meal. If necessary, process a few seconds longer. Add the contents of the work bowl to the flour in the mixing bowl and mix well. Stir in the sugar, spices, raisins or currants, and lemon zest. (From here on, follow the directions for the hand method.)

To make the dough using a stand mixer, put the flour, baking powder, salt, and fat into the mixer bowl and attach the flat beater. Beat on low speed for 2 to 3 minutes, or until the mixture has the consistency of fine meal. Rub a little between your fingertips to make sure. Add the sugar, spices, raisins or currants, and lemon zest and mix on low speed for 30 seconds.

IN A SMALL BOWL, lightly beat the egg with a fork. Beat in the lemon juice and milk.

To add the liquid by hand, scrape the liquid over the dry ingredients and begin stirring it in with the fork. Keep stirring and tossing until the dough forms medium to large clumps. It will seem to be quite dry. Reach into the bowl with both hands and, working quickly so as not to soften the fat, squeeze the dough together to form one mass that holds together. If the dough won't hold together, sprinkle on droplets of additional milk and squeeze again. The key to the success of this recipe is to keep the liquid to a minimum.

To add the liquid using the mixer, scrape the liquid into the mixer bowl and mix on low speed just until the dough masses onto the beater.

TO SHAPE THE GRIDDLE CAKES, lightly flour your work surface, place the dough on it, and roll the dough about to coat it lightly with flour. Flatten the dough a bit and roll it out until it is about ⅓ inch thick. Don't make it thicker, or the cakes will have to cook longer and they may brown too much. Stamp out circles with a sharp 2½-inch round cutter. Set the cakes on a baking sheet lined with plastic wrap. Gather the dough scraps, reroll, and cut out more cakes. Use all the dough; you may have to shape the last cake or two by hand.

PREHEAT A LARGE electric nonstick griddle to 250° to 275°F. Add as many cakes as will fit comfortably, spacing them about 2 inches apart. Cook for 5 to 6 minutes, until the cakes are a deep golden brown on their bottoms. Turn them over carefully with a pancake turner and cook them on the second side for 5 to 6 minutes, until completely cooked through. The tops will feel firm and the sides will have lost their softness; a toothpick inserted into a cake should come out clean. With a wide spatula, transfer the cakes to a wire cooling rack. While they are still hot, sprinkle each cake with a pinch of sugar. Continue with the remaining cakes the same way. Serve the cakes warm or at room temperature.

Storing

Once cool, the cakes can be stored airtight at room temperature for 2 to 3 days.

Rugelach

MAKES 36 PASTRIES

IN SOME JEWISH POPULATIONS, *this classic pastry is equivalent in popularity to the chocolate chip cookie, and some bakers even include mini chocolate chips in the filling. The buttery, rich, flaky pastry is rolled around a filling of sugar, cinnamon, and walnuts. When you bite into one, it melts in your mouth.*

Cindy Klotz learned to bake rugelach by her Russian grandmother's side. She feels her grandmother's presence every time she bakes one of her traditional recipes. Maybe that's why her rugelach turn out so sublime. The dough must be made a day ahead and refrigerated.

DOUGH

One 8-ounce package regular cream cheese, at room temperature

½ pound (2 sticks) salted butter, at room temperature

1⅔ cups unbleached all-purpose flour, plus more as needed

FILLING

⅔ cup granulated sugar

1 tablespoon ground cinnamon

1⅓ cups (6 ounces) finely chopped walnuts

4 tablespoons (½ stick) salted butter, melted

1 large egg yolk, beaten with 1 teaspoon milk for egg wash

TO MAKE THE DOUGH, in a large bowl beat the cream cheese and butter together with an electric mixer until smooth and fluffy. On low speed, gradually add about half the flour, beating only until incorporated. Scrape the bowl and beater, and stir in the remaining flour with a wooden spoon.

LIGHTLY FLOUR your work surface and scrape the dough onto it. Turn the dough to coat with the flour and shape it into a 1-inch-thick disk. Divide the dough into thirds with a sharp knife. Shape each portion into a ball, flatten into disks, and wrap each in plastic wrap. Refrigerate the dough overnight.

ADJUST TWO OVEN RACKS to divide the oven into thirds and preheat the oven to 350°F. Line two large baking sheets (18 × 12 × 1 inch) with silicone baking pan liners or cooking parchment.

TO MAKE THE FILLING, combine the sugar, cinnamon, and walnuts in a medium bowl.

ROLL ONE PORTION OF DOUGH on a lightly floured surface to a 12-inch circle. If the edges are uneven, that's okay. Brush the dough with about one-third of the butter and quickly sprinkle with ⅔ cup of the sugar and walnuts. Set a square of waxed paper over the filling and press down gently with a rolling pin to embed the filling into the dough. Use a long sharp knife to cut the dough into 12 wedges. Roll up each wedge from its wide edge, and set the rolls point side down on one of the baking sheets, spacing them about 1 inch apart. Some of the filling may fall out of the pastries as you roll them; gather it up and add it to the remaining filling in the bowl. Repeat with the remaining dough, butter, and filling, placing 18 rolls on each baking pan.

BRUSH THE RUGELACH lightly on top with the egg wash. Bake for about 30 minutes, until the pastries are a rich golden brown color. Rotate the sheets top to bottom and front to back once during baking to ensure even browning. Transfer the pastries to wire cooling racks with a wide metal spatula and cool completely.

Storing

Stored airtight at room temperature, the rugelach keep well for 2 to 3 days. They can also be frozen. When completely cool, arrange the rugelach on a baking sheet and freeze until firm. Transfer the rugelach to heavy-duty resealable plastic bags and freeze for up to 1 month. Thaw the rolls in their bags, then unwrap, set the pastries on an unlined baking sheet , and refresh in a preheated 325°F oven for 10 minutes. Cool before serving.

Variation

Mix ½ cup currants or mini chocolate chips into the filling.

5 | Savory Yeast Breads and Pies

COOKS AROUND THE WORLD HAVE TAKEN ADVANTAGE of the versatility of yeast doughs to create everything from crunchy circular rings of seeded dough to tender dinner rolls. This chapter features an eclectic collection in which pastries stuffed with a meat or vegetable filling to make a portable snack or meal predominate.

Middle Eastern cooks are champions in the individual savory pie department. Their doughs are made with little or no sugar and their fillings may contain beef flavored with onions and sumac, spinach with feta and pomegranate seeds, or spicy ground lamb, to name a few. Lithuanians like to fill their sweetish piroshki doughs with both fresh and dried mushrooms, and Russians are apt to stuff theirs with beef, mushrooms, and onions. All these pies can be baked, but piroshki tend to be at their best when fried.

On a more fundamental level are a couple of basic loaves, the Norwegian limpa and whole wheat oatmeal bread. Both are eaten every day with meals, as between-meal snacks, or used in sandwiches. The Cornish splitters fall into the same category, but they are a batter bread that is quick to make and quick to bake.

On a slightly more sophisticated level, there is kleecha, the Syrian braided dinner roll, a dense, seeded bread that is great for sopping up sauces. And when you bake Schwabisch pretzels, the real thing, all twisted and chewy, smear one with mustard and munch on it, pretending you're on a big city street.

Assyrian Spinach Pies
syrian sabanrhiyat

MAKES 24 LARGE PIES

THIS RECIPE COMES FROM RETIRED CHEF RAY RISHO, *whose Assyrian mother taught it to him while he was growing up. "She made these pies, sabanrhiyat, very often," Ray says. "I can still remember the marvelous smells coming from the oven, but it's the taste that always gets me." And what a taste it is: the tangy, slightly salty, tender, crunchy filling made with chopped raw spinach, pomegranate seeds, feta cheese, walnuts, and lemon juice. "We always eat fresh yogurt with these pies. The acidity and creaminess of the yogurt are wonderful complements to the filling."*

Susie, Ray's talented artist and poet wife, showed me how to make these pies. She, too, remembers Ray's mother, Mary, and her skill and dexterity. "The way she rolled, folded, and sealed in the filling was amazing. After all these years, I think I've finally gotten the knack of shaping them."

Ground mahlab, made from the pits of sour black cherries, adds flavor to the dough. The yeast dough is easy to make, and so is the filling. It was the raw spinach that really surprised me, though. I had expected the spinach juices to ooze out of the pies and run all over the place, but they stayed put, giving the filling a special succulence. One pie can make a meal for lunch, two for dinner. A salad of romaine, cucumbers, and tomatoes in a vinaigrette is excellent with these. Any leftover pies can be frozen.

DOUGH

- 1 package (2¼ teaspoons) active dry yeast
- 2 cups warm water (105° to 115°F)
- ½ teaspoon ground mahlab (see Sources, page 343)
- 5 cups unbleached all-purpose flour, plus more as needed
- 2 tablespoons granulated sugar
- 2 teaspoons salt
- ⅓ cup extra-virgin olive oil

FILLING

- ½ cup extra-virgin olive oil
- 1 large yellow onion, chopped
- One 1-pound package cleaned baby spinach, coarsely chopped, or 1 pound baby spinach, rinsed, dried, and coarsely chopped
- 1 cup (4 ounces) chopped walnuts
- ½ cup pomegranate seeds
- 1 cup crumbled feta cheese (about 4 ounces)
- ⅓ cup lemon juice
- 1 teaspoon freshly ground black pepper
- Salt

- Olive oil cooking spray
- Plain yogurt for serving

TO MAKE THE DOUGH, in a small bowl sprinkle the yeast into ¼ cup of the warm water. Add the mahlab and stir well. Let stand at room temperature until the yeast is dissolved, about 10 minutes.

COMBINE THE FLOUR, SUGAR, AND SALT in a large mixing bowl or in the bowl of a heavy-duty mixer. Add the remaining 1¾ cups warm water, the olive oil, and dissolved yeast and stir with a wooden spoon until the dough gathers into a mass. Let stand for 5 minutes.

To knead the dough by hand, scrape the dough onto a lightly floured work surface and knead it vigorously for about 8 to 10 minutes, until smooth and elastic. This is a soft dough and it should still be slightly sticky at the end of kneading.

To knead the dough using a stand mixer, attach the dough hook and knead on medium-low speed for 2 minutes. Increase the speed to medium and knead for about 5 minutes more, until the dough is smooth, elastic, and just slightly sticky. The dough may not clean itself from the sides of the bowl. Scrape the bowl and dough hook, then scrape the dough onto a lightly floured work surface and knead a few strokes just to get a feel for the dough's consistency.

WASH AND DRY THE BOWL and rub it lightly with olive oil. Shape the dough into a ball, place it in the bowl, turn to coat, and cover tightly with plastic wrap. Let rise until the dough has doubled in size, about 1½ hours. When you press a finger into the dough and withdraw it, the depression will remain.

SCRAPE THE DOUGH onto a lightly floured work surface. Divide the dough into 24 pieces (a scant 2 ounces each). Shape into balls, arrange on the floured work surface, and cover loosely with kitchen towels. Let rest for 30 minutes. This will make the dough easy to roll.

TO PREPARE THE FILLING, heat 2 tablespoons of the olive oil in a medium skillet over medium heat. Add the onion and cook, stirring occasionally, until tender and golden, 8 to 10 minutes. Remove the pan from the heat.

PUT THE SPINACH into a large bowl, add the walnuts, pomegranate seeds, feta, lemon juice, and the remaining 6 tablespoons olive oil, and toss to combine well. Taste and add the pepper and salt if needed, keeping in mind that the feta is salty.

ADJUST AN OVEN RACK to the center position and preheat the oven to 375°F. Line two large cookie sheets (17 × 14 inches) with cooking parchment. Cut another sheet of parchment and set it aside (or line a third cookie sheet if you have one).

TO SHAPE THE PIES, roll a ball of dough into a thin 6-inch circle, flouring the dough and work surface lightly as necessary to prevent sticking. Pile ½ cup of the filling, loosely measured, onto the center of the circle, leaving about 1 inch of dough exposed all around. Brush the exposed dough lightly with water. Imagining the circle to be a clock, lift up the edges of dough at the 10 o'clock and 2 o'clock positions to cover the top part of the filling and pinch firmly to seal, going all the way to 12 o'clock. Lift the 6 o'clock position of dough to meet in the center and pinch the two edges firmly to seal. The seams will look like an inverted Y. Set the pie on one of the prepared sheets. Working quickly, form 7 more pies, placing them on the cookie sheet with a little space between them.

SPRAY THE PIES with cooking spray and put the pan in the oven. Bake for 25 to 30 minutes, until the pies are golden brown.

WHILE THE FIRST PIES BAKE, shape the remaining pies, placing 8 of them on the second cookie sheet and 8 on the remaining parchment sheet. Coat them with cooking spray.

WHEN THE FIRST PAN of pies is baked, slide the parchment sheet of pies off the cookie sheet onto your countertop. Slide the sheet of uncooked pies onto the cookie sheet. Adjust two oven racks to divide the oven into thirds. Place the two pans of unbaked pies in the oven and bake for 25 to 30 minutes, until the pies are golden brown, rotating the pans top to bottom and front to back once during baking to ensure even browning. Let the pies cool on their parchment sheets. Serve them warm or at room temperature, with the yogurt.

Storing

Leftover pies can be frozen. When cool, arrange them on a baking sheet and freeze until solid. Transfer them to heavy-duty resealable plastic bags and freeze for up to 1 month. To reheat, thaw the pies in their wrapping, then set them on a baking sheet and pop into a preheated 350°F oven for 10 minutes. Serve warm or at room temperature.

Lithuanian Mushroom Piroshki *lithuania*

THESE HIGHLY SATISFYING AND HEARTY FRIED SAVORY TURNOVERS *are made with both fresh and dried mushrooms. They are a specialty of Ryte Kilikeviciene, a cooking teacher and caterer from Lithuania. Ryte (pronounced "Ree-TAY") means "born in the morning," which is when Ryte entered the world. She learned how to cook from her mother and grandmother, and the first thing she remembers making is mashed potatoes. "They were too thin," she says, "so I added sauerkraut to make them thicker." It may not have been the best decision, but it set her on her lifelong love of cooking.*

The dough for the piroshki is slightly sweet to complement the flavor of the mushrooms. Ryte likes to use a combination of fresh brown and white mushrooms and some dried porcini. Portobello and cremini mushrooms have more flavor than white mushrooms, so feel free to use them for the entire amount of fresh mushrooms.

The filling can be made a day or two in advance, and the piroshki can be cooked several hours or even a day ahead and reheated in a moderate oven just before serving, as part of a main meal or eaten out of hand as snacks. Pass a bowl of sour cream along with the piroshki.

FILLING

- 1 to 1½ ounces dried porcini mushrooms
- 2 pounds portobello or cremini mushrooms
- 8 tablespoons (1 stick) unsalted butter
- 2 large yellow onions, chopped medium-fine
- 2 tablespoons chopped fresh tarragon or 2 teaspoons dried tarragon, crumbled
- 2 teaspoons salt, or to taste
- ½ teaspoon freshly ground black pepper, or to taste
- ½ cup dry sherry

DOUGH

- 6 tablespoons (¾ stick) unsalted butter
- 1 cup whole milk
- ¼ cup granulated sugar
- 1 teaspoon salt
- 2 large eggs
- 4 cups unbleached all-purpose flour, plus more as needed
- 1 package (2¼ teaspoons) instant yeast

Vegetable oil for shallow-frying

Sour cream for serving

PUT THE PORCINI MUSHROOMS in a medium bowl and add about 2 cups hot water. Let stand for 1 hour, or until the mushrooms are very soft.

DRAIN THE MUSHROOMS in a strainer set over a bowl, and squeeze gently to remove excess liquid; reserve the liquid. Chop the mushrooms medium-fine. Strain the liquid through a paper coffee filter or paper towel to remove any grit, and measure ¾ cup of the liquid to use in the filling. (Save the remaining liquid for a risotto or soup, if you like.)

WIPE THE FRESH MUSHROOMS with a damp paper towel to remove any dirt. Cut the mushroom stems and caps into small dice, about ¼ inch. (Do this with a sharp knife, not a food processor.)

MELT THE BUTTER in a large sauté pan (4 to 6 quarts) over medium heat. Add the onions and cook, stirring occasionally, until they turn golden and are slightly caramelized, 10 to 15 minutes. Add the fresh mushrooms, stir well, and cover the pan. Cook, stirring occasionally, until the mushrooms release their juices, have reduced in volume, and are very tender, 10 to 12 minutes. Raise the heat to high and add the tarragon, salt, pepper, and porcini mushrooms, along with the reserved liquid. Cook, stirring, until the liquid is almost completely absorbed but the mushrooms still look moist, about 5 minutes. Add the sherry and continue cooking and stirring until the wine is absorbed, 3 to 5 minutes. Taste and adjust the seasoning with salt and pepper if necessary. Remove from the heat and let cool completely. (The filling can be made a day or two ahead, cooled, covered, and refrigerated.)

TO MAKE THE DOUGH, melt the butter in a small saucepan over low heat. Add the milk, sugar, and salt, stir well, and heat just until the liquid feels hot to your fingertip (120° to 130°F). Remove the pan from the heat.

IN A MEDIUM BOWL, whisk the eggs just to combine the yolks and whites. Whisk in the hot liquid. In a large bowl, stir together 2 cups of the flour and the yeast. Add the egg mixture and whisk for 1 to 2 minutes, until smooth. Gradually stir in the remaining 2 cups flour with a wooden spoon to make a thick, sticky dough. Stir the dough with the spoon for 2 to 3 minutes to knead it slightly; the dough does not need to be kneaded actively because it should be tender rather than elastic.

SPRINKLE YOUR WORK SURFACE with a few tablespoons of flour and scrape the dough onto it. Toss the dough about to coat it with the flour and knead it between your hands for just a few seconds to make sure it is smooth. The dough will still be slightly sticky. Wash and dry the mixing bowl and lightly oil it or coat with cooking spray. Place the dough in the bowl, turn it over, and cover tightly with plastic wrap. Let the dough rise until it has almost tripled in volume, about 1½ hours.

TO SHAPE THE PIROSHKI, gently deflate the dough by pulling in the sides and reshaping the dough into a ball. Put a long sheet of plastic wrap on your counter and coat it lightly with cooking spray. Divide the dough into 24 pieces. Shape each into a ball, placing them slightly apart on the plastic wrap. Cover loosely with a kitchen towel and let the dough rest for about 10 minutes.

PAT OR ROLL a ball of dough out on a wooden board into an oval about 4½ inches long, 3½ inches wide, and ⅛ inch thick. The dough should be very soft, easy to work with, and no longer sticky. If it is sticky, lightly dust it with flour. As you pat or roll it, lift it up and flip it over once or twice to make sure it isn't sticking to the board. Measure a scant ¼ cup of filling and place it in the center of the oval. Shape the filling into a domed oval so that it extends to about 1 inch from the edges of dough along the sides and about ½ inch from the ends. Lift the dough up and around the filling and pinch firmly to seal.

Place the piroshki seam side down on the plastic wrap. Cover again with the towel. Shape the remaining piroshki the same way, leaving space between them on the plastic wrap. The piroshki should only become slightly puffy before cooking.

TO COOK THE PIROSHKI, heat about ½ inch of oil in a large skillet over medium heat to between 350° and 360°F. A digital probe thermometer does the best job of monitoring the temperature. Line one or two large baking sheets with several thicknesses of paper towels. When the oil is ready, slip 4 piroshki seam side down into the hot oil and cook for 2 minutes. Carefully turn them over with tongs and cook for 2 minutes on the second side. Because of the sugar in the dough, the piroshki will turn a dark brown. Monitor the heat of the oil and adjust the heat as necessary. Remove the piroshki from the oil with tongs, letting the excess oil drain back into the pan, and place them on the paper towels to drain further. Cook the remaining piroshki 4 at a time.

SERVE THE PIROSHKI warm, along with sour cream. They can be cooked up to 1 to 2 hours ahead. To reheat, put them in a single layer on unlined baking sheets and reheat in a preheated 400°F oven for 5 to 10 minutes.

Storing

Piroshki can be frozen when completely cool. Arrange them in a single layer on a large baking sheet and freeze until solid. Transfer to heavy-duty resealable plastic bags and freeze for up to 1 month. To serve, thaw the piroshki completely in their wrapping, then unwrap, arrange on baking sheets, and reheat in a preheated 350°F oven for 10 to 15 minutes.

Beef Piroshki

MAKES 24 TURNOVERS

THIS IS THE WAY MY RUSSIAN GRANDMOTHER, *Baba, made piroshki. As a kid in Shanghai, I always looked forward to visiting her when I knew she'd be making them. When I wanted to re-create them, my aunt Luba sketched the recipe out for me as best she could remember. The mushrooms give the beef filling moistness and an especially rich taste. Baba fried her piroshki, and I have always preferred them that way. Baba didn't have a food processor, of course, but I use one to chop the mushrooms; I use a large sharp chef's knife, though, for the onions.*

Serve these piroshki as a main course, allowing 2 per person, along with a green vegetable or coleslaw. Be sure to pass a bowl of sour cream. Or eat them out of hand as a snack. If eating out of hand, bite an end off a piroshki and put a dab of sour cream onto the beef filling. Continue to dab on a tad of sour cream before each bite.

Dough for Lithuanian Mushroom Piroshki (page 168), made with only 2 tablespoons sugar

FILLING

¾ pound cremini or white mushrooms

4 tablespoons (½ stick) unsalted butter

Salt and freshly ground black pepper

2 tablespoons extra-virgin olive oil

2 medium yellow onions, chopped medium-fine

2 pounds ground beef (about 15% fat)

2 teaspoons salt

1 teaspoon freshly ground black pepper

½ teaspoon dried thyme

½ cup finely chopped flat-leaf parsley or dill

Vegetable oil for shallow-frying

About 2 cups sour cream for serving

LET THE DOUGH RISE while you prepare the filling.

TO MAKE THE FILLING, wipe the mushrooms with a damp paper towel to remove the dirt. Finely chop them in 2 or 3 batches in a food processor: pulse 5 or 6 times, scrape the sides of the work bowl, and pulse again 5 or 6 times; repeat until the mushrooms are chopped into very small pieces.

MELT THE BUTTER in a large skillet over medium heat. Add the mushrooms and cook, stirring occasionally with a wooden spoon, until the mushrooms are tender and moist looking, 8 to 10 minutes. Season with salt and pepper to taste, and scrape the mushrooms onto a plate.

RETURN THE PAN to medium heat and pour in the olive oil. Add the onions and cook, stirring occasionally until tender and golden, 8 to 10 minutes. Add the ground beef and break it up with the spoon. Cook, stirring, until the beef loses its pink color. Add the salt, pepper, and thyme and stir well. Add the mushrooms and parsley and combine well. Taste, and adjust the seasoning with salt and pepper if necessary. Remove the pan from the heat and let the filling cool to room temperature. (The filling can be made a day ahead; when cool, cover and refrigerate.)

TO SHAPE THE PIROSHKI, gently deflate the dough by pulling in the sides and reshaping the dough into a ball. Put a long sheet of plastic wrap on your counter and coat it lightly with cooking spray. Divide the dough into 24 pieces. Shape each into a ball, placing them slightly apart on the plastic wrap. Cover loosely with a kitchen towel and let the dough rest for about 10 minutes.

PAT OR ROLL a ball of dough out on a wooden board into an oval about 5 inches long, 4 inches wide, and a scant ⅛ inch thick. The dough should be very soft, easy to work with, and no longer sticky. If it is sticky, lightly dust it with flour. As you pat or roll the dough, lift it up and flip it over once or twice to make sure it isn't sticking to the board. Measure a packed ¼ cup of filling and place it in the center of the oval. Shape the filling into a domed oval so that it extends to about 1 inch from the edges of dough along the sides and about ½ inch from the ends. Lift the dough up and around the filling and pinch firmly to seal. Place the piroshki seam side down on the plastic wrap. Cover again with the towel. Shape the remaining piroshki the same way, leaving space between them on the plastic wrap. The piroshki should only become slightly puffy before cooking.

TO COOK THE PIROSHKI, heat about ½ inch of oil in a large skillet over medium heat to between 350° and 360°F. A digital probe thermometer does the best job of monitoring the temperature. Line one or two large baking sheets with several thicknesses of paper towels. When the oil is ready, slip 4 piroshki seam side down into the hot oil and cook for 2 minutes. Carefully turn them over with tongs and cook for 2 minutes on the second side. Because of the sugar in the dough, the piroshki will turn a dark brown. Monitor the heat of the oil and adjust it as necessary. Remove the piroshki from the oil with tongs, letting the excess oil drain back into the pan, and place the piroshki on the paper towels to drain further. Cook the remaining piroshki 4 at a time.

SERVE THE PIROSHKI warm with the sour cream. Eat the piroshki out of hand, or with a knife and fork. They can be cooked up to 1 to 2 hours ahead. To reheat, put the piroshki in a single layer on unlined baking sheets and reheat in a preheated 400°F oven for 5 to 10 minutes.

Storing

Piroshki can be frozen when completely cool. Arrange them in a single layer on a large baking sheet, and freeze until solid. Transfer to heavy-duty resealable plastic bags and freeze for up to 1 month. To serve, thaw the piroshki completely in their wrapping, then unwrap, arrange on baking sheets, and reheat in a preheated 350°F oven for 10 to 15 minutes.

Cornish Splitters

MAKES 6 BISCUITS

MARETH GUNSTREAM LEARNED THIS RECIPE *from her grandmother, Lilian Chapman, who immigrated to Canada from Cornwall, England. These are easy and quick-to-make large yeasty batter biscuits with an English muffin–like texture. Because of the working schedules of the men in Mareth's family, late dining was common. Serving big spreads of food at 10 p.m. was the norm, and splitters were almost always part of the feast. "I thought that was the time everyone had dinner," Mareth said. "It wasn't until much later I found out how weird this seemed to others." But there's nothing odd about these splitters. They are great at any time of the day—or night!*

For breakfast or brunch, split them while hot and spread with butter or jam. Or let them cool and fill them with anything you like for a luncheon sandwich. They also make excellent dinner rolls. Figure on about an hour from the time you make the batter until the splitters are ready to serve.

2 cups all-purpose flour

2 tablespoons unsalted butter, at room temperature

2 packages (1½ tablespoons) instant yeast

2 tablespoons granulated sugar

1 cup whole or low-fat milk, heated until hot (120° to 130°F)

¼ teaspoon salt

IN A MEDIUM BOWL, stir together the flour and butter with a wooden spoon until the mixture is crumbly. Stir in the yeast, sugar, and hot milk. Beat with the spoon to make a thick batter, then beat in the salt. Beat for 1 to 2 minutes more, until smooth. Let the batter stand uncovered at room temperature for 45 minutes. It will become very bubbly and will rise slightly.

WHILE THE BATTER RESTS, adjust an oven rack to the center position and preheat the oven to 400°F. Coat a large baking sheet (18 × 12 × 1 inch) lightly with cooking spray.

WHEN THE BATTER IS READY, spoon 6 large gobs onto the prepared pan, spacing them about 2 inches apart. Each blob will be about 3 inches across.

BAKE FOR ABOUT 15 MINUTES, until the splitters are pale golden brown and spring back when pressed gently in the center. Serve hot, warm, or at room temperature. These should be eaten the day they're made.

Limpa

MAKES 1 LARGE ROUND LOAF

THIS CLASSIC LIGHT-TEXTURED SCANDINAVIAN LOAF, *flavored with orange zest, anise, and cardamom, is an all-purpose bread you will be glad to have on hand. It is especially delicious warm, with butter. It also makes excellent sandwiches, particularly with cheese and deli meats, and great toast.*

I learned this recipe from Dorothy Crocker, whose uncle used to make the bread. "He always baked the bread free-form on a sheet, never in a loaf pan," Dorothy said. "I love the contrast of the crisp crust with the bread's soft insides," she added. However, Dorothy's uncle was secretive about his recipes, and it has taken Dorothy many years of experimenting to come up with this version, the closest yet to what she remembers eating as a child.

1²/₃ cups water

3 tablespoons unsulphured molasses

3 tablespoons unsalted butter

2¾ cups bread flour or unbleached all-purpose flour, plus more as needed

1½ cups dark rye flour

1 package (2¼ teaspoons) instant yeast

1 teaspoon salt

Finely grated zest of 1 large orange

2 teaspoons anise seed

1 teaspoon ground cardamom

TO MAKE THE DOUGH, heat the water, molasses, and butter in a small saucepan over low heat until the butter is melted and the temperature registers between 120° and 130°F on an instant-read thermometer. Remove the pan from the heat.

To mix the dough using a stand mixer, combine both flours and the yeast in the mixer bowl. Stir in the salt, orange zest, anise seeds, and cardamom. Add the hot liquid and stir with a wooden spoon to make a stiff dough. Let stand for 10 minutes, then attach the dough hook and knead on medium speed for 5 to 8 minutes until the dough is smooth, elastic, and still slightly sticky. It may just pull away from the side of the bowl. Transfer the dough to a lightly floured surface and knead briefly until smooth but just slightly tacky.

To mix the dough by hand, combine both flours and the yeast in a large bowl. Stir in the salt, orange zest, anise seeds, and cardamom. Add the hot liquid and stir with a wooden spoon to make a stiff dough. Let stand for 10 minutes, then lightly flour your work surface and scrape the dough onto it. Knead for about 8 minutes, until the dough is smooth, elastic, and still a bit sticky. Avoid the temptation to add more flour. The dough should be moist.

WASH AND DRY THE BOWL. Lightly coat it with vegetable oil or cooking spray. Shape the dough into a ball, place it into the bowl, and turn to coat all over. Cover the bowl tightly with plastic wrap and let the dough rise until doubled in size, about 45 minutes. When you press a finger into the dough and remove it, the depression will remain.

LIGHTLY FLOUR YOUR WORK SURFACE and turn the dough out onto it. Pat gently to remove large air bubbles, and shape the dough into a smooth ball: cup your hands around the dough and rotate it on your work surface to develop the dough's surface tension. Pinch the underside of the dough firmly to seal. Line a baking sheet with a silicone baking pan liner or coat it with cooking spray. Place the dough seam side down on the pan and cover loosely with a sheet of plastic wrap lightly coated with cooking spray. Let rise until not quite doubled in size, 30 to 45 minutes (see Note).

MEANWHILE, ADJUST AN OVEN RACK to the lower third position and preheat the oven to 450°F. When ready to bake, spritz the walls of the oven with water. Uncover the loaf, place the pan in the oven, and spritz the walls again with water. Immediately close the oven door and bake for 25 to 30 minutes, until the bread is well browned and sounds hollow when rapped on the bottom. An instant-read thermometer inserted into the center of the loaf should read 200°F. Cool the loaf completely on a wire rack, and cut the bread with a sharp serrated knife.

Storing

The bread keeps well at room temperature for several days. To freeze, place the cooled loaf in a heavy-duty resealable plastic bag and freeze for up to 2 weeks. Thaw the bread in its wrapping, then unwrap, set on a baking sheet, and refresh in a preheated 325°F oven for 10 minutes.

Note

If you have a baking stone, place the loaf seam side down onto a sheet of cooking parchment, cover it, and let it rise as directed above. As soon as you have shaped the dough, place the stone on an oven rack in the lower third position and turn the oven on to 450°F. When ready to bake, spritz the walls of the oven with water, uncover the loaf, and slide it on its parchment onto a wooden baker's peel or an upturned cookie sheet. Slip the loaf and parchment onto the baking stone and close the oven door. In 2 minutes, spritz the walls of the oven again with water. Bake for 25 minutes or so, until the loaf tests done.

Whole Wheat Oatmeal Loaves

MAKES 2 LOAVES

SPONGE

- 3 cups whole wheat flour
- 1 cup unbleached bread flour or all-purpose flour
- 1⅓ cups (4 ounces) old-fashioned rolled oats
- 1 package (2¼ teaspoons) instant or active dry yeast
- 3 cups hot water (120° to 130°F)

FINAL DOUGH

- 1 tablespoon salt
- 3 cups unbleached bread flour or all-purpose flour, plus more as needed
- Untoasted wheat germ (optional)

THESE EARTHY, HEARTY LOAVES ARE A STAPLE *in many Norwegian homes. In Norway, they are simply called "homemade bread" (hjembakt brod). Kristine Soedal, a great-granddaughter of Norwegian immigrants, learned how to make this bread from her husband, Sven, a first-generation immigrant, and from her mother-in-law, who still lives in Norway. Even with today's hectic lifestyles, bread baking is very important in Norwegian homes. Kristine says, "The Norwegians have a relationship to bread that is very different from ours." Bread is an important and integral part of Norwegian meals, and people have a respect and reverence for it, which is not the case with Americans.*

The dough is made in two stages. The first involves making a sponge, which is a wet batter that intensifies the yeast's flavor and also develops more yeast cells. After the sponge is allowed to rise, more flour is kneaded in to make the final dough, which is given a second rising before being shaped into loaves. This bread is great for all sorts of sandwiches, including open-faced ones (see Note), and it makes excellent toast.

TO MAKE THE SPONGE, in a large bowl combine the whole wheat flour, bread flour, oats, and yeast. With a wooden spoon, stir in the hot water and beat for 2 to 3 minutes. Cover the bowl tightly with plastic wrap and let the sponge rise until almost tripled in volume and very bubbly, about 2 hours.

TO FINISH THE DOUGH, beat the salt into the sponge. Gradually stir in 2½ cups of the flour to make a stiff, sticky dough. Sprinkle the remaining ½ cup flour on your countertop and scrape the dough onto it. Turn the dough to coat all surfaces with flour, and knead the dough to incorporate the flour. Continue kneading for 5 to 8 minutes, until the dough is

smooth, elastic, and only slightly sticky. Add small amounts of additional flour as necessary, but don't overdo it; the dough should still be slightly sticky at the end of kneading.

LIGHTLY COAT a large bowl with vegetable oil or cooking spray. Add the dough and turn to coat all surfaces. Cover tightly with plastic wrap and let the dough rise until doubled in size, about 1½ hours. When you press a fingertip into the dough and withdraw it, the depression should remain.

GREASE two 9 × 5 × 3–inch loaf pans or coat them with cooking spray. Turn the dough out onto your work surface and pat it gently to deflate. Divide the dough in half and shape each portion into a loaf, pinching any seams firmly to seal. For textural contrast and a nutritional boost, roll one or both loaves in untoasted wheat germ, if desired. Put the loaves seam side down into the pans and coat the tops of the loaves lightly with cooking spray. Cover loosely with plastic wrap. Adjust an oven rack to the lower third position and put the loaves in the oven, but do not turn the oven on. Let the loaves rise until their centers have domed up and are 1½ to 2 inches above the rims of the pans, about 1½ hours.

REMOVE THE PLASTIC WRAP, and turn the oven on to 400°F. Bake for 45 minutes to 1 hour, until a loaf sounds hollow when thumped on the bottom. An instant-read thermometer inserted into the center of a loaf should register 200°F. If in doubt, err on the side of longer baking; if underbaked, the bread will have a doughy texture. When the loaves are fully baked, remove them from their pans and set them upright on a wire cooling rack. Cool completely, at least 3 to 4 hours, before slicing.

Storing

Stored in plastic bags, this bread keeps well for several days at room temperature. The loaves can also be frozen in heavy-duty resealable plastic bags for up to 1 month. Thaw completely in the wrapping, then unwrap and slice.

Note

Here are some open-faced sandwich toppings Kristine recommends; use thin slices of bread for these.

- Spread the bread with butter and thinly sliced ham or other deli meat. Garnish with sliced tomatoes and cucumber.

- Spread the bread with butter and top with Havarti cheese and strips of red or orange bell pepper or sliced grapes, pears, or apples.

- Spread the bread with cream cheese mixed with garlic and chopped dill. This is good with sliced kiwi on top.

- Spread the bread with butter and top with sliced hard-boiled eggs and pickled herring.

Fatayar

MAKES 20 INDIVIDUAL PIES

FOOD WRITER MAUREEN ABOOD LEARNED HOW TO MAKE *these fragrant cinnamon-laced Lebanese lamb and onion pies from her grandmother. Maureen fondly recalls how her grandmother, who used about twenty-five pounds of flour a week for baking, made the dough and filling and shaped the pies. Fatayar are eaten out of hand as part of a meal or as a snack on their own. They are relatively quick and easy to put together once the dough has risen.*

For 20 pies, you need half the recipe for Basic Lebanese Yeast Dough (page 182). If you make the full recipe of dough, you can use some of it for Talami (page 183) and the rest for Lebanese Fried Dough (page 49)—that is what Maureen did when she taught me these recipes. (If you want to make 40 pies, use the full recipe of dough and double the filling amounts.) Ground beef can be substituted for the lamb. If serving fatayar as a meal, accompany with a green salad, a plate of olives, and a bowl of yogurt. Fatayar are especially delicious with a small spoonful of yogurt spooned onto them before each bite. Maureen likes Fage brand Greek yogurt.

DOUGH

½ recipe Basic Lebanese Yeast Dough (page 182), allowed to rise once

LAMB FILLING

2 tablespoons salted butter

½ cup pine nuts

2 tablespoons olive oil

1 large yellow onion, coarsely chopped

1¼ pounds ground lamb

1 teaspoon ground cinnamon

1½ teaspoons salt, or to taste

½ teaspoon freshly ground black pepper, or to taste

¼ cup full-fat yogurt

4 tablespoons (½ stick) salted butter, melted and kept warm

Plain yogurt for serving

TURN THE RISEN DOUGH OUT onto a lightly floured work surface and pat it to deflate the bubbles. Divide the dough into 20 equal pieces (1½ to 1¾ ounces each). Shape into balls and space them slightly apart on the countertop. Cover loosely with a kitchen towel.

TO MAKE THE FILLING, melt the butter in a small skillet over medium heat, add the pine nuts, and cook, stirring constantly, for 3 to 5 minutes, until toasted a deep golden brown. Remove from the heat and set aside to cool.

IN A LARGE SKILLET, heat the olive oil over medium heat. Add the onion and cook, stirring, for 2 to 3 minutes, just until translucent. Add the lamb and break it up into small pieces with a wooden spoon. Cook, stirring occasionally, until the lamb is browned, about 5 minutes. Add the cinnamon, salt, and pepper and cook, stirring, for 1 to 2 minutes longer. Remove the pan from the heat and set aside until the lamb is just warm, about 20 minutes, then stir in the pine nuts and yogurt. Taste and adjust the seasoning with more salt and pepper if necessary.

TO SHAPE THE PIES, lightly coat two 18 × 12 × 1–inch baking sheets with vegetable oil or cooking spray. Dust a ball of dough (the dough will have risen a bit) with flour and pat it out to a 3- to 4-inch circle, then roll to a thin 5- to 6-inch oval, about ⅛ inch thick. Turn the oval if necessary so a narrow end is nearest you. Mound a scant ¼ cup of filling in the center of the oval and pat the filling into an oval so that the filling comes to about ½ inch from the ends and 1 inch or so from the sides. Bring the sides of dough over the filling to meet in the center of the pie and pinch the center firmly to seal, then continue pinching the dough to the end of the pie farthest from you. Bring the end of dough closest to you up to meet the dough in the middle of the pie and pinch together, then pinch the remaining open edges of dough together firmly to seal. The pie will be the shape of an isosceles triangle with a triangular seam the shape of an inverted Y. Set it seam side up on a prepared baking sheet. Repeat with the remaining dough and filling, arranging 10 pies on each baking sheet, 1 to 2 inches apart. Cover the pans loosely with kitchen towels.

ADJUST TWO OVEN RACKS so one is on the lowest shelf and one is in the center position and preheat the oven to 450°F.

UNCOVER ONE PAN of fatayar (leave the remaining pan covered with the towel). If any of the seams are opening, repinch them closed. Put the pan on the lower oven shelf and bake for about 20 minutes, until the pies are nicely browned on their bottoms. Shift the pan to the center position and bake 8 to 10 minutes more, until the fatayar are a rich golden brown. Remove the pan from the oven and brush the hot fatayar lightly with half of the melted butter. Repeat the repinching with the remaining pan of fatayar, bake, and brush with the remaining butter.

SERVE HOT, warm, or at room temperature, with yogurt for spooning onto the fatayar.

Storing

Baked fatayar can be frozen when completely cool. Set the fatayar on baking sheets and freeze until solid. Pack the frozen pies into heavy-duty resealable plastic bags and freeze for up to 2 weeks. To reheat, thaw the fatayar completely in their bags, then arrange them on a baking sheet and heat in a preheated 325°F oven for 15 to 20 minutes, until piping hot.

Kleecha

MAKES 18 ROLLS

THESE EXOTICALLY SPICED SYRIAN BRAIDED DINNER ROLLS, *shaped into knots, circles, or braids, were a regular item on food scholar and former chef Ray Risho's dinner table. He remembers his Damascus-born mother, Mary, making dozens of them at a time. "She'd start with 5 pounds of flour and go on from there." For a more manageable yield, Ray's wife, Susie, who learned how to make kleecha from Mary, scaled the recipe down by two-thirds.*

For freshness and flavor, Susie grinds whole mahlab seeds (the pits of a particular kind of black cherry) with a mortar and pestle. Alternatively, you can use ground mahlab; keep it stored in the freezer or refrigerator. You can find mahlab and other spices in Middle Eastern markets or order them by mail (see Sources, page 341).

These breads are delicious when warm, split, and spread with butter. They are also great soppers of gravies and sauces, and they make terrific sandwiches filled with deli meats and cheese.

DOUGH

- 1 package (2¼ teaspoons) active dry yeast
- 2 teaspoons whole mahlab seeds, ground, or 2 teaspoons ground mahlab
- 1¼ cups warm water (105° to 115°F)
- 8 tablespoons (1 stick) salted butter
- ⅓ cup vegetable oil
- 5 cups unbleached all-purpose flour, plus more as needed

- ⅓ cup granulated sugar
- 2 teaspoons nigella seeds (also called black caraway seeds)
- 2 teaspoons untoasted sesame seeds
- 2 teaspoons anise seeds
- ¾ teaspoon ground cloves
- ¾ teaspoon freshly grated nutmeg
- 1 teaspoon salt
- 1 large egg, lightly beaten, for egg wash

TO MAKE THE DOUGH, in a small bowl stir together the yeast, mahlab, and ¼ cup of warm water. Let stand for about 10 minutes, until the yeast is dissolved.

MEANWHILE, in a small saucepan, melt the butter over low heat. Stir in the oil. The mixture should feel warm, not hot; the temperature should be no higher than 120°F when tested with an instant-read thermometer. Remove from the heat.

To mix the dough by hand, in a large bowl combine the flour, sugar, nigella, sesame seeds, anise seeds, cloves, nutmeg, and salt. Make a well in the center and add the yeast

and butter mixtures and the remaining 1 cup warm water. Stir with a wooden spoon to make a cohesive dough. Lightly flour your work surface, turn the dough out, and knead for several minutes, until it is firm and is no longer sticky. Avoid adding too much flour—the dough should feel supple and elastic.

To mix the dough with a stand mixer put the flour, sugar, nigella, sesame seeds, anise seeds, cloves, nutmeg, and salt into the mixer bowl. Add the yeast and butter mixtures and the remaining 1 cup water. Stir with a wooden spoon to make a moist dough. Attach the dough hook and knead on medium-low speed for 5 to 8 minutes, until the dough cleans the sides of the bowl and is smooth, elastic, and no longer sticky. If necessary, adjust the consistency of the dough with small additions of flour or water.

COAT A LARGE BOWL with oil or with cooking spray. Form the dough into a ball, add it to the bowl, and turn to coat all surfaces. Cover the bowl tightly with plastic wrap and let the dough rise until almost tripled in size, about 2 hours. When you press a finger into the dough and withdraw it, the depression should remain.

TURN THE RISEN DOUGH OUT onto your work surface. It will be puffy and alive looking. If the dough feels sticky, lightly dust it with flour. Pat the dough to remove the air bubbles and to redistribute the yeast cells. With a pastry scraper or a sharp knife, divide the dough into 18 equal portions (about 2½ ounces each). Shape each into a ball and arrange on the work surface. Cover loosely with a kitchen towel and let the dough rest for about 10 minutes.

TO SHAPE THE ROLLS, line two 18 × 12 × 1–inch baking sheets with cooking parchment or coat them with cooking spray. You can shape each ball of dough into a single-stranded knot, a double-stranded circle, or a three-stranded braid. *To make a knot,* roll each ball of dough into an 8-inch-long rope, form a loop, and pull one end through the loop. *For a double-stranded circle,* divide each ball of dough in half, shape each

into an 8-inch-long rope, and entwine the two. Join the ends by pinching them together, and don't be concerned with neatness. *For a three-stranded braid,* divide each ball of dough into thirds and roll each one into a 7-inch-long rope. Pinch the three strands together at one end, braid them together, and pinch the ends; tuck the ends underneath the braid. Whatever shapes you decide on, place 9 rolls on each baking sheet, about 2 to 3 inches apart. Brush with the egg wash and let the rolls rise, uncovered, until they are not quite doubled in size, about 45 minutes.

MEANWHILE, adjust two oven racks to divide the oven into thirds and preheat the oven to 350°F.

BAKE FOR ABOUT 20 MINUTES, until the rolls are golden brown. Rotate the sheets top to bottom and front to back once during baking to ensure even browning. Transfer the baked rolls onto wire cooling racks. Serve warm or at room temperature.

Storing

The rolls can be frozen once completely cool. Place on baking sheets and freeze until solid. Transfer to heavy-duty resealable plastic bags and freeze for up to 2 weeks. To refresh, thaw the rolls in their bags, then pop them into a preheated 350°F oven for 10 minutes.

Basic Lebanese Yeast Dough

MAKES ABOUT 4½ POUNDS

MAUREEN ABOOD USES THIS VERSATILE DOUGH to make Fatayar (page 178), Talami (page 183), and Lebanese Fried Dough (page 49). This recipe makes enough for all three.

2 packages (1½ tablespoons) active dry yeast	2 teaspoons salt
2⅓ cups warm water (105° to 115°F)	½ cup corn oil
1 teaspoon granulated sugar	8 tablespoons (1 stick) unsalted butter, melted and still warm
8 cups unbleached all-purpose flour, plus more for kneading	

IN A SMALL BOWL, stir together the yeast, ⅓ cup of the warm water, and the sugar. Let stand for about 10 minutes, until the yeast is foamy and bubbly. In a large bowl, stir together the flour and salt. Make a large well in the center and add the yeast, oil, butter, and the remaining 2 cups warm water. Mix well with your hands, adding more water if necessary to make a soft, smooth cohesive dough. Sprinkle a little flour on your work surface, turn the dough out, and knead for 5 to 8 minutes, adding small amounts of flour if necessary, until the dough is supple, elastic, and no longer sticky.

LIGHTLY OIL A LARGE BOWL or coat with cooking spray. Add the dough and turn the dough to coat all surfaces. Cover the bowl tightly with lightly oiled or sprayed plastic wrap and let the dough rise at room temperature until it has tripled in volume, about 2 hours. The dough is now ready to use in a recipe.

Talami

MAKES 1 LARGE FLATBREAD; ABOUT 8 SERVINGS

AN ACCOMPLISHED COOK, *Lebanese-American food writer Maureen Abood has spent her life learning and living her Lebanese heritage. She has a large family and learned how to cook from several aunts, her grandmothers, and her mother. Bread, in particular, has a sacredness, which she learned from her grandmothers. "If bread fell on the floor, you picked it up and kissed it." I told Maureen that my Iraqi granny did the same thing, and that I perform the ritual every time I drop bread too.*

As I watched Maureen make this flatbread, I thought immediately of focaccia. And, in fact, this is a Lebanese focaccia. The dough is patted out onto a baking sheet and spread with zatar (a mixture of dried thyme, sumac, and toasted sesame seeds) and olive oil. After baking, the talami is cut into wedges and served at a meal or as a snack along with labneh, Lebanese yogurt, and a plate of olives.

If you cannot find zatar, you can make your own by mixing equal amounts of the three ingredients, or order it by mail (see Sources, page 341). Sumac is available in Middle Eastern markets and by mail-order (see Sources, page 341). To make a plain talami, see the variation at the end of the recipe.

- ¼ cup extra-virgin olive oil
- ¼ recipe Basic Lebanese Yeast Dough (page 182), allowed to rise once
- ¼ cup zatar

POUR 2 TABLESPOONS of the olive oil onto the center of an 18 × 12 × 1–inch baking sheet and spread it to form a 12-inch circle. Form the dough into a ball and center it on the oil. Let the dough rest for about 10 minutes.

IN A SMALL BOWL, stir together the remaining 2 tablespoons olive oil with the zatar to make a paste. Pat the dough into a 9- to 10-inch circle and spread with the zatar paste to within ½ inch of the edges. Let the talami stand, uncovered, while the oven preheats.

ADJUST AN OVEN RACK to the lower third position and preheat the oven to 450°F. Bake the talami until golden brown, 20 to 30 minutes; check the bottom of the talami to make sure it has browned. Transfer the talami to a wire rack and cool for about 10 minutes, then cut into wedges and serve.

Variation

For plain talami, simply brush the dough with olive oil, sprinkle with kosher salt, and bake.

Iraqi Meat Pies

MAKES 20 TO 24 INDIVIDUAL PIES

THESE EXOTIC SAVORY MEAT PIES, LAHAM AGEEN, *made with a yeast dough containing nigella seeds, mahlab (ground sour cherry pits), and anise, enclosing a beef filling seasoned with sumac and allspice, are eaten out of hand as a meal or as a snack. The sumac gives an inviting tartness to the spiced meat. Evelyn Delly usually bakes dozens at a time to have on hand in case a few of her seven grown children, their spouses, and many grandchildren drop by unexpectedly. "I never know who's going to come over or how hungry they'll be, but laham ageen always are a hit," she says laughing.*

Evelyn and her family, Chaldean Iraqis, immigrated into the United States in 1976. She learned how to cook from her mother, and she has been making these pies for more than forty years. In fact, the day I visit Evelyn, her entire brood and their offspring are there. As she speaks, the kids are happily munching away on their pies. "My daughters and daughters-in-law will carry on the tradition," she says proudly.

See Sources, page 343, for nigella seeds, mahlab, and sumac.

FILLING

- 2 pounds well-trimmed boneless top round
- 3 large yellow onions (1½ to 2 pounds total), finely chopped
- ¼ cup extra-virgin olive oil
- 1½ teaspoons salt
- 1 teaspoon freshly ground black pepper
- 1 teaspoon ground allspice
- 1½ tablespoons sumac
- ⅓ cup finely chopped flat-leaf parsley

DOUGH

- 4 cups unbleached all-purpose flour, plus more for kneading
- 1 package (2¼ teaspoons) rapid-rise or active dry yeast
- 1 teaspoon salt
- 1 teaspoon nigella seeds (also called black caraway seeds)
- 1 teaspoon ground mahlab
- 1 teaspoon anise seeds, ground in a spice grinder
- 8 tablespoons (1 stick) unsalted butter
- 1 cup plus 2 tablespoons cold water
- 1 large egg, lightly beaten with a pinch of salt for egg wash

TO MAKE THE FILLING, use a sharp chef's knife to cut the meat into a medium dice, about ½ inch (partially freezing the meat first will make this step easy). Pat the meat dry on paper towels.

BEFORE COOKING THE ONIONS, you need to rid them of excess juices. You can do this, in batches, in a potato ricer or wrapped in cheesecloth. Press or squeeze firmly to get out as much juice as you can. Another way is to put all the chopped onions into a colander in a sink, cover them with a small plate, set several pounds of canned foods on top, and let stand for 10 to 15 minutes. Grasp a handful or two of the onions and squeeze firmly to make sure there's little or no juice left.

HEAT THE OLIVE OIL in a large skillet over medium heat. Add the meat and stir to coat well with the oil, then cook uncovered, stirring occasionally, until any juices released by the meat have almost evaporated and the meat is tender. This should take about 30 minutes.

ADD THE ONIONS and cook over medium-low heat, stirring occasionally, until very tender, about 30 minutes more; cover the pan during the last 15 minutes of cooking. Stir in the salt, pepper, allspice, sumac, and parsley and cook for about 5 minutes more. Remove from the heat and set aside, uncovered, to cool. (The filling can be made 1 to 2 days ahead. When cool, cover and refrigerate; bring to room temperature before using.)

TO MAKE THE DOUGH, in a large bowl stir together the flour, yeast, salt, nigella seeds, mahlab, and anise; set aside.

MELT THE BUTTER in a small saucepan over medium-low heat. Remove the pan from the heat and add the cold water. The liquid should feel almost hot to your fingertip and the temperature should be between 120° and 130°F when tested with an instant-read thermometer. Add the liquid to the flour mixture and stir well with a wooden spoon to make a very soft, slightly sticky dough. Lightly flour your work surface, place the dough on it, and turn the dough to coat with flour. Knead for 5 to 8 minutes, until the dough feels soft, smooth, elastic, and only slightly sticky. If necessary, add a bit more flour, but be cautious here—it's better to err on the side of a wetter rather than a drier dough.

COAT A LARGE BOWL lightly with cooking spray or vegetable oil. Form the dough into a ball, put it into the bowl, and turn to coat all over. Cover the bowl tightly with plastic wrap and let the dough rise until doubled in size, about 2 hours. When you press a fingertip into the dough and withdraw it, the depression should remain.

TO SHAPE THE MEAT PIES, roll the dough on a lightly floured surface to a circle measuring between 15 and 16 inches in diameter. Using a sharp 3-inch round cutter, stamp out circles of dough, as close together as possible. Gather up the scraps, reshape them into a ball, and cover loosely with a towel; let rest for 15 minutes. Meanwhile, make pies with the cut dough and filling.

LINE TWO LARGE BAKING SHEETS (18 × 12 × 1 inch) with silicone baking pan liners or cooking parchment. Roll a circle of dough to about 5 inches in diameter. Place a scant ¼ cup of filling in the center of the dough and bring up the edges to cover the filling completely. Pinch the seams to seal in the filling. Put the meat pie seam side down onto a prepared baking sheet. Continue shaping the pies, placing them about

1 inch apart on the baking sheets. When you have used all the original dough circles, reroll the scrap dough, cut, and fill more pies. You should have 10 to 12 pies on each sheet. Cover them loosely with kitchen towels while you preheat the oven. The pies will rise slightly.

ADJUST TWO OVEN RACKS to divide the oven into thirds and preheat the oven to 425°F. Brush the pies with the egg wash and place the pans in the oven. Bake for about 25 minutes, until the pies are well browned on their tops and bottoms. Rotate the pans top to bottom and front to back once during baking to ensure even browning. Use a wide metal spatula to transfer the pies to wire cooling racks. Cool for 10 to 15 minutes, and serve warm.

Storing

To freeze the baked pies, when they are completely cool, set them on baking sheets and freeze until firm. Transfer to heavy-duty resealable plastic bags and freeze for up to 2 weeks. To reheat, thaw the pies unwrapped, then place them on baking sheets and pop into a preheated 350°F oven for about 15 minutes, or until very hot. Cool for a few minutes and serve.

Variation

Evelyn sometimes adds a combination of lightly sautéed chopped green, yellow, and red bell peppers to the cooked filling, about ½ cup of each.

Two Spices for Dough

When Evelyn made the dough for these pies, she added a spice mixture containing mahlab and one other spice. She had ground both spices herself and stored the mixture in the refrigerator. When I asked her what the second spice was, she knew it only by its Chaldean name, guznache. Her son, Arith, told me that it would be no problem finding out the English name for the spice and directed me to the shop where Evelyn buys her ingredients. To make sure the clerk in the shop knew what Evelyn used, she put some of her spice mixture into a plastic bag and enclosed a slip, written in Arabic, indicating what the spices were. So off my wife and I went to Haji Baba, an Arabic store in Tempe, Arizona, in search of the elusive spice.

When I presented Evelyn's bag to the clerk, he read the Arabic and said there was no indication what the spices were. I said, "What do you mean? She wrote down what she used." "Yes," he said, "but all it says is 'two spices for dough'." I was dumbfounded. I pulled out my cell phone, called Arith, and put him on the line with the sales clerk. But Arith also knew the spice only by its Chaldean name, so he was unable to learn its Arabic name from the clerk. The clerk then told me that I needed to go to an Iranian store to buy the spice, which sounded to me like "ha-WY-itch." Since the Iranian store was nowhere nearby, I gave up for the time being.

A couple of months later, after consulting with some Middle Eastern cooks, I learned that "ha-WY-itch" was a spice mixture containing paprika. But Evelyn's mixture had a greenish-brown cast, more like curry powder, and contained only the mahlab and one other spice. I next consulted with a Syrian colleague, Ray Risho, who suggested I contact Nawal Nasrallah, author of the authoritative *Delights From the Garden of Eden*. I dashed off an e-mail, and in less than an hour I learned the spice's true identity: anise.

Schwabisch Pretzels

MAKES 12 LARGE PRETZELS

AUTHENTIC BAVARIAN PRETZELS, *with their thin, tangy, crackly surfaces and thick chewy interiors, were something that Robert and Esther Nio dreamed of many times soon after immigrating to the United States from Germany in 1997. They also missed the hearty whole-grain breads of their homeland: dense, seedy breads, thinly sliced and spread with butter and eaten simply that way, or used for various sandwiches. After several years of making a living working for various business firms, and having four children, they decided to start their own bakery: Esther's German Bakery. Since neither of them had baked commercially, they needed to find a master baker. An ad they posted on the Internet brought them more than thirty applicants. One of them was Rudy Klopp. Rudy, born near Stuttgart in Bavaria, and his wife were working in Guatemala when he happened to run across Robert and Esther's ad. To be able to bake real German breads had been a dream of his, too.*

The bakery opened in Palo Alto, California, in April 2004, and it was a success from the very beginning. There is no storefront—the breads are sold to restaurants and at farmers' markets. It was Rudy who developed their recipes, including this one for Schwabisch pretzels. What follows is a home version of what he makes at the bakery. There the pretzels are topped with salt or various seeds—sesame, poppy, and pumpkin are the most popular. Rudy is generous with the seeds. He plops a pretzel top side down into a bowl of seeds so practically the entire surface gets coated.

A traditional step in making these pretzels is dipping them into a dilute solution (3%) of lye before baking. The pretzels are perfectly safe to consume, and there really is no substitute for this step. Many bakeries that make similar types of

DOUGH

- 1 package (2¼ teaspoons) active dry yeast
- 4 tablespoons warm water (105° to 110°F) if using barley malt syrup, 6 tablespoons if using malt powder
- 4½ cups unbleached all-purpose flour
- ¼ cup light rye flour
- 4 teaspoons sea salt
- 2 tablespoons diastatic malt powder (see Sources, page 341) or 2 tablespoons barley malt syrup
- 3 tablespoons cold unsalted butter
- 1½ cups cool water (75°F)

LYE OR BAKING SODA BATH

- 1 ounce (2 tablespoons) food-grade sodium hydroxide pellets (see Sources, page 342) or 2 tablespoons baking soda
- 4 cups cool tap water

  About 1 cup coarse salt or pumpkin seeds, poppy seeds, and sesame seeds

pretzels dip them into a baking soda bath, but baking soda is sodium bicarbonate and lye is sodium hydroxide—two entirely different substances. The lye gives the pretzels a unique, glossy sheen, a crackly surface, and a special tangy taste that cannot be duplicated with baking soda. However, that said, if you do not wish to go to the trouble of buying and using lye, I've given instructions for substituting a baking soda bath. The pretzels will be dark on the outside and still be chewy on the inside.

At the bakery, the dough is shaped into pretzels soon after kneading, without allowing the dough to rise. Rudy explained that because the dough contains diastatic malt powder, a ready source of carbohydrate, the yeast cells can begin multiplying right away before they start using the carbohydrates in the flour for nourishment. Adding sugar also works, but that would sweeten the dough, which is not desirable. Barley malt syrup will also work, and I've given instructions for using it too. I've made the pretzels at home both the way Rudy does and also after allowing the dough to rise once before shaping. The pretzels have a greater depth of flavor and a slightly chewier texture if the dough has this preliminary rise, so that is what I regularly do.

At the bakery, Rudy always holds back a small portion—5 to 6 percent by weight—of the dough to add to the next day's batch of pretzels. This is an old technique, and the "old dough" imparts a unique tang to the new batch, along with some extra yeast cells. When you make the dough for the first time, Rudy suggests adding ¼ cup of light rye flour to the dough for that tang, as I describe below. Then reserve a few ounces of dough from your first batch of pretzel dough in a resealable plastic bag and refrigerate it for up to 3 days, ready to add to your dough the next time. If you don't plan on making pretzels anytime soon after your first foray, you can freeze the reserved dough for up to 1 month. Thaw it overnight in the refrigerator.

See the companion DVD for a video demonstration of pretzel making.

TO MAKE THE DOUGH, sprinkle the yeast into the 4 or 6 tablespoons warm water in a small bowl or cup. Stir well and let stand until the yeast is dissolved, about 10 minutes. Add the barley malt syrup, if using.

IN THE BOWL of a heavy-duty stand mixer, stir together both flours, the salt, and malt powder. Add the butter. Attach the flat beater and mix on low speed for 3 to 5 minutes, until the butter is in very tiny pieces and thoroughly incorporated into the flour. Add the dissolved yeast and cool water and mix for a few seconds, until the dough masses onto the beater. The dough will be very firm and there may be particles of flour that have not been completely mixed into the dough. Cover the bowl with a kitchen towel and let the dough rest for 10 minutes.

SWITCH TO THE DOUGH HOOK. Because the dough is so firm, begin kneading on medium speed to get it moving rapidly around the mixer bowl. When it looks as if it will mass around the hook, reduce the speed to low and knead the dough for about 8 minutes, until it is smooth and elastic and feels quite firm; it will not be at all sticky. Remove the dough from the mixer and knead it briefly on your work surface to feel its suppleness and firmness.

WASH AND DRY THE BOWL and replace the dough in the bowl. Cover tightly with plastic wrap and allow the dough to rise until it has doubled in size, 1½ to 2 hours. When you press a finger into the dough and withdraw it, the depression should remain.

DISLODGE THE DOUGH from the bowl with a dough scraper and set it on an unfloured work surface. Knead briefly. Divide the dough into twelve 3-ounce portions with a bench scraper or sharp knife. Reserve the extra dough in a resealable plastic bag and refrigerate or freeze it to use in your next batch of pretzels. Roll each portion of dough into a ball and set the balls slightly apart on your work surface. Cover them with a kitchen towel and let the dough rest for 15 to 30 minutes. Line two large baking sheets (18 × 12 × 1 inch) with cooking parchment.

TO SHAPE THE PRETZELS, roll a ball of dough under your palms on an unfloured surface, preferably wood, until it is about 23 inches long, with a fat middle, almost 1 inch thick, that gradually tapers to a thickness of about ⅛ inch at both ends. If the dough resists and retracts, set it aside, covered with a kitchen towel, and work on another piece of dough. In a few minutes, the first piece of dough will behave just as you want it to. When the dough is the proper shape and length, keep your hands on the ends for 2 to 3 seconds, just to hold the dough in its stretched position briefly, then lift the dough by its ends (A), give it a quick twist in the air (B), and set it down on your countertop. Pinch the two thin ends of dough firmly onto the arms of the pretzel (C). On your first few tries, you may feel this is a hopeless proposition, but with practice it goes pretty fast. If you don't want to bother with these aerial gyrations, simply twist the pretzel into its proper shape on your countertop. Set the pretzel on one of the prepared sheets. Shape the remaining pretzels, placing 6 on each sheet, spacing them about 2 inches apart. Cover the pretzels loosely with kitchen towels and let them rise for about 30 minutes, just until they've increased in size by about half. Do not let them rise more than that, or they will be light and airy instead of dense and chewy. If in doubt, err on the side of underrising.

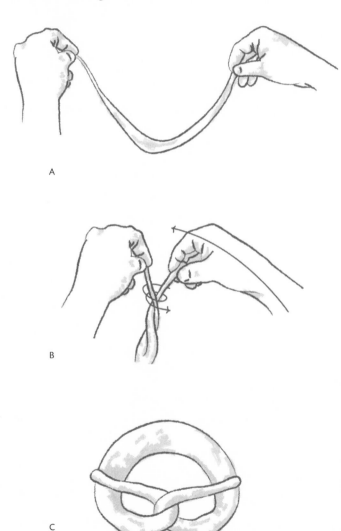

A

B

C

WHEN THE PRETZELS HAVE RISEN, place the pans in the freezer for 1 hour to firm the pretzels and make them easy to handle.

TO DIP AND COAT THE PRETZELS, (*if using lye, wear rubber gloves*), put the lye pellets in a shallow plastic, stainless steel, or glass pan measuring 12 × 8 × 2 inches or 8 × 8 × 2 inches; I use a plastic pan with a snap-on lid. Add the water and stir with a metal spoon to dissolve the lye. Wash all utensils thoroughly after using. *If using baking soda,* simply dissolve it in the water in one of the pans suggested. Lye will discolor wood, so put several thicknesses of newspaper on your countertop to protect it, and set the pretzel bath on the papers. (The lye bath can be reused several times; cover tightly between uses and store in a cool place. The baking soda bath should be made fresh for each baking.)

PUT THE COARSE SALT or the seeds in a small bowl large enough to contain a pretzel (or several small bowls if using more than one type of seeds).

REMOVE THE PRETZELS from the freezer. Dislodge 2 pretzels from the parchment, and put the pretzels into the bath you're using (using kitchen gloves if working with lye). They should be completely covered by the liquid. After 15 seconds, lift a pretzel out of the bath and let the excess liquid drain back into the bath. If salting the pretzel, set it back on the parchment-lined baking sheet top side up and sprinkle lightly with coarse salt. If coating with seeds, drop the dipped pretzel into the seeds, top side down, then lift the coated pretzel out of the seeds and replace it seed side up on its baking sheet. Continue in this way until all the pretzels are dipped and salted or seeded.

ONE OF THE HALLMARKS of a Schwabisch pretzel is a slash mark on its fat middle. During baking, the slash expands, giving the pretzels a light-colored center. To slash the pretzels, let the dipped pretzels stand at room temperature for 10 to 15 minutes, just to soften them slightly making them easy to cut. With one hand (gloved if the pretzels were dipped in lye) holding the pretzel in place, and the other holding a razor blade, make a deep cut into the side of each pretzel in a sweeping C motion (you need not work swiftly). Make the cut in an arc and go into the dough a good ¼ inch or more. Let the pretzels stand at room temperature until they are completely thawed, about 1 hour.

ADJUST TWO OVEN RACKS to divide the oven into thirds and preheat the oven to 450°F.

PUT THE PANS in the oven and bake for 5 minutes. Reduce the heat to 425°F and bake 5 minutes more. Open the oven door and quickly rotate the pans top to bottom and back to front, then continue baking for about 8 minutes more, until the pretzels are well browned and cooked through. Remove the pans from the oven and immediately, with pot holders, peel the pretzels off the parchment and set them on wire cooling racks. Cool completely before serving.

Note

To dispose of the lye bath safely, add an equal volume of distilled white vinegar to the lye to neutralize it, and flush it down the toilet.

Syrian Savory Bracelets (Kahk)

MAKES 30 RINGS

THESE CRUNCHY RINGS OF DOUGH *flavored with anise, sesame, and black caraway are eaten as a snack any time of day in many Middle Eastern homes. Also known as kahk, they go back to antiquity. Noted Mediterranean food authority Claudia Roden says the name appears in the Talmud and in medieval Arab manuscripts, but we have no idea what those kahk were like. My Iraqi grandmother had a supply on hand all the time, and I adored munching them as a child when I came home from school. The loud crunch of each bite especially thrilled me. This recipe is from retired chef Ray Risho, but the kahk ignited memories of the ones my Granny made (see her recipe on page 114).*

Typically one makes kahk by the dozens because they keep so well. I've reduced the quantity to a manageable amount, but you can double the recipe if you want to have a supply for two or three weeks. Kahk are meant to be dry and crunchy throughout, and it will take at least a week for that to happen. When first baked, they're dry on the outside and a bit soft on the inside. Kahk are excellent with all sorts of drinks.

1 package (2¼ teaspoons) active dry yeast	¼ cup room-temperature water
1 teaspoon mahlab seeds, ground, or 1 teaspoon ground mahlab (see Sources, page 343)	2½ cups unbleached all-purpose flour, plus more if needed
¼ cup warm water (105° to 115°F)	2 teaspoons toasted sesame seeds
4 tablespoons (½ stick) salted butter	1 teaspoon anise seeds
2 tablespoons olive oil	1 teaspoon nigella seeds (also called black caraway)
	¾ teaspoon salt

IN A SMALL BOWL, stir together the yeast, mahlab, and warm water. Set aside for about 10 minutes, until the yeast is dissolved.

MEANWHILE, in a small saucepan, melt the butter over low heat. Remove the pan from the heat and stir in the oil and ¼ cup water.

IN A LARGE BOWL, stir together the flour, sesame seeds, anise seeds, nigella, and salt. Make a well in the center and add the yeast and butter mixtures. Stir well to make a firm, cohesive dough. The dough may look shaggy and slightly dry, but resist the temptation to add more water. Instead, press the dough together with your hands in the bowl. If the dough forms a firm mass that is not sticky and holds together, that's what you want. If the dough is too dry, add more water by droplets, and work it in until the dough is firm and holds together.

PLACE THE DOUGH on an unfloured work surface and knead it for a few minutes, until it is smooth, elastic, and not sticky. If the dough feels tacky, dust it lightly with flour as necessary. Lightly oil a large bowl or coat it with cooking spray. Shape the dough into a ball, place it in the bowl, and turn to coat all surfaces. Cover the bowl tightly with plastic wrap and let the dough rise until it has doubled in size, about 1½ hours. When you press a finger into the dough and withdraw it, the depression should remain.

TURN THE DOUGH OUT onto an unfloured surface and pat it gently to deflate the bubbles. Pat the dough into a 6 × 5–inch rectangle, and cut it into 1-inch pieces with a sharp knife. Separate the pieces and cover them loosely with a kitchen towel. Let the dough rest for about 10 minutes.

ADJUST AN OVEN RACK to the center position and preheat the oven to 400°F. Line two large baking sheets (18 × 12 × 1 inch) with cooking parchment or silicone baking pan liners.

ROLL ONE PIECE OF DOUGH into a 5-inch-long rope about ½ inch thick. Form it into a circle, overlapping the ends by about 1 inch, and pinch firmly to form a ring about 2 inches across. Set the ring on one of the prepared baking sheets. Continue making rings of dough until you have 15 rings on the sheet, spaced about 1 inch apart.

BAKE THE KAHK for 20 to 25 minutes, until they are a light golden brown. The kahk will expand just a bit during baking and the center holes will be slightly smaller. Cool the kahk on wire racks.

WHILE THE FIRST BATCH BAKES, shape the rest of the kahk, arranging them on the second baking sheet. When the first batch is baked, bake the second sheet.

Storing

When they are completely cool, store the kahk in airtight containers at room temperature for 2 to 3 weeks. Or, to freeze, seal in heavy-duty resealable plastic bags and freeze for up to 1 month. Thaw them in their bags, then unwrap, set them on a large baking sheet, and refresh in a preheated 300°F oven for 10 minutes. Cool completely before serving.

6 Sweet Yeast Breads

SWEET YEAST BREADS, UNLIKE COOKIES, which are baked worldwide, are more likely to come from the ovens of northern cultures than southern ones. True, sourdough yeast breads—made by "capturing" wild yeast cells borne by the winds—were baked more than 5,000 years ago by the Egyptians, but the breads made in the Middle East and in other southern climates tend to be savory rather than sweet. So practically all of the breads in this chapter come from northern Europe: Finland, Germany, Poland, Slovenia, Sweden, and Russia. The one exception is Portuguese sweet bread.

All the recipes here contain, in addition to yeast, the four basic ingredients of sweet breads: sugar, butter, flour, and eggs. Flavorings and spices vary according to the country of origin. Many of the doughs begin with a sponge, a thick batter of flour, liquid, a bit of sugar, and yeast. Making a sponge provides food for the yeast cells, helping them to increase in number and develop the bread's flavor. Once the final dough is made, the recipes take off in all directions. Some are shaped by hand into buns, such as the cardamom coffee rolls and pulla, others are rolled and filled with poppy seeds (makowiec), nuts (potica), or chocolate (chocolate babka). A few of the richer doughs are formed into plain large loaves (massa sovada) or into loaves containing nuts and dried fruits (stollen and kulich). The two sweet yeast cakes are topped with sugar and almonds (bienenstich) or a crumbly mix of sugar, flour, and butter (streuselkuchen). And one bread, particularly loved by children, is a Pennsylvania Dutch version of monkey bread (pluckets), balls of dough dipped in melted butter, rolled in cinnamon sugar, and layered and baked in a tube pan.

Why did I choose these particular breads? Kulich, the tall sweet Russian cake served at Easter, was something I grew up with, and I looked forward to eating it every year. I sought out the other recipes because I had heard of them or had eaten versions of them in my travels and wanted to learn how to make them. Two Polish breads, in particular, held a fascination for me: babka, because of its shape and light texture, and makowiec, for its amazing amount of sweet poppy seed filling.

Most sweet yeast breads keep very well for days, sometimes weeks, at room temperature. And, for those of you who like to bake ahead, they can be frozen for a couple of months at least.

Babka

MAKES 1 BABKA; ABOUT 10 SERVINGS

BABKA IS A CAKE RICH WITH BUTTER AND EGGS *that may or may not contain yeast. The name means "grandmother" in Polish, and just why a babka is called a babka is pure speculation. Some say it is because the cake is so good only one's grandmother could have made it. Others say that the traditional mold the cake is baked in looks like the wide skirts a Polish grandmother was apt to wear. According to Robert and Maria Strybel, authors of* Polish Heritage Cookery, *"The only requirement for a cake to be called a babka is that it must be taller than it is wide and narrower at the top than at the bottom." To achieve this shape, many Polish bakers use a special babka tube pan, similar to a kugelhupf or Turk's head pan. But nowadays babkas may be baked in the more readily available Bundt pans or angel food cake pans, or even in loaf pans, springform pans, or brioche pans.*

Yeasted babka doughs may be flavored with vanilla, lemon, or another essence. Sometimes raisins are kneaded into the dough. I have also seen recipes where the dough is filled with fresh prune plums. In nonyeasted recipes, beaten egg whites are often folded into the batter to lighten the texture. Baking-powder batters may contain raisins, citron, figs, dates, currants, or candied orange peel. For texture and flavor, chopped walnuts, hazelnuts, or almonds also sometimes find their way into a babka. Cocoa and rum are favorite additions too, and let's not forget chocolate: see the variation that follows.

I learned this recipe from Carol Jalovec Lyons, the daughter of Polish immigrants, who bakes it regularly. She usually makes two babkas at a time, one to serve fresh and one to freeze for later use. She fills one with almond paste and brandy-soaked golden raisins, the other with finely ground chocolate and touches of almond paste and cinnamon. If you would like to do this, double the ingredients for the sponge and dough and make both fillings.

BRANDIED RAISINS

¾ cup golden raisins

⅓ cup brandy

SPONGE

¾ cup unbleached all-purpose flour

¾ cup whole milk

1 package (2¼ teaspoons) active dry or instant yeast

FINAL DOUGH

4 large egg yolks

6 tablespoons granulated sugar

½ teaspoon pure vanilla extract

½ teaspoon salt

1½ cups unbleached all-purpose flour, plus more as needed

6 tablespoons (¾ stick) unsalted butter, cut into tablespoon-sized pieces , at room temperature

ALMOND FILLING

6 ounces almond paste

1 large egg white

½ cup sliced almonds

1 large egg, beaten, for egg wash

The dough for this babka is made in two stages. For the first stage, called a sponge, a thick batter of flour, hot milk, and yeast is given a preliminary rise to increase the number of yeast cells and to help develop the yeast's flavor. To make the dough itself, egg yolks, more flour, and butter are added to the sponge. The yeasts in the sponge will help the egg-and-butter-rich dough rise efficiently. This dough is very soft and slightly sticky. Resist the temptation to add extra flour, or you run the risk of making the babka heavy and dry. A heavy-duty stand mixer will make quick work of the dough, but lacking that, you can make it with a large bowl, a sturdy wooden spoon, and elbow grease.

Carol always uses Solo brand almond paste for her babkas. I have had excellent results with both homemade almond paste (page 330) and with Solo and a newer brand from American Almond. Whichever you use, the almond paste must be moist and pliable.

Soak the raisins in the brandy before you begin the sponge to allow them to imbibe as much of the liquor as possible; this can even be done the night before.

You can serve babka at breakfast or brunch or as an afternoon pick-me-up. Although it is especially tender an hour or two out of the oven, you can wrap the completely cooled babka tightly in plastic wrap and it will be wonderful the next day too.

COMBINE THE RAISINS AND BRANDY in a small resealable bag or screw-cap jar and leave at room temperature for at least a few hours, or overnight.

TO MAKE THE SPONGE, put the flour into the bowl of a heavy-duty electric mixer or a large mixing bowl. Scald the milk in a small saucepan over medium heat—you will see steam rising from the surface and small bubbles around the edges. Pour the hot milk into the flour and whisk briskly until smooth. Measure the temperature of the batter with an instant-read thermometer. It should be between 120° and 130°F, no hotter; if it is too hot, let it cool slightly. Sprinkle on the yeast and whisk it in well, about 1 minute. Scrape the sides of the bowl and cover tightly with plastic wrap. Let the sponge rise until it has at least doubled in volume, 1½ to 2 hours. The surface of the sponge will be full of bubbles and it will look very alive.

TO MAKE THE DOUGH, in a medium bowl with a hand-held electric mixer, beat the egg yolks on medium-high to high speed until very thick and pale, about 5 minutes. Beating on medium speed, gradually add the sugar. Increase the speed to high and beat for 4 to 5 minutes, until the yolks are the consistency of mayonnaise. On low speed, beat in the vanilla and salt.

To mix the dough by hand, add the yolk mixture to the sponge and stir it in with a wooden spoon. Gradually stir in 1 cup of the flour. Beat for several minutes with the spoon to make a sticky, ropy dough. Add the butter pieces one at a time, beating until each is completely incorporated before adding the next. Continue beating for several minutes, until the dough is smooth and blistery. Gradually beat in the remaining ½ cup flour and beat with the spoon until it is smooth, shiny, elastic, and only slightly sticky.

To mix the dough with a stand mixer, add the yolk mixture to the sponge and beat it in on low speed with the flat beater, about 1 minute. On low speed, gradually add 1 cup of the flour, beating until smooth. Increase the speed to medium and beat for 4 to 5 minutes to make a sticky, ropy dough. Reduce the speed to medium-low and add the soft butter pieces one at a time, beating until each is completely incorporated before adding the next. Increase the speed to medium to medium-high and beat for 1 to 2 minutes more. At this point, the dough may clean the sides of the bowl. Scrape the bowl and beater and switch to the dough hook. With the machine on low, gradually add the remaining ½ cup flour. Increase the speed to medium and beat for 4 to 5 minutes, until the dough is smooth, shiny, elastic, and only slightly sticky.

LIGHTLY BUTTER a large bowl, preferably with straight sides, or coat with cooking spray. Scrape the dough into the bowl and turn to coat all surfaces. Cover the bowl tightly with plastic wrap. Let the dough rise until it has tripled in size, about 2 hours.

TO PREPARE THE FILLING, insert the metal blade into a food processor, break the almond paste into small pieces, and add them to the work bowl. Add the egg white and process to make a thick, pasty mixture, about 1 minute; set aside. Drain the raisins in a strainer set over a small bowl. (What to do with the liquid?—save it for making another babka, or mix it into a Coke and drink it.)

TO SHAPE THE BABKA, lightly flour your work surface. Gently dislodge the dough from the bowl with a large pastry scraper or rubber spatula and turn it out onto the work surface. The dough will be very soft, but it will be easy to work with. Dust the dough lightly with a bit more flour and pat it into a 12 × 6–inch rectangle. Roll it to a rectangle measuring about 17 × 10 inches. Check frequently to make sure the dough isn't sticking; if it is, dust it lightly with flour.

TURN THE DOUGH if neccessary so a 17-inch side is nearest you. Smear small gobs of the almond paste onto the dough, leaving a bit of space between smears and about ½ inch of dough uncovered along the 17-inch side farthest from you. Distribute the raisins and sliced almonds evenly over the almond paste and press on them gently with the palm of your hand so that they're embedded in the dough. Roll up the dough jelly-roll fashion, starting from the 17-inch side nearest you. Pinch the edges of the dough to seal, then twist the roll as if you were wringing out a towel, about 8 times— begin at the center of the roll and work your way to the ends. I'm not sure why, but this seems to distribute the filling more evenly in the babka; the twisting will also elongate the babka slightly.

COAT a 9-inch springform pan lightly with butter or with cooking spray. Shape the roll into a loose coil and lift it carefully into the pan. Don't make the coil tight, because the dough needs space to rise. The dough will half fill the pan. Coat the top of the dough lightly with cooking spray, cover the pan tightly with plastic wrap, and let the babka rise until it almost reaches the top of the pan, not quite doubling in size, about 1 hour.

ADJUST AN OVEN RACK to the lower third position and preheat the oven to 350°F. Uncover the babka and brush it with egg wash. Bake for 45 to 50 minutes, until the babka is well browned and a wooden skewer inserted into the center comes out clean. During baking, the babka will rise about ½ inch above the rim of the pan. Cool the babka in its pan on a wire rack for 30 minutes.

REMOVE the sides and bottom of the pan, and slide the babka off the pan bottom onto the wire rack. Serve the babka warm or at room temperature, cut into wedges with a serrated knife.

Storing

When it is completely cool, wrap the babka tightly in plastic wrap; it will keep perfectly at room temperature for 2 to 3 days. To freeze, place the wrapped babka in a heavy-duty resealable plastic bag, set it on a baking sheet, and freeze until firm, then remove the baking sheet. Babka freezes well for 2 to 3 weeks. Thaw the still-wrapped babka overnight at room temperature, then unwrap it, set it on a baking sheet, and refresh it in a preheated 300°F oven for about 20 minutes.

Variation

CHOCOLATE BABKA Omit the raisins (and brandy) and the almond filling. Prepare the dough as directed and let rise. To make the chocolate filling, put 4 ounces semisweet or bittersweet chocolate, coarsely chopped, into the work bowl of a food processor fitted with the metal blade and process until the chocolate is very finely chopped. Break 2 ounces almond paste into small pieces and add them to the chocolate, along with ½ teaspoon ground cinnamon. Process for about 30 seconds, until the almond paste is the same consistency as the chocolate. Transfer the filling to a small bowl. Roll out the dough as directed, and sprinkle the chocolate filling over the dough leaving about ½ inch of dough uncovered along the 17-inch side farthest from you. Press the chocolate gently into the dough with the palm of your hand to make sure it sticks to the dough. Shape the babka, let rise, and bake as directed.

German Yeast Fruit Kuchen

MAKES 1 LARGE TART; ABOUT 16 SERVINGS

GERMAN BAKING IS, PERHAPS, THE MOST INVENTIVE *when it comes to fruit tarts, or, as they are often called, kuchens. The concept is simple: a yeast dough containing butter and eggs is topped with the freshest in-season fruits, sprinkled with sugar, and baked. In some cases, a cooked custard is spread over the fruit before baking.*

Anna Lobonc, a native of the former Czechoslovakia, learned this recipe from her mother. Anna uses an electric mixer to prepare the yeast dough, which is tender and almost cake-like. The secret is to beat in some of the flour and then stir in the rest. You can use many kinds of fruit for this tart, but it is especially fine with black plums. The skin of the plums ranges from red to almost black, and the flesh is firm and not overly juicy. You can also make the tart with Italian prune plums, or apricots, or with a mixture of fruits: pitted sweet and sour cherries, blueberries, and thinly sliced plums are a good combination.

This kuchen is at its finest when freshly baked and should be eaten the day it is made. Prepare it for a large gathering when summer fruits are at their peak.

DOUGH

- ½ cup whole milk
- 1 package (2¼ teaspoons) instant or active dry yeast
- ⅓ cup granulated sugar
- 2½ cups unbleached all-purpose flour, plus more as needed
- 6 tablespoons (¾ stick) cold unsalted butter, cut into tablespoon-sized pieces
- Finely grated zest of 1 lemon
- 2 large eggs, at room temperature
- 2 large egg yolks, at room temperature

TOPPING

- 1½ to 2 pounds (6 to 8) black plums or a combination of fruits (see headnote)
- ⅔ cup granulated sugar

TO MAKE THE DOUGH, scald the milk in a small saucepan over medium heat—you will see steam rising from the surface of the milk and small bubbles forming around the edges. Remove the pan from the heat and set aside until the milk feels warm to your fingertip, about 10 minutes. An instant-read thermometer should register 110° to 120°F.

ADD THE YEAST and 1 teaspoon of the sugar to the milk and stir them in well. Let stand until the yeast is very foamy, about 10 minutes.

To mix the dough with a stand mixer, put 1½ cups of the flour, the butter, the remaining sugar, and the lemon zest into the mixer bowl. Attach the flat beater and beat on low speed for about 3 minutes, until the butter is cut into small pieces. Add the dissolved yeast, the eggs, and egg yolks and beat on medium speed for 3 minutes. Scrape the bowl and beater. Add the remaining 1 cup flour and beat it in on low speed just until incorporated, 1 to 2 minutes. The aim here is not to overactivate the gluten, or the dough will bake up too chewy. The dough will be wet and sticky. Scrape the bowl and beater.

To mix the dough by hand, put 1½ cups of the flour, the butter, the remaining sugar, and the lemon zest into a large bowl. Use a pastry blender or two knives to cut in the butter until the particles resemble coarse meal. Add the dissolved yeast, the eggs, and egg yolks and beat vigorously with a wooden spoon for several minutes, until the batter is thick and ropy. Stir in the remaining 1 cup flour. The dough will be wet and sticky. Scrape the sides of the bowl.

SPRINKLE 2 TABLESPOONS of flour over the dough and cover the bowl tightly with plastic wrap. Let the dough rise until doubled in size, 1 to 2 hours, depending on the warmth of your kitchen. Lightly flour your work surface. Dislodge the dough from the bowl with a pastry scraper, turn it out onto the work surface, and turn to coat all surfaces lightly with flour. Gently shape the dough into a ball. Cover loosely with a kitchen towel and let rest for 10 to 20 minutes.

PIT THE PLUMS and slice each half into 10 to 12 thin wedges.

LINE THE BOTTOM AND SIDES of a large baking sheet (18 × 12 × 1 inch) with heavy-duty foil, and fold the overhanging foil down around the sides of the pan. Butter the foil (do not use cooking spray—the dough must adhere to the foil). Roll the dough on a lightly floured surface to the size of the pan. Fold the dough in half, then into quarters, and place it in the pan. Unfold the dough and pat it gently to cover the bottom of the pan and extend about ⅛ inch up the sides. Prick the bottom of the dough at 1-inch intervals with a fork. Arrange the plum slices in neat slightly overlapping rows over the dough. Cover loosely with a kitchen towel and let rest for 20 minutes.

ADJUST AN OVEN RACK to the center position and preheat the oven to 350°F.

SPRINKLE THE SUGAR evenly over the plums. Bake for 30 minutes, or until the edges of the dough are golden brown. Lay a sheet of heavy-duty foil, shiny side up, loosely over the kuchen. Lower the thermostat to 300°F and bake for another 15 to 20 minutes, until the dough is completely cooked and the fruit is very tender.

REMOVE THE SHEET OF FOIL and set the pan on a wire cooling rack to cool for 10 minutes. Remove the kuchen from the pan, using the edges of the foil to help you. Set the kuchen on a countertop and loosen it from the foil with a long narrow metal spatula. Carefully slide the kuchen onto a large wire cooling rack. Cool completely before serving.

German Wedding Cakes — *jam-filled buns*

MAKES 24 INDIVIDUAL CAKES

THESE CAKES, MADE FROM A SOFT, RICH EGG-AND-BUTTER YEAST DOUGH, *can be filled with any kind of jam or preserve. Apricot is especially good (I use Solo brand). A Polish mixed fruit thick preserve containing rose hips (Krakus brand) is also excellent. Not traditional, but delicious nonetheless, is the "chocolate schmear" made by American Almond.*

Anna Lobonc's mother and grandmother made these fruit-filled streusel-topped pastries for wedding celebrations in the bucolic small town of Opava in the former Czechoslovakia, where Anna was born. Both of her parents were German, and because of the historic enmity between Gemany and Czechoslovakia, she and her family were expelled to Franconia, in southern Germany, when Anna was in her early teens. As an immigrant there, she longed for her home in Opava with its large garden and surrounding farmers' fields and forests. In 1955, she became an immigrant for the second time when she came to the United States. Now, living in rural Montana, she is surrounded by wilderness once again.

DOUGH

- ½ cup whole milk
- 1 package (2¼ teaspoons) rapid-rise or active dry yeast
- ⅓ cup granulated sugar
- 6 tablespoons (¾ stick) unsalted butter, at room temperature
- Finely grated zest of 1 lemon
- 2 large eggs, at room temperature
- 2 large egg yolks, at room temperature
- 2½ cups unbleached all-purpose flour, plus more as needed

STREUSEL

- ¾ cup unbleached all-purpose flour
- ⅓ cup confectioners' sugar
- 6 tablespoons (¾ stick) unsalted butter, cut into tablespoon-sized pieces, at room temperature

About 1 cup canned fruit fillings: apricot, prune, cherry, or raspberry (see headnote)

- 1 large egg yolk, beaten with 1 teaspoon water, for egg wash

TO MAKE THE DOUGH, scald the milk in a small saucepan over medium heat—you will see steam rising from the surface of the milk and small bubbles forming around the edges. Remove the pan from the heat and set it aside until the milk feels warm to your fingertip, about 10 minutes. An instant-read thermometer should register 110° to 120°F.

ADD THE YEAST and 1 teaspoon of the sugar to the milk and stir them in well. Let stand until the yeast is very foamy, about 10 minutes.

To mix the dough with a stand mixer, put the butter, lemon zest, and the remaining sugar in the mixer bowl and beat with the flat beater on medium speed for 2 to 3 minutes. Beat in the eggs one at a time, then beat in both the yolks. Beat in the yeast. The batter will be very liquid. Scrape the bowl and beater, add about half the flour, and beat for 2 minutes. Scrape the bowl, add the remaining flour, and beat on low speed for 2 minutes, just until the dough is smooth, soft, and still very sticky. Scrape the bowl and beater.

To mix the dough by hand, in a large bowl beat the butter, lemon zest, and the remaining sugar with a wooden spoon until smooth and creamy, 3 to 5 minutes. Beat in the eggs one at a time, then beat in both the yolks. Beat in the yeast. The batter will be very liquid. Gradually stir in the flour, beating until smooth. The dough will be smooth, soft, and still very sticky. Scrape the bowl and spoon.

SPRINKLE 2 TABLESPOONS FLOUR over the top of the dough and cover the bowl tightly with plastic wrap. Let rise until doubled in size, about 2 hours.

LIGHTLY FLOUR THE WORK SURFACE. Dislodge the dough from the bowl with a pastry scraper and turn it out onto the work surface. Shape the dough into a ball and cover it loosely with a kitchen towel. Let rest for 10 minutes.

MEANWHILE, make the streusel. Put the flour, confectioners' sugar, and butter into the work bowl of a food processor fitted with the metal blade. Pulse 5 or 6 times, then let the machine run a few seconds (no more!) until the ingredients begin to form large crumbly masses. Do not process beyond the crumb stage.

TO SHAPE the wedding cakes, take two 18 × 12 × 1–inch baking sheets. Either butter the sheets or line them with silicone baking pan liners or cooking parchment. Roll the dough into a circle about 18 inches in diameter and ⅛ inch thick. Dust the dough with flour as necessary to prevent sticking. With a sharp 3½- to 4-inch round cutter, stamp out 24 circles of dough. If you fall short, gather the dough scraps into a ball and, after a rest of 10 minutes, reroll and cut what you need. Place a rounded teaspoonful of filling in the center of one of the circles. Pick up the dough, holding it in the palm of your hand, and, with the other hand, bring the edges of the dough up over the filling in pleats and pinch firmly to seal. Turn the dough packet upside down, set it on a prepared sheet, and pat it to flatten it slightly. It will be about 2 inches across. Repeat with the remaining dough and filling, placing 12 wedding cakes about 2 inches apart on each sheet.

WITH A PASTRY BRUSH, paint the wedding cakes with a thin layer of egg wash. Press handfuls of the streusel mixture together to form larger clumps, then take a large pinch of crumbs and press it gently onto the top of each wedding cake. (Some loose crumbs will fall around the cakes—just leave them alone. During baking they'll toast up for a delicious nibble.) Let the cakes rise at room temperature, uncovered, for about 30 minutes. They will increase only a little in size.

ADJUST TWO OVEN RACKS to divide the oven into thirds and preheat the oven to 350°F.

BAKE FOR 20 TO 25 MINUTES, until the cakes are golden brown. Rotate the sheets top to bottom and front to back about halfway during baking to ensure even browning. Sometimes these cakes crack on their tops, allowing the filling to peek through—that's okay. Transfer the wedding cakes to wire cooling racks with a metal spatula. Cool completely before serving.

Storing

These are best very fresh, but day-old wedding cakes can be reheated for a few minutes in a 200°F oven. The wedding cakes can also be frozen. After they have cooled, set them on a baking sheet and freeze until solid. Transfer to heavy-duty resealable plastic bags and freeze for up to 2 weeks. Thaw them in their bags, then unwrap and refresh on a baking sheet in a preheated 325°F oven for 5 to 10 minutes.

Bienenstich

MAKES ONE 10-INCH CAKE, 8 TO 10 SERVINGS

LITERALLY TRANSLATED AS "BEE STING," *bienenstich is named for its sweet almond topping. The cake is sometimes split and filled with custard, but here it is simply served as is, the way Anna Lobonc learned how to make it in the former Czechoslovakia. Some recipes for bienenstich use baking powder instead of yeast, which gives the cake an entirely different texture. This is a fine cake to serve for afternoon coffee or tea. It is really at its best when very fresh, but it can be frozen.*

½ recipe German Yeast Dough (page 336), risen, deflated, shaped into a ball, and allowed to rest for 10 minutes

TOPPING

6 tablespoons (¾ stick) unsalted butter

¼ cup whole milk

½ cup granulated sugar

4 ounces (scant 1 cup) slivered almonds

1 teaspoon pure vanilla extract

BUTTER A 10-INCH SPRINGFORM PAN (do not use cooking spray; the dough must adhere to the pan bottom). Roll the dough to a 9-inch circle, about ¼-inch thick, and set it in the bottom of the pan. Pat the dough so it reaches the sides of the pan. Cover tightly with plastic wrap and let rise until doubled, about 1 hour.

WHILE THE DOUGH RISES, prepare the topping. Melt the butter in a small heavy saucepan over medium heat. Add the milk and sugar and bring to a boil. Add the almonds and cook, stirring occasionally, until the liquid is very thick and syrupy, about 5 minutes. Do not allow all the liquid to be absorbed, or the sugar will crystallize during cooling. Remove the pan from the heat and cool completely, then stir in the vanilla.

MEANWHILE, adjust an oven rack to the lower third position and preheat the oven to 350°F.

BECAUSE THE TOPPING is so thick, the best way to place it on top of the risen dough is with your fingers. Grab gobs of the cooled topping and carefully spread it as evenly as you can over the dough. Try not to let any topping slip between the edges of the dough and the sides of the pan.

BAKE FOR ABOUT 30 minutes, until the bienenstich is golden brown on top and a toothpick stuck into the center of the cake comes out clean. Cool the bienenstich in its pan on a wire rack for 20 minutes, then run the tip of a small sharp knife around the sides to release the cake. Remove the sides of the pan and cool the cake completely on the rack.

INSERT a wide metal spatula under the cake to release it from the bottom of the pan, and transfer the bienenstich to a cake plate. Cut into portions with a sharp serrated knife.

Storing

Bienenstich can be frozen. Set the cooled cake on a baking sheet and place in the freezer until solid, then wrap the cake securely in plastic wrap and aluminum foil, place in a heavy-duty resealable plastic bag, and freeze for up to 1 month. To serve, thaw the cake in its wrappings, then unwrap, set it on a baking sheet, and refresh in a preheated 325°F oven for about 5 minutes.

Streuselkuchen

german crumb cake

MAKES ONE 9-INCH SQUARE CAKE; 8 SERVINGS

THIS TENDER YEAST CAKE TOPPED WITH A GENEROUS AMOUNT *of streusel and a sprinkling of vanilla sugar is a German classic. Anna Lobonc learned how to make it from her mother when she lived in the former Czechoslovakia. The cake makes an excellent afternoon snack and it is ideal to serve with tea or coffee.*

½ recipe German Yeast Dough (page 336), risen, deflated, shaped into a ball, and allowed to rest for 10 minutes

STREUSEL

¾ cup unbleached all-purpose flour

6 tablespoons confectioners' sugar

6 tablespoons (¾ stick) cold unsalted butter, cut into tablespoon-sized pieces

Vanilla confectioners' sugar (see page 337) for sprinkling

BUTTER A 9-INCH SQUARE BAKING PAN (do not use cooking spray—the dough must adhere to the pan). Roll the dough on a lightly floured surface to the size of the pan. It will be about ¼ inch thick. Transfer the dough to the pan and pat it onto the bottom and into the corners. Do not make a rim; the dough should be flat. Cover with a kitchen towel.

TO MAKE THE STREUSEL, put the flour, confectioners' sugar, and butter into the work bowl of a food processor fitted with the metal blade. Pulse 5 or 6 times, then let the machine run just until the ingredients begin to form small crumbly masses, about 30 seconds. Do not process beyond the crumb stage.

UNCOVER the dough. Press the crumbs to form clumps the size of large peas, and sprinkle on top of the dough. Continue making larger lumps of streusel and sprinkling them evenly all over the dough. There will be a generous layer of streusel covering the dough. Cover the streuselkuchen with a kitchen towel and let stand at room temperature for 20 minutes.

ADJUST AN OVEN RACK to the center position and preheat the oven to 350°F.

UNCOVER THE KUCHEN and place the pan in the oven. Bake for about 30 minutes, until the kuchen has risen almost to the top of the pan and is golden brown and a toothpick inserted into its center comes out clean. Remove the pan from the oven and immediately sprinkle the top of the streuselkuchen with a generous layer of vanilla sugar. Cool completely on a wire rack. This is at its best when very fresh. Cut into portions with a sharp knife.

Cardamom Coffee Rolls

MAKES 15 ROLLS

OUR FRIEND PAM KNUTSON, A SECOND-GENERATION SWEDISH AMERICAN, *generously shared her family recipe for these delightful rolls. They are moist, light-textured, sweet, and hard to stop eating. Part of their success stems from being made with a fairly wet dough—don't be tempted to add too much flour, or the rolls will be dry. The rolls can be served for afternoon tea or enjoyed as an evening snack. They are excellent plain or split and spread with butter or jam, or both.*

Do try to use freshly ground cardamom. It adds immeasurably to the flavor of the rolls. Many markets now carry cardamom seeds that have been removed from their pods. Simply crush the seeds to a fine powder in a mortar with a pestle, or use a coffee grinder or spice mill.

SPONGE

- 1 cup whole milk
- 1½ cups unbleached all-purpose flour
- 1 package (2¼ teaspoons) active dry or instant yeast

DOUGH

- ½ cup granulated sugar
- 1 large egg, at room temperature
- 1 large egg yolk, at room temperature
- 4 tablespoons (½ stick) unsalted butter, very soft
- 1 teaspoon ground cardamom, preferably freshly ground
- ½ teaspoon salt
- 1¼ cups unbleached all-purpose flour, plus more as needed

TOPPING

- ¼ cup sliced or slivered almonds, chopped into small pieces
- 2 tablespoons granulated sugar
- ¼ teaspoon ground cardamom, preferably freshly ground
- 1 large egg yolk, beaten with 1 teaspoon water, for egg wash

TO MAKE THE SPONGE, scald the milk in a small saucepan over medium heat—you will see steam rising from the surface of the milk and small bubbles forming around the edges. Remove the pan from the heat and cool the milk until it is between 120° and 130°F.

IN A MEDIUM BOWL, whisk together the flour and yeast. Add the hot milk and whisk to make a smooth, thick batter. Bang the whisk on the rim of the bowl to remove any clinging batter, and scrape the sides of the bowl with a rubber spatula. Cover the bowl tightly with plastic wrap. Let rise until the sponge has doubled in volume, about 1 hour.

To make the dough by hand, scrape the sponge into a large bowl. Whisk in the sugar, egg, egg yolk, butter, cardamom, and salt. Beat vigorously with a wooden spoon for about 5 minutes, until the dough is smooth and very elastic. Stir in the flour and beat again for 5 minutes. The dough should be soft, elastic, and just slightly sticky. Sprinkle your work surface with 2 tablespoons flour and place the dough on it. Knead for 2 to 3 minutes, until the dough is only slightly tacky. Wash and dry the bowl, lightly oil the bowl or coat with cooking spray, and replace the dough in the bowl, turning to coat.

To make the dough with a stand mixer, scrape the sponge into the mixer bowl and add the sugar, egg, egg yolk, butter, cardamom, and salt. Attach the flat beater and beat on low speed for 1 minute. Increase the speed to medium and beat for 5 minutes, or until the dough becomes ropy, masses onto the beater, and begins to pull away from the sides of the bowl. Scrape the bowl and beater, and remove the paddle. With a wooden spoon, stir in the flour. Attach the dough hook and knead on low speed, then increase the speed to medium to medium-high and beat for 5 minutes to make a soft, elastic, slightly sticky dough. Scrape the bowl and remove the dough hook.

SPRINKLE THE DOUGH with 1 tablespoon flour. Cover the bowl tightly with plastic wrap and let the dough rise until doubled in size, about 1½ hours.

SPRINKLE YOUR WORK SURFACE lightly with flour, and scrape the dough onto it with a pastry scraper. Turn to coat both sides of the dough lightly with flour. Divide the dough into 15 equal portions with a pastry scraper or a sharp knife. Cover loosely with a kitchen towel and let the dough rest for 10 minutes.

BUTTER a 13 × 9 × 2–inch baking pan or coat it with cooking spray. Shape each piece of dough into a ball, sealing the seam on the underside of the dough firmly. Place the balls seam side down in the pan, 3 across and 5 down, leaving a bit of space between them. Coat the tops of the rolls lightly with cooking spray and drape a sheet of plastic wrap loosely over them. Let rise until the rolls have doubled in size, about 1 hour. The rolls will be touching each other with small gaps between them.

ADJUST AN OVEN RACK to the lower third position and preheat the oven to 375°F.

TO MAKE THE TOPPING, stir together the almonds, sugar, and cardamom in a small bowl.

WHEN THE ROLLS HAVE RISEN, uncover them and brush them with the egg wash. Sprinkle with the almond mixture. Bake for 20 to 25 minutes, until the rolls are nicely browned, the nuts are toasted, and the rolls spring back when gently pressed. Cool the rolls in their pan on a wire rack for 10 minutes, then, with a wide metal spatula, remove them from the pan and set them on the wire rack. Serve warm or at room temperature.

Storing

Wrapped tightly in plastic wrap or a plastic bag, the rolls can be stored at room temperature for up to 2 days. They can be reheated successfully, one at a time, in a microwave oven set on defrost for about 30 seconds. The rolls can also be frozen once completely cool. Place them on a baking sheet and freeze until solid. Transfer them to heavy-duty resealable plastic bags and freeze for up to 1 month. To refresh them, thaw them completely in their wrapping, then unwrap the rolls, place them on a baking sheet, and pop into a preheated 325°F oven for about 10 minutes.

Cinnamon Buns

MAKES 15 BUNS

DOUGH

¼ cup granulated sugar

¼ cup warm water (105° to 110°F)

1 package (2¼ teaspoons) active dry yeast

½ cup whole milk

½ teaspoon salt

3 cups unbleached all-purpose flour, plus more as needed

1 large egg, at room temperature

4 tablespoons (½ stick) unsalted butter, very soft

FILLING

⅓ cup granulated sugar

½ teaspoon ground cinnamon

3 tablespoons unsalted butter, very soft or melted

½ cup dark raisins or currants

TOPPING

6 tablespoons (¾ stick) unsalted butter

½ cup firmly packed light brown sugar

1½ tablespoons light corn syrup

½ cup coarsely chopped walnuts or pecans

KNOWN AS STICKY BUNS OR CINNAMON ROLLS *in some parts of the country, these classic American sweet yeast rolls were created hundreds of years ago by Pennsylvania Dutch bakers. Unlike the monstrous, way-too-doughy sticky buns sold in bakeries across America, these are modest affairs and can be gobbled up in three or four bites. When I first saw them in Haegele's bakeshop in Philadelphia, I was amazed how small they seemed. But one bun satisfies.*

Food historian Will Weaver told me the following:

> *Real cinnamon buns were never large. You were supposed to be able to balance them on the side of your tea saucer. They seem to be a conflation of German schnecken ("snails") and Old English Chelsea buns. They are mentioned in eighteenth-century Philadelphia records. We had bun bakers who specialized in this type of thing and sold them in the streets. They date at least to the late 1600s, maybe older. The ones made with honey are the oldest. The brown sugar–butter mix for the bottom is definitely late eighteenth century, the addition of nuts much later, twentieth century.*
>
> *Today cinnamon buns may be made with raisins or currants or nuts, or without them.*

This recipe comes from Betty Groff, a tenth-generation Pennsylvania Dutch descendant who lives in Mt. Joy, Pennsylvania. Her buns are a bit larger than the traditional ones, and she adds dried fruit and nuts. The dough is soft, smooth, supple, and slightly sticky, and it is easy to make by hand if you don't have a heavy-duty mixer. Don't bake these in a dark pan, or the sugar might burn.

TO MAKE THE DOUGH In a small bowl, stir ½ teaspoon of the sugar into the warm water, then sprinkle in the yeast. Stir to combine and let stand at room temperature until the yeast is dissolved and the mixture is very foamy, about 10 minutes.

MEANWHILE, heat the milk in a small heavy saucepan over medium heat until it is scalded—you will see steam rising from the surface and tiny bubbles all around the edges. Immediately remove the pan from the heat, add the remaining sugar and the salt, and stir to dissolve. Let stand for a few minutes until the milk feels warm to your fingertip.

To mix the dough by hand, put 2¾ cups of the flour into a large bowl. Make a well in the center and add the warm milk, yeast, egg, and butter. Stir well with a wooden spoon to make a thick, sticky dough. Sprinkle your work surface lightly with the remaining ¼ cup flour and scrape the dough onto it. Knead gently for 2 to 3 minutes, until the flour has been incorporated and the dough feels smooth, elastic, and just slightly sticky. Don't overknead. If the dough still feels too wet and sticky, add a bit more flour, keeping the dough supple and light.

To mix the dough with a stand mixer, put 2¾ cups of the flour into the mixer bowl and add the warm milk, yeast, egg, and butter. Stir well with a wooden spoon to make a thick, sticky dough. Attach the dough hook and beat on medium-high speed for about 1 minute, just until the dough masses on the dough hook. Reduce the speed to low and beat until the dough gathers into a soft ball on the dough hook and is smooth, supple, and only slightly sticky, 3 to 5 minutes. Sprinkle the remaining ¼ cup flour onto your work surface and scrape the dough onto it. Knead briefly, just until the flour is incorporated and the dough is smooth and still a bit sticky.

WASH AND DRY the bowl and butter it lightly or coat with cooking spray. Shape the dough into a ball, place it in the bowl, and turn to coat. Cover tightly with plastic wrap and let the dough rise until it has doubled in size, about 1½ hours.

DISLODGE THE DOUGH from the bowl with a pastry scraper and place it on your work surface. Flatten the dough into a rough rectangle, then fold it in thirds like a business letter. Pat the dough once more into a long rectangle and fold it again into thirds. Replace the dough in the bowl, cover tightly, and let rise again until the dough has almost doubled in size, about 1 hour.

PREPARE the filling and topping. While the dough rises, butter only the sides of a 13 × 9 × 2–inch baking pan. For the filling, stir together the sugar and cinnamon in a small bowl; set aside. The remaining filling ingredients will be used later. For the topping, melt the butter in a small heavy saucepan over low heat. Remove the pan from the heat and stir in the brown sugar and corn syrup. Keep stirring until the butter is melted and the sauce is smooth. Scrape the topping into the prepared pan and spread it evenly with the back of a teaspoon. It will be a thin layer. Sprinkle the nuts evenly over the topping.

TO SHAPE THE CINNAMON BUNS, very lightly dust your work surface with flour and place the risen dough on it. Roll the dough to a 15 × 12–inch rectangle. Turn the dough if necessary so a 15-inch side is nearest you. Spread the soft or melted butter over the dough, leaving a 1-inch border at the far edge. Sprinkle the raisins or currants over the butter, followed by the cinnamon and sugar. Set a sheet of waxed paper on the dough and press gently to embed the fruit into the dough. Remove the paper and roll the dough up tightly, like a jelly roll, starting from the side nearest you. Pinch the edges to seal. Turn the roll seam side down and cut it into 1-inch-thick slices with a sharp serrated knife. Arrange the slices cut side down on the topping, making 5 rows of buns the long way and 3 the short way. The rolls will be touching each other. Cover loosely with a kitchen towel and let rest for 20 to 30 minutes (the rolls will rise only slightly).

ADJUST AN OVEN RACK to the center position and preheat the oven to 375°F.

UNCOVER THE ROLLS and place the pan in the oven. Bake for about 25 minutes, until golden brown on top. Remove the pan from the oven and run the tip of a small sharp knife all around the sides of the rolls to release them from the pan. Cover the pan of rolls with a tray and, grasping the pan and tray with pot holders, invert the two. Wait a minute or so, then carefully lift off the pan. If any topping sticks to the pan, scrape it off with a spoon and spread it onto the rolls. Cool until warm or room temperature. To serve, pull the rolls apart with your fingers or two forks.

Storing

The buns are best when fresh, but even if a day or two old, they can be successfully revived by a brief stint in a microwave oven. Set a bun or two on a paper towel and refresh on the defrost setting for 45 seconds to 1 minute or reheat them in a preheated 300° F oven for 8 to 10 minutes.

Kulich

MAKES 12 TO 16 SERVINGS

RAISINS

⅓ cup dark raisins

⅓ cup golden raisins

⅓ cup dark rum

SPONGE

½ cup whole milk

2⅔ cups unbleached all-purpose flour

1 tablespoon granulated sugar

1 package (2¼ teaspoons) rapid-rise yeast

1 large egg, at room temperature

DOUGH

1 large egg, at room temperature

7 tablespoons granulated sugar

2 teaspoons pure vanilla extract

½ teaspoon salt

10 tablespoons (1¼ sticks) unsalted butter, cut into tablespoon-sized pieces, at room temperature

½ cup glacéed cherries, rinsed, patted dry, and halved

1 tablespoon unbleached all-purpose flour

¼ cup slivered almonds, toasted (see page 23)

GLAZE

⅔ cup confectioners' sugar, plus more if needed

2 teaspoons cold water

1 teaspoon fresh lemon juice

RUSSIAN EASTER WOULDN'T BE EASTER WITHOUT KULICH, *the tall sweet Easter yeast cake containing raisins, cherries, and almonds. Kulich's texture is light and airy yet firm. The top is covered with a thick sugar icing, and the excess runs down the sides in uneven dribbles, giving the cake a look of festive spontaneity. Kulich is always served with the rich and creamy cheesecake dessert called paskha (see page 214). The two were made for each other.*

This recipe is based on my aunt's recollection of how my grandmother, Baba, made kulich. Aunt Luba explained that in the old days in Russia, women approached the making of kulich with trepidation and let it be known that producing a flawless one demanded all the skill and know-how of a master baker.

> *Sveetie, you can't imagine how hard it was to make a really good kulich. When I was a girl in Irkutsk, we didn't have electric mixers, and the ovens didn't always work properly, and sometimes the kulich burned. But Baba's kulich, it always came out perfect. I remember how careful she was when she worked her hands in the dough, and how fussy she was about the raisins and cherries she put in. And the butter had to be the freshest and the best. I really don't know how she managed it.*

Baba was a great baker, and she would have loved the speed and ease with which a stand mixer makes the dough today. The dough is made in two stages and requires three long, slow rises for the proper development of the kulich's taste and texture. Soak the dried fruits in the rum the night before you make the kulich.

You will need a clean 2-pound coffee can to make the kulich (2-pound coffee cans contain 33 to 39 ounces of coffee, but regardless of the amount, the cans are the same size).

IN A SMALL BOWL, stir together the raisins and rum. Cover tightly with plastic wrap and set aside at room temperature to soak overnight.

THE NEXT DAY, set a strainer over a small bowl and add the raisins and rum. Let the raisins drain for about 1 hour. Reserve 2 tablespoons of the rum, and transfer the raisins to paper towels.

TO MAKE THE SPONGE, scald the milk in a small heavy saucepan over medium heat—you will see steam rising from the surface and tiny bubbles all around the edges. Remove the pan from the heat and let the milk cool until it is between 120° and 130°F.

To mix the sponge with a stand mixer, put ⅔ cup of the flour into the mixer bowl and add the sugar and yeast. Stir with a wooden spoon, and add the hot milk. Beat with the flat beater on low speed until smooth, about 30 seconds. Add the egg and beat for 1 minute. Scrape the sides of the bowl and beater. Sprinkle the remaining 2 cups flour evenly over the batter, *but do not mix it in.* Cover the bowl tightly with plastic wrap.

To mix the sponge by hand, put ⅔ cup of the flour into a large bowl and add the sugar and yeast. Stir with a wooden spoon, and add the hot milk. Beat with the spoon until smooth. Add the egg and beat it in well. Scrape the sides of the bowl and the spoon. Sprinkle the remaining 2 cups flour evenly over the batter, *but do not mix it in.* Cover the bowl tightly with plastic wrap.

LET THE SPONGE RISE at room temperature for 3 to 4 hours, until the yeast mixture has bubbled up and almost completely engulfed the flour.

To make the dough with the stand mixer, add the egg, sugar, reserved rum, vanilla, and salt to the sponge. Beat with the flat beater on low speed for about 1 minute, just to combine all the ingredients. Raise the speed to medium and beat for 1½ minutes. The dough will mass on the beater. On low speed, add the butter one piece at a time, beating until each is completely incorporated before adding the next. Increase the speed to medium and beat for 2 minutes.

To make the dough by hand, add the egg, sugar, reserved rum, vanilla, and salt to the sponge and stir, then beat well with the wooden spoon until the dough is thick and smooth. Add the butter one piece at a time, beating until each piece is incorporated before adding the next. The dough may look ropy. Beat vigorously for 5 minutes. If the dough becomes too stiff to beat, scrape it out onto a work surface and knead it rapidly with quick, short strokes.

THE DOUGH SHOULD FEEL as soft as a baby's bottom and be smooth, supple, and not at all sticky. Wash and dry the bowl, and butter it or coat it with cooking spray. Shape the dough into a ball, place it in the bowl, and turn to coat. Cover the bowl tightly with plastic wrap. Let the dough rise at room temperature until it has tripled in volume, 3 to 4 hours.

WHILE THE DOUGH RISES, cut a circle of parchment to fit the bottom of a 2-pound coffee can. Cut a rectangle of parchment big enough to line the inside of the can and to extend about 2 inches above the rim. Butter the inside of the can. Butter the pieces of parchment and line the can with them, pressing the unbuttered sides against the can.

IN A SMALL BOWL, combine the raisins and cherries. Sprinkle with the 1 tablespoon flour and toss to coat the pieces of fruit. Mix in the almonds.

LIGHTLY FLOUR A WORK SURFACE. Dislodge the dough with a pastry scraper and place it on the work surface. Flatten the dough gently with your hands. Sprinkle the fruit and nut mixture over it and knead them in gently and slowly until evenly distributed. Shape the dough into a ball and place it seam side down in the prepared coffee can. Lay a square of plastic wrap loosely over the top of the parchment, and let rise until the dough has reached the top of the can (not the top of the paper), 3 to 4 hours.

ABOUT 30 MINUTES BEFORE BAKING, adjust an oven rack to the lower third position. Place a heavy baking sheet on the rack and preheat the oven to 400°F.

TO BAKE THE KULICH, remove the plastic and place the can on the baking sheet. Bake for 10 minutes, then reduce the temperature to 350°F and bake for 50 to 60 minutes more, or until a wooden skewer inserted into the center of the bread comes out clean. The center of the bread should register 195° to 200°F on an instant-read or digital probe thermometer. If the top of the kulich is browning too fast, cover loosely with a square of aluminum foil, shiny side up. Cool the kulich in the can on a wire rack for 20 minutes.

TO REMOVE THE BREAD, rest the can on its side and tug gently on the parchment. Remove the parchment and set the kulich on its side on a wire rack to cool completely, turning it from time to time. The kulich is delicate when hot, and cooling on its side instead of upright will prevent it from collapsing.

TO MAKE THE GLAZE, whisk together the confectioners' sugar, water, and lemon juice in a small bowl until smooth. The mixture should be thick and barely runny. Adjust the consistency with confectioners' sugar or water if needed. Turn the completely cooled kulich upright on the rack and set the rack onto a sheet of waxed paper. Pour about half the glaze over the top of the kulich, covering it completely and letting the glaze run down the sides. Let stand for 5 to 10 minutes. Stir the remaining glaze and pour it over the first layer. Let the kulich stand for at least 2 hours at room temperature before serving.

TO SERVE THE KULICH, cut off the top and set it aside. Cut the kulich horizontally into ½-inch-thick slices, then cut each slice into 2 semicircles. Serve with Pashka (page 214)

Storing

Wrapped airtight, the glazed kulich will keep well at room temperature for 3 to 4 days. The cooled unglazed kulich can be refrigerated, tightly wrapped, for up to 2 days. Bring to room temperature and glaze before serving. To freeze, seal the unglazed kulich in a heavy-duty resealable plastic bag and freeze for up to 1 month. Thaw the kulich completely in its bag, then refresh it in a 300°F oven for 10 minutes. Cool completely, then glaze.

Russian Easter in San Francisco

When I was eleven, my family and I immigrated to San Francisco, home to a large population of Russians from Shanghai. Most were old friends, and many were Christian. To Russians, Easter is the most important religious celebration of the year, even more important than Christmas. On Easter Sunday, my father and I dressed up and went all over the city to visit our friends—and to eat. The women stayed at home while the men did the calling. The sheer extravagance and variety of food served at each house was dazzling: *Zakuski*, Russian appetizers, dominated the table and included a selection of vegetables; sausages and sliced meats; salads; cheeses; pickles; smoked salmon, eel, and herring; and caviar. A basket of decorated Easter eggs usually served as the centerpiece. Although the food varied from house to house, three items appeared on every Easter table: smoked ham, kulich, and paskha.

After nibbling on the *zakuski,* I headed straight for the kulich and paskha. The paskha, which had to be creamy smooth, sweet, and buttery, was crucial to the success of the kulich, because they were eaten together. I always sampled both, and over the years I got to know which of our friends made the best. Those were the ones I saved my appetite for.

Kulich and paskha are the most symbolic of the special Easter foods. Recipes for this sweet yeast cake and cheese dessert go back hundreds of years. Both are rich in eggs and butter, symbols of fertility and rebirth. So important were the *kulichi* to the Russians that the women who baked and decorated them would wrap them in clean cloths and carefully carry them to the church, where they were blessed by the priest. Often a woman would insert tall, thin candles in the kulich, light it, and place a rose alongside the candle. Then she'd whisper a prayer of her own.

Paskha

MAKES 12 TO 16 SERVINGS

THIS IS A SUBLIMELY SMOOTH, RICH, SLIGHTLY SWEET *molded cheese dessert that is always served with kulich (page 211). The name paskha means Easter. After striving for years to re-create the taste and texture of the paskha I remember eating as a young boy, I finally succeeded. The food processor produces a buttery-smooth paskha in minutes and eliminates the tedious process of forcing the cheeses through a fine-mesh sieve and beating the mixture by hand.*

Most old paskha recipes call for farmer's or pot cheese, a kind of cottage cheese. The calves born in the spring meant an abundance of milk and butter. And milk often went into making cheese, especially the pot cheese for paskha. If you can find farmer's cheese, by all means use it. Friendship brand gives the best results, and you can buy it in many supermarkets and delis or order it by mail (see Sources, page 344). Lacking it, I hit upon a combination of dry-curd cottage cheese and ricotta that works well; I also add a small amount of cream cheese for extra smoothness. If farmer's cheese is available, substitute 1½ pounds of it for the cottage cheese, ricotta, and cream cheese. You will not need to drain farmer's cheese.

The symbolism of Christ's rebirth is represented by carvings in the traditional wooden molds used for the paskha. On one side is a cross, and on another, the Cyrillic letters XB, meaning Christos voskres! *(Christ is risen!). Plastic molds are now available also, and they have become the mold of choice today because of price. To order one, see Sources, page 344. But my Aunt Luba always used a flowerpot for her paskha, so that's what I use. Small clay or plastic flowerpots with a capacity of 5 to 6 cups, about 5 to 6 inches tall and 6 inches across the top, are easy to find in mass merchant stores. Be sure the mold you use has one or more holes in the bottom.*

You will need to begin this recipe 2 days in advance. The cottage cheese and ricotta drain overnight, and the paskha must be refrigerated for 24 hours.

12 ounces (about 2⅓ cups) dry-curd cottage cheese
1 cup whole-milk ricotta cheese
⅔ cup heavy cream
4 large egg yolks
¾ cup plus 2 tablespoons granulated sugar
3 ounces regular cream cheese
2 teaspoons pure vanilla extract
½ pound (2 sticks) unsalted butter, cut into 8 pieces, at room temperature
Glacéed cherries for garnish
Blanched whole almonds, toasted (see page 23), for garnish

LINE A LARGE STRAINER with a piece of rinsed and wrung-out cheesecloth, set the strainer over a bowl, and add the cottage and ricotta cheeses. Lay a piece of plastic wrap right on the cheese, put a flat-bottomed pan or plate on top of the cheese, and add a 3- to 4-pound weight. Refrigerate overnight to remove excess moisture from the cheeses.

THE NEXT DAY, scald the cream in a medium heavy saucepan over medium heat—you will see steam rising from the surface and small bubbles around the edges. Remove the pan from the heat and set aside.

PUT THE EGG YOLKS and sugar in the work bowl of a food processor fitted with the metal blade and process for 2 minutes, stopping 2 or 3 times to scrape the bowl. With the machine running, add the hot cream in a steady stream, and process for 15 seconds. Return the mixture to the saucepan and cook over medium-low heat, stirring constantly with a heatproof rubber spatula, until the mixture thickens slightly and an instant-read thermometer registers 180°F. Do not allow the mixture to boil, or the egg yolks will curdle. Set the pan into a larger pan of ice water and stir the mixture occasionally until it reaches room temperature.

IF YOU HAVE A STANDARD FOOD PROCESSOR, proceed as follows; if you have a large-capacity food processor, there is no need to divide the ingredients before processing. With the metal blade in place, add half the drained cheeses, half the cooled egg yolk mixture, half the cream cheese, and 1 teaspoon of the vanilla to the work bowl and process until very smooth, about 1½ minutes. Stop to scrape the bowl once or twice. With the machine running, add half the butter, one piece at a time, processing for 2 to 3 seconds after each addition. Process for 1 minute more, or until very smooth.

Transfer the mixture to a medium bowl. Repeat with the remaining cheeses, egg yolk mixture, cream cheese, vanilla, and butter. Combine with the first batch and cover the bowl tightly with plastic wrap. Refrigerate for 2 to 3 hours, or until slightly firm.

TO PREPARE THE MOLD, choose a mold with a capacity of about 5 cups and with drainage holes in the bottom, such as a small flowerpot or a 7⅞ × 3⅞ × 2½–inch disposable aluminum foil loaf pan with a few holes punched in the bottom. (To measure the capacity, cover the holes and fill the mold with rice or beans, then measure the rice or beans.) Line the mold with a double thickness of cheesecloth, rinsed and wrung dry, leaving an overhang of about 3 inches all around. Put a wire rack over a pie plate and set the mold on it. Set aside.

WHEN THE CHEESE MIXTURE has firmed slightly, remove it from the refrigerator and spoon it into the mold. Smooth the top and fold the cheesecloth over to cover the cheese mixture completely. Set a flat-bottomed plate or pan on the cheesecloth (it should be smaller than the mold) and put a 3- to 4-pound weight on top. Refrigerate the mold, still on the rack over the pie plate, for at least 24 hours.

TO UNMOLD THE PASKHA, remove the weight and fold back the cheesecloth. Invert onto a serving plate and remove the mold, then pull away the cheesecloth. Decorate with cherries and almonds. Cover loosely with plastic wrap and refrigerate until ready to serve.

Storing

Paskha keeps well for at least 1 week in the refrigerator. It cannot be frozen.

Bara Brith

MAKES 1 LOAF

THE TEXTURE OF THIS WELSH FRUIT BREAD IS QUITE AMAZING, *being somehow both dense and light at the same time. The name means "speckled bread," and Tottie Parmeter, who taught it to me, says it is common to all Celtic countries. In Ireland the bread is known as barm brack, and in Scotland, Selkirk bannock; in Brittany, it goes by the name Morlaix brioche. Dried fruits and candied citrus peel partly account for the bread's speckled appearance. Older recipes call for whole wheat flour, which would also contribute to speckling. For best results, make bara brith a day ahead. The texture firms up, and it is easy to cut into thin slices. Although butter is the traditional spread for bara brith, it is also quite wonderful when slathered with Paskha (page 214).*

SPONGE	DOUGH
1 cup whole milk	1½ cups unbleached all-purpose flour, plus more if needed
8 tablespoons (1 stick) unsalted butter	½ teaspoon freshly grated nutmeg
2 cups unbleached all-purpose flour	½ teaspoon ground mace
½ cup granulated sugar	½ teaspoon ground cinnamon
1 teaspoon salt	1 large egg
1 package (2¼ teaspoons) instant yeast	¾ cup diced candied orange peel
	¾ cup currants

TO MAKE THE SPONGE, scald the milk in a small heavy saucepan over medium heat—you'll see steam rising from the surface and tiny bubbles all around the edges. Remove the pan from the heat, add the butter, and stir until the butter has melted. Let cool to a temperature of 125° to 130°F.

IN A LARGE BOWL, stir together the flour, sugar, salt, and yeast. Add the milk mixture and beat with a wooden spoon for 2 minutes. Scrape the spoon and sides of the bowl. Cover tightly with plastic wrap and let the dough rise in a warm place (85° to 90°F) until it has almost tripled in volume, about 2 hours.

TO MAKE THE DOUGH, in a medium bowl stir together the flour and spices.

ADD THE EGG to the sponge and beat it in well with a wooden spoon. Stir in the orange peel and currants. Add about half the dry ingredients and stir them in to make a thick, wet dough. Add the remaining dry ingredients and incorporate them in as best you can. The dough will be very shaggy looking. Scrape the contents of the bowl onto your work surface and knead to incorporate all of the flour mixture into the dough. At first the dough will be quite sticky, but keep pushing it and folding it on itself for 1 to 2 minutes with short, brief kneading motions (if you hold onto the dough too long, it will be sticky), and it will become smooth, slightly shiny, and no longer sticky. Try not to add any more flour, but if the dough still seems too wet to you, work in just a bit more.

BUTTER a 10 × 4½ × 3–inch loaf pan or an 11 × 4¼ × 3¼–inch baking pan or coat it with cooking spray. Shape the dough into a loaf and place it in the pan. Don't be concerned if a few pieces of fruit poke through the dough here and there. Cover loosely with lightly oiled plastic wrap, and let rise in a warm place until the center of the loaf domes up 1½ to 2 inches above the pan rim, about 1½ hours.

ADJUST AN OVEN RACK to the lower third position and preheat the oven to 375°F.

UNCOVER THE LOAF and place in the oven. After the first 30 minutes, lay a piece of aluminum foil loosely over the loaf. Bake for about 1 hour, until the bara brith is well browned and a wooden skewer inserted into the center comes out clean. A digital probe thermometer inserted into the loaf's center should register 195° to 200°F. Cool the loaf in its pan on a wire rack for 20 minutes.

REMOVE THE LOAF from the pan and set it upright on the rack to cool completely, 4 to 5 hours.

PLUCK OFF any dried fruits that have poked through the dough and are dried out. Cut the bread into thinnish slices with a serrated knife.

Storing

Wrap the cooled loaf in a heavy-duty resealable plastic bag and store it at room temperature for up to 1 week. The loaf also freezes beautifully, sealed in a heavy-duty plastic bag, for up to 1 month. Thaw completely in its bag before unwrapping and slicing.

Makowiec

poland

THIS IS A POLISH SWEET YEAST BREAD RICH WITH BUTTER AND EGGS *and with a generous amount of a special poppy seed filling. To me, it is the ne plus ultra of sweet rolls. Makowiec ("ma-KOV-yets") is traditionally served on Christmas Eve, but please don't wait until then. Krystyna Kawalec, who immigrated from Poland a few years ago, taught this to me. She makes both the dough and filling by hand.*

I have made the recipe Krystyna's way many times. But because few bakers are likely to go to these lengths, I've adapted both dough and filling to the machine. And let me assure you, the results are as excellent as those achieved manually.

What makes makowiec so special? The matched textures of the dough and filling. The two blend together seamlessly, and the effect is stunning. The usual way of making a poppy seed roll is to fill the dough with a canned filling, but canned fillings by themselves are overly sweet and sticky and they tend to fall out of the sliced roll. I've found that by grinding poppy seeds in a coffee grinder, cooking them in milk, and then combining them with a canned filling, I can duplicate Krystyna's results in a fraction of the time. A food processor will not work. You can make the filling a day ahead and refrigerate it. Bring it to room temperature before shaping and baking.

Serve slices of makowiec plain or spread with sweet butter. It is most welcome at breakfast, brunch, or afternoon tea.

FILLING

- 1¼ cups poppy seeds (see Note)
- ¾ cup whole milk
- 1½ cups canned poppy seed filling
- 4 tablespoons (½ stick) unsalted butter, at room temperature
- 1 teaspoon pure almond extract or ½ teaspoon almond oil
- 2 large eggs, separated
- 1 large egg yolk
- Pinch of salt

DOUGH

- 1 package (2¼ teaspoons) active dry yeast
- ½ cup plus 1 teaspoon granulated sugar
- ⅓ cup warm water (105° to 110°F)
- 3¼ cups unbleached all-purpose flour, plus more as needed
- 1 large egg
- 2 large egg yolks
- 4 tablespoons (½ stick) unsalted butter, at room temperature
- ½ cup whole milk, warmed to 105° to 110°F
- ½ teaspoon salt

STREUSEL

- 3 tablespoons unbleached all-purpose flour
- 3 tablespoons granulated sugar
- 2 tablespoons cold unsalted butter
- 1 large egg yolk, beaten with 1 teaspoon water, for egg wash

TO MAKE THE FILLING, grind half the poppy seeds in a coffee grinder for 10 to 15 seconds, until finely ground and slightly pasty. Transfer to a medium heavy saucepan. Grind the remaining seeds the same way and add them to the saucepan. Stir in the milk, set the pan over medium heat, and cook, stirring with a wooden spoon, for 5 to 6 minutes, until the mixture is very hot and has a thick, pasty consistency. Adjust the heat if necessary to keep the mixture from boiling. Cover the pan, remove from the heat, and let stand until completely cool, 2 to 3 hours. The poppy seeds will have absorbed the milk and the mixture will be very thick.

IN A LARGE BOWL, beat together the cooled poppy seeds, canned poppy seed filling, butter, and almond extract or oil until thoroughly mixed. In a small bowl, beat the 3 egg yolks with a hand-held electric mixer until very thick and pale, about 5 minutes. Beat the yolks into the poppy seed mixture.

WASH AND DRY the beaters. In a medium bowl, beat the 2 egg whites with the salt until they form stiff, glossy peaks. Be careful not to overbeat the whites. Fold the whites into the poppy seed filling. (The filling can be covered and refrigerated overnight. Bring to room temperature before using.)

TO MAKE THE DOUGH In a small cup, stir the yeast and the 1 teaspoon sugar into the warm water. Let stand for about 10 minutes until the yeast is dissolved and the liquid is bubbly.

PUT THE FLOUR into the bowl of a heavy-duty electric mixer and add the egg, egg yolks, butter, milk, the remaining ½ cup sugar, the salt, and dissolved yeast. Beat on low speed with the flat beater for 1 minute. Increase the speed to medium to medium-high and beat for 5 minutes, or until the dough is thick and very elastic. It will seem quite wet. Scrape the beater and bowl.

LIGHTLY BUTTER a straight-sided 3-quart bowl or coat it with cooking spray. Scrape the dough into the bowl, and turn to coat. Pick up the dough and knead it briefly between your hands. It will feel soft and not sticky. Replace the dough in the bowl, cover tightly with plastic wrap, and let the dough rise until it has doubled in size, about 2 hours.

TO SHAPE THE MAKOWIEC, butter a 13 × 9 × 2–inch baking pan or coat it with cooking spray. Lightly flour your work surface and scrape the dough onto it. The dough is soft and easy to work with. Turn the dough to coat lightly with flour and pat it gently or roll it to a 16 × 12–inch rectangle. Check periodically to see the dough isn't sticking; if it is, dust with more flour. Turn the dough if necessary so a short side is facing you. Use a narrow spatula to spread the filling onto the dough, leaving ½ inch of dough exposed on the sides and 1 inch at the far side. There will be about a ½-inch-thick layer of filling. Roll up the makowiec, starting from the short side nearest you. Don't roll too tightly, or the bread may crack during baking. Crimp the ends of the roll and place it seam side down in the prepared pan. (If you have a cookie spatula, slide it under the makowiec and transfer it to the baking pan.) Cover loosely with a kitchen towel and let the roll rise at room temperature for about 30 minutes. It will not double in size.

ADJUST AN OVEN RACK to the lower third position and preheat the oven to 375°F.

WHILE THE MAKOWIEC RESTS, prepare the streusel. In a small bowl, stir together the flour and sugar. Add the butter and cut it in with a pastry blender or two knives to make a crumbly mixture.

USE A PASTRY BRUSH to paint the makowiec with egg wash, and sprinkle with the streusel. Press the streusel gently onto the top and sides of the roll. Bake for 45 to 50 minutes, until the roll is well browned, including the bottom. A digital probe thermometer inserted into the loaf's center should register 195° to 200° F. Cool the makowiec in its pan for 10 minutes, then use a large metal spatula to transfer it to a wire cooling rack. Cool completely before slicing and serving.

Storing

The bread stays fresh for several days at room temperature if wrapped airtight. It can also be frozen. Wrap the completely cooled bread in plastic wrap and then in heavy-duty foil, and freeze for up to 1 month. To refresh, thaw still wrapped, then unwrap, set on a baking sheet, and place in a preheated 300°F oven for 15 to 20 minutes. Cool before serving.

Note

I buy poppy seeds in bulk and I've found they do not need to be washed, as Krystyna's do; I grind them straight from the bag.

Krystyna's Makowiec

Krystyna begins by making the filling. The poppy seeds she uses for the filling (a Polish brand) contain lots of husks, and they need to be removed. She puts 2 pounds of poppy seeds into a large pot, adds cool tap water, and swirls the poppy seeds about with her hand to wash them. After the seeds settle and some of the husks float to the top, she skims off the floating husks with a spoon, then slowly pours off the water (some seeds will come with it) and fills the pan again with water. Krystyna repeats the washing three or four times, until the seeds are clean and the water is virtually free of husks. After the last washing, she adds enough whole milk to cover the seeds completely, sets the pot over medium-low heat, and slowly brings the milk to a temperature of 140°F, stirring occasionally. She removes the pot from heat and lets the poppy seeds soak in the milk for about 1 hour; the seeds swell considerably during standing.

Krystyna scrapes the seeds into a large fine strainer and drains them for about 1 hour. Then the seeds must be ground. She passes them through the fine holes of a hand-cranked meat grinder one soupspoonful at a time—more than that, and it is hard to grind. For makowiec and for other poppy seed desserts and pastries, she grinds the poppy seeds three times. The second and third grindings are easier, and the final grinding results in a thick, pasty mixture.

She makes enough filling for two breads, and then she mixes the dough by hand as well. To make the filling, Krystyna separates 5 large eggs and beats the yolks until slightly thickened. She gradually adds 1 cup sugar, beating until the yolks are very thick and pale, then beats in 1 teaspoon almond oil and ¼ teaspoon salt. She adds the yolks to the ground poppy seeds, along with 8 tablespoons (1 stick) softened butter and ½ cup raisins (I omit these), mixing all this together with her hands to make a thick paste. Then she beats the 5 egg whites until stiff and folds them in.

To make the dough, she softens 1 ounce fresh yeast in ¾ cup warm milk with 2 tablespoons sugar. When the yeast is very bubbly, she puts 2 pounds (6⅓ cups) of flour into a large bowl (she eyeballs the amount) and makes a well in the flour. The yeast goes into the well along with 1 large egg, 3 yolks, 8 tablespoons (1 stick) soft butter, 1 cup warm milk, 1 cup sugar, and 1 teaspoon salt. She uses her hand to mix all of this together, and then beats for several minutes to make a soft, smooth, elastic dough. She sprinkles the dough lightly with flour, covers the bowl with a towel, and lets the dough rise until it has doubled in volume, about 1½ hours. Then she fills, shapes, and bakes the makowiec as described in the recipe.

Massa Sovada

MAKES 2 ROUND LOAVES

THIS HIGHLY ADDICTIVE CLASSIC PORTUGUESE BREAD *has traveled widely, and I've eaten versions of it in many places. Brought by Portuguese immigrants to Hawaii in the late 1880s, the bread is so popular there it is called Hawaiian Bread. You can buy it as large loaves or rolls. Some bakeries add guava or taro to the dough, tinting it a startling pink or purple.*

Massa sovada was traditionally made in huge amounts by the diligent hands of many women taking turns beating and kneading the dough (the name literally means "beaten dough"). Maria João, who regularly makes this on the island of Terceira in the Azores, does it the traditional way but in a smaller quantity. The soft bread has an especially tender, slightly open crumb, and it is excellent all by itself or spread with butter or jam or both. It also makes great toast and terrific French toast.

You must start the bread the night before, making the sponge and letting it ferment for 8 to 12 hours at room temperature. This long fermentation imparts a rich, nutty taste to the bread.

SPONGE

- ½ cup unbleached bread flour
- 1 package (2¼ teaspoons) instant yeast
- ½ cup hot water (120° to 130°F)

DOUGH

- 6 tablespoons (¾ stick) unsalted butter, at room temperature
- ½ cup granulated sugar
- Finely grated zest of 1 lemon
- 1 teaspoon salt
- 3 large eggs, at room temperature
- ½ cup whole milk, at room temperature
- 3½ cups unbleached bread flour, or as needed
- 1 large egg, beaten with 1 teaspoon water, for egg wash

TO MAKE THE SPONGE, whisk the flour and yeast together in a small bowl. Add the hot water, and whisk to make a smooth pancake-like batter. Bang the whisk on the rim of the bowl to return any clinging batter to the bowl, and scrape the sides of the bowl with a rubber spatula. Cover the bowl tightly with plastic wrap and let stand at room temperature for 8 to 12 hours, during which time the sponge will rise to more than triple its volume, then collapse back on itself into a bubbly mass. When you uncover the sponge, it will have a pleasant yeasty aroma.

To make the dough by hand, beat the butter and sugar together in a large bowl with a wooden spoon for 3 to 4 minutes, until creamy looking. Add the lemon zest and salt and beat 1 to 2 minutes more. Beat in the eggs one at a time, beating well after each. The batter will look curdled, which is fine. Stir in the sponge and the milk. Gradually stir in 2½ cups of the flour and beat vigorously with the spoon for several minutes until the dough becomes quite elastic (if you lift a spoonful of dough up from the bowl, it should stretch for about 1 foot). Stir in another ¾ cup flour to make a thick dough. Sprinkle the remaining ¼ cup flour on your work surface and scrape the dough onto it. Knead for about 5 minutes to incorporate the flour and to make a very smooth, soft, supple dough that may be slightly sticky.

To make the dough with a stand mixer, combine the butter, sugar, lemon zest, and salt in the mixer bowl and beat on medium speed with the flat beater for 3 to 4 minutes. Scrape the bowl and beater. Beat in the eggs one at a time, beating well after each. The batter will look curdled, which is fine. Stir in the sponge and the milk. Add 2½ cups of the flour and beat it in on low speed. Increase the speed to medium and beat for 5 minutes, or until the dough begins to mass on the beater. Scrape the bowl and beater and attach the dough hook. Add ¾ cup more flour and knead on low speed for about 5 minutes, until the dough is smooth, soft, elastic, and just a bit sticky. Sprinkle 2 tablespoons of the remaining flour on your work surface and scrape the dough onto it. Knead for about 2 minutes to incorporate the flour and to make a very smooth, soft, supple dough that may be slightly tacky. If it is too wet, knead in the remaining 2 tablespoons flour.

WASH AND DRY THE BOWL and rub it with vegetable oil or coat it with cooking spray. Shape the dough into a ball, place it in the bowl, and turn to coat all surfaces. Cover the bowl tightly with plastic wrap and let the dough rise at room temperature until almost tripled in size, about 2 hours.

PLACE THE DOUGH on your work surface and pat it gently into a rectangle about 1 inch thick. Divide the dough in half and shape each into a ball. Use the sides of your hands to embrace each ball of dough and move your palms all around the dough, moving from the top of the ball down to create surface tension. To maintain the surface tension, pinch the undersides of the ball tightly to seal the seams.

COAT two 9-inch round cake pans, preferably nonstick, with cooking spray, and place the balls seam side down in the pans. Coat the tops of the balls of dough lightly with cooking spray. Drape a square of plastic wrap loosely over each pan. Let the loaves rise until slightly more than doubled in size, about 2 hours. The sides of the balls of dough should be about 1 inch from the sides of the pans.

ADJUST AN OVEN RACK to the lower third position and preheat the oven to 350°F.

BRUSH THE LOAVES with the egg wash. Place the pans in the oven with a few inches of space between them and bake for about 50 minutes, until the loaves are a deep, dark brown and cooked through. Do not be fooled by the color of the bread into thinking the bread is done sooner; the high sugar content causes the early browning, but the breads won't burn. To test for doneness, insert a digital probe or instant-read thermometer into the center of the bread; it should register 195° to 200° F. Remove the pans from the oven and set them on wire cooling racks to cool for 5 minutes. Use a wide metal spatula to remove the loaves from the pans, and set them on the wire racks to cool completely. Cut with a sharp serrated knife.

Storing

The bread keeps well in plastic bags at room temperature for several days. It can also be frozen. Place the completely cooled loaves in heavy-duty resealable plastic bags and freeze for up to 1 month. Thaw the bread in its wrapping, then place the bread on a baking sheet and refresh in a preheated 325°F oven for 10 minutes.

Variation

I like to bake half the dough as a loaf and the other half as rolls. For rolls, divide half the dough into 9 large pieces and shape each into a ball. Lightly oil a 9-inch square baking pan or coat with cooking spray. Place the balls of dough in the pan seam side down and slightly apart or barely touching. Spray the tops of the rolls with cooking spray and cover loosely with plastic wrap. Let rise until doubled in size, about 1 hour. Uncover the rolls, paint with the egg wash, and bake. Baking time may be a bit less, so check for doneness with an instant-read thermometer after 40 minutes.

Pluckets (Monkey Bread) *pennsylvania dutch*

MAKES 1 LARGE CAKE; 12 TO 16 SERVINGS

THIS PENNSYLVANIA DUTCH YEAST COFFEE CAKE *has been made in Betty Groff's family for generations. Betty is a tenth-generation descendant of Pennsylvania Dutch immigrants. She has boundless energy, cooks all the time, and has written six Pennsylvania Dutch cookbooks.*

Pluckets is fun to make and even more fun to eat. The dough is shaped into small balls, dipped into melted butter, and rolled in sugar mixed with cinnamon and nutmeg. The balls of dough are layered into a tube pan and baked after rising one final time. After removing the cake from the pan, you simply "pluck" pieces from it. Kids especially love this cake. The sugar coating makes the balls of dough crisp, but the interiors are tender, a delicious contrast. This is best when very fresh. Bake it for a party or large gathering. It will disappear before you know it.

DOUGH

- ¾ cup whole milk
- ½ cup plus ½ teaspoon granulated sugar
- 1 package (2¼ teaspoons) active dry yeast
- ¼ cup warm water (105° to 115°F)
- 3½ cups unbleached all-purpose flour, plus more if needed
- ¾ teaspoon salt
- 1 large egg
- 1 large egg yolk
- 6 tablespoons (¾ stick) unsalted butter, at room temperature

COATING

- 8 to 12 tablespoons (1 to 1½ sticks) unsalted butter, melted and cooled
- 1¼ cups granulated sugar
- 2 teaspoons ground cinnamon
- ½ teaspoon freshly grated nutmeg

TO MAKE THE DOUGH, scald the milk in a small saucepan over medium heat—you will see steam rising from the surface of the milk and small bubbles forming around the edges. Remove the pan from the heat, add the ½ cup sugar, and stir to dissolve. Cool until the milk feels warm to the touch, 105° to 115°F.

WHILE THE MILK COOLS, stir the yeast and the ½ teaspoon sugar into the warm water in a small bowl and let stand for about 10 minutes, until the yeast is very foamy and bubbly.

To mix the dough by hand, put 2 cups of the flour into a large bowl. Add the salt, egg, egg yolk, butter, warm milk,

and the dissolved yeast and stir with a wooden spoon until combined, then beat with the spoon to make a thick, elastic batter, about 5 minutes. Gradually stir in 1 more cup flour, and beat with the spoon to make a thick, stretchy dough. Sprinkle the remaining ½ cup flour on your work surface, scrape the dough onto it, and knead in the flour. When all the flour is incorporated, the dough should feel soft, smooth, and not sticky. If necessary, knead in small amounts of additional flour, but try not to overdo it—the dough must be soft and malleable.

To mix the dough with a stand mixer, put 3 cups of the flour into the mixer bowl and stir in the salt. Add the egg, egg yolk, butter, warm milk, and dissolved yeast, attach the flat beater, and beat on low speed for about 1 minute to make a wet, cohesive dough. Increase the speed to medium to medium-high and beat for 5 minutes, or until the dough is smooth, elastic, and beginning to mass on the blade. Scrape the beater and sides of the bowl. Switch to the dough hook and add the remaining ½ cup flour. Knead on low speed until the flour is incorporated, then knead for 2 to 3 minutes on medium speed, until the dough is soft, smooth, elastic, and no longer sticky. If necessary, add small amounts of flour, but don't add too much—the dough must be soft and malleable.

WASH AND DRY THE BOWL and coat it lightly with oil or cooking spray. Shape the dough into a ball, place it in the bowl, and turn to coat. Cover tightly with plastic wrap and let the dough rise until almost tripled in volume, 1½ to 2 hours.

DEFLATE THE DOUGH by picking it up and working it gently between your hands for a few seconds. Reshape the dough into a ball and return it to the bowl. Cover tightly with plastic wrap and let the dough rise again until it is slightly more than doubled in size, about 1 hour.

TO SHAPE THE DOUGH, place the dough on your work surface and pat it out to an 8-inch square. Score the dough with a chef's knife into sixty-four 1-inch squares and cut the dough into pieces. Roll each piece between your palms into a ball (it will look rough), setting them, as you go, back onto your countertop.

COAT A TWO-PIECE 10 × 4–inch tube pan with cooking spray. Have the melted butter in a medium bowl. Mix the sugar, cinnamon, and nutmeg in a small bowl and transfer to a pie plate. Put about 6 balls of dough into the butter and turn them around with a spoon to coat all surfaces. Remove each piece, draining excess butter back into the bowl, and drop into the sugar mixture. Roll to coat thoroughly with the sugar, and place the balls of dough in the bottom of the prepared pan, around the central tube with a bit of space between them. To complete the first layer of dough, arrange 12 coated balls around the outer edge of the pan, leaving a bit of space between them. Continue layering the balls of dough in the pan, placing them over any spaces. You will end up with about 3 layers of dough and the pan will be slightly more than half-full. Cover the pan loosely with plastic wrap and let the dough rise until the pan is two-thirds full, 1½ to 2 hours.

ADJUST AN OVEN RACK to the lower third position and preheat the oven to 350°F.

REMOVE THE PLASTIC WRAP and put the pan in the oven. Bake for 50 to 60 minutes, until the dough is well browned and a wooden skewer inserted into the cake comes out clean; the cake will not rise much during baking. Remove the pan from the oven and let cool for 5 minutes only. Because the dough is sugared, if you let the cake cool longer, the sugar will solidify and the cake will stick to the pan.

USING A POT HOLDER, grasp the central tube and carefully lift the cake out of the pan. If the cake sticks to the sides, run a thin-bladed knife around the cake to release it. Leave the cake on the tube portion and set it on a wire rack to cool. Serve warm or at room temperature.

Potica

MAKES 1 LARGE CAKE; 16 SERVINGS

POTICA ("po-TEET-sa") MAY WELL BE THE QUEEN OF COFFEE CAKES. *It is almost five inches tall, made from a sweet yeast dough that is rolled very thin, filled with ground walnuts and honey, rolled up, and baked in a ring shape.*

For all the years that I've lived in Montana, I had never learned how to make povitica, a specialty of bakers who came to Montana from the former Yugoslavia and cousin of potica. But when I described this cookbook project to an old college buddy, Dan Hoffman, whom I have known since we were undergraduates at Berkeley, I was astounded to learn that he'd been making potica for almost forty years. So I traveled to Lewisburg, Pennsylvania, where Dan and his family live, and he taught me to make it.

Potica is moist, a swirl of the tender dough alternating with the filling of ground walnuts and honey, the textures of the two blending together perfectly. Making the dough is the tricky part, but Dan's meticulous instructions leave no surprises. The main thing to remember is that the dough should be wet and very elastic. "You must not add too much flour, or the dough will be impossible to roll and to stretch," he says. Dan always makes the dough by hand. "My mother did everything by hand," he says, "including the grinding of the walnuts, putting them through a meat grinder. But she didn't have a food processor, or I'm sure she would've used it!"

When rolling the dough, it's important that your kitchen be warm to minimize the chance of the dough tearing. Making potica is a big project, but it can be accomplished in just a few hours.

DOUGH

- ¼ cup plus 3 tablespoons evaporated milk
- About 6 tablespoons hot water (130° to 140°F), in all
- ½ cup plus 1 teaspoon granulated sugar
- 3¼ teaspoons (from 2 packages) active dry yeast
- 3 cups unbleached all-purpose flour, plus more as needed
- ½ teaspoon salt
- 6 tablespoons (¾ stick) unsalted butter, very soft
- 1 large egg
- 1 large egg yolk
- 1½ teaspoons pure lemon extract

FILLING

- ½ cup honey
- ½ cup evaporated milk
- 1¼ pounds (5½ cups) walnuts
- ½ cup granulated sugar
- 4 large egg whites
- Pinch of salt

EGG WASH

- 4 large egg yolks
- 1½ tablespoons confectioners' sugar
- ½ teaspoon ground cinnamon

- Confectioners' sugar for dusting

TO MAKE THE DOUGH, pour the 3 tablespoons evaporated milk into a 1-cup glass measure and add enough hot water to reach the ⅓-cup line. The temperature of the liquid should be between 110° and 115°F; let cool slightly if necessary. Stir in 1 teaspoon sugar and yeast and let stand for about 10 minutes, until the yeast is very bubbly and foamy. Combine the remaining ¼ cup evaporated milk with ¼ cup hot water.

To mix the dough by hand, put the flour into a large bowl. Add the salt and stir it in with a wooden spoon. Add the proofed yeast, the evaporated milk and water, the butter, ½ cup sugar, egg, egg yolk, and lemon extract and stir to make a cohesive dough, then beat vigorously for 3 to 5 minutes. The dough is too thick and wet to be kneaded on a countertop. Instead, it is kneaded in the bowl and requires substantial elbow grease. Holding the spoon in a vertical position, pull the dough from the sides of the bowl toward the center, beating the dough in an up-and-down motion as you rotate the bowl. Go all around the bowl as you do this and continue for several minutes to develop the dough's elasticity. (Dan says to "pull, pull, pull" as you beat.) By the end of kneading, the dough will be smooth, stretchy, and still quite wet. Scrape the bowl and spoon, and sprinkle the top of the dough with 1 tablespoon flour. Cover tightly with plastic wrap and let the dough rise until it has almost tripled in volume, about 2½ hours.

To mix the dough with a stand mixer, put the flour into the mixer bowl, add the salt, and stir it in with a rubber spatula. Add the proofed yeast, the evaporated milk and water, the butter, ½ cup sugar, egg, egg yolk, and lemon extract. With the flat beater, beat on low speed for 1 minute to make a cohesive, wet dough. Increase the speed to medium to medium-high and beat for 5 minutes to make a smooth, thick, wet dough that begins to mass on the blade. Scrape the bowl and beater, and sprinkle the top of the dough with 1 tablespoon flour. Cover tightly with plastic wrap and let the dough rise at room temperature until it has almost tripled in volume, about 2½ hours. (It will come almost to the top of a 5-quart mixer bowl.)

WHILE THE DOUGH RISES, prepare the filling. Stir the honey and evaporated milk together in a microwave-safe bowl and heat at full power for 1 minute.

PUT HALF THE NUTS and half the sugar into the work bowl of a food processor fitted with the metal blade. Pulse 8 to 10 times, until the nuts are finely ground. Transfer the nuts and sugar to a large bowl. Repeat with the remaining walnuts and sugar, and add to the bowl. Add the honey and milk and stir with a rubber spatula to make a thick, pasty mixture. Let stand for about 1 hour to allow the nuts to continue absorbing the liquid.

JUST BEFORE THE DOUGH IS READY, finish the filling: In a large bowl, using a hand-held electric mixer, beat the egg whites with the salt until they form stiff, shiny peaks. Fold the whites into the nuts. Do not wash the beaters.

TO MAKE THE EGG WASH, beat the yolks, confectioners' sugar, and cinnamon in a small bowl with the same beaters on medium speed until smooth, about 30 seconds.

TO ROLL THE DOUGH, spread a sheet or tablecloth on a small table about 3 feet square; the edges of the cloth should not extend more than a few inches over the edges of the table; fold it as necessary. If you have a cloth with a pattern, so much the better—you want to roll the dough thin enough so that a pattern would be visible through it. Generously flour the cloth and scrape the dough onto the center of it. Gently flatten the dough into a rectangle measuring about 12 × 8 inches. Cover loosely with a kitchen towel and let the dough rest for 10 minutes.

REMOVE the towel. If the top of the dough feels tacky, dust it lightly with flour. Roll the dough slowly and gently, pushing out rather than down, until it measures 31 × 21 inches and is less than ⅛ inch thick—not quite as thin as strudel dough, but close. Gently lift and stretch the dough occasionally to make the rectangle as even as possible and to be sure the dough is not sticking at any point. The dough is very easy to work with. In a warm kitchen, the job will be done in about 5 minutes. If the edges of the dough seem too thick, trim them away with a sharp knife.

TO SHAPE THE POTICA, work with a short end of the dough nearest you. Dip a pastry brush into the egg wash, and brush it thinly all over the dough, using quick, short strokes. Be gentle, to avoid tearing the dough. Place spoonfuls of the walnut filling all over the dough, leaving a 2-inch border at the short end farthest from you, then use a rubber spatula to spread the filling into a thin, even layer. Brush away excess flour around the edges of the dough. Lift the end of the cloth nearest you and flip about 1 inch of dough onto the exposed filling. Brush away excess flour from the dough. Continue rolling the potica in this manner, stopping to brush away excess flour as necessary. When the potica is rolled up, it will be fairly fat, about 4 inches in diameter, and 21 to 22 inches long.

COAT A TWO-PIECE 10 × 4–inch tube pan with cooking spray. Since the potica roll is fairly soft, transferring it to the pan may seem difficult, but it is not. Have the pan near you. Slip both hands under the potica near the middle of the roll. Take a deep breath and, in one continuous swift motion, lift the potica, place it into the pan seam side down, and drape the ends of the roll over each other, making a ring. The pan will be half full. Cover loosely with plastic wrap or a kitchen towel and let the potica rise until it reaches the top of the pan, 1½ to 2 hours.

ADJUST AN OVEN RACK to the lower third position and preheat the oven to 325°F.

UNCOVER THE POTICA and place the pan in the oven. Bake for about 1 hour, until the potica is well browned and a wooden skewer inserted into the center comes out clean. Cool the potica in its pan on a wire rack for 1 hour.

RUN A THIN-BLADED KNIFE all around the sides of the pan and around the central tube to release the potica. Lift the potica out of the pan by the tube. Run the knife between the potica and the bottom of the pan to release it. Cover the potica with a wire rack and invert the two. Lift away the tube portion of the pan, cover the potica with another wire rack, and invert again. Cool the potica completely right side up.

ALTHOUGH YOU CAN EAT potica as soon as it has cooled completely, it is far better if wrapped in a kitchen towel and allowed to stand at room temperature overnight. To serve, dust with confectioners' sugar and cut into thin slices with a sharp serrated knife.

Storing

Potica keeps well at room temperature for several days stored airtight. You can also freeze it. When it is completely cool, wrap it in plastic wrap, place in a large heavy-duty resealable plastic bag, and freeze for up to 2 months. To serve, thaw the potica overnight in its wrapping, then remove the wrapping, put the potica on a heavy baking sheet, and refresh in a preheated 300°F oven for 15 to 20 minutes. Let cool, then dust with confectioners' sugar and slice.

A Potica Story

I had no idea how important potica was to Slovenian baking until I read *Woman's Glory–The Kitchen*, a cookbook edited by Marie Prisland and Albina Novak and published by the Slovenian Women's Union of America (1968). I found a whole chapter on poticas, and an accompanying photo showed four beautifully decorated potica loaves that were sent to the White House to celebrate President Kennedy's inauguration in January 1961.

The introductory text to the chapter says "Insofar as baking goes, poticas can be considered primarily Slovenian. Even the name itself was developed from the Slovenian word 'povitica,' meaning 'something rolled in.' Other nationalities have kinds of bread that resemble potica, but, in entirety, the potica is considered a Slovenian specialty."

The chapter includes four different recipes for the dough, and 22 recipes for fillings, which contain various combinations of walnuts, dates, raisins, currants, honey, or chocolate.

Why was potica sent to President Kennedy's inauguration? When his sister Eunice Shriver was campaigning for him in Minnesota, she sampled a potica and said it would be nice to have it served in the White House. Mary Lenich, of Eveleth, Minnesota, obliged Mrs. Shriver's wishes by baking her Special Walnut Potica, a recipe very similar to the one here.

Pulla

MAKES 32 ROLLS, 16 ROLLS AND 1 LARGE BRAID, OR 2 LARGE BRAIDS

THIS IS A BUTTERY, RICH, CARDAMOM-FLAVORED COFFEE BREAD *with raisins. It is typically shaped into braids, but Finnish baker Soile Anderson, who owns a bakery in Minneapolis, likes to make individual rolls. Soile says pulla is one of the national breads of Finland, and it is made year-round. For the best flavor, it's important to use freshly ground cardamom seeds. Buy decorticated cardamom or cardamom pods, remove the seeds yourself, and crush them with a mortar and pestle or in a spice grinder.*

DOUGH

- 2 cups whole milk
- ½ pound (2 sticks) salted butter, cut into tablespoon-sized pieces
- 1 package (2¼ teaspoons) active dry yeast
- ¼ cup warm water (105° to 115°F)
- ⅔ cup granulated sugar, plus a pinch
- 4 large eggs, warmed in their shells in warm water for 5 minutes
- 1 teaspoon salt
- 7 cups unbleached all-purpose flour, plus more as needed
- 2 teaspoons ground cardamom, preferably freshly ground
- 1 cup dark raisins

TOPPING

- 4 tablespoons (½ stick) or 8 tablespoons (1 stick) cold salted butter, if making either 16 or 32 rolls
- 1 large egg, lightly beaten
- ½ to 1 cup sliced almonds
- About ¼ cup crushed lump sugar (see Note) or coarse sugar

TO MAKE THE DOUGH, put the milk into a medium saucepan and bring it almost to a boil over medium heat. Remove the pan from the heat, add the butter, and set aside until the butter is melted and the liquid has cooled to warm.

MEANWHILE, in a small bowl or cup, stir together the yeast, warm water, and pinch of sugar. Let stand until the yeast is very bubbly, about 10 minutes.

To mix the dough using a stand mixer, put the eggs and the ⅔ cup sugar in the mixer bowl and beat with the whip attachment on medium-high speed for 10 to 15 minutes, until the eggs have tripled in volume and are fluffy and very pale. Switch to the flat beater and add the milk and butter,

dissolved yeast, salt, and 4 cups of the flour. Beat on low speed until smooth. Switch to the dough hook, add 2 more cups of flour, and beat on low speed for 2 to 3 minutes. The dough will be very soft and sticky. Add the cardamom, raisins, and 1 more cup flour and beat for 2 to 3 minutes, until the cardamom and raisins are incorporated. The dough should be soft and only slightly sticky.

To mix the dough using a hand mixer, beat the eggs and the ⅔ cup sugar in a large bowl with a hand-held mixer until the eggs have tripled in volume and are fluffy and very pale, 10 to 15 minutes. With a wooden spoon, stir in the milk and butter, dissolved yeast, and salt. Gradually stir in 4 cups of the flour, then beat with the spoon for about 1 minute. Gradually stir in 2 more cups flour and beat for 1 to 2 minutes to make a very soft, sticky dough. Stir in the cardamom, raisins, and 1 more cup flour. Lightly flour your work surface, scrape the dough onto it, and knead briefly, 2 to 3 minutes, just until the dough is smooth and elastic and the raisins are distributed evenly. The dough should still be slightly sticky. Shape it into a ball.

COAT A LARGE BOWL, preferably with straight sides, with vegetable oil or cooking spray, transfer the dough to the bowl, and turn to coat on both sides. Cover the bowl tightly and let the dough rise until almost tripled in size, about 2 hours.

IF MAKING 32 ROLLS, you'll need four large baking sheets (18 × 12 × 1 inch) or cookie sheets; disposable aluminum foil pans are fine. For 16 rolls and 1 braid, you'll need three sheets; for 2 braids, two sheets. Line the pans with cooking parchment and coat lightly with cooking spray. Lightly flour your work surface and transfer the risen dough to it. Flatten the dough gently with your palms to deflate it. If you're using all of the dough to make rolls, divide it into 32 equal portions (a scant 2½ ounces each). For 16 rolls and 1 braid, use half the dough for each. Or divide the dough in half for 2 braids.

TO SHAPE ROLLS, form the portions of dough into balls, rounding them and tucking the sides of the balls underneath; pinch the seams firmly to seal. (The rounding and tucking helps to form a strong gluten net, giving the rolls a nice shape.) Set 8 balls of dough seam side down, spaced well apart on each prepared baking sheet. Cover loosely with a sheet of plastic wrap lightly coated with cooking spray, and let rise until not quite doubled in size, 1 to 1½ hours.

TO SHAPE A BRAID, divide the portion of dough into 3 equal pieces and roll each into an 18-inch-long strand. Braid them together, pinch the ends to seal, and tuck the ends under. Set the braid on the bias on a baking sheet. Cover loosely with plastic wrap lightly coated with cooking spray. Repeat if making 2 braids. Let rise until almost doubled in size, 1 to 1½ hours.

ADJUST TWO OVEN RACKS to divide the oven into thirds and preheat the oven to 350°F. (If you have four pans of rolls to bake and two ovens, heat them both.)

IF MAKING 16 ROLLS, cut the ½ stick of butter lengthwise in half and cut each half lengthwise again, to make 4 sticks, then cut the sticks crosswise into 4 pieces each. For 32 rolls, cut the full stick of butter lengthwise into 4 sticks and crosswise into 8 pieces each.

BRUSH EACH ROLL LIGHTLY with the beaten egg and push a piece of butter into the center of the roll, dimpling it. Grab a big pinch of sliced almonds and press the nuts onto the butter, covering the butter and some of the roll near the butter. Sprinkle each roll with about ½ teaspoon crushed sugar. For the braid(s), simply brush with egg and sprinkle with the almonds and sugar.

TO BAKE THE PULLA, if you have one oven and four pans of dough all ready to bake, you will have to stagger the baking. Refrigerate two pans while you bake the remaining two pans. When the first pans come out of the oven, put in the pans from the refrigerator. You may have to increase the baking time for the cold pans and dough. Bake the rolls for about 25 minutes, until they're a rich golden brown and spring back when pressed. Reverse the sheets top to bottom and front to back once about halfway during baking to ensure even browning. Bake the braid(s) for about 30 minutes. Cool the breads on their baking sheets. Serve warm or at room temperature.

Storing

To freeze baked pulla, put the cooled breads on baking sheets and freeze until solid, then transfer to heavy-duty resealable plastic bags and freeze for up to 2 weeks. Thaw the breads in their bags, then unwrap, place on a baking sheet, and pop into a preheated 325°F oven for about 10 minutes. Reheat breads for 15 to 20 minutes.

Note

You can crush supermarket lump sugar or use pearl sugar (pärlsocker) (see Sources, page 341).

Swedish Saffron Rolls

saffranbröd

MAKES 20 ROLLS

SAFFRANBRÖD, A SWEDISH SAFFRON BREAD *made for St. Lucia's Day, December 13, is traditionally shaped into a large loaf, into individual S-shaped scrolls, or into many other shapes, some of them quite intricate. In Gotland, where Helena Hoas comes from, it was her family's custom to shape the dough into scrolls and press a raisin into the center of each scroll before baking. According to legend, St. Lucia sacrificed her eyes to an admirer, and the raisins symbolize her eyes returning to her.*

The rolls can be served plain or with butter and jam for an afternoon tea or coffee break.

See the companion DVD for a video demonstration of saffron roll dough making and shaping.

DOUGH

- ½ teaspoon saffron threads
- ½ cup granulated sugar
- 8 tablespoons (1 stick) unsalted butter
- 1 cup whole milk
- 3 cups unbleached all-purpose flour, plus more as needed
- 1 package (2¼ teaspoons) instant yeast
- 1 teaspoon ground cardamom, preferably freshly ground
- ½ teaspoon salt
- ¼ cup currants (optional)
- 4 dark raisins
- 1 large egg, beaten for egg wash

POUND THE SAFFRON with 1 teaspoon of the sugar in a mortar with a pestle until the saffron is pulverized. If a thread or two of saffron remains, that's okay.

MELT THE BUTTER in a medium saucepan over medium heat. Add the milk and heat until the mixture reaches 120° to 130°F; it will feel hot to your fingertip. Remove the pan from the heat and stir in the saffron mixture until the sugar is dissolved.

To make the dough by hand, in a large bowl stir together the remaining sugar, 2 cups of the flour, the yeast, cardamom, and salt. Add the hot liquid and stir well with a wooden spoon to make a wet, thick dough. Beat with the spoon for about 5 minutes to make a thick, elastic dough. Stir in ½ cup more flour and the currants, if using. Sprinkle the remaining ½ cup flour on your work surface, scrape the dough onto it, and turn the dough to coat all surfaces with flour. Knead the dough until all the flour is incorporated and the dough is smooth, elastic, and slightly sticky. If necessary, add a bit more flour, but be careful—too much flour, and the rolls will be dry.

To make the dough with a stand mixer, stir together the remaining sugar, the 3 cups flour, the yeast, cardamom, and salt in the mixer bowl. Add the hot liquid and stir well with a wooden spoon to make a wet, thick dough. Scrape the spoon and sides of the bowl. Attach the dough hook and knead on medium-high speed for a few seconds, until the dough gathers onto the hook. Reduce the speed to medium and knead for 5 minutes more to make a soft, elastic, slightly sticky dough. On low speed, beat in the currants, if using.

WASH AND DRY THE BOWL and coat it lightly with cooking spray. Shape the dough into a ball, place it in the bowl, and sprinkle it with 1 tablespoon flour. Cover the bowl tightly with plastic wrap and let the dough rise in a warm place (80° to 85°F) until it has more than doubled in volume, 2 to 2½ hours. Test the dough by pressing it with a fingertip: the impression should remain after you remove your finger.

SCRAPE THE RISEN DOUGH onto an unfloured surface, and gently deflate it with the palms of your hands. Pat the dough into a 10 × 8-inch rectangle. Cut the dough into twenty 2–inch squares (about 1½ ounces each). Shape each piece into a ball, and arrange them slightly apart on the work surface. Cover them loosely with a kitchen towel and let them rest for 10 to 15 minutes.

LINE TWO LARGE BAKING SHEETS (18 × 12 × 1 inch) with cooking parchment. Roll each ball of dough into an 8-inch-long roll, then roll each end of the dough in opposite directions to form an S-shaped twist. Push a raisin into the center of each scroll. Place 10 rolls on each sheet, about 2 to 3 inches apart. Coat the rolls lightly with cooking spray and let them rise, uncovered, in a warm place until doubled in size, about 30 minutes.

ADJUST TWO OVEN RACKS to divide the oven into thirds and preheat the oven to 400°F.

BRUSH THE RISEN ROLLS with egg wash and put the pans in the oven. Bake for about 15 minutes, until the rolls are well browned. Rotate the pans top to bottom and front to back once after 10 minutes of baking to ensure even browning. With a metal spatula, transfer the rolls to wire racks to cool. Serve warm or at room temperature.

Storing

Leftover rolls keep well overnight sealed in a plastic bag. They can also be frozen. Seal them in heavy-duty resealable plastic bags and freeze for up to 1 month. To refresh, thaw the rolls in their bags, then place on baking sheets and reheat for 5 to 10 minutes in a preheated 325°F oven.

Stollen

MAKES 2 LARGE BREADS

THE RECIPE FOR THIS CLASSIC GERMAN CHRISTMAS BREAD, *shaped to resemble the blanket of the swaddled Baby Jesus, comes from Gertrude Lackschewitz. One of six children, Gertrude was born in Gelsenkirchen, in an area known as the Ruhrgebiet. She immigrated to the United States soon after marrying in 1954. Stollen was an important part of her family ritual, but she had to bake it in a wood-burning stove at first. Once Gertrude had a home with a modern range, she made stollen every Christmas, and she has been doing so for more than forty years.*

The dough for stollen has lots of butter but only one egg, which is beaten into the sponge. It is packed with liquor-soaked dried fruits, which add flavor in addition to helping preserve the bread's freshness. The baked stollen has a dense texture. Gertrude likes to enclose a log of marzipan in the stollen, as do many German bakers. The marzipan often comes as a surprise when the stollen is sliced, and people always ask what that circle is. Besides a certain level of sophistication, the marzipan contributes a welcome textural and flavor contrast to the dense dough.

Right after baking, the stollen is brushed with melted butter, which, besides softening the bread's crust and adding flavor, functions as a "glue" for the generous layer of confectioners' sugar that is then sifted onto it. The confectioners' sugar probably symbolizes snow. Gertrude uses only confectioners'

FRUIT

¾ cup dark raisins

¾ cup golden raisins

4 ounces whole candied citron (see Sources, page 342), cut into ¼-inch dice

½ cup dark rum or brandy

SPONGE

1½ cups whole milk

2 cups unbleached all-purpose flour

2 packages (1½ tablespoons) rapid-rise yeast

2 tablespoons granulated sugar

1 large egg, at room temperature

DOUGH

½ pound (2 sticks) unsalted butter, very soft

⅓ cup granulated sugar

1½ teaspoons ground cardamom, preferably freshly ground

½ teaspoon freshly grated nutmeg

1 vanilla bean, split lengthwise, seeds scraped out and reserved

¾ teaspoon pure almond extract

1 teaspoon salt

1 cup blanched whole almonds, chopped into medium-sized pieces

2½ to 2¾ cups unbleached all-purpose flour

12 ounces marzipan, homemade (page 331) or canned

4 tablespoons (½ stick) unsalted butter, melted

Confectioners' sugar for dusting

sugar that doesn't contain cornstarch, because she feels the cornstarch gives the sugar an unpleasant, chalky texture. I agree with her and, fortunately, cornstarch-free organic confectioners' (powdered) sugar is now widely available in supermarkets, so do seek it out.

Since stollen keeps well, you can bake it far in advance of Christmas and store it, wrapped securely, at room temperature. Gertrude usually bakes hers on December 12, which gives the stollen plenty of time to age gracefully.

THE NIGHT BEFORE or even 2 or 3 days ahead, combine the raisins, candied citron, and liquor in a 2-pint jar with a screw-cap lid or in a resealable plastic bag. Turn the container several times to distribute the liquor evenly. Set aside at room temperature to soak.

TO MAKE THE SPONGE, scald the milk in a small saucepan over medium heat—you will see steam rising from the surface and small bubbles forming around the edges. Remove the pan from the heat and let the milk cool to between 120° and 130°F.

PUT THE FLOUR into a large mixing bowl or the bowl of a heavy-duty mixer. Whisk in the yeast and sugar. Add the milk and whisk briskly to make a smooth batter. Add the egg and whisk to combine well. Cover the bowl tightly with plastic wrap and let the sponge rise until it more than doubles in volume and then collapses on itself, about 2 hours.

To make the dough by hand, beat the butter into the sponge with a wooden spoon in 2-tablespoon installments, beating until incorporated after each addition. Beat in the sugar, cardamom, nutmeg, vanilla seeds, almond extract, and salt. Continue beating for 3 to 5 minutes to make a thick, ropy, elastic batter. Add the raisins and citron, along with any unabsorbed liquor, and beat in well. Beat in the almonds. Gradually add 2 cups of the flour, stirring to make a stiff but wet dough.

To make the dough with a stand mixer, attach the flat beater and beat the butter into the sponge in 2-tablespoon installments on medium speed, beating until incorporated after each addition. Add the sugar, cardamom, nutmeg, vanilla seeds, almond extract, and salt and beat on low to medium-low speed until the dough masses on the blade, about 5 minutes. Scrape the bowl and beater, and stir in the raisins and citron, along with any unabsorbed liquor. Add the almonds. Switch to the dough hook. Beating on low speed, gradually add 2 cups of the flour and then knead for 3 to 5 minutes.

SPRINKLE ½ cup flour on your work surface and scrape the dough onto it. Knead the dough until all the flour has been incorporated. The dough should feel fairly firm and be only a bit tacky. If it is too sticky, knead in up to ¼ cup more flour. Push any fruit that falls from the dough during kneading back into the dough.

WASH AND DRY THE BOWL and either oil it lightly or coat it with cooking spray. Shape the dough into a ball and place it in the bowl, turning to coat all surfaces. Cover tightly with plastic wrap and let the dough rise until almost doubled in size, about 1 hour.

TURN THE DOUGH OUT onto an unfloured work surface and divide it in half with a pastry scraper or sharp knife. Shape each piece into a ball, cover with a kitchen towel, and let rest for 10 to 15 minutes.

TO SHAPE THE STOLLEN, divide the marzipan into 2 pieces. Roll each under your palms into a cylinder about 11 inches long. Pat or roll each piece of dough into an oval measuring 12 inches long and about 9 inches wide at the widest point. If the dough sticks at any point, dust it very lightly with flour.

Make a shallow depression down the center of each oval with the handle of a wooden spoon. Place a roll of marzipan in each depression. Lift one side of dough over the marzipan, covering it completely. The edge of the top flap of dough should just reach the other edge of dough.

LINE A LARGE BAKING SHEET (18 × 12 × 1 inch) with a silicone baking pan liner or cooking parchment. Put the stollen crosswise on the prepared sheet, placing them about 3 inches from each end of the sheet and leaving about 4 inches of space between them. Coat the stollen with cooking spray and cover them loosely with plastic wrap. Let rise just until they have increased in volume by about half, 45 minutes to 1 hour.

ADJUST AN OVEN RACK to the lower third position and preheat the oven to 350°F.

WHEN THE STOLLEN ARE READY, remove the plastic wrap and place the pan in the oven. Bake for 45 to 55 minutes, until the stollen are nicely browned. An instant-read thermometer inserted into the thickest part should register 195°F. Remove the pan from the oven and immediately brush each stollen with half the melted butter. Put the confectioners' sugar in a fine-meshed sieve and sift a generous layer all over the top of the stollen. Repeat in a few minutes if you see the sugar melting in spots. Cool the stollen completely on wire cooling racks. To serve, cut into ½-inch-thick slices with a sharp serrated knife.

Storing

You can leave the stollen, uncovered, on the rack overnight, which will help them dry a bit. Then wrap tightly in plastic wrap and store at room temperature for up to 2 weeks. For longer storage, put the wrapped stollen in heavy-duty resealable plastic bags and freeze for up to 2 months. Thaw completely in the wrapping, then unwrap, place on a baking sheet, and refresh in a preheated 325°F oven for 10 minutes. Cool before slicing. Dust with more confectioners' sugar, if necessary.

7 | Cookies

THE DUTCH ARE CREDITED WITH INVENTING THE COOKIE hundreds of years ago, but they probably never dreamed that their idea—one's very own small, intimate confection that is nibbled out of hand—would become a worldwide phenomenon of staggering diversity. The beautiful thing about cookies is that they're baked in batches but consumed one at a time and at one's leisure. And unlike most pastries, which are best eaten within a day or two, cookies usually stay fresh over a period of days, or even weeks.

Take the simple butter cookie that's rolled between your palms into balls, baked, and tossed in confectioners' sugar. The Lebanese, Syrians, Mexicans, Greeks, Norwegians, and other nationalities make variations of these melt-in-your mouth-nuggets. The Scottish have their own version—patting the dough to a certain thickness and cutting it into shortbread. How did this simple kind of cookie find its way into all these diverse cultures?

Many historians believe that cookie-like cakes date back to the seventh century in ancient Persia, today's Iran, where sugar was cultivated and butter was a readily available commodity. Because of an extensive trade network that formed between the countries of northern Europe, India, and the Middle East (see The Hanseatic League, page 305), and military invasions in the Mediterranean and adjoining regions, sugar spread far and wide. Each country had its own agriculture, so dairy products would have been available everywhere.

The spice trade developed at about the same time as the sugar trade, and soon each country put its stamp on various flavor combinations. Spices also have a preservative function, so before refrigeration, cookies that stayed fresh longer were favored.

Recipes from more than a dozen countries are included here. Because there are so many cookie recipes, I had difficulty deciding when to stop. I finally drew the line once I had a good international sampling of the basic categories of cookies, some molded by hand, others dropped as a batter from a spoon, still others made from a dough that is rolled and filled with nuts or fruit or both. There's a wafer cookie baked in a special iron, along with cookies shaped into logs, filled with jam, and cut into strips after baking. What you will not find are bar or refrigerator cookies, which seem to be twentieth-century American inventions.

Many of these recipes are traditionally baked for special holidays, but that doesn't mean you have to wait. Bake when the mood strikes you. And if you want to bake ahead, I've given directions for freezing those cookies that keep well. A world of cookies awaits you in the following pages.

Chinese Almond Cookies

MAKES 36 COOKIES

FOR THE BEST FLAVOR AND TEXTURE, *these classic cookies must be made with lard. The commonly available supermarket lard is not your best choice. Instead, either render your own lard (page 332) or order it by mail (see Sources, pages 342 and 343). Stella Fong, a Chinese-American food writer, learned how to bake these cookies from her mother. They are crisp and crunchy and keep well for about 1 week.*

DOUGH

2½ cups unbleached all-purpose flour

1½ teaspoons baking powder

¼ teaspoon salt

1 cup cold home-rendered lard (see page 332, or see Sources, pages 342 and 343)

1 cup granulated sugar

1 large egg

2 teaspoons pure almond extract

36 blanched whole almonds (see Note)

1 large egg yolk, beaten with 1 tablespoon water, for egg wash

---

ADJUST AN OVEN RACK to the center position and preheat the oven to 350°F. Line two large baking sheets (18 × 12 × 1 inch) with cooking parchment or silicone baking pan liners.

IN A MEDIUM BOWL, whisk together the flour, baking powder, and salt.

IN A LARGE BOWL, stir the lard with a wooden spoon to soften it a bit and make it malleable. Add the sugar and beat well with the spoon for 2 to 3 minutes, until creamy. Beat in the egg and almond extract. Gradually stir in the dry ingredients to make a firm dough. Reach into the bowl with your hands and knead briefly. The dough should hold together but not be sticky. If the dough crumbles, sprinkle in droplets of water and knead them in.

TURN THE DOUGH OUT and divide it into 3 portions. On an unfloured work surface, roll each one into a 12-inch-long cylinder. Cut each log into 1-inch pieces. Roll the dough into balls between your palms and place them about 2 inches apart on the prepared sheets. Flatten each ball into a 1½-inch circle and make a shallow depression in the center with your

thumb. Place an almond into each depression and press it gently into the dough.

WITH A PASTRY BRUSH, paint the tops of the cookies, not the sides, lightly with egg wash.

BAKE ONE SHEET AT A TIME (leave the second sheet uncovered at room temperature) for about 15 minutes, until the cookies are a pale gold color on top and the bottoms are a very light brown. Don't overbake them, or they'll be too crunchy (but still delicious). With a metal spatula, transfer the cookies to wire cooling racks to cool completely.

Storing

Store the cookies airtight at room temperature for 1 to 2 weeks. Or freeze them. Arrange on baking sheets and freeze until solid, then tranfer to heavy-duty resealable plastic bags and freeze for up to 1 month. Thaw them in their wrapping. To refresh, place the thawed cookies on a baking sheet and pop them into a preheated 325°F oven for 5 minutes.

Variation

CHOCOLATE CHIP ALMOND COOKIES Stella sometimes adds ½ cup mini semisweet chocolate chips to the batter before stirring in the flour mixture.

Note

Although you can purchase whole blanched almonds, it's a simple matter to blanch your own. Put the almonds in a small bowl, cover them with boiling water, and leave them for about 5 minutes. Remove them from the water a few at a time with a slotted spoon and slip off their skins. Pat the almonds dry on paper towels, and they're ready to use.

Anzac Cookies

MAKES 36 COOKIES

THESE DELECTABLE WAFER-THIN, CRISP AND CHEWY *oats and coconut cookies are native to Australia. Anzac is an acronym for the Australian and New Zealand Army Corps. During World War I, these troops fought in the Gallipoli campaign and suffered tremendous casualties. April 25 is known as Anzac Day, commemorating the anniversary of Gallipoli, and Anzac cookies were created some years later and named in honor of the men who fought in the war.*

Elizabeth Germaine, a cooking teacher and cookbook author who immigrated to the United States from Australia more than 20 years ago, showed me how to make them. She always keeps a supply of Anzac cookies on hand because they keep well. Lyle's Golden Syrup, an amber-colored cane syrup with a pleasant caramel flavor, is traditional in these cookies, but Elizabeth has had good results with honey and with light corn syrup. There is only 1 tablespoon of syrupy sweetener in the recipe, so the flavor of the cookie is not compromised with a substitution.

1	cup old-fashioned rolled oats
¾	cup unsweetened shredded coconut, chopped
¾	cup all-purpose flour
1	cup granulated sugar
8	tablespoons (1 stick) salted butter
1	tablespoon Lyle's Golden Syrup, honey, or light corn syrup
3	tablespoons boiling water, plus more if needed
1½	teaspoons baking soda

ADJUST AN OVEN RACK to the center position and preheat the oven to 300°F. Line a 17 × 14–inch cookie sheet with parchment and cut two more sheets the same size.

IN A MEDIUM BOWL, stir together the oats, coconut, flour, and sugar.

MELT THE BUTTER in a small heavy saucepan over low heat and stir in the syrup or honey. In a small cup, stir the 3 tablespoons boiling water and baking soda together until the soda is dissolved. Add the mixture to the hot butter, stir well, and pour the liquid into the dry ingredients. Stir with a wooden spoon until thoroughly mixed. The batter should be thick enough to hold its shape in a spoon but not at all dry. Add droplets of boiling water if necessary.

SPOON slightly rounded teaspoonfuls of batter 3 inches apart onto the lined cookie sheet, making 12 mounds. Don't make the cookies too large—they spread a lot during baking. Bake about 12 minutes, until the cookies are a deep golden brown throughout. Rotate the sheet front to back once after 8 minutes to ensure even browning. During baking the cookies will puff up and then fall. Remove the sheet from the oven, slide the parchment onto your countertop, and let the cookies cool completely on the parchment. Cool the baking sheet, or run it under cold tap water for a few seconds and wipe it dry.

MEANWHILE, shape 12 more cookies on each of the remaining two sheets of parchment. Repeat baking and cooling the cookies as described above. When the cookies are completely cool, lift them off the parchment with a wide metal spatula.

Storing

Store the cookies layered between waxed paper in airtight containers at room temperature for 2 to 3 weeks.

Cuccidati (Buccellati)

MAKES 48 COOKIES

THESE FRUIT-FILLED SICILIAN CHRISTMAS COOKIES *may remind you of Fig Newtons. A moist filling of dried figs, toasted chopped almonds, walnuts, and hazelnuts, shaped into a log, is enclosed in a buttery dough and cut into bite-sized lengths. After baking, the cookies are brushed with a thick confectioners' sugar glaze and dusted with colored sprinkles. Cuccidati are also known as buccellati or turtigliuna. The word* buccellato *comes from the Latin* buccellatum, *which means ring or wreath. Some bakers often present this as one large wreath.*

I learned how to make these hearty cookies from four Sicilian-American women in Albany, New York. Rosanna Aiuppa was born in Sicily and came to New York with her parents when only a few years old. Rosanna, her cousin Rose Padula, and her friends Santa Pasquini and Maria DeNitto gather together every Christmas season to continue the tradition of baking their families' specialties.

Rosanna says, "In the old days, mamma would grind all the fruit and nuts together in a meat grinder. Today I use the food processor. And for the dough? Mamma and her sisters mixed all of it in huge basins by hand. I do it with my KitchenAid." Since many of their traditional recipes are baked only once a year, and they don't always make notes of

FILLING

One 14-ounce package dried Kalamata or Calimyrna figs

1 cup (5 ounces) dark raisins, or a mixture of dark and golden

½ cup (2½ ounces) hazelnuts, toasted and skinned (see page 24)

1 cup (5 ounces) blanched or unblanched whole almonds, toasted (see page 23)

1 cup (3½ ounces) walnuts, coarsely chopped

Finely grated zest of 1 orange

Finely grated zest of 1 lemon

⅓ cup orange marmalade

¼ cup honey

2 tablespoons Grand Marnier or Cointreau

2 tablespoons Galliano

2 tablespoons whiskey or brandy

2 teaspoons pure lemon extract

2 teaspoons ground cinnamon

½ teaspoon ground cloves

DOUGH

3½ cups unbleached all-purpose flour

½ teaspoon salt

1 teaspoon baking powder

10 ounces (2½ sticks) unsalted butter, at room temperature

⅔ cup granulated sugar

3 large eggs

2 teaspoons pure vanilla extract

2 teaspoons pure lemon extract

ICING

2 large egg whites

3 cups confectioners' sugar

1 tablespoon fresh lemon juice

1 teaspoon pure lemon extract

Colored sprinkles

any changes, there is always some lively chatter centered on the ingredients and procedures. These good-natured exchanges, punctuated with laughter and giggles, go on all day. From moment to moment, the recipe may be transformed, which is as it should be in all cooking.

Start the cuccidati a day or two before you want to bake. A night in the refrigerator greatly improves the filling's taste and texture, and the dough needs to be well chilled before being shaped into cookies.

Serve these with hot coffee or tea.

TO MAKE THE FILLING, the figs must feel soft. If they seem dry, put them into a bowl and cover them with boiling water. Leave them for about 5 minutes, then remove one and give it a squeeze. If it seems moist, drain the figs and pat them dry on paper towels; if not, soak them a bit longer. Snip off the tough stems with kitchen shears and cut the figs in half. Put them into a bowl and add the raisins.

PLACE THE HAZELNUTS and almonds in the work bowl of a food processor fitted with the metal blade and pulse 3 times, just to begin chopping the nuts. Add the figs and raisins and pulse rapidly 8 to 10 times, until the fruit and nuts are coarsely chopped. Stir in the walnuts.

IN A LARGE BOWL, stir together the zests, marmalade, honey, orange liqueur, Galliano, whiskey, lemon extract, cinnamon, and cloves. Add the nuts and fruit and stir well with a wooden spoon or your hands until the filling is thick and pasty and holds together. It will be sticky. Transfer to a medium bowl, cover tightly with plastic wrap, and refrigerate overnight. (The filling can be refrigerated for up to 3 days.)

TO MAKE THE DOUGH, in a medium bowl whisk together the flour, salt, and baking powder.

PUT THE BUTTER in the bowl of a stand mixer fitted with the flat beater and beat on medium speed until soft and creamy, about 1 minute. Gradually add the sugar, beating for a few seconds after each addition, then beat 2 more minutes. Add the eggs one at a time, beating well after each. Stop to scrape the bowl and beater as necessary. The mixture will look curdled—that is fine. Beat in the extracts. On low speed, gradually add the flour mixture, about ⅓ cup at a time, beating only until incorporated. The dough will be stiff but slightly sticky. Remove the bowl from the mixer and stir with a wooden spoon to make sure all the dry ingredients have been incorporated and the dough is smooth.

SCRAPE THE DOUGH onto a sheet of plastic wrap and pat gently with your fingertips into a rectangle about 1 inch thick. Wrap tightly and refrigerate overnight. (The dough can be made up to 3 days ahead.)

ADJUST AN OVEN RACK to the center position and preheat the oven to 350°F. Line two large cookie sheets (17 × 14 inches) with silicone baking pan liners or cooking parchment.

DIVIDE THE CHILLED DOUGH into 4 smaller rectangles (about 9½ ounces each). Refrigerate the portions you're not working with. Sprinkle your work surface lightly with flour and coat the first piece of dough on both sides with the flour. Roll into a 12 × 7–inch rectangle, checking frequently to see if the dough is sticking; if it is, lightly flour the dough. If it cracks at any point, simply pinch it together. Use your fingertips often to square the edges and to smooth the sides. Cut the dough lengthwise in half with a long sharp knife. Separate the strips, leaving a few inches of space between them. If necessary, turn them so a long side of each one is facing you.

To shape the cookies, divide the filling into 8 equal portions (about 5 ounces each). Since the filling is moist and sticky, the easiest way to do this is to moisten your hands, pat the filling out into a rectangle on a sheet of plastic wrap, and cut it into 8 equal portions. Moisten your hands and place a portion of the filling onto a work surface (a wooden board works nicely). Gently roll one piece of the filling under your palms to form a 12-inch-long log about ¾ inch in diameter. Place the log in the center of one of the strips. Repeat with a second portion of filling and place it down the center of the second strip.

CAREFULLY LIFT UP the far side of one strip of dough and bring it over the filling, then roll the covered filling toward you to enclose the filling completely in the dough. Repeat with the second strip of dough and filling. (If your room is warm and the dough seems too soft, refrigerate briefly to firm it up a bit.) Turn the rolls seam side up and press gently with a fingertip to seal the seams completely, then turn the rolls seam side down. Gently tamp the ends of the rolls to even them. Measure them to make sure they're 12 inches long. Nick each roll with the tip of a sharp knife at 2-inch intervals, then cut each roll into six pieces, using a gentle sawing motion. Prick the top of each piece twice with a fork and place the cuccidati 1 inch apart onto a prepared cookie sheet.

REPEAT WITH A SECOND PIECE of dough and filling, so you have 24 cookies on the cookie sheet. Bake for 25 to 30 minutes, until the cookies are a pale golden brown. With a metal spatula, transfer the cookies to cooling racks to cool completely.

WHILE THE FIRST BATCH BAKES, shape the remaining cookies and place on the cookie sheet. Bake and cool as directed.

TO MAKE THE ICING, beat the egg whites with a fork in a medium bowl just to break them up. Gradually beat in the confectioners' sugar with the fork. Beat in the lemon juice and lemon extract. This is a very thick icing. Use a pastry brush to paint the tops and sides of the cookies with the glaze. Scatter a few colored sprinkles over each cookie as soon as it has been glazed. The glaze will set and harden in about 10 minutes.

Storing

Store cuccidati in airtight containers at room temperature for up to 1 week. To freeze, put no more than two layers of cookies separated by a sheet of waxed paper into each airtight container and freeze for up to 2 weeks. Thaw the cookies in their containers at room temperature, about 2 hours.

Graibi

MAKES 30 COOKIES

LEBANESE FOOD WRITER MAUREEN ABOOD shared her family recipe for these incredible cookies with me. When you bite into one, you'll think crunchy, but then, because of the amazing amount of butter, the cookie melts in your mouth—and you'll want to reach for another one immediately. The recipe calls for clarified butter, which is much lower in water content than regular butter. It gives the cookies their special taste and texture. You can easily clarify your own butter, several days ahead or longer, and store it in the refrigerator. Bring it to room temperature before using. Or you can use ghee, Indian clarified butter, available in jars in many supermarkets.

A traditional way of forming these cookies, which are popular in Syria as well as Lebanon, is to shape them into crescents, and that is the method I describe in the recipe. Maureen also likes to shape portions of dough into 1-inch-wide logs, cut them on the bias into diamond shapes, flatten them slightly, and top each with a blanched whole almond. Either way, the cookies are delicious.

¾ pound (3 sticks) unsalted butter, clarified (see page 12), or 1 cup ghee

1 cup confectioners' sugar, plus additional for dusting

1 teaspoon rose water or orange flower water

¼ teaspoon salt

2 cups unbleached all-purpose flour

ADJUST AN OVEN RACK to the center position and preheat the oven to 300°F. Line a 17 × 14–inch cookie sheet or an 18 × 12 × 1–inch baking sheet with cooking parchment.

To make the dough by hand, measure 1 cup of solidified clarified butter (reserve the remaining butter for another use), if using, and put the butter or ghee in a medium bowl. Use a wooden spoon to stir and soften the butter. Add the confectioners' sugar and beat well with the spoon until creamy and smooth. Beat in the rose water or orange flower water and salt. Gradually stir in the flour to make a firm, smooth, pliant dough.

To make the dough with a stand mixer, put 1 cup solidified clarified butter or the ghee and the confectioners' sugar in the mixer bowl and beat with the flat beater on low speed until combined, about 1 minute. Increase the speed to medium and beat for 1 minute, or until fluffy and creamy. On low speed, beat in the rose water or orange flower water and salt. Gradually add the flour, beating only until the dough masses on the beater.

TO SHAPE THE COOKIES, scoop up a rounded teaspoonful of dough for each cookie, roll the dough between your palms to form a tapered cylinder about 3½ inches long, and bend it to form a crescent. Place the cookies about 1 inch apart on the prepared sheet.

BAKE THE COOKIES for 20 to 25 minutes, just until cooked through. Do not allow the cookies to brown. Let the cookies cool on the baking sheet for 5 minutes, then transfer them to wire cooling racks with a metal spatula. Careful—the cookies are fragile at this point. Let cool completely

DUST THE COOKIES with confectioners' sugar before serving.

Storing

Store the cookies in an airtight container at room temperature, layered between waxed paper, for up to 2 weeks. The cookies can also be frozen in the same container for up to 1 month. Thaw completely before unwrapping, and dust again with confectioners' sugar before serving, if necessary.

Krumkaker

MAKES 30 TO 36 KRUMKAKER

THESE CRISP ROLLED COOKIES ARE REMINISCENT OF ITALIAN PIZZELLE, *and, like pizzelle, they're baked in a special iron (see Sources, page 341). Making cookies in an iron goes back to the sixteenth century in Norway. The oldest, an Avlett iron, had two round surfaces about the size of salad plates joined by a hinge. These irons were heavy and had long handles so they could be used in an open fireplace. Local blacksmiths who fashioned the irons were artists, and they created fancy patterns of animals (usually lions), flowers, birds, religious pictures, monograms, or important dates onto the irons, to give the cookies an attractive design.*

Karin Knight, who taught me this recipe, says her mother used an iron that was heated on top of her electric stove. "Mom had to keep an eye on it all the time, moving it on and off to prevent it from getting too hot. I use an electric nonstick iron, which takes all the guesswork out of making krumkaker." Most krumkake irons make two cookies at a time. It helps to have two people do this, one to spoon the batter onto the iron and one to roll the cookies. When the krumkaker are done, each cookie is rolled around a wooden cone-shaped mold while it's still hot and flexible. If ordering a krumkake iron, be sure to get two wooden molds for your double krumkake iron. (If you prefer, you can use foot-long wooden dowels about 1¼ inches in diameter to shape the cookies.) If your iron is new, be sure to follow the manufacturer's directions for seasoning it. Over time, the iron can be used without greasing it.

The traditional filling for krumkaker is whipped cream with cloudberries, a raspberry relative. Since cloudberries aren't often available here, you can substitute cloudberry jam (see Sources, page 345), or you can use fresh or frozen raspberries or strawberries. Krumkaker are also delicious filled just with slightly sweetened or rum-flavored whipped cream. Be sure to fill them just before serving so that the cookies will maintain their crispness. Please see the DVD for how to make Krumkaker.

3 large eggs

¾ cup granulated sugar

1 cup unbleached all-purpose flour (spooned into the cup and leveled)

¼ teaspoon salt

2 teaspoons pure vanilla extract

10⅔ tablespoons (1⅓ sticks) unsalted butter, melted and cooled to tepid

Whipped cream and fruit, for filling

IN A LARGE BOWL, beat the eggs with an electric mixer on high speed until thick and pale, 3 to 4 minutes. Beating on low speed, gradually add the sugar. Increase the speed to high and beat for 3 to 4 minutes more, until the mixture is very thick and pale in color and forms a slowly dissolving ribbon when the beaters are raised.

ON LOW SPEED, beat in the flour, salt, and vanilla. With a rubber spatula, gradually fold in the melted butter. The batter will be thick. Cover the bowl tightly with plastic wrap and let stand at room temperature for 30 minutes or a bit longer.

MEANWHILE, set an electric krumkake iron on a baking sheet lined with several thicknesses of paper towels. (The baking sheet will protect your work surface, since the iron gets very hot, and the paper towels will collect any batter that oozes from the edges of the iron.) Plug in the iron.

WHEN THE IRON IS HOT, check the batter's consistency: Spoon up a gob of batter with a regular teaspoon—it should hold its shape, and when you tip the spoon, the batter should flow off it very slowly. Make a test cookie or two to see if the batter is the right consistency. If the batter is too thin, the krumkaker will be too thin and fragile; if it is too thick, the krumkaker will be heavy instead of delicate. Adjust the consistency with pinches of flour or small amounts of warm water, if necessary.

OPEN THE KRUMKAKE IRON and quickly spoon a teaspoon of batter onto the center; if your iron makes two krumkaker, spoon a teaspoonful of batter onto each circle, working quickly. Immediately close the iron and press the handles together. If batter oozes out the sides, cut it away with a small sharp knife. Count 10 seconds and open the iron. The krumkaker should be only a very pale golden brown. Do not let them get really brown, or the delicacy of their flavor will be lost. If the krumkaker are too pale, close the iron and cook for another second or two.

IMMEDIATELY TRANSFER the krumkaker to your work surface with a narrow metal spatula, keeping the top sides up. Set the cone-shaped portions of the wooden molds onto the edge of each krumkake and roll the krumkaker around the mold to form cone-shaped cookies. The krumkaker will become crisp and firm in a few seconds; carefully slide them off the molds and set them aside. Continue making krumkaker. As you make them, the batter may get a bit thicker on standing; if so, stir in a teaspoon or so of warm water.

FILL WITH whipped cream and fruit just before serving.

Storing

Store the cooled krumkakre in an airtight container at room temperature, layered between waxed paper. They will stay fresh for up to 2 weeks.

Melomakarona

MAKES 30 COOKIES

THESE TRADITIONAL CHRISTMAS COOKIES, *flavored with olive oil, honey, orange juice, and spices, are found all over Greece. They are an ancient cookie, reaching back to antiquity. Melomakarona ("melo-ma-KA-rona") are also known as* phoenikia, *suggesting they may have originated with the Phoenicians, a people who lived where present-day Lebanon is and traded extensively with the Greeks.*

Sophie Lambros, a Greek American, learned to bake them from her mother. The dough is simple to make and easy to work with. After baking, the cookies are saturated with a syrup of honey, sugar, and water. You can find many different kinds of honey and olive oil in Greece. Whatever honey you use, be sure it is mild-flavored so that it doesn't overwhelm the spices; clover honey is a good choice. Use a fruity but nonassertive olive oil. It doesn't have to be extra-virgin—ordinary supermarket brands of pure olive oil work well. But do not use any oil labeled "light," because these lack flavor.

I have found many versions of melomakarona in Greek cookbooks. Some are made only with flour, some with semolina and flour, others with farina. Some have a nut filling or nuts added to the dough, others have nuts on top, and some have no nuts at all. Sophie adds finely chopped walnuts to the dough and sprinkles some on top for looks and for texture. "This is a plain-Jane sort of cookie to look at," she says, "but the taste just blows you away." Some recipes say to cool the cookies completely before adding the honey syrup; others have you add hot syrup to cold cookies, or vice versa. I think having both the cookies and syrup hot works the best.

Let the cookies stand overnight at room temperature before eating them if you can—they get even better on standing.

DOUGH

- 2 cups unbleached all-purpose flour, plus 1 to 1¼ cups for kneading
- 2 teaspoons baking powder
- ¼ teaspoon salt
- 1 cup olive oil
- ⅓ cup granulated sugar
- Finely grated zest of 1 orange
- ¾ cup freshly squeezed orange juice
- ⅓ cup brandy
- 1 cup fine semolina
- 1½ teaspoons ground cinnamon
- ½ teaspoon ground allspice
- ¾ teaspoon ground cloves
- ¾ cup walnuts, finely chopped

SYRUP

- ¾ cup honey
- ¾ cup granulated sugar
- 1¼ cups water
- ¼ cup finely chopped walnuts

A Montana Greek Community

Sophie Lambros, born of Greek immigrant parents in West Virginia, moved to Missoula, Montana, with her husband, Dan, in 1958. "At the time, our Greek community was just on the verge of burgeoning because we had raised the money to buy an old Mormon church, which became our Church of the Annunciation. You have to understand, Greek community life revolves around the church. At first we had to share a priest with Great Falls. But by the 1980s, our group had grown to about eighty families, so we were able to afford our own priest."

"I grew up with a strong Greek familiy tradition—learning the importance of church and family, how to cook—and at the same time I was an honest-to-goodness American gal," Sophie says with a smile. She is fluent in spoken and written modern Greek. "The thing I always loved most about the church was the community celebrations: name days, Greek Independence Day, Easter, and New Year's. My, what feasts we cooked and ate! And we all felt we were part of one large happy family."

In the 1980s, as a way to raise funds, the church began sponsoring an annual Greek Festival open to the entire Missoula community. These festivals were more ethnic rather than religious, and they became a big hit. Members of the church cooked multicourse Greek dinners, taught Greek dances post-dinner, and offered Greek baked goods, books, and art objects for sale.

TO MAKE THE DOUGH, in a medium bowl whisk together the 2 cups flour, baking powder, and salt.

IN A LARGE BOWL, whisk together the olive oil and sugar to combine well. Whisk in the orange zest, orange juice, and brandy. Gradually add the flour mixture, whisking until smooth. Use a wooden spoon to stir in the semolina, spices, and walnuts. The dough will be quite soft, oily, and wet.

FLOUR YOUR WORK SURFACE with ½ cup flour and scrape the dough onto it. Have ready another ½ cup flour. Dust the top of the dough with some of this flour, and knead the dough until the flour is completely absorbed. If the dough still feels sticky, gradually add some of the remaining flour, kneading it in until the dough feels smooth, soft, and only slightly oily; it should not be sticky. It should feel rather like a soft bread dough. Depending on the humidity, you may need to use all

of the ½ cup flour plus another ¼ cup, possibly a bit more. If in doubt, err on the side of a bit less rather than more. Slip the dough into a resealable plastic bag or wrap it in plastic and let it rest at room temperature for about 30 minutes.

ADJUST TWO OVEN RACKS to divide the oven into thirds and preheat the oven to 350°F. Line two 17 × 14–inch cookie sheets with silicone baking pan liners or cooking parchment. Have a 15½ × 10½ × 1–inch jelly-roll pan ready.

TURN THE DOUGH OUT onto your work surface. (It will have a fabulous aroma that will make you want to eat it right away.) Pat it into a rectangle measuring roughly 9 × 5 inches. Score the dough into 30 even pieces and cut them with a sharp knife. Roll each piece between your palms into an oval about 2 inches long, and place them 2 inches apart on the lined sheets, 15 cookies to a sheet.

BAKE FOR ABOUT 30 MINUTES, until the cookies are golden brown, feel dry on top, and spring back when pressed. Rotate the sheets top to bottom and back to front once during baking to ensure even browning.

WHILE THE COOKIES BAKE, PREPARE THE SYRUP. Combine the honey, sugar, and water in a medium heavy saucepan and bring to a boil over medium heat, stirring occasionally. Reduce the heat to low and simmer the syrup for 10 minutes. Remove from the heat.

AS SOON AS THE COOKIES ARE DONE, transfer them with a wide metal spatula to the jelly-roll pan, putting them close together with just a little space between them. Spoon the hot syrup evenly over the hot cookies. Let stand for 15 minutes.

CAREFULLY TURN THE COOKIES OVER and let them stand for another 15 minutes, or until the syrup is absorbed. Turn the cookies right side up and sprinkle them with the walnuts. If there is still some syrup in the pan, transfer the cookies to another pan. Cover the cookies loosely with a sheet of waxed paper, and let them stand at room temperature overnight before eating.

Storing

Store the melomakarona in an airtight container at room temperature for up to 2 weeks.

Norwegian Walnut Butter Balls *norway*

MAKES 36 COOKIES

THESE NORWEGIAN SHORTBREAD COOKIES *are made with finely ground walnuts. They are small enough to pop into your mouth, and when you bite down, the cookie crumbles and shatters into tiny pieces that soon melt into a buttery deliciousness. Cookies similar to this are found in many cultures (see page 237). Dorothy Crocker, a second-generation Norwegian American, learned how to make them from her grandmother Alma Ovidia Madsen. They are really easy to make, but you'll need a manual nut grinder or a hand-held Mouli grater to grind or shred the nuts. Do not use a food processor, or the nuts may turn pasty.*

About 3 ounces walnuts

8 tablespoons (1 stick) unsalted butter, at room temperature

2 tablespoons granulated sugar

¼ teaspoon salt

1 teaspoon pure vanilla extract

1 cup unbleached all-purpose flour

About 2 cups confectioners' sugar for coating

GRIND THE NUTS with a nut grinder or Mouli grater, and measure 1 cup.

IN A MEDIUM BOWL, beat the butter with an electric mixer on medium speed until smooth and creamy, about 30 seconds. Add the sugar, salt, and vanilla and beat for 1 to 2 minutes, until smooth and fluffy. With a wooden spoon, stir in the nuts, then stir in the flour until the dough gathers into a mass. Knead the dough briefly in the bowl until it coheres, working quickly so as not to melt the butter.

ADJUST AN OVEN RACK to the center position and preheat the oven to 350°F. Line a large baking sheet (18 × 12 × 1 inch) with a silicone baking pan liner or cooking parchment.

DIVIDE THE DOUGH into 36 equal pieces. Roll each into a smooth ball, about ¾ inch in diameter, between your palms. Place the balls 1 to 2 inches apart on the prepared sheet.

BAKE UNTIL the cookies are a very pale golden brown all over, 20 to 25 minutes. They will puff a bit during baking. Remove the pan from the oven.

PLACE THE CONFECTIONERS' SUGAR into a large plastic bag and add about half the hot cookies. Twist the top of the bag shut and gently manipulate the bag to coat the hot cookies with a generous layer of sugar. Remove the cookies from the bag with a slotted spoon and set them on wire racks to cool completely. Repeat with the remaining cookies while they are still hot.

Storing

Store the cookies in airtight containers at room temperature for up to 1 week. To freeze, place the sugared cookies on a parchment- or foil-lined baking sheet and freeze until solid, then transfer to heavy-duty resealable plastic bags and freeze for up to 1 month. Thaw the cookies completely in their wrapping. Dust again with confectioners' sugar, if necessary.

Roman Chocolate Cookies

italy

THESE SCRUMPTIOUS NOT-TOO-SWEET CHOCOLATE WALNUT BALLS, *spiced with nutmeg, cinnamon, and allspice, are an annual Christmas treat in Catherine Cavallaro Goodman's family. She learned how to make the cookies from her Aunt Marie, and over the years Catherine has modified the recipe slightly. The most recent change is the addition of chocolate chips to the dough, a tip of her hat to chocolate lovers in her family. Catherine says you could add chopped dried cherries (definitely American) or finely diced citron instead of the chocolate.*

DOUGH

- 2 cups plus 3 tablespoons all-purpose flour
- ½ cup sifted unsweetened cocoa powder
- 2½ teaspoons baking powder
- ¼ teaspoon salt
- ½ teaspoon ground cinnamon
- ¼ teaspoon freshly grated nutmeg
- ¼ teaspoon ground allspice
- 2 large eggs
- ½ cup granulated sugar
- ½ cup extra-virgin olive oil
- ½ cup whole milk
- 2 teaspoons pure vanilla extract
- ½ cup walnuts, chopped medium-fine
- 1 cup mini semisweet chocolate chips

ICING

- 1¼ cups confectioners' sugar
- 1½ tablespoons unsalted butter, at room temperature
- 2 tablespoons whole milk, plus more if needed
- ½ teaspoon pure vanilla extract

  Colored or chocolate sprinkles

TO MAKE THE DOUGH, in a medium bowl whisk together the flour, cocoa, baking powder, salt, cinnamon, nutmeg, and allspice.

IN ANOTHER MEDIUM BOWL, beat the eggs with an electric mixer on medium speed for about 1 minute, until frothy. Gradually add the sugar and beat until the eggs thicken slightly and become very pale in color, 2 to 3 minutes more. While beating, slowly drizzle in the olive oil. On low speed, beat in the milk and vanilla extract. With a wooden spoon, add the flour mixture in 2 installments, stirring until smooth after each. Stir in the walnuts and chocolate chips. The dough will be soft and slightly sticky. Cover the bowl loosely with a kitchen towel and let the dough rest for 20 to 30 minutes.

ADJUST AN OVEN RACK to the center position and preheat the oven to 350°F. Line two heavy 17 × 14–inch cookie sheets with silicone baking pan liners or cooking parchment.

TO SHAPE THE COOKIES, roll rounded teaspoonfuls of dough between your palms into smooth balls measuring about 1 inch in diameter. (The oil in the dough will keep the dough from sticking to your hands.) Set the balls about 2 inches apart on the prepared sheets, 18 cookies to a sheet.

BAKE ONE SHEET AT A TIME until the cookies smell fragrant and their tops feel dry and have numerous cracks, 10 to 12 minutes; they will almost double in size. Do not overbake—the cookies should be tender, not dry. Cool the cookies on the cookie sheets for 3 to 5 minutes, then transfer them with a wide metal spatula to wire cooling racks to cool completely.

TO MAKE THE ICING, in a small bowl combine the confectioners' sugar, butter, milk, and vanilla extract and beat with a hand-held electric mixer until smooth and thick, the consistency of heavy cream. If necessary, beat in more milk by droplets.

SET THE RACKS of cooled cookies over waxed paper. One at a time, dip the tops of 5 or 6 cookies in the icing, then set them upright on the cooling rack and dust them immediately with colored sprinkles or chocolate jimmies. Repeat with the remaining cookies. (Reuse any sprinkles that fall on the waxed paper.)

Storing

Store the cookies in an airtight container at room temperature for 3 to 4 days. To freeze, place the cookies on a parchment- or foil-lined baking sheet and freeze until solid, then transfer to heavy-duty resealable plastic bags and freeze for up to 2 weeks. Thaw the cookies completely in their wrapping.

Pennsylvania Dutch Soft Sugar Cookies

MAKES ABOUT 36 COOKIES

THESE APPEALING SUGAR COOKIES, *delicate, light, and soft, were a specialty of a certain Mrs. Kendig in Lancaster County, Pennsylvania, who baked and sold them. For many years, Betty Groff, a cookbook author and restaurateur, tried to get Mrs. Kendig to reveal her recipe, but it wasn't until she retired that she agreed to give Betty the recipe. And Betty has generously shared it with me. The true origin of this recipe is unknown, but when Betty and I made these at her home in Mt. Joy, I could not stop eating them. The cookies are at their very best when freshly made, even still warm.*

3 cups all-purpose flour (spooned into the cup and leveled)	1⅓ cups granulated sugar
1 teaspoon baking powder	1 teaspoon pure vanilla extract
¼ teaspoon salt	2 large eggs
½ teaspoon freshly grated nutmeg	¾ cup buttermilk
6 tablespoons (¾ stick) unsalted butter, at room temperature	1 teaspoon baking soda, dissolved in 1 tablespoon boiling water
	About ¼ cup dark raisins

IN A MEDIUM BOWL, whisk together the flour, baking powder, salt, and nutmeg.

IN ANOTHER MEDIUM BOWL, beat the butter with an electric mixer on medium speed until smooth, about 1 minute. Gradually add the sugar, and continue beating until light and fluffy, 2 to 3 minutes. Beat in the vanilla. Add the eggs one at a time, beating only until incorporated. Stir in the buttermilk and the dissolved soda, then gradually stir in the flour. Cover the bowl with plastic wrap and refrigerate for 30 minutes to firm the dough a bit.

ADJUST AN OVEN RACK to the center position and preheat the oven to 350°F. Line three large (17 × 14–inch) cookie sheets with silicone baking pan liners or cooking parchment. If you only have two pans, line them and cut one more sheet of parchment to fit.

PLACE WELL-ROUNDED TEASPOONFULS of dough 2 to 3 inches apart on the pans and the third sheet of parchment, about 12 cookies to a sheet. These will spread quite a bit as they bake. Top each cookie with a raisin, pressing it gently into the dough so that it sticks.

BAKE ONE SHEET AT A TIME for about 15 minutes, or until the cookies are a very light brown color. These should not get too dark—check after 12 minutes, just to be safe. Remove the pan from the oven and slide the pan liner onto your countertop. Let the cookies cool for a minute or two, then transfer them with a wide metal spatula to wire cooling racks to cool completely. When you've baked the first two batches, slide the remaining sheet of cookies onto a cooled cookie sheet and bake it.

Storing

Although the cookies are at their best when fresh out of the oven, they are still quite good stored airtight for up to 3 days.

Italian Anise-Orange Cookies

MAKES 36 COOKIES

THESE ARE TENDER, PUFFY-LOOKING COOKIES *that are not too sweet, with a pleasing anise and orange flavor. They are typically made at Christmas, but they're really welcome at any time of the year. Catherine Cavallaro Goodman, a second-generation Italian American, learned to make them from her Aunt Annie, one of many aunts who taught her how to cook. Aunt Annie said the recipe originally came from Gramma Cavallaro, who brought them from Pizzo Calabria, Italy. She added that the original fat for the cookies was melted animal lard or olive oil squeezed fresh from green olives off the trees.*

These cookies are really best the day after they're made.

DOUGH	ICING
2½ cups all-purpose flour, plus more as needed	1 cup sifted confectioners' sugar
2½ teaspoons baking powder	1 tablespoon unsalted butter, at room temperature
¼ teaspoon salt	2 teaspoons fresh orange juice
2 large eggs	5 to 6 teaspoons whole milk
½ cup granulated sugar	½ teaspoon pure anise extract
½ cup extra-virgin olive oil	
¼ cup whole milk	Colored sprinkles
Finely grated zest of 1 orange	
2 tablespoons freshly squeezed orange juice	
1½ teaspoons pure anise extract	

TO MAKE THE DOUGH, in a medium bowl whisk together 2½ cups flour, the baking powder, and salt.

IN ANOTHER MEDIUM BOWL, beat the eggs with an electric mixer on medium speed for 1 minute, or until frothy. Gradually add the sugar and beat until the eggs thicken slightly and become pale in color, 2 to 3 minutes. While beating, slowly add the olive oil. On low speed, beat in the milk, orange zest, orange juice, and anise extract. With a wooden spoon, stir in the flour mixture in 2 installments. The dough will be soft and slightly sticky. If it seems too sticky, stir in 2 to 3 tablespoons more flour a tablespoon at a time, but don't add too much. Cover the bowl loosely with a kitchen towel and let the dough rest for 20 to 30 minutes.

ADJUST AN OVEN RACK to the center position and preheat the oven to 350°F. Line two heavy 17 × 14–inch cookie sheets with silicone baking pan liners or cooking parchment.

TO SHAPE THE COOKIES, roll rounded teaspoonfuls of dough between your palms into smooth balls measuring a scant 1 inch in diameter. (The oil in the dough will keep the dough from sticking to your hands.) Set the balls about 2 inches apart on the prepared sheets, 18 cookies to a sheet.

BAKE ONE SHEET AT A TIME until the bottoms of the cookies are lightly browned and their tops have cracks and are barely colored, 10 to 12 minutes; they will almost double in size during baking. Do not overbake—the cookies should be tender, not dry. Cool the cookies on the cookie sheets for 3 to 5 minutes, then transfer them with a wide metal spatula to wire cooling racks to cool completely.

TO MAKE THE ICING, in a small bowl combine the confectioners' sugar, butter, orange juice, 4 teaspoons of the milk, and the anise extract and beat with an electric mixer until smooth and thick. Beat in 1 to 2 teaspoons more milk, until the icing is the consistency of heavy cream.

SET THE RACKS of cookies over waxed paper. One at a time, dip the tops of 5 or 6 cookies in the icing, then set them upright on the cooling rack and dust them immediately with colored sprinkles. Repeat with the remaining cookies. (Reuse any sprinkles that fall onto the paper.) Although you can serve the cookies once the icing has set, they really are best if made a day ahead.

Storing

The cookies keep well at room temperature for several days stored airtight. To freeze, place them on baking sheets and freeze until solid, then transfer to heavy-duty resealable plastic bags and freeze for up to 2 weeks. Thaw the cookies completely in their wrapping.

Kourabiedes

MAKES 36 COOKIES

THESE BUTTERY, DELICATE, CLASSIC GREEK COOKIES *are usually shaped into crescents. Kathy Papastathis Salzetti, who learned how to make them from her mother, Evanghelia, says that some Greeks shape the dough into balls. Kathy makes them for Easter, Christmas, and other special occasions, including weddings.*

The dough must be chilled for several hours, or overnight, before shaping. These are excellent keepers.

½ cup unblanched whole almonds, toasted (see page 23)

½ pound (2 sticks) unsalted butter, at room temperature

¼ cup granulated sugar

1 large egg yolk

1 teaspoon pure vanilla extract

2 cups unbleached all-purpose flour

1 teaspoon baking powder

Confectioners' sugar for coating

WITH A SHARP HEAVY KNIFE, chop the almonds into very small pieces. An easy way to achieve an even texture is to coarsely chop the nuts by hand, then finish the chopping in a food processor; pulse the nuts a few times, stir them to check their texture and then pulse a few more times, until the nuts are in very small pieces but not ground.

IN A LARGE BOWL, beat the butter briefly with a wooden spoon until smooth. Add the sugar and beat vigorously for 2 to 3 minutes. Beat in the egg yolk and vanilla. Stir in the almonds. In a medium bowl, combine the flour with the baking powder, then gradually stir it into the butter mixture until the dough gathers into a ball and pulls away from the side of the bowl. Place the dough on a sheet of plastic wrap and shape it into a 6-inch square. Wrap tightly and refrigerate for at least several hours, or overnight.

WITH AN OVEN RACK in the center position, preheat the oven to 350°F. Coat two large baking sheets (18 × 12 × 1 inch) with cooking spray or line them with silicone baking pan liners or cooking parchment.

TO SHAPE THE COOKIES, with a sharp knife, cut the dough into thirty-six 1-inch squares. Roll each piece between your palms into a ball, shape into a crescent about ½ inch wide and 3 to 3½ inches long, and place on one of the prepared baking sheets, arranging 18 cookies about 2 inches apart on each sheet.

BAKE ONE SHEET AT A TIME for 20 to 25 minutes, until the cookies are light brown on their bottoms. Check by lifting a cookie up with a narrow metal spatula. The tops of the cookies should only barely start to color; don't overbake. With a wide metal spatula, transfer the cookies to wire cooling racks to cool completely.

ONCE THE COOKIES HAVE COOLED, roll them in confectioners' sugar, coating them heavily. (Don't sugar cookies you're going to store.)

Storing

Unsugared kourabiedes can be stored in an airtight container at room temperature for 1 to 2 months. They become crisper and crunchier over time but are just as delicious as when fresh. Coat them with confectioners' sugar before serving.

Lithuanian Mushroom Cookies

lithuania

MAKES 30 COOKIES

IF YOU'RE THE ARTSY-CRAFTSY TYPE, *you'll have a ball making these charming and delicious cookies. Called* grybukai *("mushrooms") in Lithuanian, the cookies—brown, cake-like, and spicy—look uncannily like real mushrooms. They are made for special occasions, and they take patience, but they're well worth the effort. Ryte Kilikeviciene, who taught them to me, started baking because of these cookies. "I was five years old, and I remember my grandmother's second husband tossing these cookies to us kids from the horse-drawn wagon as they left the wedding party. Lithuanians celebrate for several days after a wedding. I munched on a cookie as I watched the wagon disappear, and I decided then and there that I wanted to be able to make them myself."*

As Ryte does, you can stagger the various steps over a number of days. She makes the dough one day and bakes it into caps and stems the next day. She assembles the two and lets them dry overnight at room temperature, then ices the stems and the caps the following day. The cookies keep well, stored airtight, for 1 to 2 months and, over time, they become dry and crunchy. Ryte says ideally the stems should be rounded, and in Lithuania there was a special pan for this purpose. If you have one, a breadstick pan is ideal for baking the stems—but if you don't mind stems that are flat on one side, you can bake them on a regular baking sheet.

It's important not to add too much flour to the dough, or the cookies will be doughy. Chilling the dough overnight will make it easy to handle.

DOUGH

- ⅓ cup honey
- ⅓ cup unsulphured molasses
- 6 tablespoons (¾ stick) unsalted butter
- 2 tablespoons whole milk
- 2½ cups all-purpose flour
- 1 tablespoon baking powder
- ½ teaspoon salt
- 1 to 2 teaspoons ground cinnamon (to taste)
- ¼ teaspoon ground cloves
- ½ to 1 teaspoon freshly grated nutmeg (to taste)
- 2 large eggs
- ½ teaspoon lemon oil or pure lemon extract

WHITE ICING

- 2 large egg whites
- ½ teaspoon fresh lemon juice
- 2 cups confectioners' sugar, plus more if needed
- 8 to 10 cups raw rice for assembling the cookies
- ¼ cup poppy seeds

DARK ICING

- 2 tablespoons unsalted butter
- ⅔ cup unsweetened cocoa powder
- ⅔ cup confectioners' sugar
  Pinch of salt
- ¼ cup water
- 1 teaspoon pure vanilla extract

TO MAKE THE DOUGH, put the honey, molasses, butter, and milk in a heavy medium saucepan, set the pan over low heat, and stir occasionally, until the butter is melted. Remove the pan from the heat and cool to room temperature.

IN A MEDIUM BOWL, whisk together the flour, baking powder, salt, cinnamon, cloves, and nutmeg. In a small bowl, whisk the eggs and lemon oil or extract to combine well. Stir into the butter mixture. Gradually stir in the dry ingredients to make a thick, sticky dough. Cover the pan and refrigerate the dough overnight.

THE NEXT DAY, adjust an oven rack to the center position and preheat the oven to 375°F. Line 2 large baking sheets (18 × 12 × 1 inch) with silicone baking pan liners or cooking parchment.

DIVIDE THE COLD DOUGH into 3 even portions, 2 to make the mushroom caps and 1 for the stems. Divide the dough for the caps into a total of thirty 1-inch pieces, but don't make them completely equal—they should be uneven, like real mushrooms. Shape into balls and space them 2 inches apart on one of the lined sheets, 5 across a short side and 6 down the length. Press them ever so slightly with the palm of your hand to flatten them a bit.

DIVIDE THE DOUGH for the stems into 30 pieces. Shape each one into a cylinder measuring a scant 2 inches long and tapering to a point. Don't make the stems too even, either. Place the stems about 2 inches apart on the second prepared baking sheet.

BAKE ONE SHEET AT A TIME until the cookies are lightly colored and feel dry to the touch, 8 to 10 minutes; don't overbake. Don't be concerned if cracks develop on the stems or caps. Cool the cookies completely on their pans.

TO MAKE THE WHITE ICING, in a small bowl beat the egg whites and lemon juice with an electric mixer on medium speed until foamy. On low speed, gradually beat in the confectioners' sugar, then beat on medium speed until the icing is thick enough to drip slowly off the tip of a teaspoon. Beat in more sugar if necessary. The icing should be thick but not so thick that it doesn't run. (You will have more icing than you need, but it's better to have too much than not enough.) Cover the bowl tightly with plastic wrap and keep covered when not using the icing.

FILL a 13 × 9 × 2–inch baking pan with the rice and level the rice. Use the tip of a sharp paring knife to carve out a fairly deep pointed core from the underside of each cap; it should extend about halfway into the cap. One at a time, paint the underside of each cap with the white icing and fill the core with icing dripped from the end of a teaspoon, then insert the pointed end of a stem into the core and press the cap and stem together gently but firmly. Set the assembled mushrooms cap side down into the rice. Let the mushrooms dry at room temperature, uncovered, for at least a few hours, or overnight. Cover the remaining white icing tightly and leave at room temperature.

TO COAT THE STEMS, put the poppy seeds in a small cup. Pick up a mushroom and brush off any rice grains sticking to the cap. Paint the entire stem with white icing, then dip the tip of the stem into the poppy seeds, to resemble dirt. Set the mushrooms cap side down again in the rice. Repeat with the remaining cookies, and let dry for at least several hours, or overnight.

TO MAKE THE DARK ICING, melt the butter in a small heavy saucepan over low heat. Remove the pan from the heat and add the remaining ingredients, then return to low heat and cook, whisking, until the icing is smooth, thick, and creamy looking. It should be slightly thicker than heavy cream; if necessary, add a bit more water. You want the icing thick enough to cloak the top of the caps but not be runny. The icing should be warm when used, so work at a steady clip: Pick up a mushroom, brush away any rice grains sticking to it, and dip the top of the cap into the dark icing. Swirl the mushroom once or twice, lift it out of the icing, and carefully set it stem down into the rice. (Make sure the rice is deep enough to support the mushroom without toppling.) Repeat with the remaining mushrooms. If the dark icing cools too much and thickens, rewarm it gently over low heat. Let the cookies dry completely.

Storing

Store the mushrooms airtight at room temperature for up to 2 months. They will become firmer over time. Do not freeze.

Nusssplätzchen

MAKES ABOUT 60 COOKIES

THESE COOKIES HAVE A THIN, CRISPY BASE *topped with mounds of ground hazelnuts bound together with beaten eggs and sugar. The topping is moist and chewy when fresh and becomes dry and crunchy after storage—good either way. The cookies keep well for months and are good for shipping. Gertrude Lackschewitz, who immigrated to the United States from Germany in the 1950s, learned how to make them from her mother, who came from Zell, a small town on the Mosel River. Gertrude says, "I believe these are a very local cookie, a specialty of my mother's hometown. I have not seen them in other parts of Germany. In our family, it wouldn't be Christmas without them." Gertrude, now in her eighties, has been making the cookies for more than fifty years.*

One caveat: Go easy on the lemon zest—don't be tempted to add more, or the flavor balance will be off. And start these the day before you want to bake, because both the dough and the filling need an overnight stint in the refrigerator.

COOKIE BASE

- 1½ cups unbleached all-purpose flour (spooned into the cups and leveled)
- ½ cup granulated sugar
- ½ teaspoon ground cardamom
- 1 teaspoon finely grated lemon zest
- 8 tablespoons (1 stick) cold unsalted butter, cut into tablespoon-sized pieces
- 1 large egg, lightly beaten

HAZELNUT TOPPING

- 8 ounces (2 cups) unblanched hazelnuts
- 1 large egg
- 1 large egg white
- ½ cup granulated sugar
- ½ teaspoon ground cinnamon
- 1 teaspoon finely grated lemon zest

TO MAKE THE DOUGH, in a medium bowl whisk together the flour, sugar, cardamom, and lemon zest. Add the butter and cut it in with a pastry blender or two knives until the mixture resembles fine crumbs (you can also do this with a food processor, if you wish). Add the egg and stir with a fork until the dough comes together.

PLACE THE DOUGH on an unfloured work surface and shape it into a log about 12 inches long. Turn a narrow end of the log toward you and, with the heel of your hand, smear the dough away from you in 2-inch installments, beginning at the

far end of the log. Gather the dough together, form it into a log again, and repeat the smearing process. This ensures a thorough mixing of the flour with the butter. Press the dough together and form it into a 1-inch-thick disk. Wrap it in plastic wrap and refrigerate it overnight; bring it to room temperature before using.

MEANWHILE, make the topping. Grind the hazelnuts with a manual nut grinder. Or, lacking that, put the nuts into the work bowl of a food processor fitted with the metal blade, add 2 tablespoons of the sugar (beat the remaining sugar with the eggs), and process until the nuts are finely ground. Watch carefully—you don't want the nuts to form a paste.

IN A MEDIUM BOWL, with an electric mixer, beat the egg and white until slightly thickened. Gradually add the sugar and beat until thick and pale, about 5 minutes. Beat in the cinnamon and lemon zest. Stir in the nuts. The topping will be very thick. Cover the bowl tightly with plastic wrap and refrigerate overnight.

ADJUST AN OVEN RACK to the center position and preheat the oven to 350°F. Line two large cookie sheets (17 × 14 inches) with silicone baking pan liners or cooking parchment. Roll the room-temperature dough on a lightly floured surface (a pastry cloth works best) to a thickness of ⅛ inch. No thicker! These cookies must be thin. Dip a sharp 1¾-inch round cookie cutter into flour and stamp out cookies. Arrange the cookies on the cookie sheets, spacing them about ½ inch apart. These don't spread. Gather the dough scraps together, incorporating as little flour as possible, and repeat the rolling and cutting.

DIVIDE THE COLD TOPPING into the same number of pieces as you have cookies, and shape into ¾-inch balls. Place one on the center of each cookie and press gently just to make it adhere.

BAKE ONE SHEET OF COOKIES at a time for about 10 minutes, just until the edges of the cookies are a pale golden brown color. Do not overbake. With a metal spatula, transfer the cookies to a wire cooling rack to cool completely.

Storing

Store the cookies airtight at room temperature for up to a month, or even longer.

Pfeffernüsse

MAKES 32 COOKIES

THESE SPICY GERMAN COOKIES—*the name means "pepper nuts"—are always in Gertrude Lackschewitz's larder around Christmastime. She bakes them well ahead of the holidays because they keep for two months or more, and they also pack and mail well. They make a nice nibble with afternoon tea or coffee. When fresh, the cookies are soft, like gingerbread. Over time they become drier, and that is the way most Germans prefer eating them. I like them both ways.*

Many pfeffernüsse recipes include ground black pepper. These do not. Instead, their pepperiness comes from the combination of spices. The cookies look like little igloos, with flat bottoms and domed tops. After baking, they are brushed with a sugar glaze and, once the glaze has set, rolled in confectioners' sugar.

The dough for pfeffernüsse must be made ahead and refrigerated at least 6 hours.

DOUGH

- ½ cup granulated sugar
- ½ cup honey
- 8 tablespoons (1 stick) unsalted butter
- 1 large egg
- 1½ teaspoons anise seeds
- 1 teaspoon ground cinnamon
- ½ teaspoon ground cloves
- ½ teaspoon freshly grated nutmeg
- ½ teaspoon ground coriander
- ½ teaspoon ground cardamom
- ¼ teaspoon salt
- ½ teaspoon baking powder
- ½ teaspoon baking soda
- 2¾ cups unbleached or bleached all-purpose flour
- ½ cup finely chopped walnuts or chopped slivered almonds (optional)

GLAZE

- 1 cup confectioners' sugar
- ¼ cup water

Confectioners' sugar for coating

TO MAKE THE DOUGH, put the sugar, honey, and butter into a medium heavy saucepan, set the pan over medium heat, and stir occasionally until the butter is melted and the mixture is smooth. Remove the pan from the heat and cool until tepid.

WHISK IN THE EGG until smooth. Add the anise, cinnamon, cloves, nutmeg, coriander, and cardamom, stirring them in with the whisk. Add the salt, baking powder, and baking soda and stir gently with the whisk. The mixture will thicken slightly. Gradually stir in the flour with a wooden spoon to make a stiff but wet dough. Stir in the nuts, if you wish. Cover the pan and refrigerate for at least several hours, or overnight, to firm the dough.

ADJUST AN OVEN RACK to the center position and preheat the oven to 325°F. Line two large baking sheets (18 × 12 × 1 inch) with silicone baking pan liners or cooking parchment.

SHAPE THE CHILLED DOUGH into an 8 × 4–inch rectangle about 1 inch thick. Cut it into thirty-two 1-inch squares. Roll the squares between your palms into balls and place about 2 inches apart on the prepared sheets, 16 cookies to a sheet.

BAKE ONE SHEET AT A TIME for 15 to 20 minutes, until the cookies have cracks on top, feel firm to the touch, and are golden brown on their bottoms. Cool the cookies on their pans for 2 to 3 minutes, then use a metal spatula to transfer them to wire cooling racks to cool completely.

SET THE RACKS OF COOKIES over baking sheets or over waxed paper to catch the glaze that drips off the cookies.

TO MAKE THE GLAZE, whisk together the confectioners' sugar and water in a small heavy saucepan until smooth. Set the pan over medium heat and bring to a boil, stirring occasionally. Remove the pan from the heat and immediately brush the cookies with the hot glaze. Let the glaze set.

ROLL THE COOKIES in confectioners' sugar to coat well.

Storing

Store the cookies in airtight containers at room temperature for up to 2 months. Reroll them in confectioners' sugar if necessary.

Pignoli

MAKES ABOUT 30 COOKIES

THESE SIMPLE SICILIAN COOKIES, *almond paste mixed with sugar and egg whites and rolled in pine nuts, have a deliciously chewy texture. The recipe comes from Santa Pasquini, whose father immigrated to the United States from Sicily in the early 1900s. Santa learned the recipe from a Sicilian girlfriend, who got it from her aunt, and she has been making the cookies on a regular basis for almost twenty years. Santa says, "Everytime I go back to Sicily, I always head to a pasticceria to taste some pignoli, just to make sure I'm still making them the right way."*

Santa uses a commercial variety of almond paste, made by the Saratoga Flour Company, for her pignoli. It comes in 5-pound cans, but she buys it in smaller amounts from Fiorello's, an Italian deli in Albany. I made pignoli both with her almond paste and with my homemade almond paste, and the results were entirely different. Santa used 1 cup of sugar and 8 ounces of almond paste in her recipe, and her baked cookies were about 2 inches in diameter, ⅔ inch thick, and nice and chewy. When I used the same amount of my almond paste, I had to reduce the sugar to ½ cup so the pignoli wouldn't flatten too much, but the cookies still were a bit flatter than Santa's and had a chewy-crunchy texture. But both kinds of pignoli are delicious. What almond paste should you use? It's your call. Solo and Odense are the most common supermarket brands; American Almond also makes an excellent almond paste. They all work well in these cookies, and they will give you a whole spectrum of thicknesses and delicious textures. Do not use marzipan, which has much more sugar than almond paste—it will cause the cookies to flatten excessively, brown too much, and make them totally crunchy. This isn't necessarily a bad thing, though, but the cookies won't be pignoli.

---

8 ounces almond paste, homemade (page 330) or store-bought

½ to 1 cup granulated sugar (see first step)

2 large egg whites

2 to 3 cups pine nuts, plus more if needed

BREAK UP THE ALMOND PASTE with your fingers into smallish pieces and drop them into a large bowl. Add the sugar: ½ cup if using the homemade almond paste, ¾ cup if using Solo, Odense, or American Almond brands, 1 cup if using Santa's brand. Cut it into the almond paste with a pastry blender to make a gritty mixture with the texture of very coarse, clumpy sand. Use your fingertips to help this process along. Alternatively, break the almond paste into clumps and pulse in a food processor until sandy textured. Add the sugar and pulse a few times to combine well. Transfer the mixture to a medium bowl.

IN A SMALL BOWL, beat the egg whites with a fork just until frothy. Gradually add the whites to the almond mixture, stirring well with the fork to make a thick, cohesive mass that holds its shape; it should not be runny. You may not need to use all of the whites—use only enough to give you this consistency. If there are any lumps, smooth them out with the fork. Cover the bowl tightly with plastic wrap and refrigerate for at least 1 hour. (The mixture can be made a day ahead.)

ADJUST AN OVEN RACK to the center position and preheat the oven to 350°F. Line two heavy 17 × 14–inch cookie sheets with silicone baking pan liners or cooking parchment.

PLACE THE PINE NUTS in a pie plate or medium bowl. Drop 3 or 4 scant rounded teaspoons of the almond dough onto the pine nuts and toss them about to coat all over with the pine nuts. Use your fingers to press on as many nuts as possible, and shape each cookie into a ball. Place the balls about 2 inches apart on a prepared sheet. Repeat with the remaining almond paste and pine nuts, putting about 15 cookies on each pan.

BAKE ONE SHEET AT A TIME for 18 to 20 minutes, until the cookies have flattened slightly and are golden brown. Rotate the sheet back to front once halfway during baking to ensure even browning. Remove the pan from the oven, let the cookies cool on the pan for 2 to 3 minutes to firm up slightly, then, with a wide metal spatula, transfer the cookies to wire cooling racks to cool completely.

Storing

These cookies are best when very fresh, but you can store them in an airtight container at room temperature for 2 to 3 days. To freeze, arrange the cookies on baking sheets and freeze until solid, then transfer to heavy-duty resealable plastic bags and freeze for up to 1 month. Thaw them in their wrapping.

Scottish Shortbread

MAKES 18 COOKIES

THIS RECIPE COMES FROM CAMMIE MITCHELL HINSHAW, *a third-generation Scottish American. The shortbread, buttery, crunchy, and crisp, is simplicity itself, but you must be sure of your oven temperature in order not to overbake it. Cammie makes this frequently, as did her grandmother, who cut her cookies into shapes. "She had only four cookie cutters," Cammie says, "and they were in the shapes of the symbols on a deck of cards: club, diamond, heart, and spade. I am happy to say I now have them." To make the dough, her grandmother mashed the sugar into the butter with her hands, then worked in the flour. She patted the dough out by hand and cut it into cookies. "They were delicious and melted in your mouth," Cammie adds. "I get teary-eyed just thinking of them; they bring such great memories to mind."*

Cammie also mixes her dough by hand. I've made the cookies that way, with a wooden spoon, and with a hand-held electric mixer. They turn out well by any method. For the best flavor, be sure to use top-quality butter. Cammie doesn't add vanilla, but I like to. Good strong hot tea is the perfect beverage to serve with these cookies. In Scotland many bakers use rice flour for part of the all-purpose flour to give the cookies added crunch. Substitute 1/2 cup rice flour for 1/2 cup all-purpose flour if you like.

½ pound (2 sticks) best-quality salted butter, slightly softened

½ cup granulated sugar

½ teaspoon pure vanilla extract (optional)

2 cups unbleached all-purpose flour, plus more for shaping

ADJUST AN OVEN RACK to the center position and preheat the oven to 325°F. Line a large baking sheet (18 × 12 × 1 inch) with a silicone baking pan liner or cooking parchment. Or use a nonstick pan.

WHEN YOU PRESS the butter gently with a fingertip, it should yield only slightly, leaving just a shallow dent. In a medium bowl, beat the butter with a wooden spoon or electric mixer until it is smooth and fluffy. Add the sugar and beat for 2 to 3 minutes, until the mixture is very smooth and light-textured. Beat in the vanilla, if using. Add the flour 1 cup at a time, stirring in with a wooden spoon until thoroughly incorporated. The dough will gather into a thick mass. Scrape

it onto an unfloured work surface and knead briefly until smooth.

TO SHAPE THE COOKIES INTO RECTANGLES, lightly dust your work surface with flour, place the dough on it, and pat the dough to flatten it slightly. Roll it into a ¼-inch-thick rectangle (no thinner!) measuring about 9 × 6 inches. Square the edges with your fingertips. With a sharp knife, cut the dough lengthwise into 3 strips, then cut the strips crosswise into 6 pieces each, making 18 cookies. With a metal spatula, transfer the cookies to the prepared baking sheet, leaving ½ to 1 inch between them. Prick each cookie with a fork 3 times down its length, going all the way down to the pan.

TO CUT OUT COOKIES, roll the dough on a lightly floured surface to a rough circle that is ¼ inch thick. Stamp out cookies with any shape cutters, then gather the dough scraps and reroll as necessary—but do not incorporate any more flour, or the cookies will be dry. Transfer the cookies to the prepared baking pan with a metal spatula. Do not prick them.

BAKE FOR ABOUT 25 MINUTES, only until the tops of the cookies take on a faint golden brown color and the bottoms are slightly darker. Rotate the sheet front to back once about halfway during baking to ensure even browning. Do not overbake—start checking about 5 minutes before the cookies are done to monitor their progress. Cool the cookies on their pan for 3 to 4 minutes to firm them up a bit, then transfer them to wire cooling racks with a metal spatula and cool completely.

Storing

Stored in an airtight container at room temperature, these keep fresh for a week or longer, but I doubt that any will last that long. To freeze them, place the cookies on a baking sheet and freeze until solid, then transfer to heavy-duty resealable plastic bags or put them in plastic containers, keeping them in a single layer if possible, and freeze for up to 1 month. Thaw the cookies completely in their wrapping.

Swedish Almond Jam Strips

MAKES ABOUT 48 COOKIES

THESE CLASSIC BUTTERY SWEDISH COOKIES, *called* syltängder med mandel, *are as addictive as potato chips. The tender yet crunchy cookies filled with tangy sweet raspberry jam are an irresistible taste and texture combination. Helena Hoas, who emigrated from Sweden more than twenty years ago, makes these regularly. She shapes the dough lovingly, as though she were dressing a baby. She makes the troughs to contain the jam by running a fingertip slowly up and down the lengths of dough, and she fills them with just the right amount of jam. "You have to be careful not to put in too much," she says, "or the jam will overflow and the cookies won't be as pretty as they should be."*

The cookies are best when very fresh. "They are very easy to make," Helena says. "I just make sure there'll be lots of people around to eat them all."

DOUGH

- ¾ cup unblanched almonds
- 15 tablespoons unsalted butter, at room temperature
- ¼ cup plus 3 tablespoons granulated sugar
- ¼ teaspoon salt
- 1⅔ cups unbleached all-purpose flour (spooned into the cups and leveled)
- ¾ to 1 cup seedless raspberry jam

GLAZE

- 1 cup confectioners' sugar
- ½ teaspoon pure vanilla extract
- 1 tablespoon boiling water, plus more if needed

ADJUST AN OVEN RACK to the center position and preheat the oven to 350°F. Line a large (17 × 14–inch) cookie sheet with a silicone baking pan liner or cooking parchment.

TO MAKE THE DOUGH, grind the almonds to a fine powder using a nut grinder. Lacking that, process them to a powder with 3 tablespoons of the sugar in a food processor fitted with the metal blade (beat the remaining sugar into the butter). Be careful not to overprocess them, or they may turn pasty.

IN A MEDIUM BOWL, beat the butter with an electric mixer on medium speed until smooth, about 1 minute. Add the sugar and salt and beat for 2 to 3 minutes, until fluffy. Scrape the bowl. On low speed, beat in the almonds. Gradually beat in the flour, beating only until incorporated.

TURN THE DOUGH OUT onto a lightly floured surface and shape it into a thick disk. Divide the dough into 4 portions, and roll each piece into a log about 12 inches long and 1 inch wide. Put the logs crosswise onto the prepared sheet, leaving about 3 inches of space between them.

LEAVING THE ENDS of the rolls intact, make a shallow depression down the length of each roll about ½ inch wide and ½ inch deep. You can use a fingertip or the handle of a wooden spoon, and you may need to go up and down the length of each roll 2 or 3 times. Don't make the trough too deep, or the rolls may crack. Use a small spoon to fill the depressions with the jam. The jam should be only a tiny bit higher than the rims of the troughs; if you use too much, it will run down the sides of the rolls during baking.

BAKE FOR ABOUT 25 MINUTES, until the rolls are a light golden brown. Rotate the sheet front to back once during baking to ensure even browning. Remove the pan from the oven and set it on a wire cooling rack.

AS SOON AS the rolls come out of the oven, make the glaze. Whisk the confectioners' sugar, vanilla, and boiling water together in a small bowl. Gradually add a little more water if necessary to make a glaze the consistency of heavy cream. Spoon the icing over the jam, not the sides of the rolls. You may not need to use all the glaze. Cool the rolls for 5 minutes.

USING A LARGE COOKIE SHEET as a spatula, transfer the rolls to a cutting surface. Use a sharp heavy knife to cut the hot rolls at an angle into cookies about 1¼ inches wide. Cool completely on wire racks.

Storing

Stored airtight at room temperature, the cookies will remain fresh for a few days.

Syrupy Almond Cookies

MAKES 16 COOKIES

THESE COOKIES, MADE WITH BUTTER, *sugar, egg, and a bit of yogurt for tang, are soaked in a cold sugar syrup after baking and then left to stand overnight in the refrigerator. In the cold, the cookies' texture becomes cake-like and scrumptious. Arzu Yilmaz, a charming Turkish woman who immigrated to the United States from Ankara in 1987, is an accomplished cook and cooking teacher. We had the pleasure of working together at her home in New Jersey.*

She taught me three things she loves to bake: these almond cookies, Turkish Semolina Sponge Cake (page 318), and Flaky Turkish Feta Turnovers (page 130).

Arzu says most Turkish desserts are better the day after they're made, and these cookies are no exception. To serve, remove the cookies from the syrup and arrange on a plate. Serve them chilled or allow them to come to room temperature. They're delicious either way.

SYRUP

- 2 cups granulated sugar
- 1¼ cups water
- 1 teaspoon fresh lemon juice

DOUGH

- 1¾ cups plus 2 tablespoons unbleached all-purpose flour
- ½ teaspoon baking powder
- ½ teaspoon salt
- 8 tablespoons (1 stick) unsalted butter, at room temperature
- ⅓ cup granulated sugar
- 1 large egg
- 1 large egg yolk
- 2 tablespoons plain yogurt
- 1 teaspoon pure vanilla extract
- 16 blanched whole almonds (see page 23)
- 1 large egg yolk, beaten for egg wash

TO MAKE THE SYRUP, combine the sugar, water, and lemon juice in a medium heavy saucepan, set the pan over medium heat, and bring to a boil, stirring occasionally to dissolve the sugar. Reduce the heat so that the syrup simmers and cook for 5 minutes. Remove the pan from the heat and let cool to room temperature, then cover the pan and refrigerate for 2 to 3 hours, until the syrup is very cold. (The syrup can be made up to a day ahead.)

ADJUST AN OVEN RACK to the center position and preheat the oven to 350°F. Line a large baking sheet (18 × 12 × 1 inch) with a silicone baking pan liner or cooking parchment.

TO MAKE THE DOUGH, in a medium bowl, whisk together the flour, baking powder, and salt.

IN A LARGE BOWL, beat the butter with a wooden spoon until smooth and creamy. Gradually beat in the sugar and beat until light and fluffy, 2 to 3 minutes. Beat in the egg and egg yolk, mixing well, then beat in the yogurt and vanilla. The batter may look curdled, which is okay. Gradually stir in the dry ingredients to make a firm dough.

DIVIDE THE DOUGH into 16 pieces and shape into walnut-sized balls, flouring your hands if the dough is sticky. (If the dough is very sticky, cover and refrigerate it for 1 to 2 hours to make it easier to handle.) Place the balls of dough about 2 inches apart on the baking sheet. Flatten them slightly, then dimple the center of each with a fingertip. Set an almond into each indentation and press gently so it sticks to the dough. Brush the cookies with the egg wash.

BAKE FOR 30 TO 35 MINUTES, until the cookies are golden brown. Rotate the baking sheet front to back after 20 minutes to ensure even browing.

AS SOON AS the cookies come out of the oven, use a wide metal spatula to transfer them to a 12-inch skillet or 13 × 9 × 2–inch baking pan in a single layer. Immediately pour on the cold syrup. Wait 5 minutes, then carefully turn the cookies over with your fingers and let them imbibe the syrup for a few minutes. Turn the cookies two more times; most or all of the syrup should be absorbed at this point.

PLACE THE COOLED COOKIES in a single layer into a shallow container and scrape any remaining syrup over them. Cover and refrigerate.

Storing

The cookies can be refrigerated for several days, during which time they will imbibe more syrup and develop a tender texture and deeper flavor. Bring to room temperature before serving, or serve them straight from the refrigerator.

Lebkuchen

MAKES 36 LEBKUCHEN

THIS TRADITIONAL SPICY GERMAN CHRISTMAS TREAT, *a cross between a cookie and a cake, is hundreds of years old. In taste, lebkuchen is reminiscent of gingerbread, although there isn't any ginger in it. The mixture of spices varies from recipe to recipe, and whether or not the cookies contain dried fruits, candied fruits, or nuts, or some combination of the three, depends on the baker. The rolled dough can be shaped in any number of ways—cut with cookie cutters of any design, shaped into slabs and cut after baking, or sliced into squares or rectangles and then baked. Lebkuchen is often adorned with a white sugar icing.*

This excellent recipe comes from Geri Orsi, whose husband's family came from Alsace-Lorraine, an area that passed back and forth between Germany and France. Her husband's grandparents, whose family name is Boente, immigrated to Carlinville, Illinois, and brought the recipe with them. Geri said she was told that the wealthy used dried fruits and nuts in their lebkuchen, whereas the less moneyed would use wild nuts that they had gathered. The Boente family, natural foragers, put black walnuts and hickory nuts into theirs. Over time, they modified the recipe to include pecans and English walnuts. That combination works especially well, as does one of black and English walnuts. They never included dried or candied fruits.

The dough should be made 3 to 4 days ahead and refrigerated to allow the flavor to develop fully, and the baked lebkuchen should be

---

DOUGH

½ cup buttermilk

1 teaspoon baking soda

½ cup honey

½ cup unsulphured molasses

8 tablespoons (1 stick) salted butter, at room temperature

2 tablespoons vegetable oil, such as corn or safflower

½ cup granulated sugar

2 teaspoons pure vanilla extract

1 large egg

3¼ cups unbleached all-purpose flour, plus more for shaping

1 tablespoon ground cinnamon

1½ teaspoons ground allspice

¾ teaspoon freshly grated nutmeg

½ teaspoon ground cloves

1 tablespoon unsweetened cocoa powder

½ teaspoon salt

1 cup coarsely chopped nuts—a combination of English and black walnuts, or walnuts and pecans

ICING

1 cup confectioners' sugar, or as needed

1 tablespoon salted butter, at room temperature

½ teaspoon pure vanilla extract

3 to 4 tablespoons evaporated milk

---

allowed to ripen in an airtight container at room temperature for 3 days or so. During their rest, the lebkuchen develop a wonderfully moist texture. If they are stored for longer than 2 weeks, the spiciness of the cookies intensifies.

TO MAKE THE DOUGH, in a large bowl stir together the buttermilk and baking soda with a wooden spoon until the liquid is very bubbly and has thickened to the consistency of heavy cream, about 1 minute. Stir in the honey and molasses until the mixture is very bubbly looking, about 1 minute more.

IN ANOTHER LARGE BOWL, beat the butter with an electric mixer on medium speed until smooth. Add the vegetable oil and beat it in well. Add the sugar and vanilla and beat for 3 to 4 minutes on medium-high speed, until the mixture is fluffy and pale in color. Add the egg and beat for 1 minute more. Add to the molasses and honey mixture and beat with a whisk until smooth.

SIFT 1 CUP OF THE FLOUR together with the cinnamon, allspice, nutmeg, cloves, cocoa, and salt. Stir it into the liquid mixture, then add 1 more cup flour and stir until smooth. Add the nuts and the remaining 1¼ cups flour and stir to make a thick, wet dough. Scrape the bowl and cover it tightly with plastic wrap. Refrigerate for 3 to 4 days.

ADJUST AN OVEN RACK to the center position and preheat the oven to 350°F. Line one large baking sheet (18 × 12 × 1 inch) with silicone baking pan liner or cooking parchment. Have two more pan liners or sheets of cooking parchment ready.

TO SHAPE THE COOKIES, flour your work surface (a pastry cloth is ideal), and scrape the chilled dough onto it. Dust with more flour to coat all surfaces of the dough. Roll the dough to a 15 × 10–inch rectangle about ⅓ inch thick. Square off the edges with the sides of your palms to make the rectangle as neat as you can. The dough will be soft. Using a large sharp knife dusted with flour before each cut, cut the dough crosswise into six 2½-inch-wide strips.

CUT EACH STRIP crosswise into 2-inch pieces. Transfer 12 cookies to the lined pans with a wide metal spatula, spacing them 2 to 3 inches apart. The cookies spread a bit during baking. Arrange the remaining cookies on the remaining sheets of parchment or pan liners.

BAKE THE LEBKUCHEN for 12 to 13 minutes, just until the cookies are set. Do not overbake, or the lebkuchen will be dry. Slide the pan liner onto the countertop and place a liner with unbaked cookies into the pan. Bake as directed, and repeat with the third set of cookies.

MAKE THE ICING as soon as the first sheet goes into the oven. Put the confectioners' sugar, butter, vanilla, and 3 tablespoons evaporated milk into a small bowl and beat with a small whisk until the icing is smooth, thick, and creamy. It should have the consistency of sour cream. Add more evaporated milk by droplets if necessary. Or, if the icing is too thin, add a bit more sugar.

TO ICE THE COOKIES when each batch of lebkuchen is done, let cool for 1 minute on the baking sheet. Then, with a pastry brush, paint each cookie with a generous dab of icing. With a wide metal spatula, transfer the lebkuchen to wire cooling racks to cool completely.

Storing

Lebkuchen keep well at room temperature for several weeks stored in airtight containers layered between waxed paper. The cookies can also be frozen. Place the iced cookies or uncut strips on baking sheets and freeze until solid, then transfer to heavy-duty resealable plastic bags and freeze for up to 1 month. Thaw the lebkuchen in their wrapping. Cut the strips into cookies just before serving.

8 | Cakes, Tortes, Pies, and Other Desserts

CREAM-FILLED TORTES, NUT TORTES, CAKES, PIES, PUDDINGS, WAFFLES, meringue desserts, and sponge cakes make up this collection of diverse and delicious recipes, the largest chapter in this book. Most of the desserts are from northern Europe. Colder climates tend to inspire creativity along these lines. But others come from distant parts of the world where the art of baking desserts has also flourished, such as Turkey and South Africa. And a couple of recipes came from an entirely unexpected country. I was surprised but delighted to learn of a Chinese sponge cake that is steamed instead of baked. In a culture that has no dessert-baking tradition, a mother's sweet determination resulted in a top-of-the-stove bamboo steamer becoming a moist heat chamber for "baking" a sponge cake. Years later, after emigrating to this country, where an oven became available, she transformed the recipe into something else quite wonderful.

Several of these recipes require ground nuts. I encourage you to acquire a manual nut grinder that can be clamped to the edge of a table or countertop. It is essentially a big version of a Mouli grater, with a large rotating drum that turns nuts into a dry, powdery fluff. A food processor can be used to grind nuts, but you must be careful not to overprocess the nuts into a paste.

Rigo Jancsi

MAKES 20 SERVINGS

THIS IS ONE OF HUNGARY'S MOST FAMOUS DESSERTS. *It is chocolate times three: cake, filling, and icing. It is very, very rich, of course, so serve small portions. The combination of two layers of chocolate sponge cake filled with an ultrathick layer of chocolate cream and topped with a generous amount of chocolate glaze is enough to make one's heart beat faster. And according to the story of how this dessert came to be, that's exactly what happened.*

The cake is named after Johnny Rigo (in Hungary, Johnny is Jancsi, and surnames come first), a well-known gypsy violinist around the turn of the twentieth century. He had been playing with an orchestra all around Europe, and one night he was fiddling in a restaurant in Vienna (or was it a Parisian restaurant, or possibly in Budapest at Kugler-Gerbeaud, a famous pastry shop?) when the elderly Belgian duke of Chimay was dining there with his beautiful young wife, the daughter of an American millionaire. She was totally fascinated by Johnny's music, and even more so by his passionate black eyes. They fell in love, she left her husband, and the couple lived a blissful life together, traveling around the world. (Or, as some stories say, their romance soon fizzled and they went their separate ways. But who wants to believe that?) True or not, we still have a great dessert.

Vera Eisenberg, a marvelous baker, cooking teacher, and food stylist, shared the recipe with me. She immigrated here from Hungary more than forty years ago with her mother and sister. Her father had arrived several years beforehand, at the time of the Russian takeover of Hungary. Vera learned to bake from

CAKE

- 8 tablespoons (1 stick) unsalted butter
- 6 ounces semisweet or bittersweet chocolate, chopped
- ½ cup unbleached all-purpose flour
- 3 tablespoons unsweetened cocoa powder, sifted if lumpy
- 10 large eggs, separated
- ⅔ cup granulated sugar
- ¼ teaspoon salt

FILLING

- 8 ounces semisweet chocolate, chopped
- 4 cups heavy cream
- ½ cup confectioners' sugar
- 2 tablespoons unsweetened cocoa powder, sifted if lumpy
- 2 tablespoons dark rum or Cognac
- 1 teaspoon pure vanilla extract

GLAZE

- ½ cup granulated sugar
- ⅓ cup water
- 8 ounces semisweet or bittersweet chocolate, chopped
- ⅓ cup apricot preserves, strained
- 20 candied violets or edible flowers for garnish

her mother and grandmother, and this dessert in particular brings back memories of her country and the richness of its culinary heritage. Vera's mother had a specific ratio for the ingredients in the cake: 1 egg to 1 spoonful of flour to 1 spoonful of sugar (spoonful meant heaping soupspoon). And she liked to use 10 eggs in almost everything she baked. So Vera carries on that tradition. Her cake is thicker than I've seen in other Rigo Jancsi recipes, making it an equal player with the thick chocolate cream filling.

Make this for a special occasion. You can assemble the dessert a day ahead, and you can bake the chocolate cake a day before that. Wrap the cake airtight, and leave it at room temperature. The chocolate cream filling can also be made a day ahead. This is a big hit with kids too.

TO MAKE THE CAKE, adjust an oven rack to the center position and preheat the oven to 350°F. Butter the bottom and sides of an 18 × 12 × 1–inch baking sheet and line the bottom with parchment paper. Butter the paper and dust the pan with flour; knock out the excess flour.

MELT THE BUTTER in a small heavy saucepan over low heat. Add the chocolate and stir with a heatproof rubber spatula until the chocolate is melted and the mixture is smooth. Remove from the heat and cool to tepid or room temperature.

IN A SMALL BOWL, whisk the flour and cocoa powder to combine well.

BEAT THE EGG YOLKS in the bowl of an electric mixer with the whip attachment on high speed until thick and lemon colored, 3 to 5 minutes. Beating on medium speed, gradually add ⅓ cup of the sugar. Increase the speed to high and beat for about 5 minutes more, until the yolks are very pale in color and form a slowly dissolving ribbon when the beater is raised. Scrape the yolks into a large wide bowl. Wash and dry the bowl and beaters.

IN THE CLEAN BOWL, beat the egg whites with the salt on medium speed until they increase in volume and form soft peaks when the beater is raised. Gradually beat in the remaining ⅓ cup sugar, then beat until the whites look creamy and form stiff shiny peaks that curl slightly at their tips.

WITH A LARGE RUBBER SPATULA, fold the chocolate mixture into the egg yolks. Add the dry ingredients and fold them in. Add about one-third of the egg whites and fold them in gently. Do not be too thorough at this point—it's fine if some streaks of white show. Fold in the remaining whites until thoroughly incorporated. Spread the batter into the prepared pan—be gentle so as not to deflate it—and carefully level it with the spatula.

BAKE FOR 13 TO 15 MINUTES, or until the cake is puffed and springs back when gently pressed and a toothpick inserted in the center comes out clean or with a few crumbs sticking to it. Do not overbake, or the cake will be dry. Remove the pan from the oven and immediately run the tip of a small sharp knife around the sides of the cake to release it. Lay a sheet of parchment over the cake, cover with a large wire rack, and invert the two. Working quickly, remove the pan (careful, it's hot!), and peel off the paper. Cover the cake with another large wire rack and invert again. Remove the top rack and parchment, and let the cake cool completely.

TO MAKE THE FILLING, melt the chocolate in a small saucepan set over a larger pan of hot water over medium heat, stirring occasionally with a heatproof rubber spatula until the chocolate is completely melted and smooth. Take care that no water gets into the chocolate, or it will "seize" and be impossible to work with. Remove the pan from the water and cool the chocolate to room temperature. It should still be liquid.

COMBINE THE CREAM, confectioners' sugar, cocoa, rum or Cognac, and vanilla in a large bowl and whip until the cream is slightly thickened but pourable. Gradually fold about one-quarter of the cream into the cooled chocolate, then fold the chocolate into the remaining cream. Beat on medium speed just until the filling is thick and holds a definite shape; do not beat until stiff, or the filling may separate and look curdled. If the temperatures of the chocolate and cream are about the same, the chocolate cream will be perfectly smooth and homogeneous; if the cream is a bit too cold, the chocolate may form small granules, giving the cream a speckled look. If this happens, it's fine—the filling will still be delicious. Cover the bowl with plastic wrap and refrigerate until ready to assemble the cake.

TO MAKE THE GLAZE, in a small heavy saucepan, heat the sugar and water over medium heat, stirring occasionally, until the liquid comes to a low boil. The liquid should look perfectly clear. The sugar must be fully dissolved, or the glaze will be grainy. Remove the pan from the heat and add the chocolate. Stir with a whisk until the chocolate is dissolved and the glaze is completely smooth. Let stand, whisking occasionally, until the glaze is thick enough to spread—a few minutes at most.

TO ASSEMBLE THE CAKE, cut the cake crosswise in half. Put one layer onto a serving tray or large flat platter. Use a pastry brush to coat the top with the apricot preserves. Pile the chocolate filling on top and spread it evenly, sculpting the sides with a narrow metal spatula so that they are smooth and squared off. Turn the second layer upside down and set it on top of the filling; press gently to make sure the cake sticks to the cream filling. Pour on the prepared glaze and spread it evenly over the top with a small offset spatula; do not let the glaze drip down the sides of the cake. Refrigerate for at least 1 hour.

ABOUT 30 MINUTES before serving, dip a sharp knife into hot water, shake off the excess water, and score the glaze into 20 squares, dipping the knife into hot water again as necessary. Score deeply enough so that the knife just reaches the cake layer. Then cut into individual portions, at the scoring lines. Let stand for about 30 minutes.

TO SERVE, decorate each portion with a candied violet or an edible flower and arrange on plates.

Storing

Rigo Jancsi keeps well, covered in the refrigerator, for up to 3 days.

Hungarian Walnut Torte

MAKES 16 SERVINGS

THIS IS A SPECTACULAR THREE-LAYER WALNUT TORTE, *filled and frosted with mocha whipped cream, and about 4 inches tall. The tender, not too sweet cake layers—given their structure and flavor from ground walnuts and fresh bread crumbs—are leavened only by beaten eggs. Make this for a special celebration, or any time you are feeling especially festive. Hungarian-born Vera Eisenberg, a pastry chef, food stylist, and cooking teacher in New York, learned this recipe from her stepmother, Gizi. Vera substitutes matzoh meal for the fresh bread crumbs during Passover.*

The walnuts must be finely ground. The best way to grind the nuts is with a manual nut grinder. Ground this way, the nuts are fluffy and powdery and mix into the batter easily. If you have a hand-held Mouli grater, it will also do a fine job. If grinding the walnuts with a food processor, you have to be careful that the nuts don't become pasty. To prevent that from happening, I process the nuts in batches with the fresh bread crumbs. Walnuts to be ground must be at room temperature.

For the best texture, make this a day ahead.

See the companion DVD for a video demonstration of torte making.

TORTE

Fine dry bread crumbs for the pans

12 ounces (3 generous cups) walnuts, at room temperature

3 ounces fresh bread crumbs (1½ cups loosely packed; from 3 to 4 slices of crustless day-old white bread or French or Italian bread)

12 large eggs, separated

¾ cup granulated sugar

2 teaspoons pure vanilla extract

Finely grated zest of 1 lemon

½ teaspoon salt

MOCHA WHIPPED CREAM

⅓ cup water

1 tablespoon instant espresso (I use Medaglia d'Oro)

⅓ cup granulated sugar

3 cups heavy cream

2 teaspoons pure vanilla extract

3 ounces semisweet chocolate, grated

DECORATION

16 chocolate-coated coffee beans or candied violets for garnish

TO MAKE THE TORTE, adjust two oven racks to divide the oven into thirds and preheat the oven to 350°F. Butter three 9-inch round cake pans, line the bottoms with parchment or waxed paper circles, and butter the paper. Dust the pans with fine dry bread crumbs, and tap out the excess crumbs.

FINELY GRIND THE WALNUTS with a manual nut grinder or a Mouli grater. Put the nuts in a medium bowl and stir in the bread crumbs. Or process them in 3 batches in a food processor fitted with the metal blade, adding ½ cup of the bread crumbs to each batch. Pulse the nuts and crumbs with rapid on/off bursts until the nuts feel powdery and look fluffy; you want the walnuts to be as fine as possible without any hint of their becoming pasty. Stop often to scrape the work bowl. Transfer the nut/crumb mixture to a medium bowl.

BEAT THE YOLKS in the bowl of a stand mixer with the whip attachment on high speed until thick and lemon colored, 3 to 5 minutes. Beating on medium speed, gradually add ½ cup of the sugar. Scrape the bowl, and beat on high speed for about 5 minutes more, until the yolks are very thick and pale and form a slowly dissolving ribbon as they fall off the beaters. Beat in the vanilla and lemon zest. Scrape the yolks into a large wide bowl. Wash and dry the bowl and beaters.

IN THE CLEAN BOWL, whip the whites with the salt on medium speed until they have thickened to the point that the beaters leave traces in the whites. Gradually add the remaining ¼ cup sugar and continue beating until the whites form stiff, shiny, creamy peaks that curl slightly at their tips.

SPRINKLE ABOUT ONE-QUARTER of the nuts and bread crumbs over the yolks, add about one-quarter of the whites, and fold everything together very gently, with just a few broad strokes of a rubber spatula, so as to deflate the batter as little as possible. It's all right if streaks of white remain at this point. Repeat with the remaining nuts and whites in 3 additions, folding in the last addition just until no whites show. The batter should look light and airy. Divide the batter evenly among the prepared pans (a kitchen scale is helpful for this step) and rotate each pan gently on the countertop to level the batter.

PLACE THE PANS in the oven, two on the upper rack and one on the lower rack. Bake for 20 to 25 minutes, until the layers are golden brown and spring back when gently pressed and a toothpick inserted in the center comes out clean. Be careful not to overbake. The bottom layer may be baked a minute or two before the other layers. Cool the cakes in their pans for 10 minutes. The cakes will settle on cooling and will be about 1 inch tall.

RELEASE THE LAYERS from the sides of the pan by running the tip of a sharp knife around them. Cover each layer with a wire rack and invert. Carefully lift off the pan and peel off the paper. Cover the layer with another rack and invert again to cool right side up. (The layers can be baked a day ahead; when completely cool, wrap in plastic wrap and leave them at room temperature.)

TO MAKE THE MOCHA whipped cream, put the water, instant espresso, and sugar in a small heavy saucepan (don't stir), set the pan over medium-low heat, and slowly bring the liquid to a simmer. Swirl the pan by its handle to dissolve the espresso powder and sugar and cook for 2 to 3 minutes more, until the liquid is syrupy. Remove from the heat and let cool completely.

COMBINE THE CREAM, syrup, and vanilla in a large bowl and whip on medium-high speed until the cream holds a firm shape. Fold in the grated chocolate.

TO FILL AND FROST the cake, arrange 4 strips of waxed paper in a square pattern around the edges of a cake plate. Set one cake layer right side up on the plate, with the edges of the waxed paper strips just under the edges of the cake. Use a narrow metal spatula to spread the layer with about 1 cup of the whipped cream. Place a second layer right side up and spread it with another 1 cup of cream. Set the third layer right side up on top and spread the remaining whipped cream over the sides and top of the cake, making it thicker on top than on the sides. Decorate the top of the cake with chocolate-coated coffee beans or candied violets. Carefully remove the strips of waxed paper by pulling them toward you gently by a short end. Refrigerate for several hours before serving.

TO SERVE, cut the cake into portions with a sharp knife. Let come to room temperature before serving.

Storing

This torte keeps well, refrigerated, for 3 to 4 days. Cover the cut portion with plastic wrap applied directly to the cut surface.

Piskóta

MAKES 16 TO 20 SERVINGS

THIS SOUR CHERRY TORTE *(pronounced "peesh-KO-ta")* *is a quintessential Hungarian home dessert. Vera Eisenberg, a Hungarian baker, cooking teacher, and food stylist, brought the recipe with her when she immigrated to the United States more than forty years ago. Vera says the cake can be topped with just about any fruit, but sour cherries (sometimes unpitted!) are the most common. A Hungarian housewife is likely to have piskóta on hand at all times. Serve the cake with lightly sweetened whipped cream or with ice cream.*

CAKE

½ cup plus 2 tablespoons unbleached all-purpose flour

2 teaspoons baking powder

½ teaspoon salt, plus a pinch

10 large eggs, separated

½ cup plus 2 tablespoons granulated sugar

Finely grated zest of 1 lemon

1 teaspoon pure lemon extract

1 pound sour or sweet cherries, pitted, 2 cups blueberries, raspberries, or blackberries, or 1 pound apricots, halved and pitted

Confectioners' sugar for dusting

TO MAKE THE CAKE, adjust an oven rack to the center position and preheat the oven to 350°F. Butter a 13 × 9 × 2–inch baking pan and dust the bottom only with flour. Knock out the excess flour.

SIFT TOGETHER the flour, baking powder, and ½ teaspoon salt.

BEAT THE EGG YOLKS in the bowl of an electric mixer with the whip attachment on high speed until thick and lemon colored. Beating on medium speed, gradually add ½ cup of the sugar. Increase the speed to high and beat for about 5 minutes more, until the yolks are very pale and form a slowly dissolving ribbon when the beater is raised. Beat in the lemon zest and extract. Remove the bowl from the mixer and stir in the dry ingredients. Transfer the batter to another large bowl, and wash and dry the mixer bowl and beater.

IN THE CLEAN BOWL, beat the egg whites with the pinch of salt on medium speed until they form soft peaks. Gradually beat in the remaining 2 tablespoons sugar, then beat until the whites look creamy and form shiny peaks that curl slightly at their tips. Stir one-quarter of the whites into the yolks to lighten the batter, then fold in the remaining whites in 3 additions, only until no whites show. Scrape the batter, which will look very light and fluffy, into the prepared pan.

DISTRIBUTE THE FRUIT evenly on top of the cake. If you are using apricots, arrange them cut side down. The fruit will begin to sink into the batter.

BAKE FOR 25 TO 30 MINUTES, until the cake is puffed and golden brown and a toothpick inserted in the center comes out clean. Cool the cake completely in its pan on a wire rack.

TO SERVE, cut into portions in the pan, dust with confectioners' sugar, and serve.

Storing

This cake keeps well, covered, for up to 2 days at room temperature.

Welsh Christmas Cake

MAKES 1 LARGE FRUITCAKE

THIS WONDERFUL FRUITCAKE COMES FROM TOTTIE PARMETER, *who learned how to make it from her mother in Wales. Tottie mixes the fruit with the brandy about a week before she wants to bake the cake to give the fruit plenty of time to soak up as much liquor as possible. Lyle's Golden Syrup, made from sugarcane, is sold in specialty food shops and in many supermarkets. If you can't find it, substitute light corn syrup.*

This fruitcake is best cut into thin slices and served cold.

DRIED FRUIT

2 cups (10 ounces) currants

2½ cups (12 ounces) golden raisins

2 cups (10 ounces) dark raisins

1 cup brandy

CANDIED FRUITS AND ALMONDS

1 cup glacéed cherries, halved

½ cup diced candied orange peel

½ cup diced candied lemon peel

¾ cup blanched almonds, coarsely chopped

¼ cup unbleached all-purpose flour

CAKE

Fine dry bread crumbs for the pan

2 cups unbleached all-purpose flour

¾ cup unblanched or blanched whole almonds

½ teaspoon salt

1 teaspoon baking powder

½ teaspoon ground mace

½ teaspoon freshly grated nutmeg

½ teaspoon ground cinnamon

½ teaspoon ground allspice

¼ teaspoon ground cloves

½ pound (2 sticks) unsalted butter, at room temperature

1 cup firmly packed dark brown sugar

2 tablespoons Lyle's Golden Syrup

5 large eggs at room temperature

¼ cup brandy

2 teaspoons pure vanilla extract

½ teaspoon pure almond extract

A WEEK BEFORE BAKING, put the dried fruits and brandy into a 1½- to 2-quart screw-cap jar or into a large heavy-duty resealable plastic bag. Seal the jar or bag and let the fruits macerate at room temperature for 7 days, turning the jar or bag frequently. By the end of a week, the brandy should be completely absorbed.

TRANSFER THE FRUITS to a large bowl and add the glacéed cherries, candied orange and lemon peel, and almonds. Add the flour and, using your hands, toss everything together well.

TO MAKE THE CAKE, adjust an oven rack to the lower third position and preheat the oven to 300°F. Coat a two-piece

10 × 4–inch tube pan with cooking spray and dust all over with fine dry bread crumbs. Tap out the excess crumbs.

PUT 2 TABLESPOONS of the flour and the almonds into the work bowl of a food processor fitted with the metal blade and process until the almonds are finely ground, about 1 minute. Do not process the nuts to a paste. Transfer to a medium bowl, add the remaining flour, salt, baking powder, and spices, and whisk together.

IN THE LARGE BOWL of an electric mixer, beat the butter on medium speed with the paddle attachment for 1 minute, or until soft and fluffy. Gradually beat in the brown sugar, then the syrup. Scrape the bowl and beater and beat on medium-high speed for 5 minutes. Add the eggs one at a time, beating for 1 minute after each. On low speed, beat in the brandy, vanilla, and almond extract. Scrape the bowl and beater. On low speed, gradually add the dry ingredients, mixing only until thoroughly incorporated.

REMOVE THE BOWL from the mixer and scrape the batter over the fruit and nut mixture. Stir well with a wooden spoon to coat the fruit and almonds with batter. Place about one-quarter of the batter into the prepared pan in large spoonfuls all around the central tube and spread evenly, packing the batter down to remove any air pockets. Repeat with the remaining batter in 3 more additions. Smooth the top. Bang the pan 2 or 3 times on your countertop to level it and to make sure there are no air pockets. The pan will be about two-thirds full.

BAKE for 2½ to 3 hours, until a wooden skewer inserted into the cake comes out clean.

COOL THE CAKE in its pan on a wire rack for 1 hour. Carefully remove the cake from the pan and set it right side up on a wire rack to cool completely.

WHEN THE CAKE IS COOL, wrap in two or three layers of plastic wrap and refrigerate for at least 1 day before serving. Cut into thin slices with a sharp serrated knife.

Storing

Store the cake in the refrigerator, well wrapped in plastic wrap and aluminum foil, for up to 1 month. To freeze, place the wrapped cake in a heavy-duty resealable plastic bag and freeze for up to 6 months. Thaw the cake in its wrapping and keep refrigerated until serving time.

Gâteau Basque

MAKES 8 SERVINGS

THIS IS ONE OF THE MOST FAMOUS DESSERTS *from the French Basque country. A tender, sweet, cookie-like dough encloses a thick pastry cream flavored with vanilla. It is exquisite. Bernadette Iribarren came to San Francisco about fifty years ago as an au pair. There she met and married her husband, had two sons, and continued cooking in the Basque tradition. One of eight children, Bernadette was raised on a farm in the town of Macaye. "We always had fresh eggs and butter, and I learned to use only the freshest ingredients," she said with authority. Over the years, Bernadette baked gâteau Basque regularly, often making several of them at a time to sell. Today, Bernadette makes gâteau Basque only occasionally, but she is an instinctive baker, and the practice ingrained in her during decades of baking—the deftness and skill with which she makes the pastry and filling— are exciting to watch and to be a part of.*

Bernadette makes everything by hand, and the only measure she uses is a soupspoon. Fifteen heaping soupspoons of flour and 10 to 12 soupspoons of sugar get plopped into a bowl for the dough. She adds the butter and reduces it to smaller pieces with rapid pinching movements. Then she makes a well in the dry ingredients, adds the eggs, yolks, citrus zest, and flavoring, and works them in quickly and with a light touch of a hand. She puts "enough" milk into a saucepan to heat up for the pastry cream, and she puts 10 soupspoons of sugar, 4 of flour, and the egg yolks into a bowl. She whisks these ingredients together and gradually whisks in the hot milk. Then she transfers the mixture to the saucepan and cooks the pastry cream.

Make the dough first and chill it for about 1 hour, or until it has firmed up. The high amount of sugar in the dough makes it something of a challenge to work with, but you'll be thrilled with the results. While the pastry is in the refrigerator, make the pastry cream. It needs to be cooled to room temperature before using.

Bernadette says gâteau Basque is really better the day after baking, and she never refrigerates it. I do refrigerate it after it has cooled to room temperature, then bring it to room temperature before serving.

PASTRY

- 3 cups unbleached all-purpose flour, plus more for rolling

- 1 tablespoon baking powder

- ¾ to 1 cup granulated sugar

- ½ pound (2 sticks) unsalted butter, cut into tablespoon-sized pieces, slightly softened

  Finely grated zest of 1 orange or lemon

- 2 large eggs

- 2 large egg yolks

- 1 teaspoon pure almond extract or dark rum

PASTRY CREAM

- 2 cups whole milk

- 5 large egg yolks

- ¾ cup granulated sugar

- 2 teaspoons pure vanilla extract

- ½ cup all-purpose flour

- 1 large egg yolk, beaten with 1 teaspoon water, for egg wash

TO MAKE THE DOUGH, if your kitchen is very warm, chill the flour before beginning. Put 2½ cups of the flour, the baking powder, and sugar (the more sugar you use, the more tender the dough, but the harder it is to work with) into a large bowl and mix together with your fingers. Add the butter pieces and pinch them into the dry ingredients rapidly, fluffing the mixture as you go along; your aim is to break the butter into small flakes. This step should only take 2 to 3 minutes. Make a well in the dry ingredients and add the zest, eggs, egg yolks, and extract. Beat the eggs with a fork until well combined, then gradually stir and press in the dry ingredients from the sides to make a soft, sticky, shaggy-looking dough.

SPRINKLE ABOUT HALF of the remaining ½ cup flour on your work surface and scrape the dough onto it. Sprinkle the remaining flour over the dough. Gently knead in the flour until all of it is incorporated and the dough is smooth. Small flakes of butter may be visible, and the dough may still seem a bit sticky. Flour a dinner plate, shape the dough into a disk, and set it on the plate. Cover tightly with plastic wrap and refrigerate for at least 1 hour, or up to 3 hours.

TO MAKE THE PASTRY CREAM, put the milk into a medium heavy saucepan and bring the milk almost to a boil over medium heat. Meanwhile, in a medium bowl, whisk the yolks until slightly thickened, about 1 minute. Add the sugar and whisk for another minute or two. Add the vanilla and flour and whisk until smooth and thick.

POUR ABOUT ONE-THIRD of the hot milk into the egg mixture and whisk until smooth. Add the remaining milk and whisk until smooth. Pour the mixture back into the saucepan and set the pan over medium heat. Cook, whisking constantly, until the mixture is very thick. Use a heatproof rubber spatula to scrape the sides and bottom of the pan occasionally, especially around the edges. The pastry cream will be too thick to actually boil, but you should be able to see a bubble or two pop when the cream is thoroughly cooked. This step may take 10 minutes or more. Remove the pan from the heat and let cool to room temperature, whisking the pastry cream occasionally to keep it smooth and lump-free. (The pastry

cream can be made up to 2 days ahead. Press a piece of plastic wrap directly onto the surface to prevent a skin from forming and cool to room temperature, then refrigerate. Bring to room temperature before using.)

ADJUST AN OVEN RACK to the center position and preheat the oven to 350°F. Have ready an ungreased 9 × 1½-inch round cake pan.

DIVIDE THE DOUGH IN TWO, with one piece slightly larger, and shape each piece into a disk. If the dough feels very firm, let it stand at room temperature until it has softened enough to roll easily—if the dough is too cold when you roll it, it will fragment into many pieces. Lightly dust your work surface with flour, and roll the larger piece of dough to an 11- to 12-inch circle about ³⁄₁₆ inch thick. The dough should not be too thin. Because of the high sugar content, the dough tends to fall apart. The best way to transfer the dough to the cake pan is to slide a large dough spatula or cookie sheet under the dough, move it to the cake pan, and carefully slide the dough into the pan. Do not be concerned if the dough tears; simply use floured fingers to patch the dough together. Don't stretch the dough to fit it into the pan, just carefully lift the outer edges of the pastry and nudge them gently into the pan. Leave any excess dough hanging over the edges of the pan for now.

WHISK THE COOLED PASTRY CREAM to make sure it is smooth, and scrape it into the pan. Spread it level with the back of a teaspoon. Roll the second piece of dough to a 9- to 10-inch circle about ³⁄₁₆ inch thick on the floured surface and set it on top of the pastry cream, using the dough spatula or cookie sheet. Press the edges of dough together gently to seal, and cut away excess dough from the edges of the pan with a sharp knife. Use a fork to crimp the edges of dough together. Brush the top of the dough with the egg wash, then run the fork all over the top to make an informal design. (If desired, combine the pastry scraps, wrap, and chill, then roll out to make cookies.)

BAKE THE GÂTEAU for 40 to 50 minutes, until it is well browned. Cool the cake in its pan on a wire rack for 15 minutes, then run the tip of a sharp knife carefully all around the sides to release the cake. Bang the cake pan on your countertop a couple of times to release the cake from the bottom of the pan, cover the cake with a wire rack, and invert the two. Remove the cake pan, cover the cake with another rack, and invert again to cool completely right side up.

YOU CAN SERVE the gâteau once it is cool, 3 to 4 hours, but it's really best if you can wait until the next day: Cover and refrigerate overnight. Bring to room temperature before serving.

Storing

The gâteau Basque stays perfectly fresh in the refrigerator for 3 or 4 days.

Variation

Bernadette sometimes spreads about ½ cup cherry preserves, made with a special Basque black cherry, on top of the pastry cream before putting on the top crust. Confiture de cerise noir, found throughout the Basque country, is a tradition in Itxassou. The preserves are made from Beltza, one of three local varieties of black cherries unique to the town. The cherries are not pleasant eaten raw, but they make splendid preserves. They are delicious spread on baguettes and are also excellent with sharp cheeses. You can substitute any top-quality sweet black cherry preserves.

My Quest for Bakers

I'm often asked how I found the bakers for this book. Bernadette Iribarren, an immigrant from the French Basque country, came to me through a chance encounter with a friend of hers at the Salt Lake City airport. Stranded there, my wife and I went to one of the airline clubs to see if we could find a hotel room for the night. The nearest available hotels were thirty-five miles away in Ogden, and we shared a cab with two women who also needed accommodations. We chatted about our work, and one of the women, Marie Ocafrain, who lived in the San Francisco Bay Area, asked me if I was going to include gâteau Basque in my book. I said I'd love to, but hadn't been able to locate a Basque baker. "My good friend Bernadette makes it. Would you like me to ask her for you?" This is how I came in phone contact with Bernadette. A few weeks later, I called Bernadette and told her I'd be in the city for one day the following month. Would she be able to show me how she makes her famous dessert? "Yes," she said, "I will be happy to." And that is how Gâteau Basque came to be in this book.

Torta di Limone

MAKES 8 SERVINGS

CARMELA TURSI HOBBINS, *a second-generation Italian American born in Des Moines, learned to make this lemon olive oil cake from one of her cooking teachers on a trip to Italy. Carmella, a teacher of Italian cooking herself, calls this a "tablespoon torta" because the measurements are in tablespoons. It is a sublime cake with a dramatic yellow color and spongy texture, ideally suited to serving plain with fruit or to being gussied up for fancier occasions with whipped cream. For breakfast or an afternoon pick-me-up, dust the torta with confectioners' sugar, cut into wedges, and serve with fresh fruit, such as strawberries, raspberries, or blueberries, or sliced mangoes, peaches, nectarines, or a combination. For a dessert, top the torta with heavy whipped cream flavored with limoncello, the fabulous Italian lemon liqueur.*

The olive oil gives the cake its special taste and moistness. Use a light, fruity Italian extra-virgin olive oil. Do not under any circumstances use a supermarket olive oil that has the word "light" on the label—these colorless, tasteless oils are superrefined and should be shunned.

TORTA

2 large eggs

7 tablespoons granulated sugar

7 tablespoons (¼ cup plus 3 tablespoons) whole milk

7 tablespoons (¼ cup plus 3 tablespoons) fruity extra-virgin olive oil

9 tablespoons (½ cup plus 1 tablespoon) unbleached all-purpose flour

2 teaspoons baking powder

¼ teaspoon salt

Finely grated zest of 2 lemons

3 tablespoons fresh lemon juice

Confectioners' sugar for dusting

TO MAKE THE TORTA, adjust an oven rack to the lower third position and preheat the oven to 350°F. Grease a 9-inch round cake pan or coat it lightly with cooking spray. Line the bottom of the pan with a circle of parchment. Grease or spray the parchment and dust the pan with flour. Knock out excess flour.

PUT THE EGGS, in their shells, into a small bowl, cover them with hot water, and let stand for 5 minutes. Dry the eggs and crack them into a medium bowl. Add the sugar and whisk vigorously for 1 minute. In a small bowl, whisk together the milk and olive oil just to combine well, then add to the eggs and whisk briefly.

IN ANOTHER SMALL BOWL, stir together the flour, baking powder, and salt. Add to the batter and whisk gently only until the batter is smooth. Whisk in the lemon zest and juice. Scrape the batter into the prepared pan.

BAKE FOR 20 TO 25 MINUTES, until the cake is golden and springs back when gently pressed in the center. Cool the cake in its pan on a wire rack for 10 minutes, then run the tip of a

CAKES, TORTES, PIES, AND OTHER DESSERTS   287

sharp paring knife around the sides of the cake to loosen it. Cover the pan with another wire rack and invert the two. Lift off the pan and remove the paper. Cover the cake with a wire rack and invert again to cool completely right side up.

DUST THE TORTA with confectioners' sugar before serving.

Variations

For a more intense lemon flavor, prick top of the warm torta all over with a fork and brush with a few tablespoons of limoncello. When cool, dust with confectioners' sugar, and serve portions with whipped cream and fresh fruit.

For a layer cake, double the recipe and bake the batter in two pans. Fill and frost the cake with whipped cream flavored with limoncello.

For a citrus torta, use the finely grated zest of 1 lemon and 1 orange and substitute fresh orange juice for the lemon juice.

Princess Torte

MAKES 12 TO 16 SERVINGS

THIS IS A SPECTACULAR CAKE *that is a true adventure in baking. It has three tender sponge layers. The bottom one is spread with raspberry jam and covered with a combination of custard and whipped cream. The second layer is spread with more of the custard and whipped cream. After the top layer is set in place, more whipped cream is spread on the top and sides, and then the whole thing is encased within a thin pale green layer of marzipan. I first tasted it about twenty years ago at Sweden House, a Swedish bakery and café in Tiburon, California, and fell head over heels in love with it. When I waxed rhapsodic about this cake to Helena Hoas, a Swedish friend, she said, "Oh, I know this cake well. It is one of the most special Swedish desserts." And then she said the magic words: "I can show you how to make it."*

Although it sounds complicated, the torte is not difficult to make, and you can prepare it in stages. Both the cake and the custard can be made a day ahead. On the day you want to serve the cake, prepare the marzipan and assemble and cloak the cake. Make this for a special occasion, and you'll receive raves and appreciation galore.

CUSTARD

2 tablespoons cornstarch

2 tablespoons granulated sugar

1½ cups half-and-half

3 large egg yolks

1 tablespoon pure vanilla extract

CAKE

Fine dry bread crumbs for the pan

½ cup sifted unbleached all-purpose flour

½ cup potato starch flour (spooned into the cup and leveled)

½ teaspoon baking powder

4 large eggs, separated

⅛ teaspoon salt

¾ cup plus 2 tablespoons granulated sugar

2½ cups heavy cream (use 3 cups if you want a thicker topping)

3 to 4 tablespoons seedless raspberry jam

MARZIPAN COATING

Two 7-ounce packages Odense marzipan or 14 ounces (about 1¾ packed cups) homemade marzipan (page 331)

Green food coloring

Confectioners' sugar for dusting

TO MAKE THE CUSTARD, in a small bowl whisk together the cornstarch, sugar, ½ cup of the half-and-half, and the egg yolks until smooth. Heat the remaining 1 cup half-and-half in a medium saucepan over medium heat until it is scalded—you will see steam rising from the surface and small bubbles around the edges. Very gradually, add the hot half-and-half to the egg yolk mixture, whisking constantly. Scrape the mixture into the saucepan and cook over medium heat, stirring constantly with a heatproof rubber spatula, until the custard thickens, about 5 minutes. Because it is so thick, the custard will never actually boil, and as it heats, it will gradually become lumpy, especially on the bottom. Just keep stirring, going all around the sides and bottom of the pan with the spatula. As it thickens further, the custard will look like scrambled eggs. At this point, switch to the whisk and stir, *don't beat*, until very smooth. Cook, whisking, for 1 to 2 minutes more. Remove the pan from the heat, scrape the custard into a medium bowl and stir in the vanilla. Press a piece of plastic wrap directly onto the surface of the custard to prevent a skin from forming, and cool for 30 minutes at room temperature, then refrigerate until very cold. (The custard can be made a day ahead.)

TO MAKE THE CAKE, adjust an oven rack to the lower third position and preheat the oven to 350°F. Butter a 9-inch springform pan or coat it with cooking spray. Line the bottom of the pan with a round of cooking parchment or waxed paper and butter the paper. Dust the inside of the pan with fine dry bread crumbs and tap out the excess crumbs.

SIFT THE FLOUR, potato starch, and baking powder together twice.

IN A LARGE BOWL, whip the egg whites and salt with an electric mixer on medium speed until the whites are shiny and form stiff peaks when the beaters are raised. Do not overbeat—the whites should be smooth, not lumpy. Beating on medium speed, sprinkle in about one-quarter of the sugar, then add 1 egg yolk and beat for about 10 seconds. Repeat the process 3 more times, then continue beating a few minutes more, until the mixture is thick and pale and forms a slowly dissolving ribbon when the beaters are raised.

USING A LARGE RUBBER SPATULA, gently fold in the flour mixture in 4 additions, only until no dry ingredients show. Scrape the batter into the prepared pan, and gently smooth the top.

BAKE FOR ABOUT 30 MINUTES, until the cake is golden brown and springs back when gently pressed and a toothpick inserted into the center comes out clean. Cool the cake in its pan on a wire rack for 10 minutes. Run the blade of a small sharp knife around the sides of the cake to release from the pan, if necessary, and carefully remove the sides of the pan. Cover the cake with a wire rack and invert. Remove the bottom of the pan and the paper liner. Cover the cake with another wire rack and invert again to cool completely right side up.

TO ASSEMBLE THE TORTE, use a long sharp serrated knife to split the cake into 3 equal layers; set aside.

WHIP THE CREAM in a large bowl until it is thick and holds a firm shape. Transfer one-third of the cream to a small bowl, cover, and refrigerate. Remove the chilled custard from the refrigerator; it will be very thick. Whisk it vigorously until it is smooth and creamy. Fold half the remaining whipped cream into the chilled custard, then fold the custard into the remaining cream.

ARRANGE 4 STRIPS of waxed paper in a square pattern around the edges of a serving platter. Set the bottom cake layer, cut side up, onto the platter, with the edges of the waxed paper strips just under the edge of the cake. Spread the raspberry jam onto the cake, then spread half the custard cream mixture evenly over the jam. Invert the top cake layer onto the custard cream so that its cut side is facing up. Spread the remaining custard cream over the layer and place the remaining cake layer on top. Spread about one-quarter of the reserved refrigerated whipped cream in a very thin layer around the sides of the cake. Scrape the remaining cream onto the top of the cake and spread evenly with a narrow metal spatula. Carefully remove the waxed paper strips by pulling them toward you gently by a short end. Refrigerate the cake.

TO MAKE THE MARZIPAN COATING, break the marzipan into small pieces into a medium bowl. Add 3 or 4 drops of green food coloring and knead it into the marzipan with your hands to tint the marzipan a shade of pale green. The marzipan is stiff, so be patient. Add a drop or two more of food coloring if necessary, but don't tint the marzipan a bright green. Dust your work surface with confectioners' sugar. Shape the marzipan into a 6-inch disk, place it on the work surface, and turn to coat both sides lightly with sugar. Roll the marzipan to a circle about 16 inches in diameter and less than ⅛ inch thick. Turn the marzipan over during the rolling and dust it with the confectioners' sugar as necessary to prevent sticking. (If you have 18-inch-wide plastic wrap, you can roll the marzipan between two sheets of it instead.)

REMOVE THE CAKE from the refrigerator. Fold the circle of marzipan in half and gently set it on top of the cake, with the fold on the center. Carefully unfold the marzipan so that it drapes over the cake, then fold the edges of the marzipan over and press it gently so it adheres to the sides of the cake, covering the cake completely. Try to avoid wrinkling the marzipan. Use a sharp knife to trim away the excess marzipan so that the edges are flush with the platter. Refrigerate until ready to serve.

TO SERVE, dust the top of the cake with confectioners' sugar. Use a sharp knife to score portions in the marzipan and then cut the cake.

Storing

The texture of the cake actually improves after 2 or 3 days in the refrigerator. To store leftover cake, cover the cut edges with plastic wrap.

Note

My friend Janie Hibler, author of *The Berry Bible,* served this torte after a concert in Portland, Oregon. She brushed the cake layers with framboise before filling and said it made the dessert "ethereal, almost as good as the waltzes by Strauss." As a variation, you could arrange a layer of fresh raspberries over the raspberry jam.

Tosca Cake

MAKES 8 SERVINGS

THIS IS A SWEDISH BUTTER CAKE WITH A CHEWY ALMOND GLAZE. *The cake is partially baked just until set, then the glaze is spread on top and the cake baked until the glaze caramelizes. Helena Hoas, who immigrated to the United States from Sweden, learned how to cook from her mother, and she says, "It seems that I am always baking something Swedish." No wonder. The Swedish baking tradition is long and varied, and its desserts are usually rich with butter, eggs, and almonds in one or more of their many forms.*

Serve this cake with afternoon tea or after dinner. It is delicious all by itself, but you could spoon a dollop of lightly sweetened whipped cream alongside each portion. The cake is best when very fresh.

CAKE

Fine dry bread crumbs for the pan

1 cup unbleached all-purpose flour (spooned into the cup and leveled)

1 teaspoon baking powder

2 large eggs

¾ cup granulated sugar

⅓ cup heavy cream

8 tablespoons (1 stick) salted butter (see Note), melted and cooled until tepid

TOPPING

8 tablespoons (1 stick) salted butter, at room temperature

½ cup granulated sugar

2 tablespoons unbleached all-purpose flour

2 tablespoons whole milk

1½ cups (4 ounces) blanched or unblanched sliced almonds

TO MAKE THE CAKE, adjust an oven rack to the center position and preheat the oven to 350°F. Coat a 10-inch springform pan with cooking spray and dust it with fine dry bread crumbs. Tap out the excess crumbs.

IN A SMALL BOWL, whisk together the flour and baking powder.

IN A MEDIUM BOWL, beat the eggs and sugar with a hand-held mixer on medium-high speed until thick and fluffy, about 5 minutes. On low speed, beat in the flour mixture. Add the cream and butter and beat only until incorporated. Scrape the batter into the prepared pan and rotate the pan gently on the countertop to level the batter.

BAKE THE CAKE for 20 to 25 minutes, just until the top of the cake is golden brown.

MEANWHILE, prepare the topping. Put the butter, sugar, flour, and milk in a medium heavy saucepan and stir with a wooden spoon until combined. Stir in the almonds to make a stiff mixture. Cook, stirring, over medium heat, for 3 to 5 minutes, until the mixture feels very warm to your fingertip and has the consistency of a very thick cream sauce. (The mixture will not boil.) Remove from the heat. The topping must be used while still warm.

REMOVE THE CAKE from the oven. Put dollops of the topping all over the top of the cake, and spread them together with the back of a teaspoon. Be patient, and don't rush this step—it will take 2 to 3 minutes. Return the cake to the oven and continue baking for another 15 to 20 minutes, until the topping bubbles and turns a deep golden brown. Watch closely during the last 5 minutes of baking to make sure the topping doesn't burn. Remove the pan from the oven and cool the cake completely in its pan on a wire rack.

IF THE CAKE has stuck to the sides of the pan, run the tip of a small sharp knife around the cake to release it. Remove the sides of the pan, and cut the cake into wedges to serve.

Note

If using unsalted butter, add ¼ teaspoon salt to the batter and ¼ teaspoon salt to the topping.

Boschendal Pudding

MAKES 8 TO 10 SERVINGS

THIS ULTRA-RICH, BUTTERY DESSERT WITH CARAMEL OVERTONES is a specialty of Bryony Schwan, who has been making it for almost fifteen years. It is really a cake with a pudding-like consistency, which is created by pouring a hot cream-and-butter sauce over the cake as soon as it comes out of the oven. Bryony got the recipe from the Boschendal Winery outside of Cape Town. Her ancestors came to South Africa in the late 1700s from Europe. She was born in Zimbabwe but spent many years in South Africa before immigrating to the United States. Bryony has had great success making the cake on camping trips. She bakes it in a Dutch oven over hot coals with more coals piled onto the lid. "More people have asked me for this recipe than any other," she says. Once you taste it, you'll see why.

This is excellent with fresh berries or sliced peaches. For a big crowd, you can double the recipe and bake it in a 13 × 9 × 2–inch pan. Serve small portions.

CAKE

1 cup unbleached all-purpose flour

1 teaspoon baking soda

Pinch of salt

1 cup granulated sugar

1 large egg

2 tablespoons apricot jam

1 cup whole milk

1 tablespoon unsalted butter, melted and still hot

1 teaspoon distilled white vinegar

SAUCE

12 tablespoons (1½ sticks) unsalted butter

1 cup heavy cream

1 cup granulated sugar

½ cup boiling water

TO MAKE THE CAKE, adjust an oven rack to the center position and preheat the oven to 350°F. Butter an 8 × 3–inch one-piece round cheesecake pan or cake pan or a 2-quart soufflé dish. (The pan must be deep to prevent the sauce from overflowing.)

IN A MEDIUM BOWL, whisk together the flour, baking soda, and salt.

IN ANOTHER MEDIUM BOWL, beat the sugar and egg with an electric mixer on medium-high speed for about 5 minutes, until the mixture is very thick and very pale. Add the jam and beat it in briefly on low speed. Still on low speed, add the dry ingredients in four additions alternately with the milk, beginning and ending with the dry ingredients, and beating only until the batter is smooth.

IN A SMALL CUP, combine the melted butter and vinegar, and stir into the batter. The consistency of the batter will resemble heavy cream. Scrape into the prepared pan.

BAKE FOR 45 TO 60 MINUTES, until the cake is golden brown and has a toasty aroma and a wooden skewer inserted into the center comes out clean.

MEANWHILE, when the pudding is almost done, prepare the sauce. Melt the butter in a medium heavy saucepan over medium-low heat. Add the cream, sugar, and boiling water and stir to dissolve the sugar. Keep the sauce hot over very low heat.

AS SOON AS the cake comes out of the oven, pour the hot sauce slowly over it. Let stand until the liquid is completely absorbed. This will only take a few minutes. Serve warm or at room temperature, using a sharp knife to cut portions. The dessert is best soon after it is made.

Swedish Apple Pudding

MAKES 8 TO 10 SERVINGS

APPLE FILLING

1 lemon

5 pounds late-summer apples
(see headnote)

¾ cup water

1½ to 3 cups granulated sugar

One 8-ounce can crushed pineapple
in juice, not drained

CAKE

⅔ cup bleached all-purpose flour

¾ teaspoon baking powder

1¼ teaspoons cornstarch

¼ teaspoon salt

3 large eggs, separated

¾ cup granulated sugar

3 tablespoons cold water

¾ teaspoon pure lemon extract

1½ to 2 cups heavy cream or half-
and-half, for serving

JODY ANDERSON, WHO MADE THIS FOR ME *on a late summer day when her Transparent apples were at their peak, learned the recipe from her Swedish mother-in-law, Anna Anderson, who had been taught the recipe by her mother, Beda Bood. Mrs. Bood immigrated to the United States in 1885 from Varmland, an area of Sweden with a relatively mild climate conducive to growing apples. Jody says only late-summer apples will do for this recipe, and since she has a Transparent apple tree right outside her kitchen door, that is what she always uses. Any first-of-the-season apples, available at farmers' markets and in some supermarkets, will work. Lodi, Summer Red, and Wealthy are all excellent. I have also had wonderful results with first-of-the-season McIntosh, which are available in late September into the first part of October.*

Jody's mother developed a technique for cooking the apples in batches in a microwave oven. "I just love the fact that there's no spattering," Jody says. But I have also made the applesauce in a large pot on top of the stove with minimal to no spattering.

TO MAKE THE FILLING, cut the lemon in half and squeeze the juice into a large bowl. Add 8 cups cold water and drop in the lemon halves. Quarter, core, and peel the apples, then cut into ½-inch chunks. Add them to the acidulated water as you go.

To cook the apples in a microwave oven, drain the apples and measure 4 cups. Put ¼ cup of the water into a large (6-quart) microwave-safe bowl and add the 4 cups apples. Cover tightly with plastic wrap and microwave on high power for 11 minutes. Remove the bowl and, beginning at the edge of the bowl farthest away from you, to avoid scalding yourself, carefully lift off and remove the plastic. Mash the apples a bit with a potato masher just to break them up a bit; the sauce should have some texture. Add ½ cup of sugar and ⅓ cup of the crushed pineapple with its juice, stir well, and taste. If the mixture is too tart, add more sugar to taste. Cover the bowl with plastic wrap again and microwave on high power for 3 minutes. Transfer the sauce to another large bowl. Repeat the procedure twice more, using 3 quarts apples in all. (You may have some leftover apples, which you can turn into applesauce to eat.)

To cook the apples on top of the stove, put all the apples into an 8-quart stockpot and add the ¾ cup water. Cover the pot, set over medium heat, and cook for about 10 minutes, until the liquid comes to a boil. Uncover the pot and stir well, then cover and continue cooking, stirring occasionally, for 20 to 30 minutes more, until the apples are tender. Add 1½ cups sugar and taste. If the mixture is too tart, add more sugar. Use a potato masher to break up the apples a bit, but don't overdo it; you want a sauce with some texture. Continue cooking the apples at a simmer, uncovered, over medium-low to medium heat, stirring occasionally, until they are very tender. Add the pineapple with its juices, and cook for 5 minutes more, stirring occasionally. Remove from the heat.

MEASURE 6 CUPS of the filling (if you have less, that's okay) into a large microwave-safe bowl to reheat in a microwave, or into a pot to reheat on the stove. Cover tightly with plastic wrap or pot lid and set aside.

ADJUST AN OVEN RACK to the lower third position and preheat the oven to 350°F. Have ready a 2½- to 3-quart baking dish about 3 inches deep.

TO MAKE THE CAKE, sift together the flour, baking powder, cornstarch, and salt.

IN A MEDIUM BOWL, beat the egg yolks with an electric mixer on medium-high speed until very thick and pale, about 5 minutes. While beating, gradually sprinkle in the sugar, then beat for another 2 to 3 minutes. The yolks will be very thick. Beat in the water and lemon extract. Add the dry ingredients and stir them in with a whisk just until the batter is smooth.

REHEAT THE FILLING in a microwave oven on high power for 3 to 5 minutes, or reheat it in a pot on the stovetop. The sauce must be boiling-hot when the cake batter is poured on top.

MEANWHILE, in a clean bowl, with clean beaters, beat the egg whites on medium speed just until they form peaks that hold their shape and curl softly at their tips when the beater is raised. Gently fold the whites into the cake batter only until no whites show.

CAREFULLY UNCOVER the hot applesauce, give it a stir, and scrape it into the baking dish. Spread it evenly, and immediately pour the cake batter on top. Put the pan in the oven and bake for 30 to 35 minutes, until the cake is golden brown and springs back when gently pressed.

TO SERVE HOT, let the cake cool for at least 5 minutes. To serve warm, let the cake stand for about 1 hour. Or cool the cake completely and serve at room temperature. Spoon portions of cake and applesauce into serving bowls and pass the cream at the table to be poured around the cake.

Storing

Leftover cake keeps well in the refrigerator, covered, for a day or two, and it is excellent cold.

Kransekake

MAKES ONE 18-RING TOWER

THIS IS A MAGNIFICENT NORWEGIAN TOWER *of homemade almond paste that is shaped into eighteen rings of varying sizes, baked briefly until crunchy on the outside and chewy on the inside, and stacked largest to smallest. Traditionally kransekaker were served only at weddings, but now they're made for all sorts of celebratory occasions, including birthdays. The tower can be decorated according to the whims of the baker, but poppers and paper flags are two traditional adornments. Often a bottle of wine is concealed in the tower, to be revealed (and drunk) when the topmost rings are removed.*

I learned how to make this in Brooklyn, New York, from three first-generation Norwegian American women—Linda Qualben, the late Alice Hansen, and Christine Fredricksen. They have been friends for decades, and they make kransekaker regularly to sell, then use the money to take trips together. Linda learned how to make kransekaker from her mom, who had learned the method from Norwegian immigrants after she arrived from Norway, when there was still a large and vital Norwegian community in Brooklyn.

The almond paste is made from ground unblanched almonds, confectioners' sugar, and egg whites. Linda says the almonds must be ground with a hand-cranked nut grinder. Because she and her friends make kransekaker so frequently, they looked for faster ways to grind the nuts and tried the food processor as well as a gadget they saw advertised on television, "The Ultimate Chopper." But both of these turned the nuts into tiny pebbles instead of powder; they needed to use twice as many egg whites to make the paste hold together, and even so, the paste fell apart when kneaded by hand and shaped into rings. But I was able to develop a food processor method that uses the same amount of egg whites as Linda's recipe calls for and gives virtually identical results.

After September 11, 2001, Linda created a very personal kransekake as a memorial to her brother-in-law, Lars Qualben, who perished in the Twin

ALMOND PASTE

1½ pounds (5 cups) unblanched whole almonds

6 cups confectioners' sugar

¾ teaspoon baking powder

4 large egg whites, each in a small cup

ICING

1 large egg white

1½ cups confectioners' sugar, or as needed

¼ teaspoon distilled white vinegar

Farina, to dust nonstick molds

Towers. Lars always wore bow ties, so Linda made paper bow-tie cutouts, attached them to toothpicks, and stuck them all over the kransekake tower.

You will need a set of kransekake molds, which includes 6 pans, preferably nonstick, to make the tower (see Sources, page 345).

See the companion DVD for a video demonstration of kransekake making.

To make the almond paste using a food processor, put one-quarter of the almonds (6 ounces, or 1¼ cups) into the work bowl of the processor fitted with the metal blade, and process for 20 seconds, or just until the nuts are very finely chopped, with a few larger pieces. Add one-quarter of the confectioners' sugar (1½ cups) and process for 1 minute, no longer—time this step. Scrape the work bowl and feel the mixture. It should be powdery, with the texture of fine sand. Process for 15 seconds, then scrape the work bowl and process for 15 seconds more. Add about one-quarter of the baking powder and process for 5 seconds. Scrape the work bowl, add 1 egg white, and process for about 30 seconds, until the paste forms clumps that whirl around the sides of the work bowl. (Sometimes the paste gathers into one large mass—this is to be expected, because just a minute variation in the size of an egg white can make a big difference in the paste's moistness.) Empty the paste onto your work surface—Formica, marble, or granite is ideal—and knead for 2 to 3 minutes, until it feels smooth and holds together. It will be very firm. It's okay if the paste feels "sugar sticky," but if it feels wet, knead in a small amount of additional confectioners' sugar. Put the paste into a large resealable plastic bag, and repeat with the remaining ingredients in 3 batches. (The almond paste can be refrigerated overnight; bring to room temperature before shaping.)

To make the almond paste using a manual nut grinder and a food processor, grind the almonds and put them into a large bowl. Add the confectioners' sugar and baking powder and toss everything together with your hands to combine the ingredients thoroughly. Transfer one-quarter of this mixture (12 ounces, or about 3 cups) to the work bowl

of the food processor fitted with the metal blade, add 1 egg white, and process for about 30 seconds, until the paste forms clumps that whirl around the sides of the work bowl. (Sometimes the paste gathers into one large mass—this is to be expected, because just a minute variation in the size of an egg white can make a big difference in the paste's moistness.) Empty the paste onto your work surface—Formica, marble, or granite is ideal—and knead for 2 to 3 minutes, until it feels smooth and holds together. It will be very firm. It's okay if the paste feels "sugar sticky," but if it feels wet, knead in a small amount of additional confectioners' sugar. Put the paste into a large resealable plastic bag, and repeat with the remaining ingredients in 3 batches. (The almond paste can be refrigerated overnight; bring to room temperature before shaping.)

ADJUST AN OVEN RACK to the center position and preheat the oven to 350°F. If using molds that are not nonstick, coat them lightly with cooking spray and dust them with farina. Tap out the excess farina. Nonstick molds need no special treatment.

TO SHAPE THE KRANSEKAKE, pinch off lumps of the almond paste and roll them under your palms on an unfloured pastry cloth or other work surface into long rolls about ½ inch thick—no thicker! When shaped, the rings of almond paste should not fill the depressions in the mold, because they'll puff and expand a bit during baking; if they're too thick, they will bake together and you will not be able to separate them easily. Divide the rolls into lengths to fit into the different molds and place them in the molds. Pinch the ends of the rings firmly to seal, and smooth them as best you can with your fingertips.

SET 3 MOLDS on the oven rack, spacing them about 2 inches apart. Bake for about 10 minutes, only until the rings turn a light golden brown and you can just begin to smell a fragrant almond aroma; the kransekake will feel dry when touched. It is important not to overbake the rings, because the kransekake should be moist and chewy on the inside. Sometimes cracks develop on tops of the rings; this is perfectly fine. Remove the molds from the oven with a wide metal spatula and cool the kransekake completely in their molds. Meanwhile, bake the remaining 3 molds.

WHEN THE KRANSEKAKE RINGS are cool, carefully lift off one ring at a time and arrange it on your counter. If you've used coated molds, use a pastry brush to brush off any farina.

TO MAKE THE ICING, in a medium bowl beat the egg white with a fork until frothy. Gradually add the confectioners' sugar, mixing it into the egg white with the fork until the icing is very thick, like mayonnaise; it should drop from the fork thickly, in globs. Beat in the vinegar. Scrape the icing into a small resealable plastic bag, squeeze out the air, and seal the bag. Cut a small opening in one bottom corner of the bag and squeeze a looping zigzag pattern of icing onto the largest ring. Set the ring on a doily-lined platter. Immediately ice the successive layers in the same way, carefully stacking one on the other. The icing will act as glue, holding the layers together. If you wish to hide a bottle of wine in the kransekake, add it after placing the second or third ring on the base of the tower. When completely assembled, decorate the kransekake as you like.

Storing

Once cooled, the baked kransekake rings can be frozen in heavy-duty resealable plastic bags for up to 1 month. Thaw the rings in their wrapping before assembling the kransekake.

Fyrstekake

MAKES ONE CAKE; 16 TO 20 SERVINGS

THE NORWEGIAN NAME FOR THIS CONFECTION *means "prince's cake." And what an apt description. A moist filling of toasted ground almonds and confectioners' sugar lies atop a bed of buttery short pastry, and lattice strips of the same dough arranged over the almond layer finish the cake. It is rich, rich, rich. You can cut fyrstekake into squares and serve it as a dessert or cut it into bars. I opt for the latter, because the fyrstekake keeps well for several days at room temperature and is wonderful to have on hand for breakfast or an afternoon nibble, or for unexpected company. For the best taste and texture, make this a day ahead.*

Leisha Ingdal, a first-generation Norwegian American, taught me this recipe, which she learned in Norway many years ago from her grandmother, Bestemor Johanne. When Leisha got the recipe, she followed the instructions to the letter, but the cake didn't turn out like her grandmother's. So she set up a time for the two of them to bake together and found that a couple of key details had been omitted: all ingredients should be at room temperature, and the fyrstekake must be made a day ahead.

FILLING

2 cups (10 ounces) unblanched whole almonds, toasted (see page 23) and cooled

2½ cups confectioners' sugar

6 tablespoons water

DOUGH

3 cups unbleached all-purpose flour

1½ teaspoons baking powder

¼ teaspoon salt

½ pound (2 sticks) unsalted butter, at room temperature

1 cup granulated sugar

1 large egg

1 large egg yolk

3 tablespoons heavy cream

1 large egg white, beaten with 1 teaspoon water, for egg wash

---

ADJUST AN OVEN RACK to the center position and preheat the oven to 350°F.

TO MAKE THE FILLING, finely grind the almonds using a manual nut grinder. Or grind them to a fine powder in a food processor fitted with the metal blade: Add about 2 tablespoons of the confectioners' sugar along with the nuts to prevent them from turning into a paste and process, stopping the machine every 20 seconds or so to check the progress of the nuts. Measure 2½ cups of finely ground almonds for

the recipe. (Reserve any remaining nuts to sprinkle over ice cream.)

STIR the ground almonds and the (remaining) confectioners' sugar together in a medium bowl. Add the water and stir to make a paste. Set aside at room temperature until you're ready for it; the paste will thicken somewhat while it waits.

TO MAKE THE DOUGH, whisk together the flour, baking powder, and salt in a medium bowl.

BEAT THE BUTTER and sugar in a large bowl with an electric mixer on medium speed for several minutes, until light, fluffy, and pale. Add the egg and egg yolk and beat them in well. With a rubber spatula, stir in about one-third of the dry ingredients, followed by 1½ tablespoons of the cream. Stir in half of the remaining dry ingredients, the remaining 1½ tablespoons cream, and then the last of the flour mixture. Just before the dry ingredients are completely incorporated, scrape the dough onto an unfloured work surface and knead the dough gently until it is smooth and supple.

CUT OFF about one-third of the dough and reserve for the lattice top. Roll the remaining dough between two sheets of plastic wrap to a rectangle about 14 × 10 inches. Transfer the dough, between the sheets of plastic, to a baking sheet and refrigerate 30 minutes to firm slightly.

WITH THE RACK in the center position, preheat the oven to 350°F. Line a 13 × 9 × 2–inch baking pan with foil (see Note).

REMOVE THE TOP SHEET of plastic wrap from the dough and invert the dough into the foil-lined pan. Carefully peel off the plastic and gently nudge the dough into the pan to line the bottom and come about ¾ inch up the sides, pressing and patting the dough as necessary to make an even layer. Trim away any excess dough with a small sharp knife. Spread the almond filling into the crust. If the filling is very stiff, pat it in place with dampened fingers.

ADD ANY DOUGH SCRAPS to the reserved portion of dough and roll the dough between sheets of plastic wrap into a rough rectangle about 12 × 9 inches and ¼ inch thick. With a sharp knife, cut the dough into twelve ¾-inch-wide strips and lay them diagonally over the filling in a crosshatch pattern. Press the ends of the strips to seal them to the bottom crust, and cut off excess pastry. With a pastry brush, paint the egg wash on the dough strips.

BAKE FOR 40 TO 45 MINUTES, until the lattice is golden brown and the cake smells fragrant. Cool the cake completely in its pan.

LET THE CAKE STAND at room temperature, loosely covered with a kitchen towel, overnight before serving. Then lift the cake out of the pan by the foil liner, peel away the foil, and cut into portions with a sharp knife.

Storing

Fyrstekake can be frozen for up to 1 month. Wrap in heavy-duty foil and enclose in a heavy-duty resealable plastic bag. Thaw the cake completely in its wrappings.

Note

The easiest way to line the pan with foil is as follows: Turn the pan upside down. Tear a sheet of foil about 15 inches long and place it shiny side down on the bottom of the pan. Carefully fold the foil down and over the sides of the pan. Lift the foil off the pan, turn the pan upright, and nestle the foil liner into the pan. It should fit perfectly.

Norwegian Hazelnut Torte

MAKES 12 SERVINGS

"NORWEGIAN DESSERTS ARE ALL ABOUT NUTS, CREAM, AND BERRIES," *says Leisha Ingdal, quoting a line from one of her many Norwegian cookbooks. This flourless torte is loaded with finely ground hazelnuts. The cream and berries are accompaniments.*

In Norway, fresh cloudberries, which are related to raspberries, are traditionally served with this and with other tortes. The berries, golden with a tinge of orange when ripe, thrive in parts of Norway, Sweden, and Finland. It is unusual to find them fresh in this country, but the berries are also made into jams or spreads, and whipped cream flavored with cloudberry jam or spread is another traditional accompaniment. Raspberries are an excellent substitute for cloudberries; look for the yellow berries, which are sweeter than the red ones. Leisha's husband, Geir, likes Nutella, the chocolate hazelnut spread, as a topping for this cake. You can also accompany the Nutella torte with spoonfuls of cloudberry cream or with plain whipped cream and berries.

The cloudberry spread sold under the Aquavit label, from the restaurant in New York City, is the best of its kind.

TORTE

- 2 cups (10 ounces) unblanched hazelnuts
- 1½ cups confectioners' sugar
- 1 teaspoon baking powder (optional; see Note)
- 3 large eggs, at room temperature

- 1½ cups heavy cream
- 2 tablespoons confectioners' sugar
- ⅓ cup cloudberry jam or spread (see Sources, page 344) or 3 cups yellow raspberries

TO MAKE THE TORTE, adjust an oven rack to the lower third position and preheat the oven to 325°F. Butter the sides and bottom of an 8-inch springform pan and line the bottom with a circle of parchment. Butter the parchment.

FINELY GRIND the hazelnuts with a manual nut grinder. Or grind them in a food processor fitted with the metal blade: add 2 tablespoons of the confectioners' sugar to the workbowl along with the nuts and process for about 1 minute, until the nuts are very finely ground. Transfer the nuts to a medium bowl and stir in the baking powder, if using.

BEAT THE EGGS in a large bowl with an electric mixer on medium speed until frothy, 1 to 2 minutes. Beating on low speed, slowly add the (remaining) confectioners' sugar.

Increase the speed to medium-high and beat for another 2 to 3 minutes, until the eggs have lightened in color and are fluffy but not really thick, more like very softly whipped cream. With a large rubber spatula, gradually fold in the hazelnuts.

SCRAPE THE BATTER into the prepared pan and spread it evenly. Bake for about 45 minutes, or until the torte is well browned and springs back when gently pressed. The top of the torte may have a pocked look. (At sea level the torte bakes level; where I live, at an elevation of 3,400 feet, the torte sinks—this is perfectly okay.) Cool the torte in its pan on a wire rack for 30 minutes.

RUN THE TIP of a sharp knife around the sides of the torte to release it, and remove the side of the pan. Cover the torte with a wire rack and invert. Lift off the pan bottom and remove the parchment. Cover the torte with another wire rack and invert again to cool completely right side up.

SET THE TORTE on a cake plate. In a large bowl, whip the heavy cream with the confectioners' sugar until the cream is thick. If using the cloudberry spread, fold it in. Using a narrow metal spatula, spread a thin layer of the cloudberry cream around the sides of the torte and pile the remaining cream on top. Spread the cream over the top of the torte, making a smooth, thick layer. Smooth the sides, if necessary. (The cream-covered cake can be refrigerated for 1 to 2 hours.) Or, if serving with fresh berries, place a dollop of plain whipped cream alongside each portion of torte and scatter the raspberries on top of and around the cream.

Note

The baking powder gives the torte a special lightness, but I prefer the slightly chewy texture that results from the absence of baking powder.

The Hanseatic League

It had always been a mystery to me as to why northern European countries such as Norway and Sweden used so many foods in their cooking and baking that were not native to them, especially spices from thousands of miles away. Leisha Ingdal told me it was because of the Hanseatic League. After a bit of research, this is what I learned. The Hanseatic League, or Hansa, formed in 1158/59, changed northern Europe's culinary history. Merchant associations within the cities of northern Germany and the Baltic grouped together for self-protection against pirates during trading expeditions.

Originally begun to facilitate the movement of salt via a canal between Hamburg and Luebeck, thus replacing the "Salt Road" from Kiel to Hamburg, quick transport of the prized mineral made it easy to preserve highly perishable fish and meats, allowing these commodities to be traded over great distances. Luebeck herring traveled by riverboat southward as far as the Alps.

Before the Hanseatic League came into existence, the First Crusade, 1096–1097, brought many Eastern foods, herbs, and spices to Europe. By 1200, spices had become a status symbol, although some, such as cinnamon, had been known and used since Anglo-Saxon times. But no regular way to obtain these items in Europe existed.

The Baltic Sea area was known to the Mediterranean regions for its fur and amber. The emergence of the Hanseatic League, which dominated commercial activity in northern Europe from the thirteenth to the fifteenth centuries, resulted in the export trade of grain, timber, furs, tar, honey, and flax between Russia, Sweden, and Poland to Flanders and England. Those countries, in turn, sent cloth and other manufactured goods eastward to the Slavs. Norway sent salted cod to the Mediterranean.

Over time, trade expanded to the East, and hazelnuts, walnuts, spices (especially cardamom, which became a Scandinavian favorite), saffron, vanilla, and many other foodstuffs made their way to northern Europe and were enthusiastically incorporated into the cooking of Scandinavia, as well as Germany and other countries. Cardamom's use is recorded in recipes from Scandinavian cookbooks as early as the 1300s.

Lamingtons

MAKES 24 INDIVIDUAL CAKES

LAMINGTONS ARE TO AUSTRALIANS *what chocolate cupcakes are to Americans. They are squares of yellow butter cake dipped into a chocolate sauce and coated with unsweetened coconut. Elizabeth Germaine's cooking students in Melbourne adored them, and she loved making them; she now makes Lamingtons regularly in the United States. "They're so simple, yet sophisticated in their own way, and so much fun to eat," she says. The success of a Lamington largely depends on the quality of the cake. It must be a firm-textured butter cake with a fine crumb, which is exactly what you'll get with the recipe below. For best results, it should be made a day ahead.*

The dessert is named for Baroness Lamington, the wife of an early-twentieth-century political official in Australia. Lamingtons are a national favorite, sold at almost every bake sale in Australia and practically every bakery. Kids love eating them out of hand, but you can serve them at a tea party with knife and fork. A scoop of vanilla ice cream goes very well with a Lamington.

Shredded unsweetened coconut is available in many supermarkets and in health food stores or by mail order (see Sources, page 341). If you prefer, make the variation using macadamia nuts instead of coconut.

CAKE

1¾ cups bleached all-purpose flour, plus more for the pan

2 teaspoons baking powder

12 tablespoons (1½ sticks) salted butter, at room temperature

1½ cups granulated sugar

1½ teaspoons pure vanilla extract

3 large eggs

1 cup whole milk

CHOCOLATE SAUCE

4 cups confectioners' sugar

½ cup unsweetened cocoa powder

4 tablespoons (½ stick) salted butter, melted

⅔ cup boiling water

3 to 4 cups shredded unsweetened coconut

TO MAKE THE CAKE, adjust an oven rack to the lower third position and preheat the oven to 350°F. Grease a 13 × 9 × 2–inch baking pan, dust it with flour, and knock out the excess flour.

WHISK THE FLOUR and baking powder together in a medium bowl.

BEAT THE BUTTER in a large bowl with an electric mixer on medium speed until smooth. Add ¼ cup of the sugar and the vanilla and beat for 30 seconds. While beating, gradually add the remaining 1¼ cups sugar. Scrape the bowl and beater, then beat for 5 minutes on medium-high speed. Add the eggs one at a time, beating well after each. On low speed, add the flour mixture in 3 additions alternately with the milk in 2 additions, beginning and ending with the dry ingredients and beating only until smooth. Scrape the batter into the prepared pan and smooth the top.

BAKE FOR 35 TO 40 MINUTES, until the cake is golden brown and pulls away slightly from the sides of the pan and a toothpick inserted into the center comes out clean. Cool the cake in its pan on a wire rack for 15 minutes, then cover the cake pan with a wire rack and invert the two. Remove the pan, cover the cake with another rack, and invert the cake again to cool completely right side up.

DRAPE THE CAKE loosely with a kitchen towel and leave at room temperature overnight.

WITH A SHARP SERRATED KNIFE, trim the crusts from the sides of the cake. Cut the cake into 24 squares.

TO MAKE THE CHOCOLATE SAUCE, in a medium metal bowl whisk together the confectioners' sugar, cocoa, butter, and boiling water until smooth. Set the bowl into a pan of very hot water to keep the sauce fluid. Spread the coconut in a shallow dish or pie plate. Drop a piece of cake into the chocolate sauce and use two long-tined forks to turn the cake quickly in the sauce to coat all surfaces. Lift the cake out of the sauce, letting excess sauce drip back into the bowl, and transfer the cake to the bowl of coconut. Use your fingers to sprinkle the cake with coconut, rolling it around to coat all surfaces well. Remove the cake from the coconut and set it on a wire cooling rack. Repeat with the remaining cake. Leave the cakes on the wire racks to dry for 1 to 2 hours before serving.

Storing

Lamingtons keep well for 3 to 4 days, stored in an airtight container at room temperature.

Variation

For utter extravagance, and for Lamingtons with a completely different quality, you can substitute about 1 pound salted or unsalted macadamia nuts (which originated in Australia), finely chopped, for the coconut.

Pavlova

MAKES 8 SERVINGS

MERINGUE

- ¾ cup egg whites (about 6 large), at room temperature

  Pinch of salt

- 1 cup baker's sugar (a type of fine granulated sugar) or superfine sugar

- ½ teaspoon pure vanilla extract

- ¾ teaspoon cider vinegar or distilled white vinegar

FILLING

- 2 cups quartered strawberries

- 3 kiwi fruit, peeled and cut into ¾-inch dice

- 1 large banana, peeled and sliced ¼ inch thick

- 2 fully ripe passion fruit

  Granulated sugar (optional)

WHIPPED CREAM

- 1 cup heavy cream

- 1 tablespoon granulated sugar

- ½ teaspoon pure vanilla extract

ACCORDING TO ALAN DAVIDSON IN The Oxford Companion to Food, *Australians claim that this dessert, a meringue case filled with whipped cream and cut fresh fruits, was created in 1935 by Herbert Sachse, an Australian chef, in honor of the Russian prima ballerina Anna Pavlova. To some, the built-up sides of the meringue suggest the appearance of a tutu. But the actual facts of pavlova's origin are far from clear. Be that as it may, it is a luscious dessert.*

I learned how to make this from Elizabeth Germaine, a cookbook author and cooking teacher from Melbourne. She always made it for special occasions in her home country, and she has continued to do so since she came to the United States more than thirty years ago.

The hallmark of a well-made pavlova is a meringue with a crisp exterior and a marshmallow-like interior. "Do not make this on a humid day," Elizabeth cautions, "it will just not be right." The traditional fruits for pavlova are strawberries, bananas, kiwi, and passion fruit. Passion fruit, the fruit of a tropical vine, is about the size of a large egg. The most common variety, grown in Australia and New Zealand, has a deep purple skin. The rind of the Hawaiian passion fruit is yellow. In either case, the fruit is ripe only when it is wrinkled and shriveled looking. The soft orange pulp contains dozens of tiny edible black seeds. Since passion fruit can be hard to find, or quite pricey, many bakers leave it out, but passion fruit gives pavlova its unique tang.

TO MAKE THE MERINGUE, adjust an oven rack to the lower third position and preheat the oven to 250°F. Line a baking sheet with a sheet of cooking parchment, set an 8-inch round cake pan on the parchment, and trace a circle around its base with a pencil. Turn the parchment over.

IN A SCRUPULOUSLY CLEAN LARGE BOWL, beat the egg whites and salt with an electric mixer on medium speed until they form soft peaks that droop at their tips when the beater is raised, about 2 minutes. Add ⅓ cup of the sugar and beat until the sugar is dissolved and the whites resemble thick marshmallow cream, about 2 minutes. Beat in the remaining ⅔ cup sugar in 6 installments (scant 2 tablespoons each), beating for 30 seconds after each. Increase the speed to medium-high and beat for about 3 minutes, until the meringue stands in stiff, straight peaks. On low speed, beat in the vanilla and vinegar.

USE SMALL DABS of the meringue to glue the corners of the parchment to the baking sheet. Scoop the remaining meringue into the traced circle and shape it into a 3- to 4-inch-tall casing a little over 8 inches in diameter. With a soupspoon, make a depression in the center about 1 inch deep. The sides of the case should be about 1 inch thick. A narrow metal icing spatula is useful but not essential for smoothing the sides.

BAKE THE MERINGUE for 1½ hours, or until it is a pale golden brown. Cracks may develop in the top—this is fine. Turn off the oven, prop the door slightly open, and leave the meringue in the oven until it is completely cool, 2 to 3 hours.

TO MAKE THE FILLING, put the strawberries, kiwi, and banana into a large bowl. Cut the passion fruit crosswise in half and spoon the seedy pulp over the fruit. Fold everything together gently. Taste and add a little sugar if you feel it needs it. (The fruit can stand at room temperature for 1 to 2 hours.)

TO MAKE THE WHIPPED CREAM, beat the cream with the confectioners' sugar and vanilla until very thick. Refrigerate if not using immediately.

JUST BEFORE SERVING, assemble the pavlova. Set the meringue on a dessert platter and spread the whipped cream into the depression. Spoon the fruit onto the cream, piling it in the center. Bring to the table and cut into portions. The cream and fruit will not stay put, but that is part of the dessert's charm. It's best to eat all of this at one sitting.

Variation

You can substitute raspberries for the strawberries or use a combination of the two. Elizabeth also likes to use diced mango in place of the kiwi. Well-drained canned apricots can also be used.

Chocolate Cinnamon Pavlova

MAKES 8 SERVINGS

THIS VARIATION OF PAVLOVA, *a favorite of Elizabeth Germaine's, who taught it for years in her cooking classes in Australia, will become an instant hit with you and your guests. It is a special party dessert that is not at all difficult to make. A cinnamon-flavored meringue case—tender on the inside, slightly crunchy on the outside—cradles a thin layer of melted chocolate spread with cinnamon-flavored whipped cream and a thick layer of chocolate custard cream filling, also flavored with cinnamon. Just before serving, the chocolate is masked with a thin layer of vanilla-flavored whipped cream. Although lavish and sumptuous, the dessert is light on the tongue.*

You must assemble this pavlova a few hours before serving to give the chocolate custard time to set. Make the meringue in the morning and the fillings in the early afternoon.

MERINGUE

- ¾ cup egg whites (about 6 large), at room temperature
- Pinch of salt
- 1 cup baker's sugar (a type of fine granulated sugar) or superfine sugar
- 1 teaspoon ground cinnamon
- 1 teaspoon distilled white vinegar

CHOCOLATE FILLING

- 8 ounces semisweet or bittersweet chocolate, coarsely chopped
- 4 large egg yolks
- ½ cup warm water

CINNAMON CREAM FILLING

- 1¼ cups heavy cream
- ½ teaspoon ground cinnamon

WHIPPED CREAM

- ¾ cup heavy cream
- 1 tablespoon granulated sugar
- ½ teaspoon pure vanilla extract

   Chocolate curls for garnish

TO MAKE THE MERINGUE, adjust an oven rack to the lower third position and preheat the oven to 250°F. Line a baking sheet with a sheet of cooking parchment, set an 8-inch round cake pan on the parchment, and trace a circle around its base with a pencil. Turn the parchment over.

IN A SCRUPULOUSLY CLEAN LARGE BOWL, beat the egg whites and salt with an electric mixer on medium speed until they form soft peaks that droop at their tips when the beater is raised, about 2 minutes. Add ⅓ cup of the sugar and beat until the sugar is dissolved and the whites resemble thick

marshmallow cream, about 2 minutes. Beat in the remaining ⅔ cup sugar in 6 installments (scant 2 tablespoons each), beating for 30 seconds after each. Increase the speed to medium-high and beat for about 3 minutes, until the meringue stands in stiff, straight peaks. On low speed, beat in the cinnamon and vinegar.

USE SMALL DABS of the meringue to glue the corners of the parchment to the baking sheet. Scoop the remaining meringue into the traced circle and shape it into a 3- to 4-inch-tall casing a little over 8 inches in diameter. With a soupspoon, make a depression in the center about 1 inch deep. The sides of the case should be about 1 inch thick. A narrow metal icing spatula is useful but not essential for smoothing the sides.

BAKE THE MERINGUE for 1½ hours, or until it is a pale golden brown. Cracks may develop in the top—this is fine. Turn off the oven, prop the door slightly open, and leave the meringue in the oven until it is completely cool, 2 to 3 hours.

WHILE THE MERINGUE cools, make the chocolate filling. Melt the chocolate in the top of a double boiler over medium heat, whisking occasionally, until perfectly smooth. Remove from the heat and let cool slightly.

USING THE BACK OF A TEASPOON or a small offset spatula, spread ¼ cup of the warm chocolate in a thin layer over the depression in the meringue. Add the egg yolks and water to the remaining chocolate, whisking them in vigorously until smooth. The mixture will be thin. Return the pan to the double boiler and cook for 8 to 10 minutes, stirring occasionally with a heatproof rubber spatula, until the chocolate thickens into a soft pudding-like consistency. Pour it into a bowl and refrigerate uncovered, stirring occasionally, until the chocolate is cool to the touch and has thickened further, 20 to 30 minutes or so. The chocolate should be smooth and thick, like very softly whipped cream, no thicker. If the chocolate custard gets too firm, set the pan over a bowl of hot water and stir gently and constantly with a rubber spatula until it has softened to the proper consistency.

JUST BEFORE ASSEMBLING the pavlova, make the cinnamon cream. Whip the cream with the cinnamon until thick enough to hold a firm shape. Spread half the cream into the chocolate-lined meringue depression. Fold the remaining cream into the chilled chocolate mixture, and spread it over the cinnamon cream. If the chocolate extends above the rim of the depression, smooth the sides with a small metal spatula. Refrigerate for 3 to 4 hours.

JUST BEFORE SERVING, make the whipped cream topping. Whip the cream with the sugar and vanilla until thick. Spread smoothly over the chocolate layer, masking it completely. Decorate with chocolate curls.

TO SERVE, dip a sharp knife into hot water and shake off the excess water before making each cut.

Storing

Leftover pavlova can be refrigerated overnight, but the meringue will soften and ooze a sugar syrup. Although the dessert will still taste sensational, it won't look terrific.

Buttermilk Cardamom Waffles

THESE CRUNCHY YET TENDER WAFFLES *are served for dessert in many parts of Norway. Kristine Soedal's in-laws make them all summer long at their cabin by the sea. The waffles are a sort of nightcap to the long summer days, where it is still light after 10 p.m. Cardamom is one of Scandinavia's favorite spices. Kristine likes to use a lot of it, but she tends to use less if people are unfamiliar with its taste. Use the amounts in this recipe as a guide, according to your likes.*

Waffles are so popular in Norway they are often made at school fundraisers. Kids sit at tables and bake them to order while people line up and wait for them. The waffles are typically served with fruit or jam and sour cream, just as these are.

FRUIT TOPPING

2 pints strawberries, hulled and sliced, or any fruit jam

Sugar to taste

WAFFLES

2 cups unbleached all-purpose flour

½ cup granulated sugar

1 teaspoon baking soda

½ teaspoon salt

1 to 2 teaspoons ground cardamom

4 large eggs

2 cups buttermilk or plain kefir

4 tablespoons (½ stick) unsalted butter, melted

About 2 cups sour cream

IF USING THE BERRIES, mix them an hour or so ahead, or even the day before, with sugar to taste in a bowl. Cover and refrigerate.

PREHEAT a waffle iron.

TO MAKE THE WAFFLES, in a medium bowl whisk together the flour, sugar, baking soda, salt, and cardamom.

IN A LARGE BOWL, whisk the eggs to combine the yolks and whites well, and whisk in the buttermilk or kefir. Add the dry ingredients and whisk gently only until the batter is smooth. Fold in the melted butter. Do not overmix, or the waffles will be tough.

BAKE THE WAFFLES following the manufacturer's instructions, buttering the grids or coating them with cooking spray before making each waffle. Spread the baked waffles with the berry topping or with jam, top with dollops of sour cream, and serve.

Blueberry Meringue Torte

MAKES 16 SERVINGS

THIS CLASSIC GERMAN DESSERT RECIPE *was taught to me by Anna Lobonc, who immigrated to the United States from Germany more than fifty years ago. She learned it from her mother, and she often makes it when she entertains. A thin layer of a rich butter-and-egg-yolk pastry serves as the base for a generous amount of meringue-shrouded blueberries. The meringue acts both as a sweetener and thickener for the blueberries. This torte is an excellent choice for an informal outdoor party in the summertime, when blueberries are at their best. In the winter, frozen blueberries may be substituted. Huckleberries work well too.*

Anna's mother also made the torte with strawberries from her garden. Strawberries make a fine torte provided they are small and sweet. You'll have the best results with locally grown berries.

Dusting the top of the slightly sticky meringue with confectioners' sugar both adds a nice flourish and makes cutting the torte easy. Serve with a spoonful of softly whipped cream, if you wish. The torte is best when very fresh.

DOUGH

- 1½ cups unbleached all-purpose flour
- 1 teaspoon baking powder
- 6 tablespoons (¾ stick) unsalted butter, at room temperature
- ⅓ cup granulated sugar
- Finely grated zest of 1 lemon
- 3 large egg yolks
- ⅓ cup whole milk

MERINGUE

- 3 large egg whites
- Pinch of salt
- ½ cup granulated sugar
- 4 cups (20 ounces) fresh or frozen unthawed blueberries

WHIPPED CREAM (OPTIONAL)

- 1½ cups heavy cream
- 2 tablespoons granulated sugar
- ½ teaspoon pure vanilla extract

- Confectioners' sugar for dusting

TO MAKE THE DOUGH, adjust an oven rack to the center position and preheat the oven to 400°F. Butter a 15½ × 10½ × 1–inch jelly-roll pan (do not use cooking spray; the dough must adhere to the pan).

IN A MEDIUM BOWL, whisk the flour and baking powder together to combine well.

IN ANOTHER MEDIUM BOWL, beat the butter briefly with an electric mixer until smooth. Add the sugar and beat for 2 to 3 minutes on medium speed, until fluffy. Add the lemon zest and egg yolks and beat in well. On low speed, alternately add the flour mixture in 3 additions with the milk in 2 additions, beginning and ending with the flour and beating only until smooth. The dough will be stiff and wet and mass up on the blades.

PLACE TABLESPOON-SIZED GOBS of the dough all over the bottom of the prepared pan. Lightly coating your fingers with cooking spray as necessary, pat the dough into a thin even layer over the pan bottom, making the edges a bit thicker, then press the dough about ⅓ inch up the sides of the pan. Prick the dough with a fork at 2-inch intervals.

TO MAKE THE MERINGUE, beat the egg whites with the salt in a large bowl with an electric mixer on medium speed until soft peaks form. Beating on medium-low speed, add the sugar 1 tablespoon at a time, beating for 10 seconds after each addition. Increase the speed to medium-high and beat until the meringue forms stiff peaks.

PUT THE BLUEBERRIES into a large bowl and scrape the meringue over them. Fold them together to completely enrobe the blueberries. Place large spoonfuls of the blueberries onto the crust and spread them into a smooth, even layer.

BAKE FOR ABOUT 25 MINUTES, until the edges of the crust are golden brown, the meringue is lightly browned, and drops of blueberry juice are peeking through. Rotate the pan front to back once during baking to ensure even browning, Cool the torte completely on a wire rack.

TO MAKE the optional whipped cream, whip the cream with the sugar and vanilla until it holds a soft shape.

DUST THE TOP of the torte with confectioners' sugar. Cut into portions with a sharp knife, and serve with the whipped cream, if you have it.

Steamed Chinese-Style Sponge Cake with Chocolate Ginger Sauce

china

MAKES 16 SERVINGS

STELLA FONG REMEMBERS OFTEN FINDING THIS CAKE *awaiting her for a snack when she came home from school. She calls it a sponge cake, but unlike a classic sponge cake, which has an open, porous texture, this is firm and dense with a pleasant doughy, chewy texture, very similar to that of a Chinese steamed bun. Stella says that because of this "foreignness," many people don't know quite what to make of the cake when they first bite into it. I like it a lot. It is very different from any other cake I've ever eaten, and it is particularly good with the chocolate ginger sauce. Stella's mother often served the cake with Hershey's chocolate sauce, and Stella sometimes dunked slices of the cake into hot Ovaltine. Over time, Stella's mother came up with a ganache-like sauce flavored with orange and ginger, and that is what Stella usually serves with the cake today. If you love chocolate, double the recipe.*

Stella's parents had immigrated to the United States from Kowloon, a city across the harbor from Hong Kong. People in Kowloon didn't have ovens, so any "baking" had to be done on top of the stove. Stella's mother used a bamboo steamer set into a wok with boiling water. This allowed her to make several layers of cake, each one in its own compartment of a stacked steamer. Bamboo steamers come in various sizes. Stella uses one measuring 10 inches in diameter, with just enough space inside each basket to hold an 8-inch round cake pan; see Sources, page 341.

When Stella makes the batter, she uses chopsticks, just as her mother taught her. They are extremely effective at beating the eggs, beating in the sugar, and stirring in the flour. You can use a whisk, if you prefer, but making the cake Stella's way will connect you more effectively with the cake's Chinese origins. The original recipe calls for evaporated milk, undoubtedly because refrigeration was not widespread decades ago in Kowloon. You can use regular milk, half-and-half, or heavy cream instead.

CAKE

- 7 large eggs
- 1 cup granulated sugar
- ¼ cup peanut, corn, or canola oil
- 3 tablespoons evaporated milk (or use whole milk, half-and-half, or heavy cream)
- 1 teaspoon pure almond extract
- 2 cups unbleached all-purpose flour
- 2 teaspoons baking powder

SAUCE

- 6 ounces semisweet chocolate, coarsely chopped
- ⅓ cup heavy cream
- 1 teaspoon finely grated orange zest
- 2 tablespoons fresh orange juice
- 1 tablespoon minced crystallized ginger

This cake is best when served slightly warm. If made a few hours ahead, it can be resteamed briefly to refresh its texture. If you prefer, you can divide the recipe in half and make just one layer; use 3 large eggs plus 1 egg yolk.

TO MAKE THE CAKE, if your wok has a round bottom, set it on its support over a burner on your stovetop; if your wok is flat, simply set it directly on the burner. Put the base of a bamboo steamer (see Note) into the wok and mark the bottom of the base with a fingertip, then remove the steamer and add water to the wok so that it almost reaches your fingertip (4 cups is about right). Set the base of the steamer back into the wok and turn the heat on high.

PUT THE EGGS (in their shells) in a medium bowl and add hot tap water to cover. Let stand for 5 minutes to warm the eggs a bit. Meanwhile, line the bottoms of two 8-inch round cake pans with waxed paper. Pour a few drops of oil into each pan and rub with a paper towel to coat the pans and paper with a thin layer of oil.

REMOVE THE EGGS from the water, pat them dry, and crack them into a large mixing bowl. Using chopsticks or a whisk, beat the eggs for about 1 minute, until the whites and yolks are thoroughly combined and look frothy. Add the sugar and beat for about 1 more minute until the sugar is dissolved, or almost dissolved. (Rub some of the egg between your fingers to see if you detect any grittiness—a little is fine.) Beat in the oil, then the milk and almond extract.

PUT THE FLOUR and baking powder into a strainer and sift it into the eggs, stirring to make a thick, creamy batter. Scrape the sides of the bowl. Divide the batter evenly between the prepared pans.

WHEN THE WATER in the wok is boiling, put one cake pan into the base of the steamer. Set the second steamer basket over it, place the second cake pan into the basket, and cover with the bamboo top. Cook for about 20 minutes, until a toothpick inserted into the center of the cakes comes out clean. The layers will dome up during steaming.

CAREFULLY REMOVE THE CAKES from the steamer baskets—using tongs is a good idea—and set them onto pot holders to cool for about 10 minutes. Run the tip of a sharp knife around the cakes to release them from the sides of the pans. Holding one pan with a pot holder, tip the cake out of its pan onto a pot holder in your other hand, then set the cake top side up onto a wire cooling rack. Repeat with the second layer. Cool the cakes for about 30 minutes.

MAKE THE CHOCOLATE SAUCE while the cake cools. Put the chocolate into a small metal bowl and set it over a saucepan of simmering water over medium heat. Stir occasionally until the chocolate is melted and smooth. Remove the bowl from the water and stir in the cream. Add the orange zest, juice, and ginger and stir to combine well. Scrape the sauce into a serving bowl.

SERVE THE CAKE slightly warm, cut into wedges, drizzled with the sauce.

Note

You can still make this cake if you don't have a steamer. Stella showed me how one can use an empty tuna fish can, opened at both ends. Set it in the bottom of the wok, add water until it almost reaches the top of the can, and set a wire cake rack on top of the can. Then set a pan of batter onto the rack, place a second wire rack on top of the cake pan, and set the second cake pan on top. Another method is to criss-cross chopsticks in the wok, tic-tac-toe fashion, to make a support for the first cake pan. Set the pan in place, place a wire rack over it, and place the second cake pan on the rack. Cover the wok with its top, and steam away!

Chinese-Style Almond Sponge Cake *china*

MAKES 8 SERVINGS

WITH ITS SUBTLE ALMOND FLAVORING, *this cake makes a delightful light dessert. The cake has an extremely fine crumb and looks dense when cut, but its texture is moist and tender. Food writer Stella Fong, who shared this recipe with me, learned how to make it from her mother, who immigrated to the United States from Kowloon in the 1950s. For the topping, use the finest in-season fruit you can find. Peaches or strawberries are ideal, but blueberries, raspberries, or even sliced bananas or kiwifruit will work well too.*

Make this cake the day you plan to serve it.

CAKE

- 1 cup cake flour
- ½ cup granulated sugar
- ½ teaspoon baking powder
- Pinch of salt
- 3 large eggs, separated
- 6 tablespoons water
- ¼ cup vegetable oil
- ½ teaspoon pure almond extract
- ⅛ teaspoon cream of tartar

TOPPING

- 2 cups sliced strawberries or sliced peeled peaches (see headnote for other suggestions)
- 1 cup heavy cream
- 2 tablespoons confectioners' sugar
- ¼ teaspoon pure almond extract

TO MAKE THE CAKE, adjust an oven rack to the center position and preheat the oven to 350°F. Line the bottom of a 9 × 2–inch round cake pan with cooking parchment or waxed paper.

SIFT TOGETHER the cake flour, ¼ cup of the sugar, the baking powder, and salt.

IN A MEDIUM BOWL, beat the egg yolks, water, oil, and almond extract with an electric mixer on medium speed for 30 seconds. Add the dry ingredients and beat on low speed until the batter is smooth. Increase the speed to medium and beat 1 to 2 minutes more, until the batter is creamy. Wash and dry the beaters.

IN ANOTHER MEDIUM BOWL, beat the egg whites on medium speed until foamy. Add the cream of tartar and beat until the whites form soft, droopy peaks. Gradually add the remaining ¼ cup sugar, then continue beating until the whites form stiff, creamy-looking peaks that curl slightly when the beaters are raised. Carefully fold the egg yolks into the whites in 3 additions just until evenly combined. Scrape the batter into the prepared pan.

BAKE FOR ABOUT 30 MINUTES, until the cake is golden brown and springs back when gently pressed. Set the cake pan on a wire rack to cool for 20 minutes. The cake will settle considerably and will pull away from the sides of the pan.

IF THE CAKE is sticking to the sides of the pan, release it with the tip of a sharp knife. Cover the pan with a wire rack and invert. Lift off the cake pan and peel off the paper liner. Cover the cake with another wire rack and invert again to cool completely right side up. When it is completely cool, wrap the cake in plastic wrap if not ready to serve.

TO SERVE, set the cake on a cake plate and spoon the fruit onto the cake. Whip the cream with the confectioners' sugar and almond extract until the cream holds a firm shape. Spoon and spread the cream over the fruit, leaving a border of fruit exposed. Cut the cake into portions with a sharp knife.

Turkish Semolina Sponge Cake

turkey

MAKES 15 SERVINGS

THIS SWEET CAKE, REVANI, IS EXTREMELY POPULAR IN TURKEY. *Arzu Yilmaz, a talented Turkish cooking teacher, taught me the recipe. Like many Turkish desserts, it is soaked with a sugar syrup, which adds sweetness as well as keeping properties. In fact, the cake is best the day after it is baked, and it keeps well for about 1 week in the refrigerator. Make the syrup ahead of time, because it must be cold when used.*

Fine semolina, made from durum wheat, adds a great depth of flavor to the cake. You can find it in health food stores and in well-stocked supermarkets. Serve the cake with whipped cream or, if you can get it, with kaymak, a Turkish cream.

SYRUP

3 cups granulated sugar

3 cups water

1 tablespoon fresh lemon juice (grate the zest for the cake first)

CAKE

½ cup all-purpose flour

1 teaspoon baking powder

1 cup fine semolina

10 large eggs, separated

½ cup granulated sugar

1 teaspoon pure vanilla extract

Finely grated zest of 1 lemon

½ cup whole milk

¼ teaspoon salt

8 tablespoons (1 stick) unsalted butter, melted and still hot

¾ cup unsalted pistachios, coarsely chopped

Lightly sweetened whipped cream for serving

TO MAKE THE SYRUP, combine the sugar, water, and lemon juice in a heavy medium saucepan over medium-high heat and stir almost constantly until the liquid comes to a full rolling boil. Reduce the heat so that the syrup boils slowly and cook, without stirring, for 10 minutes. Remove the pan from the heat and cool to room temperature. Cover and refrigerate until cold, at least several hours, or overnight.

TO MAKE THE CAKE, adjust an oven rack to the center position and preheat the oven to 350°F. Butter a 13 × 9 × 2–inch baking pan.

SIFT THE FLOUR together with the baking powder and semolina twice.

IN THE BOWL of a heavy-duty mixer, use the whip attachment to beat the egg yolks with the sugar on medium speed for 1 minute. Increase the speed to high and beat for another 3 to 4 minutes, until the yolks have increased in volume and are very pale and thick. On low speed, beat in the vanilla, lemon zest, and milk. Add the dry ingredients and beat just until incorporated. Scrape the batter into a large wide bowl. Wash and dry the mixer bowl and whip.

PUT THE EGG WHITES and salt into the clean mixer bowl and beat on medium-low speed until the whites are frothy. Increase the speed to medium-high and beat just until the whites form puffy, droopy peaks that curl slightly at their tips when the beater is raised. With a large rubber spatula, gradually fold the whites into the yolks—about 3 additions— only until no whites show. Scrape the batter into the prepared pan and smooth the top.

BAKE FOR 30 TO 40 MINUTES, until the top is an even golden brown, the cake springs back in the center when gently pressed, and a toothpick inserted in the center comes out clean.

SET THE CAKE PAN on a wire rack and immediately begin brushing the hot melted butter all over the top of the cake, using it all. This will take a couple of minutes. Cut the cake, in its pan, into 15 portions with a small sharp serrated knife. Slowly pour the cold syrup all over the cake, using it all. Sprinkle the top of the cake with the pistachios. Let the cake stand at room temperature until it has cooled completely.

COVER THE CAKE with plastic wrap and refrigerate overnight before serving.

Storing

The cake gets even better over a few days in the refrigerator. Let come to room temperature before serving, with the whipped cream.

The Original Shoofly Pie   *pennsylvania dutch*

MAKES 8 SERVINGS

SUCH A STRANGE NAME FOR A PIE. *Did it have anything to do with bakers who had to shoo flies away from it? In fact, the name comes from the Shoofly Molasses Company, which made the molasses originally used in the pie. Food historian Don Yoder says, "The key ingredient in this pie is molasses, and prior to refrigeration, it was never available during hot weather due to its perishability. Shoo-fly pie was invented for the U.S. Centennial in 1876, and Pennsylvania Dutch cookbooks from the 1870s and 1880s call it Centennial Cake."*

Food historian Will Weaver generously shared this recipe for shoofly pie, which he got from his grandmother. She, in turn, got it from an old lady in Ephrata, Pennsylvania, who got the recipe at the 1876 Centennial. Will says the pie "is a molasses crumb cake baked in a pie shell. It is supposed to be eaten like cake, so you can pick it up with your fingers and dip it into coffee." The pie's delightful texture and flavor will remind you of tender gingerbread. It is eaten as a breakfast cake, or it can be served as a dessert with fresh fruit. Will says it is particularly good with pureed pawpaws and with strawberry or raspberry wine or with pear brandy.

DOUGH

- 1¼ cups unbleached all-purpose flour
- 5 tablespoons cold salted butter, cut into tablespoon-sized pieces
- 2 tablespoons extra-virgin olive oil
- 1 large egg yolk
- 3 to 5 tablespoons dry white wine

TOPPING

- 1 cup plus 2 tablespoons unbleached all-purpose flour
- ½ cup granulated sugar
- 1 teaspoon ground cinnamon
- ½ teaspoon freshly grated nutmeg
- 8 tablespoons (1 stick) cold salted butter, cut into tablespoon-sized pieces

FILLING

- ½ teaspoon baking soda
- ¾ cup warm coffee
- ¾ cup unsulphured molasses

TO MAKE THE DOUGH, put the flour in a medium bowl and cut in the butter with a pastry blender or two knives until the mixture is the consistency of medium-fine crumbs. In a small bowl, combine the olive oil, egg yolk, and 3 tablespoons wine with a fork. Add the liquid to the flour and stir with the fork until the dough just gathers into a ball. If it is too dry, add more wine a teaspoon at a time. Shape the dough into a disk about 1 inch thick, wrap in plastic wrap, and refrigerate for at least 1 hour. (The dough can be made up to 1 day ahead.)

UNWRAP THE DOUGH and put it between two squares of waxed paper. Tap gently on the dough with the rolling pin to soften it slightly and make it easy to roll. Roll the dough to a 12- to 13-inch circle, rolling from the center outward and flipping the crust over from time to time; readjust the waxed paper as necessary as creases develop. Remove the top sheet of waxed paper and invert the dough, centering it as best you can, into a 9-inch pie plate. Carefully peel off the paper. Nudge the edges of the dough into the pan, without stretching, so that the crust fits snugly into the bottom and up the sides of the pie plate. Trim the excess pastry with scissors, leaving a ½-inch overhang. Fold the edge of pastry back on itself to make a double thickness all around and turn it upright to make a high standing rim on the edge of the pie plate. Flute it by pinching it at ½-inch intervals into an attractive zigzag pattern. Refrigerate for 1 hour.

ADJUST AN OVEN RACK to the lower third position and preheat the oven to 425°F.

TO MAKE THE TOPPING, put the flour, sugar, cinnamon, nutmeg, and butter into the work bowl of a food processor fitted with the metal blade. Process to the texture of fine crumbs, 15 to 30 seconds.

TO MAKE THE FILLING, in a small bowl dissolve the baking soda in the warm coffee. Stir in the molasses and keep stirring for 1 to 2 minutes, until the molasses is completely mixed in and the top layer of the liquid is lighter in color and very bubbly. Patience—this will happen!

POUR THE FILLING into the unbaked pie shell. Gradually sprinkle on the crumb mixture. Begin at the edges and work your way to the center, making the crumb layer a bit thicker around the edges to prevent the filling from bubbling over.

PUT THE PIE into the oven—be careful, the liquid will slosh around in the pie shell—and bake for 15 minutes. Reduce the temperature to 350°F and bake for another 35 to 40 minutes, until the crumb topping is golden brown and the center of the pie is firm and cake-like. When pressed gently, the top of the pie should spring back and a toothpick inserted into the center will come out clean. Cool the pie on a wire rack and serve warm or at room temperature.

Storing

Leftover pie keeps well for 2 to 3 days, covered, at room temperature.

Betty's Shoofly Pie

MAKES 8 SERVINGS

THIS RECIPE COMES FROM COOKBOOK AUTHOR, *cooking teacher, and tenth-generation Pennsylvania Dutch descendant Betty Groff. She is an energetic, big-hearted, and caring lady, eager to share her knowledge and recipes. Her ancestors came to the area before 1730, and every generation has lived in Pennsylvania since then. Betty's Shoofly Pie differs from the classic (see page 320) in that she uses a golden table syrup, a mixture of corn syrup and refiner's syrup, instead of real molasses. The syrup has just a faint molasses flavor, and the pie has a caramel-like taste.*

It is this version that I found in all the bakeshops I visited in Pennsylvania Dutch country. Just why this is so puzzles me. Perhaps, over the years, tastes have changed, and the assertiveness of molasses was deemed too strong. Whatever the reason, this is a fine pie. It will be welcomed at any breakfast or dessert table. Serve it with whipped cream or vanilla ice cream, or, for breakfast, serve it plain.

½ recipe Basic Pie Dough (page 335), chilled

TOPPING

1 cup unbleached all-purpose flour

½ cup firmly packed light or dark brown sugar

5 tablespoons cold unsalted butter, cut into tablespoon-sized pieces

Pinch of salt

FILLING

¾ teaspoon baking soda

¾ cup warm water

¼ teaspoon salt

¾ cup Golden Barrel Table Syrup (see Sources, page 342) or Lyle's Golden Syrup

LIGHTLY FLOUR your work surface. Set the chilled dough on it and tap gently on the dough with the rolling pin to soften it slightly and make it easy to roll. Roll the dough to a 12-inch circle, rolling from the center outward and flipping it over from time to time. Fold the dough in half and center it in a 9-inch pie plate. Carefully unfold the dough. Nudge the edges of the dough into the pan, without stretching, so that the crust fits snugly over the bottom and up the sides

of the pie plate. Trim the excess pastry with scissors, leaving a ½-inch overhang. Fold the edge of pastry back on itself to make a double thickness all around and turn it upright to make a high standing rim on the edge of the pie plate. Flute it by pinching it at ½-inch intervals into an attractive zigzag pattern. Refrigerate for 1 hour.

ADJUST AN OVEN RACK to the lower third position and preheat the oven to 425°F.

TO MAKE THE CRUMB TOPPING, put the flour, butter, brown sugar, and salt into the work bowl of a food processor fitted with the metal blade. Pulse rapidly 6 to 8 times, then process for about 15 seconds, until the butter is cut into small pieces. Transfer the topping to a sheet of waxed paper.

TO MAKE THE FILLING, put the baking soda into a small bowl and add the warm water. Stir to dissolve the soda. Add the salt and golden syrup and stir until thoroughly combined.

POUR THE FILLING into the pie shell. Grab handfuls of the crumb topping and sprinkle evenly over the filling, beginning at the edges, then filling in the center.

BAKE FOR 15 MINUTES. Reduce the temperature to 350°F and bake for another 30 to 40 minutes, until the topping is nicely browned and set. It may have a few cracks. A toothpick inserted into the center of the pie will come out clean. Cool the pie on a wire rack.

Storing

Leftover pie keeps well for 2 to 3 days, covered, at room temperature.

Amish Vanilla Pie

MAKES 8 SERVINGS

HERE IS ANOTHER DESCENDANT OF SHOOFLY PIE *(see pages 320 and 322). Betty Groff made this for me, and she got the recipe from her friend Ruth Clark. Ruth is not Amish, but she lived among Amish people. (Historian Will Weaver told me that the word "Amish" was not attached to things until after the 1940s, when it became used commercially in Pennsylvania as a label to denote old-fashioned, wholesome country ways. It has to do with tourism, he says.) The crumb topping for this pie, made with white sugar and butter, contains a bit of baking powder to give it a slight airiness. The filling, which has a mild caramel flavor, is made with golden table syrup, as in the shoofly pie on page 322. The egg and a little flour give it added body, and it is cooked on top of the stove before going into the pie shell to be baked.*

Serve the pie with whipped cream or vanilla ice cream if you like.

½ recipe Basic Pie Dough (page 335), chilled

TOPPING

1 cup all-purpose flour

½ cup granulated sugar

6 tablespoons (¾ stick) cold unsalted butter, cut into tablespoon-sized pieces

¼ teaspoon baking soda

¼ teaspoon cream of tartar

Pinch of salt

FILLING

½ cup Golden Barrel Table Syrup (see Sources, page 342) or Lyle's Golden Syrup

¼ cup granulated sugar

1 large egg

1 tablespoon unbleached all-purpose flour

⅛ teaspoon salt

1 cup hot water

2 teaspoons pure vanilla extract

LIGHTLY FLOUR your work surface. Set the chilled dough on it and tap gently on the dough with the rolling pin to soften it slightly and make it easy to roll. Roll the dough to a 12-inch circle, rolling from the center outward and flipping it over from time to time. Fold the dough in half and center it in a 9-inch pie plate. Carefully unfold the dough. Nudge the edges of the dough into the pan, without stretching, so that the crust fits snugly over the bottom and up the sides of the pie plate. Trim the excess pastry with scissors, leaving a ½-inch overhang. Fold the edge of pastry back on itself to make a double thickness all around and turn it upright to make a high standing rim on the edge of the pie plate. Flute it by pinching it at ½-inch intervals into an attractive zigzag pattern. Refrigerate for 1 hour.

ADJUST AN OVEN RACK to the lower third position and preheat the oven to 425°F.

TO MAKE THE CRUMB TOPPING, put the flour, sugar, butter, baking soda, cream of tartar, and salt into the work bowl of a food processor fitted with the metal blade. Pulse rapidly 6 to 8 times, then process for about 15 seconds, until the butter is cut into small pieces. Transfer the topping to a sheet of waxed paper.

TO MAKE THE FILLING, put the syrup, sugar, egg, flour, and salt in a small heavy saucepan and whisk together well. Gradually whisk in the hot water. Set the pan over medium heat and cook, stirring constantly with a heatproof rubber spatula, going all around the sides of the pan and all over the bottom, until the filling is just barely thickened, about 8 minutes. Wisps of steam will rise from the surface of the liquid to let you know it's almost ready; do not allow the filling to boil. An instant-read thermometer should register 180°F. Remove the pan from the heat and stir in the vanilla. Cool, stirring occasionally, until warm.

POUR THE FILLING into the pie shell. Grab handfuls of the crumb topping and sprinkle evenly over the filling, beginning at the edges, then filling in the center.

BAKE FOR 15 MINUTES. Reduce the temperature to 350°F and bake for another 30 to 40 minutes, until the topping is nicely browned and set; a toothpick inserted into the center of the pie should come out clean. Cool the pie on a wire rack.

Storing

Leftover pie keeps well for 2 to 3 days, covered, at room temperature.

Pennsylvania Dutch Crumb Cake

MAKES 12 TO 16 SERVINGS

THIS IS A CLASSIC CRUMB CAKE, or streuselkuchen, with a lot of streusel. A buttery mildly spiced crumb topping lies atop a tender, moist cake, also flavored with spices. The cake comes together very quickly because the batter is based on the same streusel base. The cake is often served at breakfast or for a brunch. This and a yeast version (see page 205) share the same name for this quintessential coffee cake. Betty Groff, a tenth generation Pennsylvania Dutch descendant, restaurateur, and a prolific cookbook author, remembers this cake from her childhood. "I don't know how long this cake has been in my family," she says, "but I learned how to make it from my mother and grandmother. I always have it on hand for company, expected or not!"

CRUMB BASE

- 4 cups unbleached all-purpose flour
- ½ teaspoon salt
- ½ pound (2 sticks) cold unsalted butter, cut into tablespoon-sized pieces
- 1 cup granulated sugar
- 1 cup firmly packed light or dark brown sugar
- 2 teaspoons ground cinnamon

TOPPING AND CAKE

- 6 tablespoons (¾ stick) unsalted butter, melted
- ½ teaspoon ground ginger
- ½ teaspoon freshly grated nutmeg
- ¼ teaspoon ground cloves
- 1 teaspoon baking soda
- 1 cup buttermilk
- 1 large egg
- 2 teaspoons pure vanilla extract

Confectioners' sugar for dusting (optional)

ADJUST AN OVEN RACK to the center position and preheat the oven to 350°F. Butter a 13 × 9 × 2–inch baking pan or coat it with cooking spray.

To make the crumb base by hand, in a large bowl stir together the flour and salt. Add the butter and rapidly work it into the flour with your fingertips to the consistency of medium-fine meal. Or cut the butter into the flour with a pastry blender or two knives until the crumbs are the consistency of medium-fine meal. Add the granulated sugar, brown sugar, and cinnamon and stir well.

To make the crumb base with a stand mixer, put the flour, salt, and butter into the mixer bowl and attach the flat beater. Mix on low speed until the dry ingredients are the consistency of medium-fine meal, about 3 minutes. Add the granulated sugar, brown sugar, and cinnamon and mix on low speed until thoroughly combined, about 1 minute more.

TO MAKE THE TOPPING, transfer 4 cups of the crumb base to a medium bowl. Add the melted butter and stir it in with a rubber spatula only until incorporated. Then reach into the bowl with your hands and fluff and crumble the mixture with your fingertips to make coarse, buttery crumbs.

To make the batter by hand, add the ginger, nutmeg, cloves, and baking soda to the remaining crumb base and stir in well with a wooden spoon. Add the buttermilk, egg, and vanilla and beat with the spoon to make a smooth, thick batter.

To make the batter using a stand mixer, add the ginger, nutmeg, cloves, and baking soda to the remaining crumb base in the mixer bowl. Mix on low speed for 30 seconds. Add the buttermilk, egg, and vanilla and beat on low speed only until the batter is smooth and thick, about 1 minute.

SPREAD THE BATTER evenly in the prepared pan. Sprinkle the streusel topping evenly over the batter. It will make a thick layer.

BAKE FOR 40 TO 45 MINUTES, until the topping is lightly browned and a toothpick inserted into the center of the cake comes out clean. Cool the cake in its pan on a wire rack.

SERVE THE CAKE warm or at room temperature. If you wish, dust the top of the cake with confectioners' sugar before cutting it into portions.

Storing

This cake keeps well at room temperature for 3 to 4 days, loosely covered with a sheet of waxed paper. It can also be frozen. After it has cooled completely, wrap it, still in its pan, in two or three layers of aluminum foil and freeze for up to 1 month. To serve, thaw the cake in its wrapping, then unwrap and refresh in a preheated 300°F oven for 15 to 20 minutes. You can also remove the cooled cake from its pan, wrap it in foil and freeze. Thaw and refresh as above. Serve warm or at room temperature.

9 | Basic Recipes

i'VE INCLUDED BASIC RECIPES HERE that have many uses and are called for in other chapters. Because the homemade versions of almond paste, marzipan, and ricotta, as well as the home-rendered lard, are superior to most of their commercial counterparts, I encourage you to try these recipes. Making them does not require much time, and you'll be glad to have staples of your own creation at hand.

329

Almond Paste

I BASED THE FORMULA IN THIS RECIPE on the one used by American Almond Products Company. The proportions here result in an almond paste that is about 66 percent almonds. It is best to make the almond paste at least a day ahead and refrigerate it so that the texture and almond flavor can develop. If you want to make more almond paste, simply repeat the recipe, but you will not have success if you simply attempt to double the recipe.

2½ cups (12½ ounces) blanched whole almonds

⅔ cup granulated sugar

¼ cup water

IF YOU HAVE A MANUAL NUT GRINDER, use it to grind the nuts, then transfer to the work bowl of a food processor fitted with the metal blade. If you don't have a nut grinder, put the almonds into the work bowl of a food processor fitted with the metal blade and process for about 20 to 30 seconds, only until the nuts are very finely chopped, almost ground. Rub the nuts between your fingertips—they should feel like tiny pebbles. Pulse the machine 5 or 6 times, about 1 second each, then scrape the work bowl and continue pulsing, about 1 second each, until you see the nuts at the upper edges take on a slightly pasty look; do not process until the nuts actually gather into a paste. Stop the machine and rub the nuts between your fingers again. They should feel powdery and only look as if they're beginning to become pasty. If you check the bottom of the work bowl, you may see that some of the nuts have formed a paste around the edges. Scrape the work bowl again, and leave the nuts in the bowl.

PUT THE SUGAR AND WATER into a small heavy saucepan, no larger than 1 quart; don't stir or agitate the mixture. Set the pan over medium heat and bring to a boil, without stirring. Swirl the pan by its handle to make sure the sugar is dissolved, cover the pan, and cook for exactly 3 minutes. Uncover the pan, swirl it by its handle two or three times, and take the temperature of the syrup with a digital probe thermometer. You want the syrup to be between 236° and 240°F—chances are it won't be this hot yet, but it'll be close. Cook the syrup for another minute or so, swirling the pan gently from time to time and monitoring the temperature of the syrup frequently. As soon as the syrup is ready, remove the pan from the heat.

START THE FOOD PROCESSOR and add the hot syrup through the feed tube in a steady stream, taking about 10 seconds. Don't scrape the bottom of the pan, or the syrup may crystallize. Continue processing for 1 to 2 minutes. The almonds will form a ball of paste whirling around the work bowl. Transfer the ball of almond paste to a work surface. Scrape the work bowl clean and add the bits of almond paste to the ball. Knead them together for 2 to 3 minutes, until smooth and malleable. You'll notice as you knead that the almonds will release an oily slick—this is fine.

SHAPE THE PASTE into a disk about 1 inch thick and wrap it in plastic wrap. Refrigerate for at least 1 day to allow the paste to ripen before using. Wrapped airtight, the almond paste keeps well in the refrigerator for at least 2 to 3 weeks.

Note

Priscilla Martel, culinary director at American Almond Products Company, says, "While there is no official standard of identity for almond paste and marzipan, there are some general guidelines. Almond paste is an ingredient and marzipan is a finished confection. Almond paste is made from 1 part or more almonds to 1 part sugar. Marzipan can be made with 1 part or more almonds to 3 parts sugar."

Marzipan

MARZIPAN IS ALMOND PASTE *containing more sugar. It typically contains 1 part or more almonds to 3 parts sugar, but there can be huge variations. Marzipan's most common use is to tint it with food coloring and to shape it into confections representing various fruits or animals. Another major use for marzipan is to roll it into sheets and drape it over cakes, giving the cakes a smooth professional look and adding a delicious thin layer of almond flavor. I tint marzipan green and use it in Princess Torte on page 289.*

- 1 cup (5 ounces) blanched whole almonds
- 1 cup granulated sugar
- 2 tablespoons corn syrup
- ¼ cup water
- ½ teaspoon pure almond extract

IF YOU HAVE A MANUAL NUT GRINDER, use it to grind the nuts, then transfer to the work bowl of a food processor fitted with a metal blade. If you don't have a nut grinder, put the almonds into the work bowl of a food processor fitted with the metal blade and process for 20 to 30 seconds, only until the nuts are very finely chopped, almost ground. Rub the nuts between your fingertips—they should feel like tiny pebbles. Pulse the machine 5 or 6 times, about 1 second each, then scrape the work bowl, and continue pulsing, about 1 second each, until you see the nuts at the upper edge take on a slightly pasty look; do not process until the nuts actually gather into a paste. Stop the machine and rub the nuts between your fingers again. They should feel powdery and only look as if they're beginning to become pasty. If you check the bottom of the work bowl you may see that some of the nuts have formed a paste around the edges. Scrape the work bowl again, and leave the nuts in the bowl.

PUT THE SUGAR, corn syrup, and water into a small heavy saucepan, no larger than 1 quart; don't stir or agitate the mixture. Set the pan over medium heat and bring to a boil, without stirring. Swirl the pan by its handle to make sure the sugar is dissolved, cover the pan, and cook for exactly 3 minutes. Uncover the pan, swirl the pan by its handle two or three times, and take the temperature of the syrup with a digital probe thermometer. You want the syrup to be 240°F—chances are it won't be this hot yet, but it will be close. Cook the syrup for another minute or two, swirling the pan gently from time to time and monitoring the temperature of the syrup frequently. As soon as the syrup reaches 240°F, remove the pan from the heat.

START THE FOOD PROCESSOR and add the hot syrup through the feed tube in a steady stream, taking about 10 seconds. Don't scrape the bottom of the pan. Stop the machine, add the almond extract, and process for 1 to 2 minutes. The almonds will form a ball of paste whirling around the work bowl. Transfer the ball of marzipan to a work surface. Scrape the work bowl clean and add the bits of marzipan to the ball. Knead them together for 2 to 3 minutes, until smooth and malleable. You'll notice as you knead that the almonds will release an oily slick—this is fine.

SHAPE THE MARZIPAN into a disk about 1 inch thick and wrap it in plastic wrap. Refrigerate for at least 1 day to allow the marzipan to ripen before using. The marzipan keeps well in the refrigerator for up to 1 month.

Rendering Lard

TO RENDER LARD *(or for that matter any animal fat), you chop or grind chunks of fatty tissue, heat them slowly with a little water to cause the fat to be released, and then continue cooking gently to evaporate the water, leaving pure fat. Strain out the browned bits and cool the golden liquid to room temperature, then refrigerate it; chilled, it solidifies and turns white. The rendered lard will keep for up to 3 weeks in the refrigerator or up to 6 months in the freezer. The "cracklings," the crunchy, crusty fatty bits, are delicious spread on toast or crackers for an appetizer.*

Lard is an ancient fat, and in many parts of the world it was used extensively in baking and in cooking. I urge you to render your own lard. It makes tender, flaky piecrusts and pastries, and I suggest its use in some of the recipes in this book. Many butchers will save pork fatback and kidney fat for you if you tell them what you want it for. If you can only get small amounts at a time, wrap tightly and freeze until you have 5 to 10 pounds, then render it. You'll be very glad you did.

The fats in home-rendered lard are about 39 percent saturated, 11 percent polyunsaturated, and 45 percent monounsaturated. Monounsaturated fats, the type present in olive oil, have been shown to be beneficial to our cardiovascular systems. The fats in butter are about 51 percent saturated, 3 percent polyunsaturated, and 21 percent monounsaturated. So, on the basis of fat composition alone, home-rendered lard turns out to be more healthful for us than butter. Why do I specify home-rendered lard? Because store-bought lard, the kind that comes in 1-pound boxes, is hydrogenated to help keep it shelf-stable, and so it contains undesirable trans fats.

To render lard, you will need a large heavy casserole, a digital probe thermometer or candy/deep-fat thermometer, and a fine-meshed strainer.

FOR 2 TO 4 QUARTS LARD

5 to 10 pounds pork fatback or kidney fat (leaf lard)

1 cup water

PICK OVER THE FAT, cutting away any rind and membranes.

To chop the fat by hand, use a sharp chef's knife to cut the fat into ½-inch pieces.

To use a meat grinder, fit the grinder with the large-holed disk. Cut the fat into strips that will fit into the grinder, and grind.

To use a food processor, cut the fat into 1-inch chunks. Arrange them in a single layer on a baking sheet lined with plastic wrap and freeze for 20 to 30 minutes, until the fat is firm. Insert the metal blade into the work bowl of the processor and process the fat in 2-cup batches, pulsing repeatedly until the fat is chopped into small pieces; stop to scrape the work bowl as necessary.

TRANSFER THE FAT to a large heavy-bottomed casserole (a 4- to 6-quart enameled cast-iron pot is ideal). Add the water and give the fat a stir. Set the pot over low heat and very slowly bring the water and fat to a simmer. As the fat renders, it will sputter and hiss, and the fatty pieces will turn golden brown. Check the temperature periodically. Ideally, it should be between 250° and 275°F. It should never get above 325°F, or the fat will lose its clarity and pale yellow color. The rendering time will depend on how much fat you're rendering and your heat, but you may need to allow anywhere from 1½ to 3 hours. It's ready when the fat is golden and no longer sputtering.

SET A FINE-MESH STRAINER over a large bowl and carefully pour the fat into it. Scrape the cracklings into the strainer and press gently on them to extract as much fat as possible. Let cool. You can chop the cracklings and reserve them to spread on crackers or toast.

TRANSFER THE COOLED FAT to storage containers. Sealed airtight, it can be refrigerated for up to 3 weeks or frozen for up to 6 months.

Homemade Ricotta

HOMEMADE RICOTTA IS EXQUISITELY SMOOTH AND RICH ON THE TONGUE. *I use it in cannoli fillings, to make the Russian cheese dessert paskha if I can't find farmer's cheese, and in cheesecakes and tarts. It is also delicious with ripe melon and fresh strawberries. Homemade ricotta is especially good when just made and still warm.*

Making ricotta is not difficult, but you'll need some special equipment. To cook the milk and cream, you need a large pot; a pot with a heavy bottom is essential to prevent the liquid from scorching. My first choice is enameled cast iron, but a heavy stainless steel pot will also work well. You'll need a candy thermometer or digital probe thermometer to monitor the temperature as the milk and cream heat slowly. You'll also need some cheesecloth, a large wire strainer or colander, and a heatproof rubber spatula.

2½	quarts whole milk
1	cup heavy cream
⅓	cup fresh lemon juice
¼	teaspoon salt

COMBINE THE MILK, cream, and lemon juice in a heavy 5½- to 6-quart pot. Stir well with a heatproof rubber spatula and set the pot over medium-low heat. Attach a candy thermometer or digital probe thermometer to the side of the pot and bring to a simmer. Simmer, without stirring, for 40 minutes, or until the thermometer registers 170°F.

INCREASE THE HEAT to medium and continue to cook, stirring very gently with the rubber spatula only two or three times, until the temperature registers 205°F. (Medium to large curds of cheese will form as the milk heats; to keep the curds this size, it's important to stir as little as possible.) The liquid will seethe and be on the verge of boiling. Remove the pot from the heat and let stand for 10 to 15 minutes.

RINSE A DOUBLE THICKNESS of cheesecloth, squeeze out the excess water, and line a large strainer or colander with it. Set the strainer in the sink and slowly ladle the ricotta mixture into it. Let the cheese drain for about 1 hour, without stirring, until it is quite thick. Discard the liquid.

TRANSFER THE CHEESE to a medium bowl and gently stir in the salt. The ricotta is ready to use, or it can be refrigerated, covered, for up to 3 days. It can also be frozen for up to 1 month. Thaw completely before using.

Basic Pie Dough

THIS IS ONE OF MY FAVORITE ALL-PURPOSE PIE DOUGHS. It is excellent for any filling. I use half butter and half homemade lard, but vegetable shortening works just fine instead of lard.

See the companion DVD for a video demonstration of making, rolling, and forming a pie shell.

2 cups unbleached all-purpose flour	½ cup chilled home-rendered lard (page 332) or vegetable shortening, or commercial lard (see Sources, pages 342 and 343)
¼ cup cake flour	
½ teaspoon salt	
8 tablespoons (1 stick) cold unsalted butter, cut into tablespoon-sized pieces	6 tablespoons ice water
	1½ teaspoons cider vinegar

IN A LARGE BOWL, stir together both flours and the salt. Add the butter and cut it into the flour with a pastry blender or two table knives until the fat is in pea-sized pieces. Add the lard or shortening and work it into the flour until cut into pea-sized pieces.

COMBINE THE ICE WATER and cider vinegar. Add to the dry ingredients 1 tablespoon at a time as you toss the mixture about with a table fork, then continue mixing just until the dough holds together.

TURN THE DOUGH OUT, form it into a rough ball, and divide it in two. Shape each piece into a 1-inch-thick disk, enclose tightly in plastic wrap, and refrigerate at least 1 hour before using. The dough can be refrigerated for up to 2 days. For longer storage, put each disk of dough into a small heavy-duty resealable plastic bag and freeze for up to 1 month. Thaw overnight in the refrigerator before using.

German Yeast Dough

MAKES A SCANT 1½ POUNDS, ENOUGH FOR ONE STREUSELKUCHEN AND ONE BIENENSTICH

THIS IS A VERSATILE SWEET DOUGH RECIPE *used in many German yeast pastries. It was given to me by Anna Lobonc. Its tender texture is particularly suited to Streuselkuchen (page 205) and to Bienenstich (page 204).*

½ cup whole milk

1 package (2¼ teaspoons) active dry or rapid-rise yeast

¼ cup granulated sugar

2¼ cups unbleached all-purpose flour, plus more as needed

4 tablespoons (½ stick) cold unsalted butter, cut into 4 tablespoon-sized pieces

Finely grated zest of 1 lemon

2 large eggs, at room temperature

SCALD THE MILK in a small saucepan over medium heat—you will see steam rising from the surface of the milk and small bubbles forming around the edges. Remove the pan from the heat and let stand until the milk feels warm to your fingertip, about 10 minutes; an instant-read thermometer should register 110° to 120°F.

SPRINKLE THE YEAST and 1 teaspoon of the sugar into the milk and stir well. Let stand for about 10 minutes, until the yeast is bubbly and foamy.

To make the dough using a stand mixer, combine 2¼ cups of the flour with the remaining sugar in the bowl of the mixer, and add the butter and lemon zest. Attach the flat beater and mix on low speed for about 3 minutes, until the flour looks mealy. Remove the bowl from the mixer stand, add the yeast and eggs, and stir with a rubber spatula to make a moist, thick dough. Switch to the dough hook and beat on low speed for 1 minute. Increase the speed to medium and beat for 5 minutes, or until the dough becomes sticky and elastic and begins to pull away from the sides of the bowl. Scrape the bowl and dough hook.

To make the dough by hand, stir 2¼ cups of the flour with the remaining sugar in a large mixing bowl. Add the butter and cut it in with a pastry blender or two knives until the flour looks mealy. Add the lemon zest, then add the yeast and eggs and stir with a wooden spoon to make a moist, thick dough. Beat vigorously for 5 to 8 minutes, until the dough becomes smooth, sticky, and elastic. When you pick up some of the dough with the spoon, it will be very stretchy. Scrape the bowl and spoon.

SPRINKLE 1 TABLESPOON FLOUR over the dough and cover the bowl tightly with plastic wrap. Let the dough rise until doubled in size, 1 hour or more depending on the warmth of your kitchen.

LIGHTLY FLOUR YOUR WORK SURFACE. Dislodge the dough from the bowl with a pastry scraper, scrape it out onto the work surface, and turn to coat all surfaces lightly with flour. Divide the dough in half. Shape each half into a ball, cover loosely with a kitchen towel, and let rest for 10 minutes. The dough is now ready to use.

Note

If you are using only half the dough, place the second ball of dough into an airtight container and refrigerate it. The next day, shape and bake it into a streuselkuchen or bienenstich.

Vanilla Sugar

VANILLA SUGAR IS SIMPLE TO MAKE *and keeps forever. I keep jars of vanilla-flavored confectioners' sugar and granulated sugar on hand at all times. I shake the confectioners' sugar onto Pennsylvania Dutch Crumb Cake (page 326) and Streuselkuchen (page 205), use it in icings, and anywhere I want an extra hit of vanilla. I often coat doughnuts, such as Puff Puff (page 54), in vanilla granulated sugar, and I also stir some into hot tea. You'll be glad you have both these sugars in your kitchen.*

2 to 3 cups confectioners' sugar
   or granulated sugar

1 vanilla bean, split lengthwise

PUT THE SUGAR into a screw-cap jar, and bury the vanilla bean halves in the sugar. Seal the jar and wait 3 to 4 days before using; the vanilla aroma and flavor will permeate the sugar.

After you've used a cup or so of the sugar, replenish it. The beans will continue flavoring the sugar for months. Shake the jar every once in a while to distribute the flavored sugar evenly.

Index of Recipes by Country or Region

Index of Mail Order Sources by Company

Many department stores and specialty cookware shops will have what you need, but here are a few retail and mail-order sources that sell all kinds of baking equipment. And don't forget eBay.com—it is an excellent source for hard-to-find kitchen equipment.

Amazon.com

Search under Gourmet Food, and you'll be directed to an appropriate site for farmer's cheese, tuna packed in oil, capers, pine nuts, dried porcini mushrooms, and lots more.

Aquavit

This is an excellent brand of cloudberry spread and is available in 10-ounce jars. See Sarabeth's Kitchen for ordering information.

The Baker's Catalogue

P.O. Box 876

Norwich, VT 05055-0876

800-827-6836

web site: www.bakerscatalogue.com

A publication of King Arthur Flour, *The Baker's Catalogue* is issued several times a year. It offers all kinds of baking pans, including Magic Line, Doughmakers, and Chicago Metallic brands, baking stones, measuring cups, spoons, bench scrapers, marble slabs, cherry pitters, cookie and doughnut cutters, pastry brushes, pastry canvases, silicone liners, and many more baker's needs, including ingredients. If you can't find King Arthur flours locally, you can order them by mail. The catalog also offers nuts (including black walnuts), dried fruits (including diced citron), flavoring extracts, chocolate, cocoa, various seeds, unsweetened shredded coconut, pearl sugar, and much more. The company also has an excellent retail store, in Norwich.

Bridge Kitchenware

711 Third Avenue (entrance on 45th Street)

New York, NY 10017

212-688-4220

web site: www.bridgekitchenware.com

This venerable New York City institution is a cook's heaven. Bakers will find just about anything they might need there. Visit the retail store or shop online.

Cooking.com

This site offers all manner of kitchen equipment, including Chinese bamboo steamers, electric krumkake makers, griddles, and more.

Dairy Fresh Candies

57 Salem Street
Boston, MA 02113
800-336-5536
web site: http://dairyfreshcandy/stores.yahoo.com

This company offers excellent citron, in halves or diced. I prefer the halves because I can cut them into any size I want, and they also keep better than cut citron. The company also sells many kinds of nuts, extracts, dried and candied fruits, and baking chocolate and cocoa.

Fisher Scientific

web site: www.fishersci.com

Fisher sells food-grade lye (sodium hydroxide) pellets. Minimum order is a 500-gram container, but it lasts forever if kept tightly closed and dry.

Flying Pigs Farm

Shushan, NY 12873
518-854-3844
web site: www.flyingpigsfarm.com

An excellent source for lard and other pork products.

Golden Barrel

4960 Horseshoe Pike
Honey Brook, PA 19344
800-327-4406
web site: www.goldenbarrel.com

This is the place to order golden table syrup for shoofly pie.

igourmet.com

Founded in 1997, this online store sells a huge variety of foods from many countries, including Italian tuna packed in olive oil and dried porcini mushrooms.

Importfoods.com

888-618-THAI

web site: importfoods.com

Offering Thai ingredients and equipment, this is a good source for limestone, tamarind, fine rice flour, chiles, and more.

Indiablend.com

770-442-3818

web site: Indiablend.com

An excellent site for atta flour (the hard durum wheat used to make Indian flatbreads), this site also sells ghee, saffron, Indian spices, and more.

Kalustyan's

123 Lexington Avenue
New York, NY 10016
212-685-3451
web site: www.kalustyans.com

Shop here for all sorts of spices, including asafetida, garam masala, nigella, mahlab, sumac, saffron, and five-spice powder, as well as almond and anise oils, rose water, orange flower water, rice flour, and more.

lacuisineus.com

This venerable store sells all manner of baking equipment and ingredients. Visit their web site to see an online catalog. Check with them for manual nut grinders.

Mother Linda's

P.O. Box 7
Bladensburg, MD 29710
e-mail: momlinda@motherlindas.com
web site: www.motherlindas.com/lard_for_sale.htm

This site occasionally has organic homemade lard available. E-mail for availability and prices.

New York Cake and Baking Distributor

56 West 22nd Street
New York, NY 10010
800-942-2593
web site: www.nycake.com

This is the mother of all baking stores. Just about anything you could want is here, including baking ingredients. Pay them a visit, or shop online.

nextag.com/nut-mill/search-html

A source for the Leifheit 23130 nut grinder. It is listed online as a nut and vegetable mill and comes with three interchangeable drums.

Otto's Hungarian Import Store & Deli

2320 West Clark Avenue

Burbank, CA 91506

818-845-0433

This emporium sells Hungarian food products and kitchen equipment, including nut grinders and poppy seed grinders. The nut grinders come in various sizes. Call to order.

Penzeys Spices

P.O. Box 933

W19362 Apollo Drive

Muskego, Wisconsin 53150

800-741-7787

web site: www.penzeys.com

The company is famous for pure extracts of vanilla (including double-strength), almond, lemon, and orange; whole vanilla beans and nutmegs; nigella; zatar; sumac; cinnamon sticks, ground cinnamon (real Ceylon cinnamon, Vietnamese cassia cinnamon, and others); cardamom; and many other spices. Catalog available.

Polishharvest.com

An online store for many Polish food products, shipped from Poland, this company offers Krakus Multifruit Powidła, a thick jam made with rose hips that is excellent for pączki and for kolacky.

Russian Foods

web site: www.russianfoods.com

Excellent source for equipment and foods shipped directly from Russia, including wooden and plastic paskha molds.

Sarabeth's Kitchen

web site: www.mailordercentral.com

Many food products including Aquavit Cloudberry Spread.

Spices, etc.

P.O. Box 2088

Savannah, GA 31402

800-827-6373

web site: www.spicesetc.com

This company carries a huge range of spices, many natural extracts, and other food items.

Swedensbest.com

A source for Swedish cloudberry jam and other Swedish food and cooking items.

Sweet Celebrations

7009 Washington Avenue South

Edina, MN 55439

800-328-6722

web site: www.sweetc.com

Formerly known as Maid of Scandinavia, this company sells all kinds of baking equipment, including tartlet molds, Bethany lefse griddles, other lefse-making equipment, silicone liners, and sets of nonstick kransekake molds. It also sells ingredients for baking and candy making.

The Vanilla Company

800-757-7511

web site: www.vanilla.com

This online company, founded and owned by Patricia Rain, is dedicated to promoting and selling pure, natural vanilla worldwide as extracts and whole beans. The site is also a source of vanilla lore, history, and recipes.

Williams-Sonoma

P.O. Box 7456

San Francisco, CA 94120-7456

800-541-2233

web site: www.williams-sonoma.com

Although Williams-Sonoma made its reputation selling well-made cookware, cooking utensils, and baking equipment, in recent years the company's focus has shifted to high-end cookware and food products. However, it still sells food processors and heavy-duty mixers and some baking equipment, including LaForme and Chicago Metallic bakeware.

Index of Mail Order Sources by Specialty Ingredient

Listed below are specialty ingredients and companies that sell them. For more information about each of these retailers, see Index of Mail Order Sources by Company on page 341.

Almond Oil
Kalustyan's
Spices, Etc.

Anise Oil
Kalustyan's
Spices, Etc.

Black Walnuts
The Baker's Catalogue

Citron
The Baker's Catalogue
Dairy Fresh Candy

Cloudberry Spread
Aquavit
Sarabeth's Kitchen
Swedensbest.com

Coconut, Shredded Unsweetened
The Baker's Catalogue
Kalustyan's

Extracts and Flavorings (Almond, Lemon, Orange, Vanilla)
Penzey's Spices
Spices, Etc.

Farmer's Cheese
Amazon.com

Five Spice Powder
Kalustyan's

Flours
Atta (also called chapati flour or durum wheat flour)
Indiablend.com
Kalustyan's

Rice
The Baker's Catalogue
Kalustyan's
Importfoods.com

Semolina, Fine
The Baker's Catalogue

Ghee
Indiablend.com
Kalustyan's

Golden Table Syrup
Golden Barrel

Indian Spices (Asafetida, Garam Masala, Cumin, Turmeric)
Indiablend.com
Kalustyan's

Lard

Flying Pigs Farm

Mother Linda's

Lye (Pure, Food Grade)

Fisher Scientific

Middle Eastern Spices and Seeds (Mahlab, Nigella, Sumac)

Kalustyan's

Penzey's Spices

Multifruit Povidła

Polish Harvest

Orange Blossom (Orange Flower) Water

Kalustyan's

Porcini Mushrooms, Dried

igourmet.com

Rose Water

Kalustyan's

Saffron

Kalustyan's

Thai Ingredients (Limestone, Tamarind Concentrate, Chiles)

importfoods.com

Tuna Packed in Olive Oil

igourmet.com

Zatar (Zahtar)

Penzey's Spices

Bibliography

Baboian, Rose. *Armenian-American Cook Book*. Lexington, MA: Baboian, 1964.

Bremzen, Anya von, and John Welchman. *Please to the Table: The Russian Cookbook*. New York: Workman, 1990.

Brown, Linda Keller, and Kay Mussell. *Ethnic and Regional Foodways in the United States*. Knoxville: University of Tennessee Press, 1985.

Coetzee, Renata. *The South African Culinary Tradition*. Johannesburg: C. Struik Publishers, 1977.

Corey, Helen. *The Art of Syrian Cookery*. New York: Doubleday, 1962.

Davidson, Alan. *The Oxford Companion to Food*. Oxford: Oxford University Press, 1999.

FitzGibbon, Theodora. *A Taste of Wales*. London: J. M. Dent, 1971.

Fredrickson, Karin, ed. *The Great Scandinavian Cook Book*. New York: Crown, 1967.

Groff, Betty. *Betty Groff's Pennsylvania Dutch Cookbook*. New York: Galahad Books, 1990.

Harris, Jessica B. *The Welcome Table: African-American Heritage Cooking*. New York: Simon & Schuster, 1995.

Helou, Anissa. *Lebanese Cuisine*. New York: St. Martin's Press, 1995.

Hess, Karen. *The Carolina Rice Kitchen: The African Connection*. Columbia: University of South Carolina Press, 1992.

Kaplan, Anne R., Marjorie A. Hoover, and Willard B. Moore. *The Minnesota Ethnic Food Book*. St. Paul: Minnesota Historical Society Press, 1986.

Legwold, Gary. *The Last Word on Lefse*. Cambridge, MN: Adventure Publications, 1992.

Morton, Mark. *Cupboard Love: A Dictionary of Culinary Curiosities*. Toronto: Insomniac Press, 2004.

Ozan, Özcan. *The Sultan's Kitchen: A Turkish Cookbook*. Hong Kong: Periplus, 1998.

Roden, Claudia. *The Jewish Book of Food*. New York: Knopf, 1996.

Shoemaker, Alfred L. *Christmas in Pennsylvania*. Mechanicsburg, PA: Stackpole Books, 1999.

Sokolov, Raymond. *The Jewish-American Kitchen*. New York: Wings Books, 1989.

Strybel, Robert and Maria. *Polish Heritage Cookery*. New York: Hippocrene Books, 1997.

Weaver, William Woys. *Pennsylvania Dutch Country Cooking*. New York: Abbeville Press, 1994.

Wright, Clifford A. *A Mediterranean Feast*. New York: Morrow, 1999.

Index

F

JOHN WILEY & SONS, INC.

CUSTOMER NOTE: IF THIS BOOK IS ACCOMPANIED BY SOFTWARE, PLEASE READ THE FOLLOWING BEFORE OPENING THE PACKAGE.

By opening the package, you are agreeing to be bound by the following agreement:

This software product is protected by copyright and all rights are reserved by the author, John Wiley & Sons, Inc., or their licensors. You are licensed to use this software as described in the software and the accompanying book. Copying the software for any other purpose may be a violation of U.S. Copyright Law.

This software product is sold as is without warranty of any kind, either express or implied, including but not limited to the implied warranty of merchantability and fitness for a particular purpose. Neither Wiley nor its dealers or distributors assumes any liability for any alleged or actual damages arising from the use of or the inability to use this software. (Some states do not allow the exclusion of implied warranties, so the exclusion may not apply to you.)

To place additional orders or to request information about other Wiley products, please call (800) 879-4539 or visit Wiley.com online.

© 2007 John Wiley & Sons, Inc.